HALLS OF FAME

OF

MY BOOK HOUSE

EDITED BY

OLIVE BEAUPRÉ MILLER

PUBLISHERS

THE BOOK HOUSE for CHILDREN

LAKE BLUFF, ILLINOIS

PREFACE

When the child reads the stories in "Halls of Fame" he will see that behind every great achievement is one person's struggle to accomplish it. We hope he will see that outstanding men and women, as children, were much like himself. One of the important goals of "Halls of Fame" is to bring to the young person the realization that many of the most interesting things in life are attainable goals for him. "Halls of Fame" is full of possible dreams.

"The Royal Page" is a story about Chaucer. He was the first recognized poet to write in English in an era when educated English people spoke and wrote French. An interesting sidelight is a description of how the English language evolved from a composite of Anglo-Saxon and French words. "Down by the River Avon" gives a colorful description of Elizabethan England. The story makes it easy to visualize how young Will Shakespeare felt when working as an actor and how, out of his closeness with the people of London, he was able to write plays of interest to the great mass of English people. In the following century Charles Dickens was the interpreter of the poor and novelist for all. It is interesting to read how this came to be.

Washington Irving was named after George Washington six years before our first president took office. Young would-be authors will be interested in Irving's growth as a writer, influenced by his wanderings through the countryside. Also influenced by their American surroundings were authors Louisa May Alcott, Joel Chandler Harris, James Whitcomb Riley, Joaquin Miller, and Vachel Lindsay. Stories about them will be found in this volume.

The tales of Jackie Robinson, Jessie Owens, and Babe Didrikson are similar in that each person had success in sports as his or her goal. Each achieved the goal by personal effort and determination, often surmounting personal, financial, or racial barriers. Boys and girls who aspire to be top athletes can read with interest just what qualities are necessary for success in competitive athletics.

Students will be fascinated to learn about the early life of Albert Einstein, who is known throughout the world as one of the great minds of all time. Andrew Carnegie, "Telegraph Boy," grew up with a thirst for learning at a time when books were hard to borrow and harder to own. His determination resulted in the possession of one of the largest private libraries ever, in addition to a great personal fortune. One of the greatest success stories in this volume is that of Frederick Douglass who had to break a slave law in order to learn to read. This tale is told in "Learning to be Free."

Boys and girls who love animals and nature will be fascinated by the story of Jane Goodall, who took care of many beloved pets when she was a little girl. As a young woman she journeyed to an isolated game reserve in Africa to live among the apes. She studied their habits and learned things no one had known before about chimpanzees. Thor Heyerdahl, who had always loved hiking and living in the great wildernesses of Norway, became enthralled by theories of the migration of peoples from one continent to another and decided to see if he could cross the Pacific ocean in a balsa raft. His adventures on the high seas provide excitement and suspense.

Pioneers need not be those who live a primitive life. Daniel Hale Williams, who began his surgical career operating on a kitchen table, was the first man to enter the chest cavity and repair tissue around the heart. This pioneer black surgeon was a founder of the National Medical Association. Pioneers Neil Armstrong, Buzz Aldrin and Mike Collins blazed a trail to the moon. "The First Moon Landing" is an accurate account of the challenges of their daring voyage and stunning photographs of what they found there.

Browsing through the three indexes will be a pleasant and rewarding experience for parents and the somewhat older child. Those in special subjects will discover stories they might otherwise have missed. The Character Building Index is helpful to a parent who may wish to find a painless way to prove a point. Favorite authors, personalities, and illustrators can be easily found. The older child who uses the index may well find himself turning back to enjoy a story he missed in an earlier volume. Although these twelve volumes are graded for age level interest and reading difficulty, children of any given age will inevitably enjoy the stories in various volumes.

It is to be remembered that all of literature has many functions. It touches off the creative fire of fancy, it enriches our lives with a fund of beauty, humor, truth and ever expanding knowledge. Above all, it is always moulding and reshaping our concepts of what is good and what is not good, not only presenting a wider and truer understanding of life but stirring in our hearts a strong emotional reaction to that understanding, so, instead of merely knowing something, we actually *feel* something. And it is this *feeling* rather than knowledge of facts alone, it is this drive of the emotions behind the intellect, which becomes the dynamo, the motive power for action—the *do*-something behind the *know*-something. Thus My BOOK HOUSE not only enlarges the child's knowledge and his understanding of life but helps to plant within his heart and spirit that dynamo which impels him to live life fully, wisely and well.

CONTENTS

PAGE

BOY IN RUSSIA, A 190
              Leo N. Tolstoy

COIN, THE . . . . *Sara Teasdale* 212

DOWN BY THE RIVER AVON 15
             William Shakespeare

FIRST MOON LANDING, THE . . . . *Margaret Waldorf* 30
      Neil Armstrong, Buzz Aldrin and Mike Collins

GENTLE GENIUS, THE . . . . *Tamsin Murphy* 218
           Albert Einstein

HARVARD PROFESSOR, THE 135
         Henry Wadsworth Longfellow

HOOSIER POET, THE 141
         James Whitcomb Riley

INTERESTING HISTORY OF OLD MOTHER GOOSE, THE 213

JANE AND THE WILD CHIMPS . . . . . . *George Crossette* 70
      Baroness Jane van Lawick-Goodall

LEARNING TO BE FREE . . . . *Mildred Barger Herschler* 198
        Frederick Douglass

LIFE IN CONCORD 122
        Louisa May Alcott

LONDON STREETS 102
        Charles Dickens

LONELIEST BATTLER, THE . . . . *George Vass* 79
        Jackie Robinson

LONE STAR TEAM OF TEXAS, THE . . . . . . *George Vass* 170
        Babe Didrikson

MAN WHO MADE ADOLF HITLER RUN, THE . . . . *George Vass* 104
        Jesse Owens

PAGE

NEGRO SPEAKS OF RIVERS, THE . . . . *Langston Hughes* 188

PIONEER IN SURGERY . . . . *Louis Haber* 154
              Daniel Hale Williams

POET OF THE SIERRAS, THE 143
             Joaquin Miller

ROVER IN THE CATSKILLS, A 99
             Washington Irving

ROYAL PAGE, THE 11
             Geoffrey Chaucer

SENOR KON-TIKI. . . . . *Arnold Jacoby* 45
             Thor Heyerdahl

TELEGRAPH BOY. . . . . *Clara Ingram Judson* 60
             Andrew Carnegie

TRAMP OF THE MIDDLE WEST, A 147
             Nicholas Vachel Lindsay

'WAY DOWN SOUTH IN DIXIE 138
             Joel Chandler Harris

INDEX TO MY BOOK HOUSE PLAN 226

AUTHORS, TITLES, AND LEADING CHARACTERS INDEX . . 227

SPECIAL SUBJECTS INDEX 248

CHARACTER BUILDING INDEX 288
             A Guide for Parents

GUIDE TO THE PRONUNCIATION OF PROPER NAMES . . . 299

The Royal Page

GEOFFREY CHAUCER (*English*, 1340-1400)

IN days when all the great people of England were Norman-French and the poor people were Anglo-Saxons, a swine-herd met a cow-herd and a sheep-herd on a green sweep of rolling meadow beyond which rose the gray towers of ancient castle walls.

"All the good things in the land be for the Norman-French since the days when William the Norman conquered our Saxon England," said the swine-herd, pointing to the castle. "When these beasts of ours be out here in the meadow and a poor man must work to tend them, how do you call them, friend?"

"Why, man, I call them *swine*," the cow-herd answered thickly.

"And *swine* is Anglo-Saxon—good Anglo-Saxon," the swine-herd nodded with emphasis, "but how call you that same beast when he is served up at table before lordly ladies and gentlemen?"

"Why, then I call him *pork*."

Read *The Chaucer Story Book*, by Eva M. Tappan, and *The Canterbury Pilgrims*, by F. J. H. Darton.

"And *pork* is Norman-French!" The swine-herd continued to grumble. "The beast is Saxon when a poor man by the sweat of his brow must tend him, but French when lords and ladies may take their pleasure of him! And you, friend cow-herd, your *cow* and likewise your *ox* are Saxon. They're lowly Saxon beasts when you tend them in the field, but look you, they change, as by magic, to lordly French *beef* at table!"

"Aye,'' interrupted the sheep-herd. "The very word *pleasure* is French but *work* is Anglo-Saxon! Right you are, friend swine-herd. Even the language we speak since the days of William the Conqueror shows all the good things of life be for the Norman-French. Whatever is noble and courtly and giveth joy and pleasure, that must have a French name, but for everything lowly and homely there must be a Saxon word!" The cow-herd, the swine-herd and the sheep-herd solemnly shook their heads.

Now in these days there dwelt at the court of King Edward the Third of England a young page named Geoffrey Chaucer. Clad in red and black breeches, with a short cloak and elegant shoes, he attended upon his mistress, the wife of King Edward's son, at many a gay festivity. Often in some chamber with beautiful tapestried walls he sat amid lords and ladies while someone read a poem to entertain the party and though it was three hundred years since William the Norman had come with a mighty army from France and conquered the Saxon King Harold in the bloody battle of Hastings, the poems read in these chambers were always written in French. Who would use Saxon English, the language of churls and peasants? True, the common people of England already spoke a mixture of Anglo-Saxon and French, but their common English was vulgar, the tongue of the man in the streets! It was rude. It was not for nobles. In the court one must speak only French. Ere long young Geoffrey himself began to write poems in French, in the slight, graceful, shallow manner of the poets across the water.

H A L L S   O F   F A M E

Living like any young page, Geoffrey was barely nineteen when he went with the King to France to fight England's battles there. In the stress and struggle and bloodshed he bore himself right nobly till the days of the English retreat. Then he was taken captive and for months he languished in prison. But King Edward held him so dear that he paid a ransom to free him. Thereafter, behold young Geoffrey again returned to England and in the King's own household, risen to be a squire with an annual salary and a gift of handsome clothes at every Christmastide. Soon there were wedding bells and Geoffrey was taking a bride, the beautiful young Philippa, a lady-in-waiting to the Queen.

As years went by, his master sent him on important missions to many a foreign port, to Genoa, to France, to Flanders. A deal of the world Geoffrey Chaucer saw on his travels for the King! In Italy he was touched by the warm, glowing charm of the land and by the rich depth and color of Italy's powerful writers, Dante, Petrarch and Boccaccio. Now he could no more be satisfied with the poems he wrote in French. They might be graceful and tender, but they were slight and shallow. Henceforth he wished to write with all the depth and fire of the great Italian poets.

As a new departure in time he devoted himself to business. Being made Comptroller of Customs at the busy port of London, he spent his days at the wharves, recording trade in wool and hides, talking with stevedores and sea-going men and seeing human nature of quite a different sort from that he had known at court. He began to know the common man and to hear almost altogether the language he spoke, the vulgar tongue of the English.

A courtier, a poet, a diplomat, a man of business was Chaucer, ever active in many affairs. In 1386, at the very height of his glory, he sat in Parliament as a Knight of the Shire from Kent. But thereafter misfortunes befell him. He lost all his friends at court; his offices were taken from him and he was obliged henceforth to live among common people with a purse exceedingly lean.

But now what new life for his poetry! At last he wrote no more after the French or Italian fashion. He was out of life at the court. He was living with the common man. For him he would write in English. He would use the despised English tongue! Save for the poems of a ploughman or some such man of the people, English had heretofore never been used in literature. But Chaucer now burst forth with beautiful poems in English, vivacious, full of humor, tender and delighting in nature, singing of all the "smale foweles" that "maken melodye," of sunshine and soft breezes, of April's fresh, sweet showers. His greatest work was *Canterbury Tales*, a rich and colorful picture of Old England in those days. Down along the white and dusty Kentish road, a company of pilgrims wended their way on horseback, journeying to the shrine of St. Thomas Becket at Canterbury. From every walk of life they came,—knight, squire, miller, monk, doctor merchant, churl; and as they journeyed they told the stories Chaucer related, now one all courtliness of phrase, now one overflowing with the broad coarse humor of the churl.

Thus it was that Chaucer made the homely English tongue the language of a new and splendid literature which was to follow him through the years. This was the great thing he did. English literature really began with Geoffrey Chaucer.

In the Sixth Century, Anglo-Saxon invaders drove the original Britons, who spoke Celtic, into Wales, Cornwall, and the Scottish Highlands. Their Saxon England ended with the Norman Conquest, 1066. Gradually English became a mixture of Anglo-Saxon and Norman-French with some remaining Celtic words. See pages 22, 44, Vol I. Tales of King Arthur are Celtic. Saxon poems by Caedmon 665, A. D.; works of the Venerable Bede; *Beowulf*, the oldest English epic; the Anglo-Saxon *Chronicle*, systematized by King Alfred; *The Vision of Piers the Ploughman;* and Wyclif's translation of *The Bible* constitute the literature of Saxon-England before Chaucer. The first English printing, by William Caxton, 1475, made books more widely read. He printed *Canterbury Tales*.

Down by the River Avon

WILLIAM SHAKESPEARE (*English*, 1564-1616)

BEYOND Sir Hugh Clopton's noble old stone bridge that spans the Avon with fourteen splendid arches, rise the quaint gables and cathedral spire of Stratford town. In the days of good Queen Bess the houses were ancient plaster buildings crossed with timber and each had at the sides or rear a gay little garden, bright with flowers. In one of the best of those houses on Henley Street lived Master Will Shakespeare, a high spirited lad with a fine, courtly bearing and very pleasant eyes. His father, John Shakespeare, once High Bailiff or Mayor of Stratford, was a well-to-do merchant, a trader in hides, leather-goods, wool, meats, and goodness knows what besides. His mother, Mary Arden, was a blithe and womanly matron, who shed a warmth of tenderness through the merry, little home circle.

Over in the old, old grammar school, with its jutting second story abutting on the street, Master Will and the other Stratford urchins learned their lessons. There they conned arithmetic, a bit of Latin and Greek, and the precepts of good manners, from six o'clock in the morning till five-thirty in the evening, and the schoolmaster sitting over them was all too well versed in the use of the birchen rod.

But it was a gay and joyous life, in spite of lessons, that they led in Stratford town. Warwickshire in those days was divided into two well marked divisions by the river Avon. To the south lay the rich green pasture land of Feldon, stretching away to the blue line of the distant Cotswold hills, and dotted here and there by herds of cattle and flocks of snow-white sheep. Amid little clumps of protecting elms nestled cozy homesteads, and past the well tilled fields flowed placid rivers, their limpid waters overhung by alders and silverwillows. To the north of the Avon, however—Ah! there was no cultivated land, but the wild, free forest of Arden, sweeping out over hill and dale for twenty miles, the delight of all boyish hearts. When school time was over, then for Will Shakespeare and the other Stratford boys, it was Heigh the doxy over the dale! We're off for the Forest of Arden!

O, the sweetness of those woodland haunts, the exhilaration and breadth and joy! The boys raced through leafy covert and sunny glade, past giant oaks and tangled thickets, now skipping from stone to stone across the brawling brooks, now cleaving the woodland stillness with their shrill young voices. Sometimes a dappled herd of deer swept away before them across an open lawn or twinkled through the leaves amid the shadowy bracken, while groups of timid rabbits fed here and there on the tender leaves. In the air was the melody of birds, the warble of wren and throstle. Will Shakespeare talked with every keeper and woodsman in the forest till he knew intimately all the ins and outs of that glorious sylvan life and could carol a tirra-lirra with the merriest of the larks.

At times, too, young Will wandered through the picturesque towns and little forest villages round about, past the old gray castles and abbeys that loomed within their parks shut off by palings from the wilderness of Arden. Some of these castles had been abandoned and dismantled during the Wars of the Roses. Silent now as the surrounding forest they stood, half ruined, and haunted with shadowy memories of lords and ladies and all the stately revelry that had once held sway within their walls. It was a country full of interest, full of history, full of stirring border legends of the days when the English stood sturdily against the insurgents of Wales. Every hill and stream, every grim old abbey and castle had its heroic tale of long ago.

On market days and fair days there was great excitement in the town itself for Master Will, for Stratford was the center of a famous agricultural and grazing district. On a bright summer's day, Will would rise with the sun and make off from Henley Street to see the countrywomen come in, jogging along on horseback, their panniers laden with chickens, butter and eggs, or to watch the droves of slow oxen come crowding over Clopton Bridge, and the herds of Herefordshire cows, lowing anxiously after their skittish young calves. Then he would follow the cattle to Rother Market, where the cattle dealers gathered about Market Cross, and observe the humors of the ploughman and drovers, scarcely less stolid and deliberate of movement and speech than their oxen.

At the jovial Fair-season, the streets of Stratford were alive with jugglers and minstrels, harpers singing old ballads, and lads and lassies dancing their country measures. At such times it seemed as though the wealth of the world had been dumped into Stratford-town. There in the booths were wheat and wool, cheese and wax, clothes and stout linen napery. Besides all this, there was many a wandering peddler, carrying trinkets and trumpery such as country swains buy for their sweethearts—ribbons and gloves, masks and coifs, stomachers and bracelets.

Not far from Stratford lay the little forest village of Snitterfield, where Will's grandfather and Uncle Henry Shakespeare

had their farms. Every boundary tree and stone, every pond
and sheep-pool, every barn and cattleshed on the way to his
Uncle Henry's farm, Will knew by heart, for he dearly loved
the place and spent many a happy day there. At Snitterfield
Will trotted around after his uncle, poking with eager interest
into all the byres and barns and poultry yards. Now and again,
from a safe nook on the bushy margin of a pool, he enjoyed the
fun and excitement of the sheep washing, or watched the mysteries of the sheep shearing. Then he would remain to the shearing feast, eat the cheese-cakes and warden-pies, and see the young
maid who was chosen Queen of the Festival receive her rustic
guests and distribute among them her gifts of flowers. Indeed,
Will Shakespeare's youth was passed amid the labors and pas-
times, the recurring festivals and varying round of a rural community. Each incident of the year, seedtime and harvest, summer and winter, brought its own group of picturesque merry-
makings in those forest farms and villages.

The best loved holiday of all was May-day, a spontaneous
outburst of joy, a gladsome welcome to the re-awakening life
and freshness of the spring. Very early in the morning, before

dawn, lads and lassies went out into the woods
and brought back branches of trees and garlands
of flowers to build leafy bowers and arbors in the
streets of the city. Then, with twenty sleek yoke
of oxen, each one bearing a nosegay of blossoms
on his horns, they dragged home the Maypole,
all bound around with flowers. When the Maypole was reared in the center of the city with
streamers and banners flying, men, women and
children fell to dancing and feasting about it.

Hey ding-a-ding! Sweet lovers love the spring!

On May-day there were the Morris dancers,
dancing their jovial measures, and masquerading

as Robin Hood, Friar Tuck and
Little John. And there was Maid
Marian, Queen of the May, and
the Fool in his motley dress with
cap and bells. There was the Hobby Horse performing ridiculous
antics and the comical, waddling
dragon, and jolly Tom Piper, the
musician of the troop. It was well
that May-day was a holiday in the
Stratford schools, so that Master
Will Shakespeare did not have to
play truant to witness such scenes
as these.

Christmas was merry, too, though it had a deeper note as well befitted the season. The great Yule log, like the Maypole, was dragged in with shouts and music and joyously laid on the hearth. On Christmas Eve, the waits, their noses red from cold, went round from door to door through the snow, singing their carols and hymns,—"As Joseph was a-walking, he heard an angel sing."

The great cross of Stratford was garnished with holly, ivy and bay, and in every household hospitality reigned. The manor house of the Cloptons among the trees overlooking the town, was a-bustle with preparations, its chimneys belching smoke, the sounds of pipe and trumpet issuing from its doors. Long tables were spread for the guests; the master and mistress took their seats at the head of the board with their friends and principal tenants about them; the Boar's head was brought in with solemn ceremony, and the Lord of Misrule with his jovial attendants became the master of the feast. Thereafter was dancing till curfew, then home through the moonlight to Stratford.

So went the joyous round of life in Stratford-town and each recurring holiday brought its own particular mumming and masking and playing of parts, but there were real players, too, sometimes to be seen in the city.

The very oldest form of play loved by the people in England was the miracle or mystery play, presenting some tale from the Bible. At first, long years before Shakespeare's time, these plays had been given in the churches by the clergy, but gradually they had moved out to the church yard. Then the actors had changed from the clergy to citizens, members of the various trade guilds of the towns. Later still they were presented on a pageant cart, which was moved about from place to place, and gave a performance wherever it stopped. The actors would play the story of Noah's flood, or Adam and Eve, or indeed any tale from Creation to the Last Judgment.

20

These carts had two stories, an upper one for the stage, and a lower one which was curtained to provide a dressing room for the actors. Over all was a canopy of carved and gilded woodwork cut into battlements and a-flutter with bright-colored banners. Usually men dragged these carts through the streets, but at times they were drawn by horses, and their approach was heralded by jesters and tumblers who ran along before them.

The action of the play took place on the upper platform, but sometimes the actors stepped down into the street, particularly if they wished to present such a scene as the grim and gaping jaws of Hell. This Hell-mouth was the most elaborate and costly theatrical property owned by the trade guilds. It was used in several plays but especially in the Last Judgment,—a huge and grotesque head of canvas with a vast gaping mouth armed with fangs. The jaws were made to open and shut, a light within gave the effect of flames, and whenever the devil carried off a lost soul, there was a great noise in the beast's interior made by the rattling of pans and kettles, while thick smoke issued from his mouth. The making and repairing of this Hell-mouth was a constant expense to the trade guilds, and frequent entries like the following appear in their books of accounts:

Paid for making and painting Hell-mouth..........12 pence
Paid for keeping of fire at Hell-mouth............ 4 pence

Lost souls were dressed in black or yellow to represent flames, saved souls were robed in white. The Devil wore a grizzly mask, was shaggy and beast-like, with horns, cloven feet, and forked tail, and he carried a club with which he laid about him vigorously. He was attended by a company of little demons, their coats covered with horsehair to make them look like awesome monsters. Vice was likewise a constant attendant on the Devil, but he gradually became no more than a mere buffoon or clown to set the crowd a-laughing. Indeed, the plays themselves in time acquired parts that were all too hilarious. Noah's wife

became a comic character, a shrew who laid about her with a cutting tongue and sent the audience into an uproar before she could be dragged off into the ark.

The representative of Jesus wore a gilt wig and a coat of white leather, painted and gilded. King Herod, who was a very important character and blustered about the stage in a manner that became proverbial, was dressed like a Turk and bore a sword and helmet. Herod and Pilate, Cain and Judas, Turks and infidels, as well as the Devil, were favorite characters of these mysteries.

In time, however, morality plays became even more popular than the mysteries. In the moralities, Bible stories were no longer presented, but all manner of Vices and all manner of Virtues were portrayed as persons who did battle with each other in order to gain possession of man's soul. It was some such performances as these that Will Shakespeare used to see as a boy, though in his day it was customary to draw the pageant cart up in the courtyard of some inn, rather than to leave it in the street. The common people then crowded around it, standing, while the richer ones paid a large fee to have seats in the balconies or windows of the inn that overlooked the yard.

Coventry, a town near Stratford, was one of the chief centers for the production of miracle plays, and Shakespeare must certainly have gone over there at times to see them. Moreover, the various trade guilds, plasterers, tanners, armourers, hosiers, etc., who presented the plays were in the habit of visiting neighboring cities, and doubtless performed in Stratford.

Noye's Flude
by
ye Guild of Fiʃhmongers

When Will was only five years old, his father, then Mayor of Stratford, especially invited to the city some of the real stage players, who made a business of acting and were beginning to replace the old performers of the guilds. Later, the best companies in the kingdom came to Stratford, including the Earl of Leicester's Company from London. So young Will had plenty of opportunity to study the making and presenting of plays, to acquire a deep love for the theatre, and perhaps sometimes even to act himself and make friends with the strolling players.

But now when Will was still little more than a boy, his father began to have business failures and his affairs to go down, down, down in the world. Soon it became necessary for the lad to be taken from school and put to work to help out in his father's business. John Shakespeare had been imprudently extravagant in his prosperity, and now he lost his grip and let himself sink beneath misfortune. He would not go to church, he would not see his friends, he would not show himself at any public meeting. Sweet Mary Arden, however, bore up nobly under their troubles, her spirit as calm and serene in the dark days as it had been in the bright. How the boy loved and admired his mother! All his life long she lived in his heart as the very embodiment of every womanly virtue.

Will sympathized ardently with his parents in their troubles, and was willing to do any kind of work to help them. Moreover, those very troubles awakened his independence and taught him to be scrupulously honorable in his own business dealings with others, a trait which he never forgot. An open, frank, generous young fellow was Will Shakespeare in those days, innately courteous and wholly lovable.

When Will was only eighteen, he was many a day to be seen making off across the fields, with daisies pied, to the little hamlet of Shottery, which lay half concealed by aged elms, its cozy homesteads nestling amid blossoming fruit-trees and brilliant gardens. Here in a lovely old cottage, with a quaint thatched roof, lived Anne Hathaway, the daughter of a friend of Will's father, a maid whom he had known all his life. In the garden and through the primrose lanes the two lingered often together, and soon there was news of their wedding.

Boy that he was, Will was only nineteen when his first daughter, Suzanne, was born. Now what was there to do? He had a family on his hands to support and his father's business grew every day worse and worse. Two years later twins were born to him, a boy and a girl, Hamnet and Judith, and then an event occurred which made the young man decide that the only thing for him to do was to be off to London and seek his fortunes there.

He was out hunting one day with some comrades when they pursued a fine deer into Fullbroke Park, or perhaps across the shallow ford of the river to Charlecote Park. Now Charlecote Park was the property of a sour and gloomy old Puritan, Sir Thomas Lucy, a man of aristocratic pride and narrowness who hated all youthful frolics and merriment. Just as they had killed the buck, the youths fell in with one of Sir Thomas's keepers, who insisted violently that they had no right to hunt where they were and accused them of being deer-stealers. Master Will defended himself right spiritedly against the charge, indeed it is even said that he posted certain none too respectful placards on Sir Thomas Lucy's gate. Sir Thomas in high dudgeon complained to the authorities in Stratford. These honorable gentlemen, fearing to offend so rich and powerful a man, doubtless let it be known to Will that it would be better for him to leave town for a time. Accordingly, behold young Will, bidding his wife and babes farewell and off for London town.

It was about 1585 or 1587 when Will Shakespeare arrived in London. In those days players were just beginning to be recognized as respectable folk. Heretofore, they had been looked down upon as wandering, beggarly fellows. Certain writers of education,

such as Greene and Peele and Marlowe, had been among the first to think the writing of plays a vocation worthy of their dignity, and were turning out dramas more like our modern ones than the old moralities and mysteries. Ten years before, Queen Elizabeth I had given the Earl of Leicester's players the first legal permit to act in certain places in London, and James Burbage, the leader of these players, had built *The Theatre* at Shoreditch, just outside the boundaries of the city, for mayor and common council still frowned darkly on the presentation of plays within the sacred precincts of the town.

In building his theatre, Burbage took his plan from the old courtyards of the inns where it had been customary to draw up the pageant carts. The square yard where poorer people stood, became the pit of the theatre, the pageant cart the stage, the balconies whence the wealthier class had looked on, the gallery or boxes. The stage and galleries were the only part of the building covered, which was none too comfortable for the people in the pit if a sudden storm came pelting down.

It was at *The Theatre* that Master Will first found occupation by holding the horses of the gaily dressed young gallants who attended the performances. There he stood before the door in all kinds of weather, with Hey, ho, the wind and the rain! But he soon advanced from this work to acting. Then he began to write over faulty old plays, and at last he took to writing splendid new dramas of his own. In a very short time he had surpassed all the dramatists of his day and held the foremost place in the hearts of the playgoing public.

Before Shakespeare's plays were produced, the merry farces *Ralph Roister Doister*, by Nicholas Udall, and *Gammer Gurton's Needle*, by William Stevenson, had been entertaining the English public. The plays of Greene and Peele, of Christopher Marlowe and the "rare" Ben Jonson were written in the days of Shakespeare.

H A L L S   O F   F A M E

Many a time in those days, however, amid the noise and babble of London, there flashed upon his inward eye, quiet pictures of willows "growing aslant a brook," of orchards when "the moon tips with silver all the fruit tree tops." Many a time he thought of the blue-veined violets, the cowslips and ladies-smocks that grew in the meadows by the Avon. He heard again the "throstle with his note so true, the wren with little quill," and the very notes of those songsters warbled their way into the music of his words. Indeed, he carried the meadows of the Avon, the forest of Arden, the sunburnt sicklemen and merry maidens of his homeland with him to London, and these came forever glancing out here and there in his plays. Aye, his home on the Avon was the beacon that loomed ever before him, beckoning, and the craving always lived in his heart for his beautiful native heath.

But, withal, young Will kept his head marvelously well in spite of his success, and he avoided the wild dissipations that were ruining his fellow-dramatists, though he loved life and mirth as well as any and had no smallest trace of harshness in

27

his blithe and genial nature. He worked hard, studying at French and Italian in his spare time, saving money for his family and making visits every year to his beloved Stratford.

He was first a member of the Earl of Leicester's players which later became the Lord Chamberlain's Company and the favorite company of the Queen. All the players in London in those days, save for certain bands of children, were divided into two companies, the Lord Admiral's and the Lord Chamberlain's, and many a time they went to perform before Queen Bess herself.

The theatres where Shakespeare's plays were given were *The Globe* erected outside the city, and *Blackfriar's* which was practically in the town. The actors played at *The Globe* in summer and at *Blackfriar's* in the winter. *Blackfriar's* was completely roofed in and lit by torchlight so performances could be given there in the evening, but at *The Globe* the pit was uncovered and performances were only given by day.

The common people had a merry time standing in the pit, munching apples and nuts, jostling and chaffing good-naturedly under the open sky, while the fine ladies and gentlemen, who did not wish to mingle with these "groundlings," had their own boxes in the covered balconies, the ladies occupying the seats, the gentlemen reclining at their feet. If they chose, they played cards during the performance and there were always pages ready to attend upon their needs. Whoever paid extra could sit upon the stage itself. There was no scenery on that stage and a simple printed placard announced the name of the place where the scene was supposed to be laid. Women's parts were taken by men. It was not until long after Shakespeare's time that women appeared on the stage. The hoisting of a flag and the blowing of a trumpet bade all be still to hear the play.

What an age of awakened national life and stirring spirit was that of good Queen Bess, when the minds of men had burst the

HALLS OF FAME

bonds of the Dark Ages and were eagerly inquiring and adventuring everywhere. Along the river side and in noble houses on the Strand were the hardy mariners and adventurous sea captains, Drake, Hawkins and Frobisher, who had driven their dauntless keels fearlessly into the unknown seas of the new world, in order to push back the limits of man's knowledge. The greater number of eager and excited listeners who crowded the rude theatres from floor to roof had shared the adventurous exploits of the age and felt the keenest interest in life and vivid action. So the drama of the day became the mirror in which all these active forces were reflected.

But, besides the Americas, there was another new world which men were most anxious to explore in that age of awakened inquiry, that is, the world of human nature, heretofore left so little questioned and understood. All the traits and impulses of that nature, good and bad, its high hopes and aspirations, its fears and sorrows, its bigness and its littleness,—there was need of a map to point them all out. Into that unknown sea sailed the intrepid mariner, Shakespeare, and he charted it in his mighty dramas as none other has ever done, the great Columbus of the newly discovered world of man's heart and mind and spirit.

For twenty years he worked actively in London, twenty long years, but at last a great wave of home-yearning called him back forever to the primrose lanes of Stratford. He had already bought a fine house there for his family, and here he settled down, to spend his remaining years in peace and quiet, honored and loved by all. No other man ever knew the hearts of men and women as Shakespeare did. He still remains the greatest dramatist of all ages who wrote "not for an age but for all time."

Under the Stuart Kings, James I and Charles I, who followed Queen Elizabeth I, the vitality and joy of this period found expression in the graceful poems of Robert Herrick and the Cavalier poets, Richard Lovelace and Thomas Carew, courtiers in the reign of Charles I (1625-1649). In sharp contrast to the Cavalier poets was the intense and majestic John Milton with his magnificent *Paradise Lost*. Milton embodied all the Puritan feeling which ruled England under Oliver Cromwell, whose battles with the Cavaliers ended in the beheading of Charles I. Richard Lovelace, cast into prison for his Cavalier sympathies and still blithely singing, "Stone walls do not a prison make nor iron bars a cage," is a noble figure on one side. Opposite him is the dignified stateliness of the blind Milton, dictating *Paradise Lost* to his daughters or pouring forth out of his blindness his longing for the fight he had lost in "Hail, holy light!" Milton (1608-1674) was the great figure of the period following Elizabeth.

29

The First Moon Landing
Neil Armstrong, Buzz Aldrin, and Mike Collins
By Margaret Waldorf

H A L L S   O F   F A M E

The spaceship *Apollo 11* hurtled around the backside of the moon on its eleventh orbit. Three astronauts, strapped securely to their couches, sat next to each other in the cabin of the craft and faced the instrument panel. Their mission was to land men on the moon for the first time.

Commander Neil Armstrong glanced over the glowing dials and then looked out the porthole window into the black space through which the ship traveled. *Apollo 11* rotated slowly and the moon's cratered surface came into view. Armstrong spotted several smooth dark areas on the moon called "seas" which were surrounded by ridges and craters. He hoped to land in one of the many seas on the other side of the moon—the side facing earth.

Buzz Aldrin and Mike Collins, the other two astronauts seated beside Armstrong, were busy reading dials and calculating *Apollo 11's* velocity and distance from the moon.

"Sixty miles from the surface," Aldrin reported to Armstrong.

"Check, Buzz. You and I better suit up and move into the LM," he answered. LM (pronounced *lem*) stood for Lunar Module. This small spacecraft would separate from the command ship and carry Armstrong and Aldrin to the moon. Collins was to remain in orbit with the command ship and pick up the LM and her two-man crew after they had completed their mission and blasted off from the moon's surface.

Armstrong and Aldrin put on their bulky white pressure suits in the cramped quarters of the cabin. Aldrin pushed himself gently away from his seat and floated weightlessly to a hatch which opened onto a narrow tunnel leading to the LM. He opened the hatch, crawled through the tunnel, and entered the LM. Armstrong followed and closed the hatch.

The cabin of the LM was even smaller than that of the command ship. It had no room for seats. One wall was covered with gauges, dials, and computer keys. There were only two small triangular windows on either side of the instrument panel.

Apollo 11 emerged from the backside of the moon and the earth rose into view over the lunar horizon. Its cloud-streaked surface was a welcome sight to the astronauts. Mission Control Headquarters in Houston, Texas, which directed the flight from earth, was now able to radio to the crew of *Apollo 11.*

"Hello, *Apollo 11*, this is Houston. We're wondering if you have started into the LM yet. Over."

"Okay, Houston, we're in the LM. Over." Armstrong replied.

"We copy," Houston answered, meaning that Mission Control had received the message. "You are now 99 hours and 31 minutes into the mission." *Apollo 11* had rocketed off the launch pad at Cape Kennedy, Florida, almost four days ago.

Astronomers, engineers, and physicists crowded the control room in Houston and followed every maneuver of the spacecraft and every heart beat of the astronauts.

"*Apollo 11*, this is Houston. We currently show a velocity on the *Apollo 11* spacecraft of 3,625 miles per hour."

"Roger, Houston. I can see the entire landing area looking out the left window," Aldrin radioed back from the LM as *Apollo 11* swept across the moon's equator.

"Roger, *Eagle*. This is Houston and we read you." *Eagle* was the name chosen for the LM. The command ship was named *Columbia*, a name which, like *Eagle*, symbolized the United States. Mission Control double-checked the information relayed through space from *Eagle's* systems and radioed to the astronauts, "Looks super to us. We're go for undocking."

Armstrong fired *Eagle's* rockets and the mooncraft pulled away from *Columbia*. "*Eagle's* undocked," he announced to Mission Control.

"Roger. How does it look?" Mission Control asked.

"The *Eagle* has wings," replied Armstrong.

From the window of *Columbia*, Collins inspected *Eagle's* gold, silver, and black body. "I think you've got a fine looking flying machine there," he said, "despite the fact that you're upside down." The four landing legs which stretched out from *Eagle* pointed away from the moon's surface and made the LM appear upside down.

"You guys take care," Collins said to his two friends as *Columbia* moved farther and farther from *Eagle* and continued in lunar orbit.

"See you later," Armstrong radioed back. He fired the descent engines, and *Eagle* plunged toward the moon's surface. "We're going right down Highway U.S. One, Mike."

The earth rises above the lunar horizon as the LM prepares to land.

NASA

Eagle dropped rapidly, following a sloping course. Armstrong turned the ship right-side up and triggered the descent engine again. Flames blasted out from the base of *Eagle* to slow down the craft for a soft landing. Aldrin studied the radar screen and calculated the ship's altitude.

"We are now 50,000 feet from surface, ten minutes to touchdown time," Aldrin reported.

Armstrong scanned the gray landscape slipping by below him for landmarks. They passed over a crater which he recognized as Maskelyne W. So far they were right on course. In the distance, on the lunar horizon, he spotted the landing site on an apparently smooth plain in the Sea of Tranquility.

The numbers "12 02" suddenly flashed across the computer screen in *Eagle*. This warned that something was wrong with the computer, a vital part of the landing equipment. Armstrong immediately radioed Houston. "We're getting a 12 02 alarm. Repeat, 12 02 alarm from *Eagle*."

The ground crew in Houston, 250,000 miles away, had to analyze the problem quickly. If they couldn't discover where the breakdown had occurred, the astronauts would have to return to moon orbit without landing. The error was spotted in a matter of seconds. Too much information had been feeding into the computer at one time. Mission Control corrected the error and radioed, "Okay, *Eagle*. You are go for landing."

Eagle had fallen from 30,000 feet to 3,000 feet. Armstrong had been so absorbed in the computer problem that he had had no chance to watch for landmarks on the surface. When he looked out the cabin window again, he didn't recognize the terrain. The automatic landing system was taking *Eagle* down in front of a large crater. As the ship dropped closer Armstrong realized that a boulder field surrounded the crater. Some of the boulders were as large as cars. If *Eagle* slammed down on such a rough surface the fragile legs could break or the ship might topple over, strand-

34

ing the astronauts on the moon. No rescue was possible if that happened.

Armstrong gripped the control stick on the instrument panel. He pushed the stick forward and took over command of the ship from the automatic pilot. *Eagle* skimmed over the tops of the boulders and across the rock-strewn crater. A red emergency light flashed beneath the fuel gauge, warning that they had only 60 seconds of fuel left. They had less than a minute to find a landing site.

Straight ahead they spotted a level plain ringed by craters. It was only about the size of a football field, but it had a smooth surface. Armstrong aimed the ship for the clearing. *Eagle* approached the field slowly and sank toward the ground.

"Forty feet from surface and dropping," Aldrin reported. "Only thirty seconds of fuel left." Flames from the engine reached to the surface and churned up lunar dust.

"Twenty feet," Aldrin called. From the windows they could see *Eagle's* shadow on the ground. The astronauts grabbed a hand rail mounted above the instrument panel to brace themselves for the touchdown. *Eagle's* footpads settled onto the lunar soil, sending a slight quiver through the ship.

"Touchdown!" Armstrong said.

The astronauts released their grip on the hand rail. Aldrin grinned and reached out to shake Armstrong's hand. "We made it," he said.

"Tranquility Base here," Armstrong radioed. "The *Eagle* has landed."

"Roger, Tranquility, we copy you on the ground. You got a bunch of guys about to turn blue. We're breathing again. Be advised there are lots of smiling faces in this room."

"There are two of them up here," said Aldrin.

Collins listened to the landing report and added, "Don't forget one in the command module. You guys did a fantastic job."

"Thanks, Mike," answered Armstrong. "Just keep that orbiting base ready for us up there now. Houston, we were a little busy worrying about program alarms and things like that . . . I can't tell you precisely where we are."

"Roger, Tranquility. No sweat. We'll figure it out."

The dust kicked up by the engine during the landing scattered, and the astronauts could see clearly out *Eagle's* windows. Aldrin described what he saw to the men at Mission Control. People all over the world listened on radio and TV. "It looks like a collection of just every variety of rock you could find. Some of the rocks and boulders look pale purple, but the general color is tan."

Aldrin and Armstrong were anxious to get out of the small cabin and move around on the surface. They unstowed their moon-walking gear and helped each other struggle into helmets, gloves, and boots. There were many levers, keys, and buttons on the instrument panel, and the astronauts had to be careful not to hit any of them with their clumsy equipment. They strapped oxygen tanks onto their backs and began pressurizing their suits.

Aldrin flipped a switch on the panel and soon the cabin was depressurized. He pulled the hatch handle down and opened the door. Armstrong crawled out onto a small platform, called the porch, outside the hatch. Then he carefully backed down the ladder mounted on one of the landing legs.

A television camera mounted on another leg of *Eagle* began sending pictures to earth of Armstrong's slow climb down the ladder. Viewers around the world waited to watch man's first moon walk.

Armstrong reached the last rung of the ladder and stepped off the LM. His boot sank slightly into the fine-grained moon dust. "That's one small step for a man, one giant leap for mankind," he said. The radio headset in his helmet transmitted his voice a quarter of a million miles through space back to earth.

NASA, courtesy Newsweek

In the photograph at the right, astronaut Neil Armstrong makes the historic first step on the moon. Above, Colonel Aldrin inspects a particle-collecting apparatus. "The sky is black," Armstrong said, "but it seems more like daylight than darkness. It's a peculiar thing, but the surface looks very warm and inviting. It would be a nice place to take a swimming suit to get a little sun. The surface seems like desert sand." However, there is no oxygen on the moon and life outside the pressurized cabin without spacesuits would be fatal.

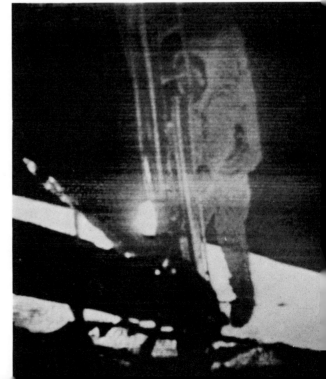

"It's quite dark here in the shadow of the LM and a little hard for me to see if I have good footing." He worked his way out of the shadow and into the light, being careful not to look directly into the blinding sun. "It's very pretty out here," he added.

The television picture was fuzzy, but viewers could see Armstrong move into the light.

Scientists on earth were eager for Armstrong to collect rock samples from the moon. Man had observed and studied the moon from earth but did not know how it was formed or where it came from. Was it a fragment of the earth flung into space as earth was formed billions of years ago? Or was it an asteroid trapped into earth orbit as it journeyed through the solar system eons ago? If rock samples could be returned to earth they could be analyzed to help solve this riddle.

His bulky space suit made it hard for Armstrong to bend over to pick up rocks around *Eagle*. He had to use a long aluminum pole with a scoop on the end to collect rock samples.

"It's no trouble to walk around," he said. "The surface is very soft, but here and there where I plunge with the sample collector I run into a hard crust." Armstrong stuffed the rock samples he gathered into a zippered pocket on the leg of his suit.

Aldrin watched Armstrong from the window of *Eagle*. He was impatient to get out on the moon and asked, "Are you ready for me to come out?"

"All set," Armstrong answered, "I'll try to watch you from underneath."

Aldrin backed out on the porch and closed the hatch. He hopped down from one step to the next and jumped from the last step. He leaped back up to the end of the ladder and then jumped down again to show how easy it was.

"Beautiful view," he said to Armstrong.

"Isn't it something? Magnificent sight out here."

"Magnificent desolation," replied Aldrin.

HALLS OF FAME

Across the level landing plain they could see a low ridge on the horizon. Shadows on the moon were velvet black, as was the sky, but the sun focused on the stark landscape like a high-intensity spotlight.

Aldrin walked a few steps away from the LM and then tried running. He found that the easiest and fastest way to get around was to take long, leaping strides. Because the moon's gravity is less than earth's, he could lope along in a near-run without becoming exhausted.

"The rocks are covered with powdery dust and are rather slippery," Aldrin reported to Mission Control. "My boot tends to slide easily. To keep our balance we have to lean forward slightly with our arms dangling down in front of us. Neil and I look like apes stalking around up here."

The astronauts took pictures of each other and gathered many different types of rocks which they packed into sample boxes. Armstrong assembled a seismograph near the LM. This instrument could detect vibrations caused by meteors hitting the moon's surface and transmit this data back to earth.

The only wind on the moon was solar wind—a stream of atomic particles from the sun which constantly bombards the surface. Aldrin set up a small screen designed to trap some of these solar particles. The screen would be brought back to earth for analysis.

A plaque was mounted on the landing ladder and would remain on the moon to mark the landing site. Armstrong removed the covering which protected the plaque and read the inscription aloud. "Here men from the planet Earth first set foot upon the Moon, July 1969 A.D. We came in peace for all mankind." Beneath this inscription the crew members and the President of the United States, Richard M. Nixon, had signed their names.

The astronauts then unrolled an American flag which was wrapped around an aluminum pole and hammered the pole into the moon's crust.

Tranquility Base is shown with all scientific gear in place. Aldrin inspects the seismometer with blue solar panels and gold-colored beryllium container. Beyond the seismometer is the laser reflector. In the rear stand the flag and TV tripod.

Armstrong looked for a place to set up a laser reflector which would be used to bounce back a narrow beam of light aimed at it from earth. Scientists could then determine the exact distance of the moon from the earth. Armstrong loped toward a small hill a few hundred feet from the LM and said to Aldrin, "I think straight out on that rise is as good a place as any for the laser. It'll probably stay on the high ground there and . . ."

"Watch it!" Aldrin yelled to him, "The edge of that crater drops."

Armstrong stopped abruptly and sank several inches into the lunar soil. He looked down and saw that he had almost toppled over the edge of the crater. "That's kind of a drop-off there, isn't it?" he said and backed away slowly to set up the laser reflector on less treacherous ground.

"It's easy to get disoriented out here," he reported to Mission Control. "The horizon is so close on the moon that you can't see very far ahead of yourself. It's kind of like being tossed around on the open sea in ten-foot waves."

Armstrong walked back to *Eagle* and stacked the boxes of rocks they had collected. Their oxygen supply was running low and it was time for the astronauts to return to their cabin. Aldrin climbed the ladder first, opened the hatch, and entered *Eagle*. Armstrong passed the rock boxes up to him and then joined Aldrin in the cabin.

When the LM was pressurized again, the astronauts were able to take off their helmets and gloves. Moon dust had collected on their suits and boots. Some of this dust now floated around in the cabin. They noticed that the dust had a peculiar pungent odor, "like gunpowder," Aldrin said.

"Mission Control, this is *Columbia*. What is the report on the moon expedition?" Collins, in orbit 60 miles above the moon, had not been in touch with his fellow crew members since they landed.

"*Columbia*, this is Houston. The crew of Tranquility Base is

back inside their cabin, repressurized. Everything went beautifully. Over."

"Hallelujah!" radioed Collins.

It was twelve-thirty in the morning in Houston. The ground
crew at Mission Control was tired but elated with the success of
the landing. The astronauts had been awake and working hard
for almost twenty-four hours. Aldrin aimed his camera at Armstrong for a souvenir snapshot. Armstrong's eyelids were swollen
from fatigue and his face was unshaven, but he smiled broadly
and Aldrin snapped his picture.

Lift-off from the moon was scheduled in six hours and the

Astronaut Neil A. Armstrong, Apollo 11 commander, right, and astronaut
Edwin E. Aldrin, Jr. are shown back inside the Lunar Module soon after both
have walked two hours and twenty minutes on the lunar surface. Each one
posed while the other snapped his picture. The pipelike appliances near their
mouths are part of their communications headsets.

NASA

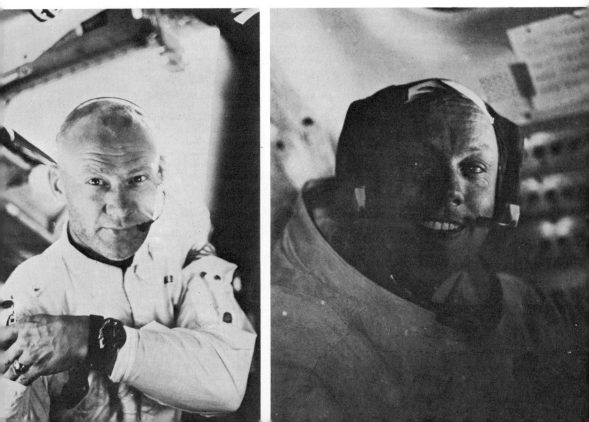

astronauts had a few hours to sleep. After a light meal Aldrin curled up on the cabin floor and fell asleep while Armstrong rigged up a hammock facing the window. He could see the earth, a blue and white disc surrounded by black space. Armstrong slept restlessly. The mission was not over yet and he had much on his mind.

Four hours later the astronauts were awake and ready to blast off for the rendezvous with *Columbia*. Armstrong fired *Eagle's* rocket and pulled back on the throttle. The moonship lifted off the surface and climbed into orbit.

From *Columbia*, Collins picked up *Eagle* on his radar screen and waited for the craft to come into view from his window. He reported to Mission Control, "It's a nice crisp lunar day. The moon is a warm tan color and doesn't look sinister or forbidding as it can when the sun hits it at an angle."

Then Collins spotted *Eagle* heading towards him. "Houston, this is *Columbia*. I've just sighted *Eagle*. She's getting closer and larger, brighter and shinier, right smack dab where she should be. Now all we have to do is dock and get home."

An abrupt jolt shook *Columbia. Eagle* was docked. Collins floated up to open the hatch and then pushed himself into the tunnel to greet Armstrong and Aldrin.

"Welcome home," Collins smiled and shook their hands.

Armstrong and Aldrin smiled back from the LM and passed Collins the rock boxes. He handled them as if they were packed with rare jewels.

When all three astronauts were back in the cabin of *Columbia*, Collins ignited the large thrust rocket, and *Apollo 11* broke away from the moon's gravity and began its journey home. The astronauts watched as the moon, framed by their cabin window, grew smaller and smaller.

For the first time human beings had walked on land that was not earth and explored the fringe of a dusty, lifeless lunar sea.

Sẽnor Kon-Tiki
THE STORY OF THOR HEYERDAHL
BY ARNOLD JACOBY

It was summer holiday, and as always, young Thor Heyerdahl was spending the season in the open moors of the lofty Norwegian inland mountains where he could walk in the woods and see all about him signs of the animals in which he was so interested.

Thor's kingdom was the mountain plateau, nearly three thousand feet above sea level, a boundless playground with adventures waiting for him everywhere. The true Norway—his Norway—was the moors where the last rugged trunks of pine, fir, and birch stopped and handed over the barren soil to windswept dwarf birch and juniper, wild flowers, rock clothed with gray, green and yellow lichen, and isolated groups of hill farms

From the book *Señor Kon-Tiki* by Arnold Jacoby. Copyright 1967 by Arnold Jacoby. Printed in the United States of America by Rand McNally & Company.

or shepherds' huts, with gray, weathered, log walls and roofs of turf on which the grass still grew. There were jagged peaks, far away in a blue haze and, deep in a kind of underworld below, thickly forested valleys with sparkling strips of rivers.

Nevertheless, all the loveliness of Norway did not make life perfect for young Thor. He could not swim. Once he fell through the ice in a nearby pond and nearly drowned before his friends could rescue him. Another time he went with the gang to Kirkebuten (Church Bay), a gloomy cleft in the mountain south of the town church. Thor, who had had a fear of water since his close call in the pond, would not go swimming with the others; he joined them afterward in a game and, in his excitement, slipped off a narrow plank bridge and fell into the sea. Paralyzed with fright his friends watched him splashing wildly. Then one of them rushed off to the nearest bathhouse for a life belt. Thor had already been under twice before the boys hauled him up.

Another tragedy at this time increased still more his fear of water. A schoolmate of the same age, the son of the head watchman in the brewery, was lost in Kirkebuten. Full of morbid curiosity, Thor hurried there with the other boys; but when he stood and looked down at the dark waves washing the seaweed at the foot of the cliff, he was overcome by a fear that came from another and a nameless world. Without a word to his companions he turned away from the yawning abyss and ran the long way home until he stood behind locked doors. From then on, the depths of the sea were to him like the gate of death, and the sea with its quiet rollers became a living creature that with invisible hands drew its helpless victims down below.

This boy who feared water so dreadfully was to grow up to be the young man who found that the only way to prove his beliefs was to cross part of the Pacific Ocean with only a few balsa logs between him and the sea.

HALLS OF FAME

One day, when Thor and his mother were on a long hike in the mountains they came upon a tumbledown log hut. It had recently become the home of Ola Bjorneby, a weather-beaten man, the son of a wealthy landowner who had lost all his money. Ola could not bear the thought of staying in his former surroundings under these conditions, so he packed his few possessions in a knapsack and went into the wilderness to live as a hermit by hunting and fishing.

The hut, which Ola had borrowed from a shepherd, had an earth floor. On one side the space between the ground and the bottom log was so wide that sheep could get through. On some stones in a corner of the shack stood an iron pot. This was his kitchen. The only other furniture was a homemade table and a couple of stools. Beneath a heap of blankets and hides on a bunk close under the roof, Ola slept all year.

As their friendship grew, Thor was allowed to join Ola during the summer and be his helper. Now the fourteen-year-old was able to see how an intelligent man could so accustom himself to the wilderness that he was perfectly at home there, just as much as a hare or elk. For the first time in his life Thor had to work hard, carrying heavy loads of wood, hay, fish, and game, and he would not show signs of fatigue, even if sometimes he were ready to drop. If they had been fishing all night, they slept all day on a flat rock at the edge of the marsh.

In the time he spent with Ola Bjorneby, Thor learned about tracks in the grass, about what can be read from a tuft of fur caught high up in a tree, and of how to live in the wilds in all weather and under every condition. He often said later that his lessons from Bjorneby were among the most important in the whole of his upbringing.

When Thor got back to school that year, he shared with his schoolmates the feelings of adventure and joy of being able to live completely with nature, with none of the newfangled things which man had invented to make his life softer. He wanted to experience life for himself, in close contact with nature, to set out on journeys of discovery to strange and distant lands. His friends pointed out that there were very few places left to discover, but Thor had heard of the mystery of the Polynesian Islands, far from the coast of South America. Scientists were confused about who the people were who had settled the islands, and were awed by the great stone statues which stood there. At fourteen, Thor Heyerdahl decided to find out for himself.

Meanwhile, Thor was able to write and illustrate stories of his own about children who left home for tropical countries and islands. Reading was a passion with him. He read the usual boy's adventure stories of the period, but of much greater interest to him were the illustrated books about foreign lands and peoples.

As he grew up, Thor retained this strong interest in the Polynesian people and their origin, and studied everything he could find that was related to this interesting problem.

When he was just twenty, Thor married a young woman who felt as he did about living close to nature. Together, they decided to spend a year on a completely natural island, that is, with no modern aids or conveniences, an island where they could explore and study plants and animal life. This island was to be Fatu Hiva. Before they set out on the final leg of their journey to this Pacific island they spent some time on Tahiti with the Tahitian Chief, Teriiero. There they prepared for life in the wilderness.

With Chief Teriiero they had their first education in native ways of life. They learned to eat with their fingers—everything from sweet potatoes to soup—to light a fire with two sticks, to catch crayfish with a three-pronged spear, to roast breadfruit in the embers, and to bake fish and root vegetables in the stone-lined earth oven. They also learned to make tools of bamboo, bark, and different sorts of leaves.

One time, when he was catching crayfish in the Papenoo river below Teriiero's house, Thor stepped on a prickly river snail and lost his balance. The next moment the current swept him down toward the mouth of the river. He struggled frantically. When he saw the ocean breakers beyond, his old fear of water completely paralyzed him. But he told himself that he must keep calm; he must remember everything about learning to swim that he had heard over and over again when he was a boy. He began to use the strokes, found himself gliding smoothly through the water and was soon washed up on a sunbaked sandbank, surprised at how easy it had been when compelled by necessity and determination. Although waves and breakers still filled him with panic, from that day on his fear of deep water vanished.

On Fatu Hiva, Thor and his wife had many adventures, learning how to live by primitive means and studying the life of the island. One day they were cutting a path through the jungle accompanied by natives when they came upon a huge slab entirely covered with strange symbols and menacing human figures with raised arms . . . No doubt magic had been associated with it once upon a time, for the natives became frightened and solemn.

"Tiki," they said in low voices. "Menui tiki." ("Gods. Many gods.")

Thor wrote that night in his journal: "The forest was quiet after the rain, and just behind us hung a reddish peak of lava above the roof of the jungle, menacing and sharp as a knife. We felt as if it was watching our work and guarding the ancient secret of the stones. And at our feet the grotesque figures danced their motionless dance as if petrified by the sunshine. They had stood like this for centuries, since the time when an unknown civilization ruled the Marquesas Islands. They were a mysterious people, who remain an unsolved enigma of science. Where they came from and who they were no one knows. The only traces we have are huge walls and terraces of enormous stones, left by a branch of the unknown race who once raised the colossal stone statues on Easter Island . . . We suspect that there were many hidden clues here in the deserted jungles of Fatu Hiva, the island which has been overlooked by science." An old islander, Tei Tetua, spoke of Tiki, the god and chief who had brought his ancestors to the islands from "a great land far beyond the sea."

"As I pursued my research," said Thor, "I was impelled to go on digging deeper and deeper, trying to identify the place or origin of the all-Polynesian tribal god Tiki."

In later discovery trips through the island Thor found many more carvings, all of which resembled in style and workmanship carvings found among the primitive Inca Indians who had at one time been known to inhabit Peru and the South American coast as far north as Central America. The Spanish explorer, Francisco Pizarro, had seen fair-skinned, bearded men among the Inca Indians. Was this only a coincidence?

When they finally returned to civilization, the Heyerdahls became interested in the similarities between the Polynesian natives and the Indians on the northwest coast of Canada. Others had discovered this similarity but when Thor suggested that the Polynesians, the Indians of northwest Canada, and the Indians of Peru might all be closely related, he found it difficult to get anyone to listen to him. He wrote papers describing his findings and backing them up with archeological discoveries he had made, but it was hard to get anyone influential to read them, and no one would accept his theory.

Thor had learned about a white chief-god who had made an unexplained departure from Peru.

"I am no longer in doubt," said Thor, "that the white chief-god Sun-Tiki who left Peru was identical with the white chief-god Tiki, son of the sun, who reached Polynesia and became the legendary founder of the earliest island culture. And the details of Sun-Tiki's life in Peru and the ancient names of places in Peru crop up again in historical legends about the ancestral homeland still current among the natives of the Pacific islands."

But how did the sun-king and his followers reach Polynesia?

The conclusion was that they arrived on balsa rafts with sails. Many old Spanish documents have left descriptions of their construction and efficiency.

When the first explorers reached Peru they met a whole flotilla of such rafts putting to sea full sail toward an island off Ecuador and loaded with Inca troops. However, at the end of the nineteenth century this seagoing type of raft disappeared, and when modern scholars took an interest in the voyages of the Incas, the balsa raft had been forgotten in Peru.

Now, no one would believe that it would have been possible for early South Americans to sail balsa rafts to the Polynesian Islands. "Well, if you think a trip from Peru to the Pacific Islands on a balsa-wood raft is possible, try it!" is what Thor heard from many people in many languages. His lonely struggle to be believed led only to contempt and mistrust. Thor resolved that he would indeed show the skeptics—scientists and laymen alike. He finally got enough financial backing to enable him to do the job. He rallied five able-bodied and congenial men, and together they made the trip to Peru. Thor and one of his men went into the jungle to choose and fell the balsa logs which would go into their raft. On these logs would depend the success of their voyage, the proof of his theory, and their very lives.

To assist in the raft construction, they hired some Peruvian seamen with Inca blood in their veins. Nine balsa logs, two feet in diameter, were lashed together with lengths of rope, and across these, thinner logs were placed at intervals of about three feet. Deep grooves were cut in the circumference of the logs to prevent the ropes from slipping.

H A L L S   O F   F A M E

A cabin was erected amidships to shelter the crew, their personal possessions, the radio equipment, and the technical instruments. It measured eight by fourteen feet, and to diminish the pressure of wind and sea it was built so low that a man could not stand upright under the ridge of the roof. The walls, roof, and floor were all made of woven bamboo.

A large bipod mast of heavy mangrove wood, on which the square sail was to be hoisted on a bamboo boom, was raised forward of the cabin. They used the same form of keel as was used by the Incas on all of their rafts for navigational purposes.

In the whole construction of the raft not a single spike, nail, or wire rope was used. It was laboriously fastened together with about three hundred different lengths of one-inch and quarter-inch hemp rope, each firmly knotted.

The projected voyage produced a variety of reactions from specialists and the general public alike. Many thought it was simply the product of a boyish thirst for adventure. Others thought it a mere advertising stunt. Most people laughed at the whole business, and continued to laugh even when the raft was a good way out at sea.

But ahead lay a whole complexity of known and unknown perils. The heavy and violent storms in southern latitudes could tear both sail and rigging from the raft. Waves as high as battleships could reduce the logs to matchwood. The raft could be driven off course and lie adrift long after provisions had been exhausted. Hurricanes could wash the crew overboard, or they might be sucked down into the depths by the giant octopuses that climbed on board at night.

The raft was christened with coconut milk and named *Kon-Tiki* after the legendary sun-king who had led his fair-skinned people westward to Polynesia more than 1,500 years ago.

On April 28 the *Kon-Tiki* was towed out to sea by the tug *Guardian Rios* and on the following day they entered the Hum-

boldt Current which comes up from the Antarctic, sweeps its
cold waters along the coast of Chile and Peru, and swings west
just below the equator. The tug hove to, the towrope was cast
off, and the *Kon-Tiki* was left alone. The sail was hoisted, but
hung slack, showing *Kon-Tiki's* bearded head painted in red, a
copy of an ancient stone statue of the god. When the *Guardian
Rios* disappeared over the horizon, the raft still lay dipping up
and down on the same spot. But the breeze came, blowing up
from the southeast, and by late afternoon the trade wind was
blowing at full strength.

"We were at sea at last!" Thor wrote. "When darkness crept
over the waters, our first duel with the elements began. We were
still uncertain whether the sea would show itself a friend or an
enemy. When, swallowed up by the darkness, we heard the
general noise from the sea around us suddenly deafened by the
hiss of a roller close by and saw a white crest come groping
toward us on a level with the cabin roof, we held on tight and
waited uneasily to feel the masses of water smash down over us
and the raft.

"But every time there was the same surprise and relief. The
Kon-Tiki calmly swung up her stern and rose skyward unper-
turbed, while the masses of water rolled along her sides."

As the days and nights passed, the six men steadily gained
confidence in their raft. What did it matter if a mountain of
water rose high around them, so long as they knew the raft
stayed on top? However, the next question was—how long could
they count on it staying on top?

After a week or so the sea grew calmer, and they noticed that
it became blue instead of green. Hardly a day passed without
the raft receiving visits from astonishing or alarming creatures
from the deep. Whales and porpoises appeared everywhere.
Shoals of three or four big whales came right up to the side of
the raft, so close that only part of the whale was visible in the

viewfinder of the camera. Sharks, too, paid them many visits, and they captured as many as possible as a following shark would be dangerous if any man should fall overboard.

The marine creature against which the experts had warned them the most was the giant octopus, which could get onto the raft. For protection each of the crew armed himself with a long machete knife which he took with him into his sleeping bag at night. Yet they were to see few of these monsters, and then mostly just the shine of the phosphorescent eyes staring at them from the water after dark.

On a couple of occasions the raft sailed over a great dark mass like a reef under the surface of the ocean. Presumably, this was the dreaded giant ray, but they never got close enough to make out its shape clearly.

Thor was constantly busy with observations and experiments. He recorded the expedition's daily life on 16 mm. film, wrote a detailed logbook, experimented with fishing methods and the extraction of thirst-quenching fluids from raw fish, and collected and prepared samples of plankton and other marine life. He never tired of studying this miniature world with its countless variety of incredible shapes and colors when viewed under his magnifying glass.

On July 4 the *Kon-Tiki* sailed into her first storm. As the towering waves built up, the men watched with anxiety. In an incredibly short time the seas around them were flung up to a height of fifteen feet, while single crests were hissing twenty and twenty-five feet above the trough of the sea. But the astonishing raft took everything with ease, and the combat with the storm became an exciting form of sport.

After a second storm, however, the *Kon-Tiki* had become weaker in the joints. In fact, the strain had stretched all the ropes, which in turn had dug themselves deeper into the balsa wood. Thor recorded:

"We thanked Providence that we had followed the Incas' custom and had not used wire ropes, which would simply have sawed the whole raft into matchwood in the gale. And, if we had used bone-dry, high-floating balsa at the start, the raft would long ago have sunk into the sea under us, saturated with sea water. It was the sap in the fresh logs which served as an impregnation and prevented the water from filtering in through the porous balsa wood."

Toward the end of the third month the first signs appeared of land ahead somewhere out in the boundless ocean ahead of the *Kon-Tiki*. First they spotted some frigate birds; then in the stomach of a shark they found an undigested starfish, a certain sign of coastal waters ahead. From then on they observed an increasing number of sea birds every day.

When the crew awoke on July 30 the first island was visible as a short blue pencil line against the red morning sky behind them. This had to be the atoll of Puka Puka, the first outpost of the Tuamotu group, and they had passed it in the night. The trade wind and the current carried the raft farther on into Polynesia, although the men tried unsuccessfully to change course to get back to Puka Puka.

On August 3 another coral island, identified as Angatau, was sighted, and they set their course for it. However, they soon realized there was a dangerous coral reef a hundred yards from land. They circled the atoll, but finally had to give up in their attempts to find an opening which they could navigate.

One of the crew decided to go in the dinghy to fetch more help from land. He found a village, but his sign language did not suffice to make the villagers realize that the strange craft now drifting farther and farther out to sea had no propeller and needed their help to return to their island. It was completely dark before he managed to persuade three canoe-loads of natives to guide him back through the reef and only through signals flashed from the mast were they able to find and catch up with the drifting raft. Only one man had landed in Polynesia after exactly ninety-seven days on the raft, the period calculated by Thor back in New York to reach their destination.

Three days later the raft was drifting toward the dangerous Takume and Raroia reefs. The crew made great effort to steer clear and for awhile it looked as if they would succeed. But as the dawn rose on their hundred and first day at sea, the watch hurried into the cabin and roused all hands: Land Ahead!

The wind had changed and they were drifting straight toward the Raroia coral reef, lying part above and part under water, like a breakwater where the sea was white with foam and leaped high into the sky. Behind the reef idyllic islets lay in a string around the still lagoon inside. It was obvious that they had now only a few hours more on board the *Kon-Tiki*. Everything was prepared for the push through the thundering inferno ahead. Each man was told precisely what he was to do. Life itself was at stake, and there was not a minute to waste.

Thor recorded, "The breakers thundered in the air and the sea rose and fell furiously. All hands were at work on the deck, and the radio operator got word through that we were drifting toward the dangerous Rarioa reef.

"The swell grew heavier and heavier, with deep troughs between the waves, and we felt the raft being swung up and down, up and down, higher and higher.

"A sea rose straight up under us, and we felt the *Kon-Tiki* being lifted up in the air. The great moment had come; we were riding on the waveback at breathless speed, our ramshackle craft creaking and groaning as she quivered under us. The excitement made one's blood boil. I remember that, having no other inspiration, I waved my arm and bellowed 'Hurrah!' at the top of my lungs. On we ran with the next enormous sea rushing in behind us; this was the *Kon-Tiki's* baptism of fire: all must and would go well."

Again and again the seas grasped the balsa raft and tumbled over it and its weakening crew with tremendous force. Each time they thought that the raft might now have been washed past the murderous reef they looked up and saw still another wall of green about to strike them.

When they hit the reef there was barely a bump. Again and again they were struck by the force of the waves and pushed toward the calm on the other side of the reef and again and again they were sucked back into its thundering purgatory by the backwash.

There was nothing that the men could do but cling to the ropes which held the raft together. Their very existence consisted of hanging on against the force of the waves.

They all had one single thought—hold on, hold on, hold, hold, hold! At last the punishing waves relented and they were in the calm of the lagoon.

Thor's final entry that day read, "I shall never forget that wade across the reef toward the heavenly palm island that grew larger as it came to meet us. When I reached the sunny sand beach, I slipped off my shoes and thrust my bare toes down into the warm, bone-dry sand. Soon the palm tops closed over my head, and I went on, right in toward the center of the tiny island. In the interior two quite tame terns flew about my shoulders. They were as white and light as wisps of cloud . . ."

The strange journey was over and all hands were alive!

Thor had proved that the trip from Peru to the Polynesian Islands on a primitive balsa raft was possible. No one could deny it now. But there were other, related theories to be tested and new people to be convinced. Thor's adventures had just begun.

Telegraph Boy
A STORY OF ANDREW CARNEGIE
BY CLARA INGRAM JUDSON

Andrew Carnegie was twelve years old in 1848 when his father decided to move his family from Dunfermline, Scotland to America. Modern weaving machines had forced Mr. Carnegie out of the weaving business, and he hoped that America would give him a new start. Young Andrew was eager to go to America because of the many opportunities there. He was quite a little businessman already, having raised rabbits with his friends. Also, he and his cousin Dod had peddled gooseberries for his Uncle Lauder.

Although they hated to be in debt, the Carnegies borrowed $100 from a friend, Ella Henderson, to help pay for their trip to America. Andrew, his parents, and his brother Tom sailed across the Atlantic to New York City. From there they went to Pittsburgh, Pennsylvania, where they had relatives. In Pittsburgh, Andrew began working to help pay the debt.

One day, when Andrew was almost fifteen years old, he heard that there was a delivery-boy position available at the telegraph office. The pay for this job would be higher than he had ever earned before. That night Andrew asked to be allowed to talk to Mr. Brooks at the telegraph office, but his father said no. Mr. Carnegie was not sure that the boy could do the work because he was so small for his age. That night Andrew went to bed wishing sadly that he could have taken the job. He did not know that his father would feel differently in the morning.

In the morning, Mr. Carnegie seemed to have changed his mind. "We will go early to see about that job, Andra," he said, as they ate their porridge. "You will need me with you to make sure no advantage is taken of your youth."

Andrew was pleased in a way, but concerned, too. He knew that his father, like many of the neighbors, had pride in keeping his Scottish brogue and ways. Of course Scots spoke English, but in their own way, often hard for Americans to understand. When the Carnegies had first come and Andrew was looking for a job, boys had shouted "Scotchie!" at him unkindly. Now many of those same boys were his friends. He was careful to say his words the way they did. But he could not hurt his father; he loved him. They left together.

As they came near the end of their two-mile walk, Andrew saw that his father was getting more and more nervous. Near the telegraph office, Andrew thought of a plan.

"You wait here, Father," he said quietly. "I'll go in and see if Mr. Brooks is there."

"Well . . . if you're not afraid. But remember, I'll wait right here, Andra."

"I'll be sure to call you if anything goes wrong," Andrew promised.

The brief interview with Mr. Brooks went well.

"When can you start?" Mr. Brooks asked.

"Right now, sir," Andrew said.

"Then sit on that bench. You'll get a message to take soon."

Messages came in fast that time in the morning. It wasn't ten minutes until Andrew was called. He picked up the message and hurried down the stairs and to the place where his father was standing.

"I got the job, Father," he said proudly. "I'm working now."

"Good laddie! Then I'll be getting back to my work," William Carnegie said.

Andrew found the new job different and the hours long. But none of that surprised him. He was getting more money. His greatest problem was his ignorance of the streets, even though George McLain, the first telegraph boy, helped him. He saw he must learn the streets and the people quickly.

Pittsburgh in that year, 1850, was a city of some 40,000 people. It had grown up on a point where two rivers, the Allegheny and Monongahela, meet to form the Ohio River. The big business of Pittsburgh was sending merchandise from east to west and west to east. In this business, telegraphing had become very important.

As Andrew walked back to the telegraph office on Wood Street near Fourth he memorized the name of each street he passed. And when he went out with the second message, he committed to memory the names of all the firms in the block. Most of the stores and offices were in cheap wooden buildings, hastily put up after the terrible fire of 1845.

On his job Andrew found out that his smallness seemed not to be noticed. He had friendly ways. Men noticed that the little Scottish boy was always ready and willing to do an extra bit of work. In this busy city men liked that.

On a Saturday evening not long after Andrew took his new job, Mrs. Carnegie counted out their earnings as usual. Then she brought out the sock. Proudly she tipped it and spilled out the silver fifty-cent pieces.

"Count them!" she ordered. They all counted.

"Two hundred!" Andrew exclaimed.

"Two hundred!" Mr. Carnegie cried, astonished.

"I was sure it was two hundred," Andrew's mother said. "Andra, Monday morning you are to take this money to the bank you told of. Get a draft—isn't that what you called it? Safe, you said it was. And I shall send it to Ella Henderson."

"Then we'll have no more debt!" Carnegie's voice actually shook with relief. This was the happiest evening they had known for years.

"Now if you could only have some of your money yourself, Andra," his mother mused. "You need cloth for shirts . . ."

"Don't you fret, Mother," Andrew said. He didn't want their fine evening spoiled. "I'll think of something."

He didn't say what he had already thought of.

As the telegraph business increased, Mr. Brooks needed more boys, and Andrew suggested friends who lived near his home on Rebecca Street. All his life Andrew liked to have his friends work with him.

The plan that had come to Andrew concerned the ten cents extra the boys got for delivering messages outside the city limits. Each boy could keep that ten cents himself. There were often quarrels about these dimes.

One morning when Mr. Brooks had ordered the loud talking to stop, Andrew remarked quietly, "We could put all our dimes together and at the end of each week divide up fairly. The walking and the money evens up—I've been keeping track."

"Who'd keep the record of our money?" David asked. The others eyed Andrew thoughtfully.

"I could do that," Andrew told him. "I know how to keep books. You can see the record and the money."

The boys agreed to the plan and gave him their dimes. On each Saturday Andrew spread the money and the record on the counter, and they watched while it was counted and divided— each boy getting an equal sum. In America, this was Andrew's first business deal that was with money and people. It was quite a different thing from rabbit feeding or selling gooseberries.

Mr. Brooks was pleased with the new plan, too.

Working hours were long. Andrew had to be at the office at seven in the morning and take his turn at sweeping out. Three nights a week he must stay till the office closed; he seldom got home before eleven. These evenings were trying because there was so little to do; he simply had to be there in case a message came.

While he sat waiting, Andrew thought about his education. No one had mentioned school since the Carnegies left Dunfermline. If I want to read books and to learn, Andrew thought, I must find the way myself.

Before he had solved this problem, an exciting day came for Andrew. The local superintendent of the Telegraph Line came by to inspect the corps of messengers. Not only had this man, Mr. James D. Reid, come from beloved Dunfermline, but he ordered the boys to be measured for uniforms of dark green jackets and knickerbockers. Andrew was so proud of his as he walked the streets of Pittsburgh that he organized a visit of the messenger boys to Mr. Reid's to thank him.

Messages often had to be delivered by the green-clad boys to the Pittsburgh Theatre. Here leading actresses and actors were presenting plays of Shakespeare. If delivery of the messages came near performance time, the kind-hearted manager would let the boys slip upstairs to the gallery and see the play.

Arriving home late one evening, Andrew explained his good luck to his mother. "I got to see a play at the Theatre. You never saw such a beautiful place, Mother. There are great chandeliers that sparkle when the lights go on, grand golden curtains, and crimson velvet trim on the seats."

"What play were they giving?" asked his mother, watching her son's glowing face.

"It was *Hamlet*. Listen, I can even remember one of the fine speeches." Young Andrew drew himself up tall and proclaimed slowly,

> *To be, or not to be: that is the question:*
> *Whether' tis nobler in the mind to suffer*
> *The slings and arrows of outrageous fortune*
> *Or to take arms against a sea of troubles,*
> *And by opposing end them?*

"Isn't that grand? Oh, I hope I get a chance to deliver another message there soon."

Andrew had found a way to continue his education. He learned the plays of Shakespeare by ear before he had a book to read them in, just as he had learned the poems of Burns from hearing Uncle Lauder read and recite them before he read them himself. Gradually the thrill of the words and the drama of the stories made him long for books to read and a chance to learn.

Then he heard of Colonel James Anderson. Colonel Anderson had books—400 of them—that he was willing to lend to working boys. Andrew found out about the books from his friend Tom Miller, who lived near the Andersons. On his first free evening, Andrew went to see Colonel Anderson.

"Yes, I am glad to lend books to working boys. Come on Saturday evening, and you may choose one to have for a week," Colonel Anderson said kindly.

"Oh, thank you, sir," said Andrew. "I'll be sure to have it back on time."

In the weeks that followed he borrowed Bancroft's "History of the United States," Macaulay's essays, and even some of Shakespeare's plays.

Then one day the treasure was closed to him. Colonel Anderson had purchased more books and had persuaded the town of Allegheny to supply him with a building. He employed a librarian to manage the "Mechanics' and Apprentices' Library."

When Andrew went to get a book, the librarian asked, "What is your trade?"

"I'm a telegraph boy," answered Andrew proudly.

"Oh, we don't loan to such boys!" the librarian said firmly. "We lend to boys who *work*."

"But I work, sir!" Andrew protested. "I work hard."

"You just run with messages. That's not work. He wants to lend books to boys with a trade—carpenters, bakers, and such. Sorry, son, but that's the rule."

As he walked home, Andrew figured his money in his mind. Could he possibly buy a book? It would be wonderful to own one. But he wanted to read many books, not just one. And he needed clothes. Anyway, the telegraph business was important. Why was it not as important as building a house or baking bread?

A new thought popped into Andrew's mind. As soon as he

got home, he begged a piece of paper and a pen from his mother. He wrote a letter to the newspaper, the *Pittsburgh Dispatch*. In it he said about the library, ". . . its means of doing good have recently been greatly circumscribed by new directors who refuse to allow any boy who is not learning a trade and bound for a stated time to become a member. I rather think that the new directors have misunderstood the generous donor's intentions." At the end he signed it "A Working Boy though not bound."

In the morning, on the way to work, he left the letter at the newspaper office. The very next day his letter was printed in the paper. Andrew was so pleased he could hardly keep his secret—but he did.

Two day later there was an answer in the paper. It explained that the library could lend books only to apprentices, but others could subscribe two dollars a year for the privilege. They did not offer to change their rules. Gleefully Andrew noticed that men discussed the two letters. So people *did* read the printed letters; he'd wondered. He wrote a reply defending all kinds of work and again urged that the managers "have certainly misunderstood the generous donor's intentions." This he signed "A Working Boy" and dropped it in the box at the newspaper office.

The next day the newspaper carried a notice, "'A Working Boy' will confer a favor by appearing at our office." He found that the rules were changed. He could call Saturday and borrow a book. Andrew's first attempt at changing a man's opinion was successful.

Andrew was soon so impressed by his new learning that he and his friends formed a debating club of six members. They met in Mr. Phipps's shoeshop. They chose a different topic for each meeting and debated it hotly. This gave purpose to Andrew's reading, for he tried to find books in the library that would help him in the debates. After a while he made rules for himself: Feel at home while speaking; talk *to* your audience, not *at* it. And never orate; be yourself. Their interest led the boys to joining the Webster Literary Society of Pittsburgh.

One day, Mr. Glass, the downstairs office manager, stopped Andrew as he went by.

"I have to be out of the office for a while, Andy," he said. "Think you could take my place for an hour?"

"Yes, sir," Andrew replied quickly, but he was so astonished that he wondered whether he said the words or thought them. Mr. Glass took messages that were to go out, checked the written words, and figured the cost. Andrew had no idea that Mr. Glass had even seen him! And now he was gone, and almost at once a man came in to send a telegram. Andrew did his best, and when the manager returned, he seemed pleased. After that he was often called downstairs, and his pay was raised.

Upstairs at the office the messages arrived in the Morse code of dots and dashes; Andrew decided he would learn this. But the operator objected to having a boy touch his tapes. Then Andrew heard there was a man down the line who could read messages by sound.

He began paying attention to sounds, teaching himself the meaning of combinations of long and short. Often he had a chance to check himself by reading scraps of paper thrown away. The knack was easier than he expected.

Mr. Brooks called to him one day. "Andy, come here a minute. Our business is growing so fast we need another operator. I hear you've been learning to take messages. Think you could be an assistant operator?"

"Yes, sir, I can do it," Andrew said quickly, trying to hide his surprise and delight. What would his mother say? Maybe she could stop making shoes now that her son would be on his way to earning a fortune.

HALLS OF FAME

He proudly wrote Dod, "I have got past delivering messages now and have got to operating. I am to have four dollars a week and a good prospect of getting more soon."

In his letters to Dod or Uncle Lauder, it wasn't enough to tell about the improving financial situation of the family. He said, "I have the characteristics of 'our folks' rather strongly developed, as Aunt Aitken would say, and am of course therefore a great, or rather small, dabbler in politics. . . ." He thought it would be "beneficial to us both (Dod and Andrew) to examine into the systems of government by which we are ruled." They could debate the subject by letter.

Andrew enjoyed having new experiences to write them about. But he never failed to have a word to say about the "Young Republic" he now lived in. "We believe we have a mission to fill," he wrote. "Our mission as the representative of a new era, as the pioneer of liberty, is to serve as an example to other nations, to incite them to come up to the true standard, to impel people to ask and obtain new reforms and go on steadily until the world can bear a peace congress or a simple Republic."

Andrew Carnegie did well as a telegraph delivery-boy, and that was only the beginning of his career. He knew how to get along with people, and he had an inborn ability to manage money. In a few years he became one of the most successful businessmen in America. While making a fortune in railroads, oil, iron, and steel, he helped to build the nation. In doing this he pioneered some business practices that became widely used during the industrial age.

After his retirement, Andrew Carnegie gave nearly all of his money to various people and organizations. Having gained much of his education from borrowed books, he believed that educational materials should be available to those who could not afford to buy them. He contributed money to build thousands of libraries all over the world, and aided numerous educational institutions. He used his good business sense in giving away money just as he had in earning it. He tried to give only to those who would use the money wisely. Often the donation was in the form of a trust, so that its benefits would continue over a long period of time.

Carnegie felt indebted to America for the opportunities he had received to better himself, and he felt it was his duty to help others to succeed as he had. Today many Americans still benefit from his generosity.

Jane and the Wild Chimps
THE STORY OF BARONESS JANE VAN LAWICK-GOODALL
BY GEORGE CROSSETTE

Ever since she was a very little girl, Jane Goodall loved animals of all kinds. When Jane was only nine years old her mother took her to a lecture given by a gentleman who had a large golden eagle. He asked if anyone would like to hold the huge bird and Jane was the first one from the audience to reach its side.

When she was still a young woman, Jane Goodall became the world's foremost authority on chimpanzees. During the first three years of her study she discovered facts about these intelligent primates that other scientists had overlooked for many years. Armed with this new knowledge we may wonder, as we laugh at the chimps in the zoo, if perhaps they are also laughing at us.

Born in London, England, on March 4, 1934, Jane came from a family with many interests. Her father was a successful business executive whose exciting hobby was racing motor cars. Her mother was a well-known author. Her only sister, Judy, developed a business of her own making reproductions of artifacts for museums.

While growing up in London and Bournemouth, Jane spent most of her free time watching mammals, birds, and insects. She kept notes on the animals living around her home and recorded everything she noticed about their activities. Her favorite subjects were mice, squirrels, various birds and their eggs, turtles and sea shells. At one time she published a little

Flo, right, a chimpanzee, holds her baby while his older sister Fifi nuzzles and plays with him. Fifi was a devoted baby sitter for several months until her brother became too independent. Then she left him to their mother.

MY BOOK HOUSE

Making Friends With the Chimps

At right, this chimpanzee mother must be reassured that Jane will not harm her baby. Jane gently extends the back of her hand, being careful to keep her fingers turned away. This is a chimpanzee sign for "no harm intended." Even so, the ape's mother, Flo, keeps an arm around his waist, alert to whisk him to safety if he is endangered. By watching the wild chimps for a long time Jane was able to learn many of the signs by which they communicate with each other.

Below, when Flo allowed her eleven-month-old baby to seek Jane out, Jane knew she had finally gained the complete confidence of the chimps. Not seen in the photograph, Flo is near by, watching his every move. Jane spent months waiting patiently for the chimpanzees to become accustomed to her. It was worth the long wait when they accepted her as a friend. Like many children, this little chimp is shy with strangers. But because Jane is so patient, he is overcoming his fear, and will soon be in her arms.

Photos by Baron Hugo van Lawick © National Geographic Society

magazine containing stories about her wild friends. She even
started a small museum in her home. Seeing creatures caged
bothered her but Jane realized that thousands of people would
never have a chance to see certain animals if it were not for the
world's many fine zoos. She appreciated the importance of zoos
to science and learning.

Jane's spending money went to buy books about animals
living all over the world. She longed to visit the places she read
about where exotic beasts were plentiful. Before she really
knew where Africa was, Jane told everyone, "When I grow up,
I'm going to Africa to study animals." With this ambition in
mind, she worked as a secretary until she had earned enough
money to go to Africa and see her beloved animals.

While visiting a friend in Kenya, Jane met the world-famous
anthropologist Dr. Louis S. B. Leakey, who was in charge of
Kenya's Natural History Museum. She was delighted when
asked to become Leakey's secretary because it brought her one
step closer to her childhood dream.

Her work with Dr. Leakey began at Olduvai Gorge where the
riddles of early man were slowly being solved by study of newly
unearthed prehistoric remains. Jane often took long walks with
the Leakeys' dogs near the digging site. On one occasion she
came face to face with a lion. It growled and followed her for
some distance as she tried to walk away. She said, "The moment
of seeing the lion was terrifying. After that, it was exciting."

To round out his program of research on evolution, Dr. Leakey
had been trying to find someone to study the behavior of chimpanzees. He needed a person with patience, someone willing to
spend a great deal of time observing these animals. He finally
decided Miss Goodall was the one to undertake the task. At Dr.
Leakey's urging, Jane began what was to become the longest
continuous field study of chimps on record.

In June, 1960, Jane settled into her new home, the thirty-

square-mile Gombe Stream Game Reserve in Tanzania. Here a
large number of chimps lived protected by law. Conditions were
rugged and supplies hard to obtain. Jane worked long hours,
from dawn well into the chilly night. Often her only meal for the
day was a can of cold beans. At one point both Jane and her
mother, who stayed with her for the first few months, fell desperately ill. Without proper drugs or care, they lay in bed for
ten days with high fevers until their bodies could fight off the
sickness.

In spite of the hardships, Jane did not give up. She went on
looking for the chimps day after day, armed only with a pair of
binoculars. Time passed and she had almost despaired of ever
spotting one of the elusive chimps. Finally, from the top of a
high hill, Jane saw dark specks moving through the trees below
her.

Naturally, the chimps fled from Jane at first, but since she
worked alone and quietly, they gradually came to accept her
presence. She stationed herself near them each morning for an
entire year before the shy animals would allow her to observe
them from a distance of thirty feet. It took two years to get
them to come into her camp for bits of food. Jane forgot all the
long hours of sitting in blazing sun and pouring rain the day a
chimp first took a banana from her hand.

In order to understand the chimps better, Jane experimented
with imitating them. She stayed in the trees a great deal, studied
and tested their nests, and tasted their foods including the insects they seemed to enjoy so much. In fact, one of Jane's most
important discoveries was that wild chimpanzees are not strictly
vegetarian. She found that they hunt, kill, and eat not only
insects but chickens and small monkeys as well.

Jane did not allow visitors to her camp at first for fear the
chimps, which had become accustomed to her, would be frightened by strangers. It was vital for Jane to make friends of her

subjects because the strong apes could be dangerous enemies. Friends they became, and Jane fondly gave the chimps such fitting names as David Greybeard, Fifi, old Flo, Mr. Worzle, Pepe, and Merlin. She studied them as individuals and as a society, noting every detail of their behavior from bedmaking to throwing stones. Bananas and blankets began to disappear from camp as the chimps grew bolder. A chimp would clutch a blanket and suck on one corner like a small child. Jane felt that at long last she was making progress and discovering valuable new information about chimpanzees.

Before Jane came to the Gombe Stream Game Reserve, the chimpanzees had never had bananas to eat. She brought them with her and used them to make friends with the chimps.   Photo by Baron Hugo van Lawick © National Geographic Society

Chimpanzees often remove the leaves from sticks and use them to fish for termites. When the ends of the sticks are bent, the chimps break them off to make a new point. Their ability to make such tools was undiscovered before Jane lived with them in the jungle.

Jane's findings changed a number of ideas people had about chimpanzees. It had been stated that the difference between man and animals is that man is able to make and use tools, whereas animals cannot. But Jane watched the chimps strip leaves from twigs and poke the sticks into termite nests to draw out the insects for food. Surely this could be called making and using a tool. When the chimps gathered leaves, crushed them, and used them to sponge up water or to clean their furry bodies, they were certainly using a tool. Therefore, as Dr. Leakey said, we must either classify the chimpanzee as man or change our definition of what man is supposed to be.

In 1962, Jane permitted the National Geographic Society to send Baron Hugo van Lawick, a Dutch wildlife photographer, to the reserve to record on film some of the amazing facts she had uncovered. When Hugo arrived in camp, Jane was most favorably impressed by his great concern for the wild animals. He was anxious to learn how to avoid frightening them. Jane and Hugo the working partners became husband and wife in 1964.

The couple's first son was born in March, 1967. Jane found she had a wonderful opportunity to compare a human baby's behavior with that of the infant chimps. She noted that male chimps took no part in family life but that a mother chimp kept her baby at her side for about three years and did not completely release it for another three years. Jane observed that chimp mothers demanded and obtained strict obedience. Both young and adult chimps recognized and responded to certain sounds. Touch was also important in communicating. The animals seemed to find a sense of security in touching or hugging each other. The most distressing fact Jane learned was that she could usually predict a baby chimp's next move but she could seldom outguess her son's actions.

Jane received her doctor's degree in a science called ethology in 1965 and, working with a number of assistants, she began to study various phases of animal behavior. Her findings were published in many journals, including the *Annals of the New York Academy of Science, Nature,* and the *National Geographic Magazine.* The National Geographic Society also published her book *My Friends the Wild Chimpanzees* in 1967. Although her husband was the team's official photographer, Jane became expert with a camera and had many pictures published.

Jane certainly fulfilled her childhood aim of studying animals. Her career gave her such great satisfaction that she said of it, "As far as I'm concerned I don't work. I just do what I enjoy. It's a good life."

The Loneliest Battler
THE STORY OF JACKIE ROBINSON
BY GEORGE VASS

The hotel clerk pointed at Charley Thomas, a member of the
Ohio Wesleyan University baseball team of 1910.

"We don't register blacks in this hotel," the clerk told Coach
Branch Rickey, a former major league catcher. "I can't give
that boy a room."

Rickey tried to stifle his anger. He knew what he was up
against. This was 1910, and he was in South Bend, Indiana,
where his team was to play a game. Few people then would have
criticized the hotel clerk for refusing a room to a black man. In
those days Negroes were not permitted to stay in the same hotels

From the book *Champions of Sports: Adventures in Courage* by George Vass. Copyright © 1970 by George Vass.
Published by Reilly & Lee Books, a division of Henry Regnery Company. Reprinted by permission of publisher.

as white men, eat in the same restaurants or even, in many cases, attend the same schools.

But Rickey was determined. Either Thomas would stay at the same hotel as the rest of the team, or they would all leave. The clerk, fearing to lose the whole team, finally consented to put a cot for Thomas in Rickey's room.

Thomas couldn't fall asleep. He sat on the cot crying and staring at his hands. He began to tear at one hand with the other, as if he were trying to scratch off the black skin with his fingernails.

"Charley, what are you doing?" cried Rickey.

"It's my hands," sobbed Charley. "They're black. If only they were white. If it weren't for my skin, I'd be as good as anyone, wouldn't I, Mr. Rickey? If only my hands were white!"

Rickey felt sorry for Charley and indignant at a world that could humiliate a man because of his color. He tried to soothe Charley's hurt feelings.

"The day will come, Charley, when your hands won't have to be white," he said.

That day was not to come until thirty-five years later. By that time Rickey had become one of the most important men in major league baseball.

Rickey developed the powerful St. Louis Cardinal teams that won National League pennants in 1926, 1928, 1930, 1931, 1934, 1942, 1943 and 1944.

He was considered the finest judge of talent baseball had ever known. He introduced such great players as Pepper Martin, Dizzy Dean, Jim Bottomley, Enos Slaughter, Terry Moore, Stan Musial, Morton and Walker Cooper, Red Schoendienst and many more.

Yet all these players were white men. In those days, by unwritten law, Negroes were not allowed in professional baseball.

Black men were limited to their own leagues. Rickey, a deeply religious man, waited for the right moment to give the Negro his chance in baseball.

That moment came during World War II, which the United States entered in 1941. Rickey left the Cardinals at the end of the 1942 season to become president and general manager of the Brooklyn Dodgers.

As the war continued, more and more men went into the armed forces. Baseball began to run short of talent, and Rickey saw his opportunity. He suggested to the Dodger board of directors that this would be a good time to scout Negro players. After hearing Rickey's arguments, the directors agreed.

Rickey saw that the war against Hitler had changed the racial attitudes of many Americans. How could a country fighting for human rights and freedom continue to consider baseball the national game as long as it excluded the black man?

The time was ripe for bringing the Negro into organized baseball. But Rickey was a smart man, perhaps the most brilliant baseball has ever known. He wanted to be sure everything would be ready for the introduction of the black man.

More than anything else, he had to have the "right" black man. The player he chose would have to be sufficiently qualified for the major leagues. He also would have to have unusual intelligence and moral courage. He would have to be able to take great abuse without losing self-control.

"We have to find a man who is right off the field," Rickey told the Dodger directors. "We will know about his playing ability in uniform, but what about out of uniform? Will he be able to take it? What about his habits, his associates, his education, his intelligence?"

Rickey considered these things important. He knew the first Negro player would be faced with many insults and challenges.

81

Most major league players were Southerners, men who, because of their upbringing, were prejudiced against Negroes. Some of them would treat the first black player with contempt and perhaps even try to injure him physically.

Rickey also considered it important that no one know his intentions in advance. If bigots found out he intended to bring a Negro into organized baseball, they would try to stop him. He needed a way to hide his plans.

In the Spring of 1945 Rickey announced he was forming a new Negro baseball league. He sent out scouts, supposedly to find players for the new league. Actually, he was looking for the man who would be the first Negro player in major league baseball. The scouts did not know this. They were told to find the best Negro baseball player in the country.

Scout after scout came up with the same name: Jackie Robinson. They gave Rickey a complete report on Robinson, then twenty-six years old and a shortstop for the Kansas City Monarchs, an all-Negro team.

Robinson was born on a sharecropper's farm near Cairo, Georgia, on January 31, 1919, the youngest of five children. Six months after Jackie was born, his father deserted the family. His mother, Mrs. Mallie Robinson, was left to raise the youngsters.

Life was difficult on the Georgia farm, and in 1920, at the invitation of a brother, Mrs. Robinson moved the family to Pasadena, California. She got a job as a domestic, scrubbing floors and ironing clothes so the family could afford food and a place to live.

Mrs. Robinson was a forceful, religious woman and a great believer in education. Her faith assured her the Negro could improve his lot through hard work. She tried to make sure her children would have an opportunity to rise above poverty.

Even though there wasn't always enough food in the house

for more than two meals a day—sometimes consisting of only bread and sweet water—Mrs. Robinson made sure the children got their schooling. The youngsters also filled out the family budget by selling newspapers and running errands.

Jackie did his share of work, but he also took a great interest in sports. He idolized his brother Matthew (Mack), who was six years older than he, because he was such a fine athlete. Mack was a track star and finished second to the great Jesse Owens in the 200-meter run at the 1936 Olympic Games.

Yet there was a time when Jackie could have gone wrong. Like many poor youngsters, in his teens, he belonged to a gang. While the boys in the "Pepper Street Gang" never did anything seriously wrong, they were mischievous and occasionally got into trouble with the Pasadena police.

Fortunately, a teacher took an interest in Jackie.

"Jack, you know in your own heart that you don't belong in a gang—at least, with a crowd that might steer you into trouble," the teacher told Jackie. "Most of you youngsters who fall into the gang habit do so because you're afraid to be considered different, afraid not to follow the crowd.

"Well, let me tell you something. Only first-class suckers let themselves be pressured into doing what they don't want to do. It takes guts and imagination and intelligence to go your own way, to be different, to stand on your own two feet. You'll not only be a much better person but better off, too, if you resist doing wrong and forget about being called 'chicken.'"

Jackie never forgot the teacher's advice. It gave him a new outlook on life. He never followed the crowd again just to be a "good guy." He was able to resist the temptations to smoke and drink because he knew that a good athlete could not afford to do things that might weaken his endurance and slow his reflexes.

By the time he entered Muir Technical High, Jackie's life

revolved around sports. He excelled at football, baseball, basket-ball and track. He was a rare combination of coordination and competitive fire.

He was so aggressive that some people thought he was "too cocky." If they were prejudiced, they said he was "too uppity" for a Negro. Yet the coaches were delighted with Jackie. He was a "holler guy" and the team "spark plug."

From Muir he went on to Pasadena Junior College, where he set a world record for junior college athletics with a broad jump of 25' 6", and on the same day helped the baseball team to the conference championship. All told, he batted .417 and stole twenty-five bases in twenty-four games.

Jimmie Dykes, then manager of the Chicago White Sox, saw him play.

"That boy could play major league baseball at a moment's notice," said Dykes.

The "moment" was to be a long one. In the fall of 1939 Jackie entered the University of California at Los Angeles, where he won national fame. He excelled in five sports, adding tennis to his skills. As a halfback one year he averaged twelve yards per carry.

"It's my honest opinion that Jackie Robinson will go down in history as the greatest all-around athlete in Pacific Coast history," wrote George T. Davis of the *Los Angeles Herald Express*.

Unfortunately, his participation in so many sports—he was the first athlete in UCLA history to win letters in four sports—hurt Jackie's grades. His mother was disappointed because she wanted him to become a professional—a doctor, lawyer or coach. He preferred the last, often using it as an excuse to go out and play.

"If I am going to be a coach," he would tell his mother, "I'll have to keep on playing. You can't teach a game if you don't know it."

But in the spring of 1941 his grades were low. He was worried about his family's financial situation. He wanted to be able to help his mother; he also wanted to get married.

The girl's name was Rachel Isum. She was preparing to become a nurse. Rae—as Jackie called her—was as attracted to him as he was to her. She quickly sensed what a proud young man he was, why he reacted so strongly to the people who insulted him because he was a Negro.

They fell in love and planned someday to be married. Rae didn't want Jackie to quit school. However, he wouldn't listen. He had to get ahead. He left UCLA, played professional football for a while, then was drafted into the U.S. Army.

Before he was discharged from the Army in late 1944, he had been promoted to lieutenant, a rare feat for a Negro in those days.

Robinson returned to civilian life first as a basketball coach, then as a player for the Kansas City Monarchs, where Rickey's scouts found him.

But even before Rickey got in touch with Robinson, Jackie had had a major league "tryout." No real test of his ability, it was closer to a farce. The Boston Red Sox, yielding to political pressure, called Robinson and two other Negro players to Fenway Park in mid-1945. The Red Sox officials watched the three players for a few minutes, then sent them home. They weren't about to be the first to have Negro players on their team.

The memory of this experience in Boston was still fresh in Jackie's mind in August, 1945, when the Monarchs were to play a game against the Chicago American Giants in Chicago's Comiskey Park.

Clyde Sukeforth, one of Rickey's scouts, was in the stands. He introduced himself to Jackie. Jackie was suspicious, but Sukeforth was insistent. He said that he represented the Brooklyn Dodgers and told Jackie of Rickey's plans to organize a team of players to be called the Brown Dodgers.

Reluctantly, thinking of the Boston farce, Jackie agreed to accompany Sukeforth to Brooklyn to meet Rickey.

Rickey was an impressive man, with bushy eyebrows, deepset, brilliant eyes and a round belly. His voice was resonant, reminding one of a prophet's, especially since he frequently used Biblical expressions. His first question was to the point.

"Do you drink?" he demanded.

"No, I don't," replied Jackie.

"You got a girl?"

Jackie was embarrassed at first, hesitantly replying, "I don't know."

"What do you mean, you don't know?"

"I mean that I had a girl, one to whom I'm engaged, but the way I'm traveling around with the Monarchs, never seeing her or anything, a fellow can't be sure if he's got a girl or not."

"Is she a fine girl, good family background, educated girl?"

"They don't come any finer, Mr. Rickey."

"Then you know doggone well you've got a girl. When we get through today, you may want to call her up, because there are times when a man needs a woman by his side. By the way, are you under contract to the Monarchs?"

Jackie explained he merely had an agreement from payday to payday to play with the Monarchs. Rickey asked him if he knew why he had been invited to Brooklyn. Jackie said he thought he was to play for the Brown Dodgers.

"No, Jackie, that isn't really it," said Rickey. "You were brought here to play for the Brooklyn organization—perhaps, as a start, for Montreal."

"Me, me play with Montreal?" Jackie was stunned.

"If you can make it. If you can make the grade."

While Robinson sat in a daze, Rickey continued to speak, explaining the difficulties, all the hostility they would both face. He portrayed scenes in which Jackie would be made conscious of his color, in which he would be cursed because he was black.

"You're playing shortstop and I come down from first, stealing, flying in with my spikes high, and I cut you in the leg," said Rickey. "As the blood trickles down your shin I grin at you and say, 'Now, how do you like that, nigger boy?' What do you do?"

Jackie seethed as Rickey spoke. He was a black man with tremendous pride and self-respect. All his life he had tried to convince white people that he was not a coward, that he was as good a man as any other, no matter what the situation.

"Mr. Rickey, do you want a ballplayer who's afraid to fight back?" he burst out.

Rickey shouted, "I want a player with guts enough not to fight back!"

Then he continued his explanation. "We're tackling something big here, Jackie," said Rickey. "If we fail, no one will try it again for twenty years. If we succeed . . . well, we're dealing with the right of any American to play baseball—the American game."

He glared at Jackie, as if trying to read his mind. "This is one battle we can't fight our way through," Rickey said. "Remember what I said, Jackie: no army, no owners, no umpires, virtually no one is on our side. This is a battle in which you'll have to swallow an awful lot of pride and count on base hits and stolen bases to do the job. That's what'll do it, Jackie. Nothing else."

For three hours Rickey prodded, tested, exhorted and evaluated Jackie. He concluded by offering Jackie a thirty-five hundred dollar bonus and a salary of six hundred dollars per month to play the next season for the Montreal Royals, a Dodger farm club.

He also warned Jackie not to reveal the agreement until Rickey was ready to announce it in October. The only people he could tell were his mother and Rae. When the meeting with Rickey was over, Jackie telephoned them, telling them he had accepted the challenge.

But there was no way he could tell them how hard it would be for him to take abuse in the effort to show that a black man could succeed in the major leagues. He would have to stifle his urge to strike back and protest. Yet his mother and Rae understood instinctively the sacrifice in pride that Jackie had been asked to make.

On October 23, 1945, Jackie appeared at a press conference in Montreal, where it was announced that he had been signed to a contract. The announcement caused a furor among baseball people and sportswriters.

Jackie Robinson and Branch Rickey agree on a contract for Jackie to play in the major leagues.

HALLS OF FAME

William G. Bramham, commissioner of minor league baseball, was angry.

"Father Divine (a Negro minister) will have to look to his laurels," said Bramham, "for we can expect Rickey Temple to be in the course of construction in Harlem soon."

Jimmie Powers, sports editor of the *New York Daily News*, predicted: "Robinson will not make the grade in the big league this year or next . . . Robinson is a 1000-1 shot."

But there were people on Jackie's side, too. Red Smith, a famous sports columnist, wrote: "It has become apparent that not everybody who prattles of tolerance and racial equality has precisely the same understanding of the terms."

The controversy raged all winter. Meanwhile, Jackie went on a barnstorming tour of South America. Then he returned to California to marry Rae on February 10, 1946. They decided to face the ordeal together.

After the honeymoon, they flew to Daytona Beach, Florida, where the Montreal Royals were to train after a week of preliminary drills at Sanford, a small town twenty miles away.

When he reached Sanford, the newspapermen were waiting for Jackie.

"What will you do if one of these pitchers throws at your head?" one writer asked.

"I guess I'll duck, just like anyone else." replied Jackie.

"If you're going to play shortstop with Montreal, you want to become a Dodger and take Pee Wee Reese's job as a shortstop for Brooklyn, don't you?" asked another writer.

"I'm not after anyone's job," replied Jackie. "I'm going to do my best to make the team and play where I'm assigned to play. Right now, I haven't got time to think about Brooklyn. I haven't made Montreal yet."

He hadn't even made Sanford. The population of the small

town objected to the Negro's living there. Rickey ordered Jackie back to Daytona Beach to wait for the rest of the Royals.

There was more trouble ahead. In mid-March the Royals played an exhibition game with Indianapolis in Deland, Florida. When Jackie scored a run in the first inning of the game, a policeman ran onto the field.

"Get off the field right now," the policeman ordered Jackie, "or I'm putting you in jail."

Jackie turned and walked toward the dugout. Clay Hopper, manager of the Royals, came out to face the policeman.

"What's wrong?" Hopper asked.

"We don't allow Negroes to mix with whites in this town," the policeman said. "You can't change our way of living. Negroes and whites can't sit together and they can't play together."

Hopper didn't answer.

"Tell that black man to leave," said the policeman. Jackie left.

Hopper, too, suffered, but in a different way. He was from Mississippi and had little regard for Negroes. When Rickey had told him that Jackie was to play for Montreal, he was shocked.

"Please don't do this to me," he begged, "I'm a white man. I've lived in Mississippi all my life. If you do this to me, you're going to force me to move out of Mississippi."

Yet from the start Hopper was courteous and pleasant to Jackie. He tried desperately to control his deep-seated prejudices. Only occasionally did they break out. An instance came when Jackie made a remarkable play while Hopper and Rickey watched.

"No other human being could have made that play," exulted Rickey.

Hopper whirled around. "Mr. Rickey, do you think he's a human being?"

But being a sound and experienced baseball man, Hopper

tried to be fair in judging Jackie's skills. He soon saw that
Jackie, because of an arm injury, would be better off throwing
from the second-base position than from shortstop. That's why
Jackie opened the 1946 International League season for the
Royals at Jersey City, New Jersey, at second base.

The large crowd at first greeted him with boos. But by the
time he had grounded out in his first time at bat the cheers had
begun to drown out the jeers.

Jackie responded to the encouragement. The second time up
he hit a home run with two men on base. Before the day was
over, in five times at bat he had had four hits, stolen two bases
and driven in three runs. Montreal won 14-1, and Jackie was on
his way. The crowd roared its appreciation.

But almost every step was difficult. In 1946 a Syracuse
player held up a black cat and shouted, "Hey, Robinson! Here's
one of your cousins!"

Jackie gritted his teeth and remembered Rickey's plea to
answer insults with base hits. He cracked out a double, and when
he reached second base, he shouted to the Syracuse player, "I'll
bet my cousin's pretty happy now, huh?"

Perhaps the worst moment of that first year came in Baltimore, then a minor league town with Southern prejudices. The
Baltimore players and fans were unbelievably vicious in their
name-calling. But although Jackie came close to a nervous breakdown, he played on, steadily improving as the season progressed.

With Jackie leading the way, hitting .349, Montreal won the
International League championship. The Royals went on to take
the Little World Series from Louisville, champions of the
American Association.

At times during the season Rickey would visit Montreal for
talks with Jackie.

"For as long as you are in baseball you must conduct yourself as you are doing now," said Rickey. "You will always be on trial."

Jackie did so well that first year that press opinion swung strongly in his favor. His fine playing indicated that he was almost certain to succeed as a major leaguer the next season if Rickey gave him a chance.

But Rickey was cautious as always. He had chosen Montreal as the site of Jackie's introduction into baseball because it was a Canadian city, with little prejudice against Negroes. Brooklyn and the other cities in the National League might present a different problem.

After the 1946 season, Rickey called his people together to discuss the next step to be taken with Robinson. Hopper was on hand. He hadn't said much about Robinson and just listened as Rickey spoke.

"Sure, the boy has hit minor league pitching," said Rickey. "But the majors are something else. And how about off the field? Can he handle the problems and the praise he's going to get in the majors?"

Hopper could no longer bear Rickey's indecision. He whirled on his boss, earnestly thrusting his face close to Rickey's.

"Mr. Rickey," said Hopper, "you don't have to worry about that boy. He's the greatest competitor I ever saw, and what's more, he's a gentleman."

Rickey smiled. He could see that Jackie had scored a major victory by winning over Hopper, who just a few months before didn't really think of Jackie as a human being. It was just what the Dodger boss wanted to hear. He knew Jackie was ready for the majors in 1947.

All that winter Rickey laid ground. He met with Negro leaders and explained that, just as Jackie would be on trial as a major leaguer, so would black people as major league fans. He made certain there would be as little friction in the stands as possible.

Rickey also shifted the Dodger and Montreal training sites to Havana, Cuba, where there was little probability of racial trouble. Nothing was left to chance.

One thing Rickey could do little about was the attitude of the Dodger players who were to be Jackie's teammates. For a moment it looked threatening. Outfielder Dixie Walker wanted the Dodgers to join him in a protest against Robinson. When they refused, he asked to be traded but then agreed to wait until season's end.

Reese, the Dodger shortstop and captain, helped Rickey's cause by standing up for Jackie's right to a trial with the Dodgers.

There was one final complication. Since the Dodgers had Reese at shortstop and Eddie Stanky at second base, Rickey and Leo Durocher decided Robinson would have a better chance as a first baseman. When training started, Jackie had to learn how to play first base.

Jackie quickly showed he could play first base well enough, and he got off to a good start as a hitter in training. He was still on the Royals' roster, and Rickey waited for the right moment to move him to the Dodgers.

On April 10, 1947, the Dodgers announced they had acquired Jackie from Montreal. The announcement came a day after Manager Durocher had been suspended from baseball for a year by the commissioner. This took the spotlight away from Jackie and eased the pressure a little.

When Manager Burt Shotton took over the Dodgers, Jackie made his way into the Dodger lineup. He was greated coolly by his new teammates.

His first major league game, against the Boston Braves at

Ebbets Field in Brooklyn on April 15, 1947, was hardly startling. The Dodgers won 5-3, but Jackie failed to hit, grounding out to third, flying out to left and hitting into a double play. He was safe on an error when his bunt was booted.

The next day he beat out a bunt for his first major league hit. His next hit was a home run against the New York Giants. Then he fell into a slump and went hitless for five straight games. After a time the hits began to fall in, but his average was still below major league standards.

The pressures were mounting in other ways. The Philadelphia Phillies, managed by Ben Chapman, a Southerner, came to Ebbets Field.

As Jackie took his first turn at bat, some Phillies began shouting: "Go back to the bushes, black boy." "Hey, nigger. Go back where you came from." "They're waiting for you in the jungles. We don't want you here, black boy."

As the game continued, the Philly remarks became worse. Jackie's teammates, who until then had been cool to him, began to get angry at the Phillies. Dodger second baseman Stanky called time and ran over to Jackie.

"Jack, play this fellow a little closer to the bag," said Stanky, "and don't let those bums get you down."

Jackie nodded. It was the first time Stanky had given him advice. He reacted to the encouragement. The game was scoreless until the Dodgers came to bat in the eighth inning. Jackie came to bat, and the Phillies renewed their insults. He singled, then stole second and third and scored on a hit by Gene Hermanski.

The run decided the game. Jackie's response was just what Rickey had ordered. Hits and stolen bases were his answer to insults.

The press and Commissioner Happy Chandler had another response. The newspapermen criticized Chapman and the Phillies for the viciousness of their attacks on Jackie. Chandler warned Chapman to tone down his remarks.

There were other problems. The St. Louis Cardinals planned to strike in protest against Jackie's playing in the majors. But National League President Ford Frick found out about their plans and interfered. He informed the players, in part:

"I don't care if half the league strikes. Those who do it will encounter quick retribution. They will be suspended and I don't care if it wrecks the National League for five years. This is the United States of America and one citizen has as much right to play as another. The National League will go down the line with Robinson whatever the consequences. You will find if you go through with your intentions that you have been guilty of complete madness."

Rickey and Jackie had found powerful support. The wisdom of Rickey's plan was borne out. Not that everything went smoothly from then on. But Jackie proved equal to every test.

When Lenny Merullo, a Chicago Cub infielder, insulted him, Jackie checked the punch he wanted to throw. When Ewell Blackwell, a Cincinnati Reds pitcher, stopped pitching to call him a long series of names, Jackie said only, "Come on. Throw the ball." Then he singled.

More and more people started to line up on his side. Jeep Handley, a Philadelphia infielder, apologized for the way his teammates had treated Jackie. Hank Greenberg, the great slugger with the Pittsburgh Pirates, befriended him.

"Let's have a talk," suggested Greenberg. "There are a few things I've learned through the years that can help make it easier for you."

When bench jockeys became particularly vicious in one game, Pee Wee Reese came over to Jackie.

"Look, don't pay any attention to them," said Reese. "We're on your side, Jack. Just keep cool and everything will be all right."

Stanky turned on Jackie's tormentors. "You yellow-bellied cowards," Stanky yelled at the opposition bench, "why don't you yell at someone who can answer back."

His teammates' rallying to his side bore out Rickey's prediction: "The day your teammates take up the fight for you is the day we will have begun to win the battle of integration in baseball."

Off the playing field, the battle seemed to go easier. Fan reaction was mostly in Jackie's favor. There were scattered boos, but white and Negro fans in general applauded him. There were nasty notes and letters, but they were far outnumbered by favorable ones.

Heartened, Jackie began to play better. In mid-season he hit in twenty-one straight games. He improved as a first baseman, and the Dodgers began to move toward a pennant. The greatest challenge came from the Cardinals, but in a September series the Dodgers won two games out of three, with Jackie hitting .462.

Jackie overcame every barrier. At season's end he stole twenty-nine bases to lead the league, batted .297 and hit a dozen home runs. The Dodgers won the pennant—although they lost the World Series—and Jackie was chosen Rookie of the Year.

The most unexpected tribute came from Dixie Walker, the teammate who had asked to be traded when Jackie joined the team.

"No other ballplayer in this club, with the possible exception of (catcher) Bruce Edwards, has done more to put the Dodgers

up in the race than Robinson has," said Walker. "He is every-thing Branch Rickey said he was when he came up from Montreal."

Rickey exulted in Jackie's success. He knew, more than any-one else except Jackie himself and his wife, Rae, just how difficult it had been to integrate baseball. He knew how much self-control had been required of Jackie. He appreciated the courage and great moral strength of this unusual young man.

"Only those on the team know the great patience and self-control Robinson exercised continually throughout the season," said Rickey. "For this exemplary conduct, displayed both off and on the field during the entire season, he deserves the com-mendation of everyone."

Jackie played nine more fine seasons with the Dodgers. He was the league's most valuable player in 1949, when he hit .342 to lead in batting. His lifetime average for ten seasons, when he retired after the 1956 campaign, was .311.

Despite his late entry into the majors (he was twenty-eight years old), Jackie had a wonderful career. In 1962 he became the first Negro elected to baseball's Hall of Fame. As he said, "Every-thing is complete."

It was also complete for Branch Rickey. He had fulfilled his pledge to Charley Thomas, the young man who wept in 1910 because his hands weren't white. Rickey had opened baseball to black men, who followed Jackie Robinson into the game in ever increasing numbers.

But the fight was mostly Jackie's. He bore the brunt of the pain and anguish. He suffered the most.

As Rickey said: "It took an intelligent man to understand the challenge—it took a man of great moral courage to accept it and see it through. He was both."

A Rover in the Catskills

WASHINGTON IRVING (*American*, 1783-1859)

LONG, long ago, just at the close of the American Revolution, when New York was a little old town with all the air of an overgrown village, a small boy was born there whose mother named him Washington Irving in honor of General Washington. When the little fellow was about six years old his nurse took him one day to see the procession escorting General Washington to Federal Hall to take his oath as first President of the United States. Pressing through the throng, the nurse dragged her small charge up to the great man and told him that the boy had been given his name. With a kindly smile Washington stopped to give his young namesake his blessing.

Washington Irving grew to be an adventurous lad. He liked to visit new scenes and observe strange manners and customs. When he was still the merest slip of a child he made long tours of discovery into foreign parts, the foreign parts of his own little city, and more than once his parents had to employ the town-crier to hunt up their wandering son by crying his name through the town. He loved to roam around the Battery, and to wander out on the piers to watch the out-going ships departing to distant climes. With what longing eyes did he gaze after their lessening sails and waft himself in fancy to the very ends of the earth. As he grew into boyhood, Washington extended the range of his adventures. He now spent his holiday afternoons in rambles far out into the country round about New York, visiting the little villages where the descendants of the old Dutch settlers continued to dwell, and pushing on, on to the very distant hills. He made voyages, too, in a sail-boat up the lordly Hudson River whose

Irving was the first great figure in American letters. Before his time, the New World had produced no writer of note. Intensely American in spirit, he still wrote in the style of English authors preceding Queen Victoria.

cliffs and towering highlands breathed forth the very spirit of old
Dutch and Indian legends. He penetrated into the heart of the
Catskill Mountains, that rise to the west of the river, changing
their magical hues with every hour of the day.

At times he peered into some dark glen, lonely and wild and
tangled, or stood at the foot of a waterfall, a sliding sheet of silver,
slipping down over mossy rocks; again he came out on the edge of
a precipice, whence he could look out for miles and miles over all
the sun-flooded valley and see far down below the twisting ribbon
of the Hudson. He knew those mountains in sunshine and in
storm—now in the calm of evening when they threw their long
blue shadows peacefully over the valleys, or gathered a hood
of gray vapors about their heads to glow in the setting sun like a
crown of glory—now when the thunderclouds lowered, the lightning went leaping from crag to crag and peal after peal of thunder
rolled crashing down their heights. And at the foot of these fairy
mountains, its smoke curling up through the trees, would nestle
a little Dutch village, where the houses had latticed windows and
the gable fronts were surmounted by the quaintest of weathercocks.
Here in the shade of some great tree before the old tavern, Irving

could always find a club of worthies smoking their pipes and whiling away the long, lazy summer's day by telling endless stories.

But as the boy grew to young manhood, he began to long to go further still in his travels. He had seen and loved so much of the natural beauty of America, her mighty lakes and mountains, her valleys and trackless forests, her broad, deep rivers and boundless plains, but now old Europe beckoned him. He longed for her treasures of art, her quaint and different customs, her poetic associations. He longed to loiter about her ruinous old castles, and reconstruct in his fancy all the shadowy grandeur of her past. And so when the young maid who had been his sweetheart died and there was nothing more to hold him in America, off he went to England. Already he was known there as the author of *Salmagundi Papers* and that humorous mixture of fact and fancy, *Knickerbocker's History of New York*. And so in England he found a place ready made for him. He could travel now as much as he pleased and he set down in his *Sketch Book* all the interesting things he saw—little home scenes of rural repose and sheltered quiet, peasants in country lanes, as well as the solemn magnificence of grand old Westminster Abbey.

A journey to Spain gave him the rich store of Spanish and Moorish legend to put into *The Alhambra* and *The Conquest of Granada*.

After seventeen long years abroad, Irving returned to New York and bought the beautiful place called Sunnyside at Tarrytown on the Hudson, not far from Sleepy Hollow. No woman ever replaced the sweetheart of his youth and Irving never married, but here at beautiful Sunnyside he passed all the rest of his days, quitting it only once for any length of time, and then to serve for four years as American Minister to Spain. But however great was the volume of work that Washington Irving put forth, his name always calls first to mind the magic of the Catskills and the Hudson, gleaming through mists of romantic old Dutch legends. THE LEGEND OF SLEEPY HOLLOW   RIP VAN WINKLE

London Streets

CHARLES DICKENS (*English*, 1812-1870)

IT WAS a crazy, tumble-down old building on the river, the blacking factory where Charles Dickens worked, and it was literally overrun with rats. Charles was only ten years old, shabbily dressed and underfed. He lived in a garret and he had a sausage and a slice of cold pudding for his dinner. Day after day he sat before a little table in the factory and covered pots of blacking with oiled paper, for which work he received the magnificent sum of six shillings a week. Poll Green and Bob Fagin, a rough boy in a ragged apron and paper cap were his companions.

Sometimes, before work began in the morning, Charles would sit on a flight of steps leading down to the Thames and tell stories to a quaint little cockney girl, a slavey who scrubbed floors and washed dishes all day long. Then the dingy warehouses that bordered the river would give way to castles of romance and knights and ladies would cross a bridge of splendor. But when the clock struck, play time was over. The boy went off to his pots of blacking, the girl to her scrubbing, and little did either dream that Charles would some day make that little slavey famous as the "Marchioness" in one of his stories.

Charles Dickens' father was a regular Mr. Micawber, always confidently expecting something to turn up, and always going steadily down in the world. Once he had been a clerk in a navy pay office. There had even been fortunate days when Charles could go to school and read *Robinson Crusoe* and *Don Quixote*. Then for weeks at a time he was not Charles Dickens at all, but one of his heroes. Armed with a broken rod from an old

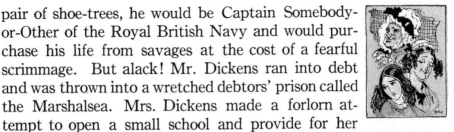

pair of shoe-trees, he would be Captain Somebody-or-Other of the Royal British Navy and would purchase his life from savages at the cost of a fearful scrimmage. But alack! Mr. Dickens ran into debt and was thrown into a wretched debtors' prison called the Marshalsea. Mrs. Dickens made a forlorn attempt to open a small school and provide for her eight children, but soon the whole family followed the father, and Charles went to work in the factory.

The little fellow felt a bitter sense of neglect and wasted talents. Sometimes, full of fancies and secret ambitions, he would tramp for miles just to look at an elegant red brick house on Gad's Hill, to imagine that it was his and he lived there. After a few years Mr. Dickens inherited enough money to get him out of prison and send his son for a brief time to school. Nevertheless, it was little enough schooling the boy could get. In dark days of grinding toil he would wander, if he had the leisure, through the British Museum to learn what he could by himself.

By the time he was nineteen Charles had fitted himself to be a reporter and, sitting up in the gallery, he reported discussions in Parliament. When he was twenty-five *Pickwick Papers* made him famous. A novelist of the poor before all else was Charles Dickens.

What a procession of characters he gives us from the London streets, ludicrous or grotesque, pathetic or lovable. Only those hard days in the blacking factory could have taught him to know these types so well, and his appeal to the hearts of men brought about more than one reform in England in the courts, in the schools, and in wretched debtors' prisons. So at last the little boy was able to buy for his own the elegant house on Gad's Hill.

DAVID COPPERFIELD   GREAT EXPECTATIONS   OLIVER TWIST   A CHRISTMAS CAROL

The Man Who Made Adolf Hitler Run
THE STORY OF JESSE OWENS
BY GEORGE VASS

Jesse Owens was too shy to push his way through the crowd of youngsters reading the bulletin board in the lunchroom of Fairmount Junior High School in Cleveland, Ohio.

He got on tiptoe to peer over the taller youngsters in front. But it was no use. Jesse, at fourteen, was small and slight for his age.

"What's it say up there?" he asked another freshman at Fairmount.

"Mr. Riley put it up," replied the friend. "It's about the track tryouts. Mr. Riley's going to hold them on the sidewalk in front of the school tomorrow. I'm going because we'll get out of the last class if we do. You going to try out, Jesse?"

"I don't know," Jesse said slowly. "I don't know if I should do that. Mom might not like it. I guess I'd better not."

"Aw, come on Jesse," urged his friend. "You'll just miss half an hour of math. And I bet you can make the team. I bet you can."

"You think so? No, I wouldn't have a chance." Jesse shook his head. "Not against those big boys. They can really run."

But Jesse, like most of the Fairmount boys, was in front of the school the next afternoon. The sidewalk had been swept clean, and the distances for events had been marked off with chalk lines. Several boys had been given stopwatches by Charles Riley, a math teacher who also coached track, to act as official timers.

First came the preliminary races. One by one the events were run off, and the excitement mounted as the names of the finalists were read. By the time the finals were reached, school had been

dismissed, but many pupils and teachers stayed to watch the races.

The freshmen were excited and shouting because one of their classmates, little Jesse Owens, had reached the finals in the 100-yard dash. His classmates were proud of Jesse but didn't expect him to win because the other two finalists were upper-classmen and had been winners in the event many times before.

Coach Riley gave the starting signal, but one of the competitors jumped the gun. Jesse's classmates started to yell. They wanted the older boy set back a few yards as a penalty. But Coach Riley refused.

He set the boys on their marks again. This time everybody waited for the signal. When it came, Jesse stumbled. For a moment his heart sank. In a short race like this a lost step could be costly. But in an instant he regained his stride and caught up with his rivals. Near the finish line he pulled away and easily won the race.

Coach Riley couldn't believe the time shown on his stopwatch.

"It can't be right," he said in amazement. "Ten seconds flat. Why, that's a new junior high school record. What's that boy's name again? Jesse Owens!"

That name was to become world famous, and Jesse was to set many more records. There was to come a period during which he set a record almost every time he ran or jumped. It may be that the most important thing he ever did in his life was to try out for track that spring day in 1928 at Fairmount Junior High.

Jesse's real name was James Cleveland Owens. He was born one of seven children on a tenant farm near Decatur, Alabama, on September 12, 1913. As a small boy, he was called J.C. for short.

He was shy and spoke so softly it was sometimes difficult to understand what he was saying. On his first day in school, when the teacher called the role, he gave his name as "J. C. Owens." She did not understand what he said and wrote down "Jesse." He was too shy to correct her, and from that time on was known as Jesse.

Like most Negroes in the South at that time, Jesse's parents, Henry and Emma, were desperately poor. Henry Owens finally decided he could better provide for his big family by moving north. In 1924, when Jesse was eleven, the family moved to Cleveland, where the father got a job in a foundry. But he could not keep it long, and the Owenses were little better off in Cleveland than they had been in the South.

If Jesse wanted to go to a movie or buy some candy, he had to earn his own money. He did it first by running errands and by scrubbing kitchen floors. But he wanted a steady job, and when he was twelve, he got it at a shoeshine shop. The owner wouldn't hire him at first because he wanted Jesse's mother to give her permission. Mrs. Owens was reluctant to let Jesse work at the shop because she was afraid he would be mistreated. She gave in only after Jesse pleaded with her and the owner promised to be good to the boy.

"I'm going to let you have Jesse," said Mrs. Owens. "But I don't want him punched around. If he gets ornery let me know and I'll paddle him."

Mrs. Owens need not have worried. Jesse was a hard worker and the owner was satisfied with him. Jesse tried to learn all he could about mending shoes. He thought someday he might become a cobbler and open a shoeshine and repair shop of his own.

But that race on the sidewalk in front of Fairmount Junior High was to change Jesse's life more than he could imagine. Coach Riley, from the moment he looked at the stopwatch, realized he had discovered an extraordinary runner. There was no telling how good this boy could become. If he could run 100 yards in ten seconds as a freshman without coaching, what might he be able to do with training as he grew bigger and stronger?

Coach Riley taught Jesse the proper way to start, how to pace himself, how to jump and how to stay in condition. It was not a difficult task, for Jesse was willing and was quick to pick up everything that Coach Riley told him. He was never out of condition and at times ran so effortlessly that people complained he wasn't trying as hard as he could.

Jesse replied to the criticism by winning and continuing to set records. Coach Riley began to hope that someday his young friend might become an Olympic champion sprinter.

When Jesse graduated from Fairmount and entered East Technical High School, also in Cleveland, he thought he had left Riley behind. But to his surprise, Coach Riley also had moved. He was now track coach at East Technical.

Under Riley's coaching, Jesse continued to improve as a sprinter. He competed in seventy-nine races as a high school boy and won seventy-five. The four defeats were understandable. In two of them he was a sophomore competing against juniors and seniors. The other two he lost were in Ohio Interscholastic finals in competition with the best runners in the state.

By 1932, when Jesse was nineteen, people were talking about him. The Cleveland newspapers ran stories about his running and jumping. He was a junior at East Tech in 1932 when the Olympic tryouts were held at Dyche Stadium in Evanston, a suburb of Chicago. His home-town fans expected to see Jesse make the team for the Olympic Games in Los Angeles.

But 1932 was not to be Jesse's Olympic year. He lost three races, two of them to Ralph Metcalfe, the great runner from Marquette University. Metcalfe, who later was to become Jesse's close friend, went on to become the standout Olympic sprinter and gold medal winner of 1932. Jesse's turn came four years later in Berlin, Germany.

Still, the years between 1932 and 1936 were successful. In 1933, at the National Interscholastic meet at Soldier Field, Chicago, Jesse had one of his greatest days. He gave a record performance for a high school boy.

Jesse ran the 100-yard dash in 9.4 seconds, tying the world record for the event. His broad jump of 24' 9-5/8" had been surpassed by few collegians and never by a high school boy. He ran the 220-yard dash in 20.7 seconds, also close to a world record.

"This is the greatest one-man track-team record in the history of schoolboy games," wrote a newspaper reporter. His neighbors in Cleveland held a celebration upon Jesse's return from Chicago.

But Jesse seemed glum during the party.

"What's the matter, Jesse?" asked a friend. "This is really something. Look how proud everybody is of you."

"I wish everybody would stop all this soft-soaping and give my dad a job," replied Jesse.

It was the time of the Great Depression, and Jesse's father, like so many millions of other Americans, was out of work. When Jesse's complaint became known, a job was found for the famous athlete's father. It was no problem for Jesse to continue his education. He had excellent marks in high school, and about thirty colleges offered him scholarships because of his track skill. He chose Ohio State University and earned pocket money by working in a filling station.

He was as successful as a college athlete as he had been in high school. Under a new coach, Larry Snyder, he broke so many records that he led Ohio State to one track championship after another.

Jesse had many outstanding days in college track, but two

of them were particularly noteworthy.

On May 25, 1935, Jesse had "the greatest day in track history," according to one newspaper account. That was the day the National Collegiate track and field championships were held at Ann Arbor, Michigan. Jesse was almost the whole show.

He again equaled the 100-yard record with 9.4. He smashed the 220-yard mark with 20.3. His time for the 220-yard low hurdles was 22.6 seconds, also a record. To top it all, he broke the broad-jump record with a leap of 26' 8-1/4".

The other outstanding performance was given in 1936 at the National Amateur Athletic Union meet in Princeton, New Jersey. Jesse revenged his defeat in the 1932 Olympic trials by out-running Ralph Metcalfe by a full yard in the 100-meter dash. His broad jump of 26' 3" beat the listed world record. Just a week later, at the Olympic trials of 1936, Jesse proved his right to compete in the 1936 games by winning every event that he entered. He set a world record for the 200-meter run.

Jesse was busy with track, study and work, but he also had time for romance at Ohio State. He married Minnie Ruth Solomon in Cleveland. They were to have three daughters, the first while he was still attending school.

In those days in Columbus, Ohio, the site of Ohio State, Jesse left his apartment at 6:30 each morning. His classes started at 8:00 A.M. and finished at 2:50 P.M. By 3:00 P.M. he was in his track uniform, working out until 4:00. Then he changed clothes and ran for the trolley to take him to work in downtown Columbus. He worked from 5:00 P.M. until 1:00 A.M., when he caught the trolley home. That gave him four hours a day with nothing to do except sleep.

It was not an easy life, but it showed Jesse's great determination. The time was at hand when that determination would be tested to the limit.

H A L L S O F F A M E

Adolf Hitler was dictator of Germany in 1936. He had made great preparations for the Olympic Games in Berlin because he planned to use them to show off the "new Germany" he was building. He hoped the games would help prove that the Germans were superior to everyone else, especially the Jews and Negroes, whom he classed as "inferior" races.

Hitler had spent many millions of dollars in preparing Berlin for the Olympics. In addition to the vast Olympic Stadium, seating more than 100,000 spectators, three other stadia had been built. There were also basketball courts, an outdoor theater, swimming pools, polo fields and a gymnasium. A huge Olympic Village was erected to house athletes from all over the world.

This elaborate preparation was intended to show the superiority of the German "master race," which consisted of those people who believed in Hitler and joined his Nazi party. The Nazis tried to bar Negroes from competing in the Olympics but discovered that if they wanted to hold the games, they would have to let blacks enter.

On August 1, 1936, the U.S. team arrived at Berlin's Olympic Stadium. They were to be dazzled by the huge show Hitler planned for the Olympics.

Jesse had his first look at the stadium the day before the event in which he was to compete in a preliminary heat. While working out, Larry Snyder, his coach from Ohio State, pulled him aside. He was worried about how Jesse would react to the Nazis' attitude toward Negroes.

"Don't let anything you might hear from the stands upset you," said Snyder. "Ignore the insults and you'll be all right."

Jesse shook his head to show he understood. He had read enough about Hitler and the Nazis to know what to expect. The Nazi-controlled newspapers attacked the U.S. team because one-third of it was composed of Negroes. The Nazis mocked the

Negroes as "Black Auxiliaries." They argued that the United States must be in sad shape because it had to rely on "sub-humans."

Jesse shook off his anger. "I came here to run," he said to himself. "All I have to do is run."

Run he did, from the opening events on. His first competition was in a preliminary heat of the 100-meter dash. The competition was weak, but he spurred himself on, finishing far ahead. Metcalfe, his old rival, met him at the finish line.

"Take it easy, Jesse," said Metcalfe. "You'd better save a little for later. This is just your first day."

Jesse laughed. "I ran that one pretty fast, didn't I?"

He was fast. His time was announced at 10.2 seconds. He would have set a new world record except for a technicality. But the records were to come later.

The next day Hitler made his first appearance at the games. Jesse glanced with curiosity at the dictator's box, trying to catch a glimpse of Hitler and his chief aides. He wondered whether they would congratulate him if he won a gold medal. It would be like a slap in the face to them if they had to honor a black man.

The first gold medal of the day was won by a German, Hans Luebke, a shot-putter. It was the first time a German had ever won an Olympic track and field gold medal, and the Nazis roared their appreciation. Luebke was triumphantly conducted to Hitler's box and congratulated.

The next two winners were Finns, followed by another German. Each man was personally congratulated by Hitler.

Cornelius Johnson and Dave Albritton, both Negroes and Jesse's friends, finished first and second in the high jump. Jesse heard a commotion and glanced up again at Hitler's box. The dictator was leaving. An announcement was made over the loud-speaker that Der Fuehrer wasn't feeling well and had decided to leave early.

H A L L S   O F   F A M E

Hitler wasn't fooling anybody. Everybody knew that he left to avoid having to congratulate the Negroes. The insult was so obvious that the International Olympic Committee had to warn the German officials that it would be unsportsmanlike for Hitler to congratulate some winners and ignore others. His answer was to meet the winners he liked privately and ignore the others. That was fine with Jesse.

Jesse had only one thought as he dug his starting pits, awaiting the gun. He remembered his mother's frequently repeated request: "Do right, Jesse, and do good."

When the gun sounded, Jesse started flying. He was 20 yards down the track before he knew he was running. His rivals flanked him for a moment, then fell behind. He was all alone, feeling the power flow from his legs onto the track. He hit the tape in 10.3 seconds tying the world record.

More than 100,000 people were on their feet, many cheering. Jesse was brought to the winner's platform and given his gold medal. He was also given a small potted German oak tree as a living memorial to his victory. The officials shook his hand. Holding the trophies he had won fairly and honestly, Jesse glanced up at the empty box of the dictator.

The next day was the fourth of the Olympics. Jesse was to compete in the preliminaries and finals of the broad jump and a heat of the 200-meter run. Coach Snyder was anxious lest Jesse burn himself out.

"Don't go all out," said Snyder. "Pace yourself. You've got a big day ahead. Just win, that's all. You can go after the records later."

It was difficult for Jesse to pace himself. At times, it seemed, he broke records almost without trying. He couldn't help himself in the 200-meter heat. He was out of the starting blocks like an explosion and won without challenge. His time was 21.1, an Olympic record.

He went right to the jumping pit. Each contestant was permitted three broad jumps, with the longest counting toward qualification. Jesse made the first jump incorrectly, and a foul was called. Once again he made his approach, but he was off stride and, stepping beyond the take-off, committed another foul.

Almost unbelievably, Jesse, the finest broad jumper in the world, the only man ever to clear 26 feet, was one try away from disqualification. His teammates were nervous. Coach Snyder moved over to pat Jesse on the back.

"You can still do it," said Snyder. "Don't let it worry you. Just keep your mind on what you're doing. You'll be O.K."

"I know it," said Jesse. "It won't happen again."

The third time his approach was perfect, and his jump well beyond the qualifying distance. Coach Snyder sighed his relief.

There was a brief rest after the morning events. Then came another heat, the semifinal of the 200-meter run. Jesse ran it in exactly the same time with which he had set the Olympic record in the morning.

An official remarked, "Owens' records don't last long. He breaks them himself even before they become official."

He walked back to the jumping pits again. He still felt strong, but his first broad jump fell short of what he expected. He wondered if he was more tired than he felt. His muscles didn't seem to be responding.

While he was waiting for his next leap, the other jumpers made theirs. The only one to challenge Jesse was Lutz Long, a German. His second jump equaled Jesse's first, and the crowd began to buzz.

The American coaches were worried. One of them walked up to Jesse.

"How do you feel, Jesse?" he asked. "Are you getting tired? You didn't look like yourself on that first jump."

Jesse smiled. "You don't have to worry about me. I feel real good, real strong."

He proved it by sprinting down the runway as if he were taking off on the 100-yard dash. He was all grace and power as he soared through the air, his arms and legs helping his momentum. When the distance was announced, the crowd roared its astonishment and appreciation. The German crowd roared as the loudspeaker said the Negro had leaped 26' 1/16"—a new Olympic record. Lutz Long smiled at Jesse in admiration.

Long was a great competitor, though, and he had one jump left. The crowd held its breath as he soared through the air. His distance was 25' 9-3/4", a new record for a European but not enough to catch Jesse, who thus was assured of his second gold medal.

Jesse had one leap left. There was no pressure on him. He had no one to beat but himself. Yet he soared through the air with an even greater effort than before. This time he went 25' 5-5/16".

The first man to greet him as he scrambled out of the sawdust was Lutz Long. The German, disregarding the Nazis, held out his hand to Jesse.

"You are magnificent," said Long to Jesse. "I have never seen anything like this before. You are incomparable."

The crowd could sense the comradeship between the two men and cheered, despite the disapproval of the Nazis. Hitler had seen the black man defeat the German. Two of his aides were sent to the jumping pit. They did not fetch the winner. They came to get Long, who had finished second. Hitler wanted to congratulate him on his fine effort. He chose to ignore Jesse. Long protested for a moment, arguing with Hitler's aides that Jesse deserved the congratulations. But he could do nothing. Long waved at Jesse as he left, as if to demonstrate his admiration for the Negro.

H A L L S   O F   F A M E

That night, despite Hitler's disapproval and all the attacks on Negroes in the newspapers, Jesse was the hero of Berlin. Everywhere he went people sought his autograph. Everybody wanted to talk with him, to express their admiration.

The next morning, on the day in which Jesse was to compete in the 200-meter finals, his barracks in the Olympic Village was besieged by autograph hunters. People rapped on the windows of the room in which he was staying to get his autograph or merely because they wanted shake hands with him.

Coach Snyder was worried that Jesse would be too tired to do his best that afternoon.

"Jesse, you've got to ignore these people," said Snyder. "Go someplace where they can't find you and you can get some rest. You'll be worn out by the time you have to run."

"I can't do that, Coach," said Jesse. "These people are my friends. I owe it to them to be as friendly as I can. Don't worry about me. I'll be all right."

Still, by the time Jesse started warming up for the finals he felt a little tired. It was late in the afternoon, and the weather had been damp and chilly, hardly ideal conditions for a sprinter. Yet a few exercises and some preliminary jogging seemed to refresh Jesse.

Just before the race there was a commotion in the crowd, and everybody's head turned toward Hitler's private box. The dictator, to everyone's surprise, had decided to watch the 200-meter finals although the likely winner was a Negro, either Jesse or Mack Robinson, Jackie Robinson's elder brother.

Hitler showed himself to the crowd and raised his hand in the Nazi salute.

"I think he's waving to me, Mack," said Jesse to Robinson, who joined in his laughter.

"I hope your legs are better than your eyes," replied Robinson.

It was drizzling by the time Jesse, Mack and the other 200-

meter finalists entered their starting blocks. The huge crowd had to strain to see them through the rain and the growing darkness. But Jesse felt good in the cool rain.

When the starter's gun went off, he flung himself forward as if shot out of a cannon. His muscles were loose, and the soggy track felt springy. He floated on it, moving smoothly, almost effortlessly, his strides gliding over vast spans of distance. He was unaware of the crowd, of Hitler's eyes upon him. Every fiber of his being was concentrated on running as he had never run before.

At the turn he was two yards ahead and gaining strength. The rain trickled down his body and seemed to stimulate him. He was almost sorry to feel the tape break as he reached the finish line.

In a moment everybody was hugging him, slapping him on the back, reaching out to shake his hands. The crowd was on its feet, cheering wildly.

Then Jesse's time was announced: 20.7 seconds, a new world record, 0.4 seconds faster than the 200-meter distance had ever been run before.

More than 100,000 throats roared anew at the announcement. The clamor was indescribable as Jesse was almost carried to the victory stand.

He glanced up again at Hitler's box. It was empty. The dictator had been forced to flee from a Negro in his own city.

Hitler's absence did not affect Jesse as he stood on the victory stand, accepting his third gold medal and another potted German oak tree. "It's a good feeling standing up here," he told the crowd. "I never felt like this before."

He felt even better when Lutz Long once again came to congratulate him. It was a brave thing for Lutz to do. Jesse knew this and appreciated Lutz's gesture.

There was one more gold medal. Jesse, Metcalfe, Foy Draper

and Frank Wykoff won the 400-meter relay in 40-seconds, also a world record.

After Berlin came the busy years of post-Olympic track. Jesse was the most famous track and field athlete the world ever had known. After an exhibition tour of Europe, he was greeted in New York City with a ticker tape parade up Broadway.

Jesse enjoyed all the acclaim, but his head was not turned by it. He knew that he had to begin to think of his future. He could not rely forever on his Olympic fame.

For a while he ran for a living. He had a wife and growing family to support. He was billed as "The World's Fastest Human." Everybody wanted to see him run. His last race came in Barcelona, Spain, in 1948. He was thirty-nine years old, and yet he ran 100 yards in 9.7 seconds. It was a tremendous feat.

He also tried a lot of other ways to earn a living. One year he conducted a band. He stood on the bandstand, and the dancers crowded up to see him—not because his band was so fine, but because he was Jesse Owens.

When World War II came, Jesse worked for the Ford Motor Company in Detroit, dealing with the firm's many thousands of Negro employees. Later, he appeared across the country with the Harlem Globetrotters, the famous Negro basketball exhibition team. Jesse did not play basketball. He appeared in his track suit and gave exhibitions at half-time.

He moved from job to job, finally settling in Chicago, where he was a disc jockey, businessman and public official.

Despite World War II, the memories of Berlin and Lutz Long in 1936 remained strong. They were to be revived in a most dramatic way.

On August 22, 1951, Jesse, now balding and dressed in a business suit, again stood in the tunnel leading into Berlin's Olympic Stadium. It had been fifteen years since his triumph here, and he was surrounded by memories. Seventy-five thou-

. sand people were waiting to greet him. Many of them, no doubt, had been there fifteen years before.

The signal came, and Jesse moved out of the tunnel into the bright sunlight of the Olympic Stadium. Slowly, he jogged around the track as the crowd gave him an ovation. Then he turned and mounted the speaker's platform, and the crowd hushed to hear him. He spoke distinctly.

"Words often fail on occasions like this. But I remember the good that happened here. I remember the fighting spirit and sportsmanship shown by German athletes on this field, especially by Lutz Long. . . . I believe the real spirit of Germany, a great nation, was exemplified here on the field by athletes like Long.

"I want the young people here to be like those athletes. I want to say to all of you to stand fast with us and let us all work together to stay free, and God Almighty will help us in our struggle. That is what the United States stands for, and I know you are with us. God bless us all."

Once more the crowd cheered, and Jesse felt a hand on his shoulder. It was Walter Schreiber, the acting mayor of West Berlin, who turned to the microphone.

"Hitler wouldn't shake your hand," said Schreiber, "but I will give you both hands."

Jesse was exhausted from emotion as he left the platform and turned into the tunnel leading to the dressing rooms. As he walked along, a boy in his teens ran up to him, holding out a book and a fountain pen.

"Mr. Owens, will you please sign an autograph for me?" asked the boy. As tired as he was, Jesse smiled and reached for the book. He scribbled his name almost without looking and gave the autograph book back to the boy.

"Thank you, Mr. Owens," the boy said, turning away. But Jesse's hand shot out to hold him back. Something in the autograph book had caught his eye.

H A L L S   O F   F A M E

"Son, let me see that book again for a moment," said Jesse. The boy gave him the book, and Jesse opened it to the page where he had just signed his name, under an old photograph. The face was familiar; Jesse's heart beat a little faster.

"That's a picture of Lutz Long," Jesse exclaimed. "Son, how did you come to put that picture in your autograph book?"

"That's my father, sir," said the boy.

Jesse's eyes dimmed with tears. He looked at the boy closely. The resemblance was there. He reached out to shake the boy's hand.

"Yes, you are Lutz's boy," he said. "He and I were pals. Where is he? I want to see him, to talk over old times."

"My father is dead, sir," said the boy. "He died in the war. He was a soldier and I hardly knew him. He left home when I was young."

The boy trembled. His eyes were filled with tears, and Jesse's heart went out to the blond boy, who tugged at his cap and started to back away.

"No, don't go, son," said Jesse. He put his arm around the boy's shoulder. "We have to talk, son. We have to talk about your father and get to know each other. I want to tell you what a fine man your father was, how he stood up for what was right."

Jesse guided Lutz Long's son into the dressing room. They talked and talked and later wrote letters to each other. The bond between Jesse and Lutz Long, made in 1936, was too strong to be broken.

As the years rolled on and one Olympic Games followed another, Jesse Owens was always on hand. Each time he appeared the crowd rose to give him its tribute.

He was the man who had made Hitler run. He had flung a challenge to a tyrant with his unsurpassed skill as an athlete.

Life in Concord

LOUISA MAY ALCOTT (*American*, 1833-1888)

IN THE historic old town of Concord, Massachusetts, there lived once a strong, sturdy, jolly girl named Louisa Alcott. Louisa's home was a shabby, dingy old house, but it was full of merry laughter for Louisa had a good mother, a devoted father, and three lively sisters, Anna, Beth, and May. Over the hills behind Old Concord and down by the rush-bordered river that meandered through the town, the little girls romped and played.

They weren't very well off so far as money goes, for Mr. Alcott was a schoolteacher with very peculiar ideas as to how children ought to be taught, so all too often he couldn't get pupils enough to keep his family well-fed. In days when the birch rod, well-applied to a naughty boy, was highly thought of as discipline, Bronson Alcott flogged himself to punish an unruly child! Moreover, he took children walking, swimming, and rowing; he showed them the world around them instead of keeping their noses always glued to their books. Such methods did not make him popular. That was no way to teach children, grown-up people said.

From his earliest days, Bronson Alcott had been a dreamer. As a young man, he had traveled as a peddler with the tin trunk in his wagon full of Yankee notions, pins, scissors, combs, thimbles, puzzles, and what-not; and always as he traveled, he looked for some school where he might be able to stop and exercise his ideas.

Moreover, this strange young man believed and earnestly preached that people should lead simpler, truer, more useful lives than they do and his opinions as to how they should set about doing this were so different from those held by others, that people made fun of him generally. They said he was odd and called him a crank.

"He's bent on saving the world by a return to acorns and the Golden Age!" one man said.

"But no man can laugh at him without loving him," the same man added.

So Louisa's father went about Concord with his mild eyes radiant, working by the day for his neighbors, chopping their wood, digging gardens, and laboring like a farmhand, to provide food for his family when he didn't have pupils enough.

At least the Alcotts had plenty of apples. A basket of golden russets always stood on the table. Usually there was also bread, potatoes, and boiled rice with grated cheese when the family sat down to dinner.

True, when Mrs. Alcott's cousins came for a visit, they had to bring their own tea and pepper, for the Alcott's rarely had such expensive trimmings on their table. As soon as they were able to provide rice and turnips for themselves, they were sure to cut their meals down to two a day in order to share what they had with some neighbor who had a drunken husband or was otherwise in trouble.

But Concord was a better place for Bronson Alcott to live than the city of Boston had been where the family had lived before, for there were other people in Concord, whom the world might, perhaps, call queer.

There was Ralph Waldo Emerson, poet and philosopher, writing his essays on Love and Friendship and dreaming of life in the spirit. There was that strange man, Henry Thoreau, who went off and lived alone for two years in a hut on Walden Pond, just to prove to himself and others the joys of simple living close to the heart of Nature. And there was Nathaniel Hawthorne, earnestly pondering like old Puritans of Pilgrim days, the problems of right and wrong and writing of the stern punishments that overtook evildoers. All these men loved Louisa's father and held him in high esteem.

Shoulder to shoulder with Bronson Alcott stood his wife, always upholding him, working day and night with her capable hands to make his burdens lighter, cooking, sewing, cleaning. And in spite of all the hard work she did, she was never too tired to be gay and jolly and interested in all that interested her daughters. So the four little girls were brought up from their infancy in a world of simple living and high thinking. They had plenty of joyous, carefree fun in which both mother and father joined, but they began to understand very early the necessity for being useful and bearing their share in the household tasks. Thus, though the house where they lived was poor and shabby, it was very rich in love and loyalty and simple homey joys.

Louisa was a strong, active, handsome girl with blue eyes and a perfect mane of heavy chestnut hair. She could run for miles and miles and never get tired and she was as sturdy as a boy. Indeed, her mother used sometimes to call her Jo in fun and say that Jo was her only son. Jo loved to climb trees and leap fences, run races and roll hoops, and when she was not playing with her sisters she liked best to play with boys. But beside all these lively sports, Louisa liked, too, to curl herself up in a chair and read or study. Sometimes she would go off alone into the garret, taking a pile of apples with her and her favorite book. There she would read and munch away in happy solitude. All day long she had interesting thoughts and often she made up stories with which she held her sisters spellbound.

On occasion, little Louisa could be a turbulent miss and her high spirits often led her into paths of strange adventure. Once when she was very small and lived in Boston, she ran away from home and spent the day with some Irish children. They shared a very poor and very salty dinner with her, after which they all went to play in the nice, dirty, ash heaps. Late in the afternoon they took a daring trip as far away as Boston Common. When it began to grow dark, however, Louisa's little Irish friends deserted her, and there she was left all alone in a strange place with the dusky shadows deepening and the night lights twinkling out. Then, indeed, she began to long for home, but she hadn't the smallest idea which way to go and so wandered helplessly on and on. At last, quite wearied out, she sat down on a welcome doorstep beside a friendly big dog. The dog kindly allowed her to use his back for a pillow and she fell fast asleep. From her dreams, she was roused by the voice of the town crier who had been sent in search of her by her distracted parents. He was ringing his bell and calling out loudly:

"Lost! Lost! A little girl six years old, in a pink frock, white hat, and new green shoes!"

Out of the darkness a small voice answered, "Why dat's me!"

Next day the little runaway was tied to the arm of a sofa to cure her of her wandering habit. But, whenever Louisa was naughty, she was always terribly sorry and pondered over her sins in a way that would have done credit to Nathaniel Hawthorne, himself, pondering with tense moral earnestness over the sins of the world. In the intervals of working off steam in the liveliest adventures, she worried over her faults. Sometimes, then, she had a little game she played. She made believe that she was a princess and that her kingdom was her own mind. When she had hateful or self-willed thoughts, she tried to get rid of these by playing that they were enemies of her kingdom. She would marshal her legions of soldiers and march them against the foe. Her soldiers, she said, were Patience, Duty, and Love. With these she fought her battles and drove out the enemy. When she was only fourteen years old, she wrote a poem about this:

A little kingdom I possess,
Where thoughts and feelings dwell,
And very hard I find the task
Of governing it well.

Nevertheless, after many a hotly contested battle, she did succeed in taking command and governing her kingdom like a queen.

The house where the four girls lived in Concord had a yard full of fine old trees and a big barn which was their most particular delight. Here they produced many marvelous plays, for Anna and Louisa both had a wonderful talent for acting. They made the barn into a theatre and climbed up on the haymow for a stage, while the grown people who came to see their plays sat on chairs on the floor. One of the children's favorite plays was Jack and the Beanstalk. They had a ladder from the floor to the loft, and all the way up the ladder they tied a squash vine to look like the wonderful beanstalk. When it came to the place in the story where Jack was fleeing from the giant and the giant was hot on his heels, about to plunge down the beanstalk, the girl who took the part of Jack would cut down the vine with a mighty flourish while the audience held their breath. Then, crashing out of the loft to his well-deserved end below, came the monstrous old giant. This giant was made of pillows dressed in a suit of funny old clothes, with a fierce, hideous head made of paper.

HALLS OF FAME

Another play which the children acted was Cinderella. They made a big pumpkin out of the wheelbarrow trimmed with yellow paper. Thus the pumpkin could easily become a golden coach in which Cinderella magnificently rolled away at a single stroke of the fairy godmother's wand. The tale of the foolish woman who wasted her three wishes was illustrated in a way to make the beholders scream with laughter, by means of a pudding which was lowered by invisible hands until it rested upon the poor lady's nose.

The costumes used in these performances were marvelous affairs; for Louisa, Anna and Mrs. Alcott had a wonderful knack for rigging up something out of nothing. A scrap found its use. A bright colored scarf, a table cover, a bit of old lace, a long cloak, a big hat with a plume stolen from some departed bonnet, would afford a regal costume in which to come sweeping on the stage. Furthermore, the children were never at a lack for scenery; for their ready wit was quite capable of providing castles, enchanted forests, caves or ladies' bowers, and barns offered splendid opportunities for a hero or a villain to make desperate but

safe leaps from the beams, or to sink out of sight at short notice.

There was one other beautiful and much more serious story which the Alcott children loved to play, though they did not give this to an audience in the barn, but played it alone for their own amusement. This story was Pilgrim's Progress, in which the pilgrim, Christian, loaded down with his burden of sins, finds his way through toil and danger from the City of Destruction to the Celestial City. Their mother used to tie her piece-bags on their backs to represent Christian's burden. Then they would put on broad-brimmed, pilgrim hats, take a stick for a staff and start out on their journey. From the cellar, which was the City of Destruction, they mounted to the housetop where was the Celestial City, and they acted out on the way, in most dramatic form, every step of Christian's upward progress. Sometimes, instead of playing Pilgrim's Progress indoors, they played it out of doors, wandering over the hills behind the house, through the woods and down the lanes.

There could not have been a more beautiful place than Concord for four hearty, simple girls like these to live. It was a typical New England village, quiet and homelike, with its plain, white houses and its shady elm trees, nestling in its circle of peaceful hills. There were no very rich people there and none very poor. The inhabitants were honest and friendly, with simple occupations and amusements and very few worldly ambitions. In the winter the place rang with the happy voices of young people skating on the hardened snow in the pine woods. In the summer the river was alive with gay bathing or boating parties.

Concord was an historic old place, too, with its memories of the first gun-shots of the Revolution, and many a time in the days of the Alcott girls, there were masquerades on the river to celebrate the anniversary of that great event. Gay barges full of historic characters in costume glided down the stream, and sometimes savages in their war-paint darted from the lily-fringed river banks to attack the gay masqueraders. Hearty and healthy was the life in Concord, and it produced a fine race of people, among them three, at least, of most remarkable character. These three were Emerson, Hawthorne, and Thoreau, the friends of Louisa's father, who belonged to the great New England group of writers, the most distinguished local group America has ever produced.

Ralph Waldo Emerson, living in the big white house on the turnpike, was a thinker, philosopher, and poet, strong, gentle, and serene. He had stood by Mr. Alcott when everybody else laughed at him and deserted him, and, from her earliest recollections, Louisa had adored him. Once she went to school with the little Emersons in their father's barn; for, in those days of no public schools, teachers used frequently to gather their pupils together in barns. The illustrious Mr. Emerson was often the children's playfellow. He would pile all the youngsters on a hay-cart and take them off to picnic or go berrying in the woods.

The favorite place for such picnics was the hut which Emerson's friend, Thoreau, had built on the edge of Walden Pond when he wanted to retire from the world. This hut stood in a beautiful spot among the fragrant pines and it overlooked the clear, green depths of the water, which Thoreau, from its gleaming expressiveness, called the "Eye of the Earth." All about rose tall, green hills and around the pond, through the woods, there ran an old Indian trail which had been worn hard through the centuries when the red men tramped over it on the hunt. When they came to this beautiful spot, Emerson showed the children all the places he loved; all the wood people Thoreau had introduced to him; or the wild flowers whose hidden homes he, himself, had discovered. So, years later, when the children read Emerson's beautiful poem about the sweet rhodora in the woods, his "burly, dozing bumblebee," or his fable of the Mountain and the Squirrel, they recognized old friends of these beautiful woodland jaunts.

To the turbulent, restless, half-grown Louisa the calm philosopher, with his gentle ways and practical common-sense, was an anchor indeed. In her warm little heart he was held so sacredly that he himself would have smiled at such worship. She went to him often for advice about her reading, and was at liberty to roam all around the book-lined walls of his library, there to select whatever pleased her most; for Emerson was never too busy to help her.

Hawthorne, too, handsome, shy man that he was, always steering away from the society of grown-ups, had much to do with Louisa and the Concord children. He was always at his best with children, and his stories never failed to hold Louisa spellbound. Doubtless she was one of the children to whom he first told the *Tanglewood Tales* and the stories in the *Wonder Book*. She pored over his books, and love and admiration for him grew with her growth.

Henry Thoreau was the last of those great Concord friends who had such an influence on Louisa's life. From him the Alcott

girls learned to know intimately the nature they already
loved, and many a happy day
was spent with him in the
woods, studying the secrets of
the wildflowers and the language of the birds. It was
down by the river that Thoreau was most often to be found.
There he would row his boat
or paddle his canoe with Indian skill through the many
windings, stopping now and
then to gather some rare plant
from among the grasses on the
shore. In his company the
girls took long, long walks,
even tramping the twenty

miles from Concord to Boston. There was not a single flower or
tree that the gentle woodsman did not know; birds, squirrels and
insects were his comrades. Hunted foxes would come to him for
protection; wild squirrels would nestle in his coat; birds and chip-
munks gathered about him as he sat at rest on the river bank;
he seemed able even to coax the fishes up to the surface to feed
out of his hand. And so for him all Nature had a voice, and the
Concord children loved the simple friend who taught them the
poetry of the woods.

As Louisa grew up into a tall young girl she began to come
into prominence as a story teller. Her nature studies gave her
material, and out in the Concord woods she would gather about
her the little Emerson children, Ellen, Edith and Edward, and
the three Hawthorne children, Una, Julian and Rose, and many
another, too. Then, under the spreading branches of some great

tree, with the sunshine filtering down on her head and lighting up all the eager little faces about her, she would tell stories that made the very woods alive—wood-sprites and water-sprites and fairy queens dancing in and out through the greenery of those cool forest glades.

But in spite of all the delights of Concord, Louisa was beginning to feel the weight of the family troubles. She saw her father struggling day by day, earning a little here and there by the work of his hands when his talents as a teacher were running to waste. She saw her mother carrying burdens too heavy for her and working far too hard. She had always helped her mother as much as she could with the housework, but the greatest need of the household now was for money. A splendid purpose took root in Louisa's heart. She would set out into the world, earn a living, and mend the family fortunes. She would give this dear devoted mother the comforts that had been denied her so long.

Once determined to accomplish this, Louisa never rested. True, she was only a girl, and there were very few lines of activity open to girls in those days. The way seemed dark before her and full of obstacles. But Louisa was never daunted. Full of energy and pluck, she set forth. First she went up to Boston and lived in a wretched little sky-parlor. There she wrote stories for various magazines and papers, taught in a kindergarten and did sewing or anything else that came to her hand. Only one thing mattered to her henceforth, to help her mother, father and sisters. Night and day she worked, never sparing herself, and every penny that she did not absolutely need for the barest necessities of life, she sent home to her mother and father. James Russell Lowell was the editor of the *Atlantic Monthly* in those days and he praised her stories and took them for his magazine. Yet, as the years passed, she wrote nothing that had any very lasting merit. She merely labored unceasingly and earned money enough by her own self-sacrifice to keep her dear ones in greater comfort at home.

HALLS OF FAME

Then one day Louisa's publisher asked her to write a book for girls. Louisa was very worn and weary, and she hadn't the smallest idea that she could really write an interesting book for children. All these years she had written for grown-ups only. But she had never yet said, "I can't" when she was asked to do anything. So in spite of her misgiving she answered the publishers simply, "I'll try."

When she began to think about what she should write, Louisa remembered all the good times she used to have with her sisters in the big, bare house in Concord, out in the old barn, and over the hills. So she began to write the story of *Little Women* and to put in all those things. Besides the jolly times and the plays they had, she put in the sad, hard times too, the work and the worry and the going without things. It was a simple story of simple girls, of their daily struggles, their joys and sorrows, but through it all shone the spirit of that beautiful family affection that the Alcotts knew so well, an affection so strong and enduring that neither poverty, sorrow, nor death could ever mar it. And the little book was so sweet and funny, so sad and real, like human life, that everybody bought it and it brought in a great deal of money for Louisa.

There were Mr. and Mrs. March in the book, true as life to Mr. and Mrs. Alcott, and there were all the four sisters, too Meg, the capable house-wifely one, was Anna; Jo (the old pet name for Louisa) was Louisa, herself, the turbulent, boyish one, who was always "going into a vortex" and writing stories; Beth was the sweet, sunny little home-body, Lizzie or Beth; Amy was May, the pretty, golden-haired, blue-eyed one, with the artistic tastes, whose pug nose was such a sore trial to her beauty-loving soul that she went about with a clothespin on it to train it into proper lines. There was a real John Brooke, too. He was a portrait of that gentle, kindly, lovable John Pratt, who really married Anna. And Laurie was a mixture in whom Louisa combined a handsome Polish boy she once met in Europe, with a certain New England lad who was her friend in girlhood. So, many of the good times in *Little Women* are true, and many of the sad times, too—the marriage of Meg and John Brooke, and the death of little Beth.

Louisa was hardly prepared for the immense success of this book. It made her almost rich; and, besides that, she suddenly found herself so worshipped and idolized by young people and old alike that crowds began haunting her path, hanging about the house to get just a glimpse of her, popping up in her way to bow reverently as she went for a walk or a drive, deluging her with flowers, and writing her sentimental verses.

All this attention drove Louisa nearly distracted, so she had to run away from it for a year's rest in Europe. But, ever after that, the children considered Louisa their especial property and she devoted herself henceforth to writing for them entirely. She loved them very dearly, too, boys and girls alike; and no American author has ever held a warmer place than she in the hearts of American young people.

Thus, after so many years of hard and devoted labor, Louisa's dream came true. She was able to give her family all they needed and wanted. She bought a comfortable home for them in Concord, she sent May to study art in Europe, she gave her father books; but, best of all, she was able at last to give her beloved mother the happiness and rest which she had so nobly earned. Never again did "Marmee" have to do any hard work. She could sit from that time forth in a comfortable chair beside the sunny window, with beautiful work and beautiful things about her.

Through endless toil and effort, Louisa's life ended in success and it had been her privilege to live much of it in company with the greatest group of literary men America ever produced.

Read the *Life of Louisa May Alcott*, by Belle Moses,
and Miss Alcott's own books:

| *Little Women* | *Little Men* | *Jo's Boys* | *An Old-Fashioned Girl* | *Rose in Bloom* | *Jack and Jill* |
| | | *Eight Cousins* | *Silver Pitchers* | | |

HALLS OF FAME

The Harvard Professor

HENRY WADSWORTH LONGFELLOW (*American*, 1807-1882)

ACROSS the Charles River, from Boston, and some twenty miles from Concord, lay the quiet old city of Cambridge, with its splendid, wide-spreading elms and all the rosy brick buildings of Harvard University. Here, in an old wooden house where Washington had stayed when he took command of the American army, lived a young Harvard professor, Henry Wadsworth Longfellow. He was scholarly and gentle, his home was simple and elegant, and he traveled now and then in Europe. Life for him was pleasant and peaceful as was life in Cambridge generally, where rooms were full of books, conversations were of bookish things, and the sharpest sounds to be heard were the musical tinkling of bells as the cows ambled home at twilight, the lullaby of the crickets, or the creaking of sleds in the snow.

Afternoons, after lectures, the young professor rode horseback. Then all his vivid fancies took shape in poetry. He had been born in Portland, Maine, and had never forgotten his old home town with its glimpses of the sea. He was forever thinking of

> *"Spanish sailors with bearded lips*
> *And the beauty and mystery of the ships*
> *And the magic of the sea."*

His house was full of children. Every evening at twilight he heard, in the room above him, the patter of little feet. Then he saw by the lamplight his children on the stairs. A rush and a raid from the doorway, they were climbing over his chair—Alice, laughing Allegra, and Edith with golden hair. The poet had friends in Cambridge, James Russell Lowell and Oliver Wendell Holmes, who were writers like him. And, over in Concord, were Emerson, Hawthorne, and Thoreau. They were a congenial group.

Of all seasons in the year, the poet loved October. When the leaves turned scarlet and yellow and the haze of Indian summer

Standing apart from New England writers of his time, was Edgar Allan Poe with his love of the supernatural as in short stories like *The Goldbug* and his magically interpretive rhythms as in *The Bells*.

lay over all the meadows, he was most deeply stirred. *Hiawatha*, his Indian love story, is a poem of October; a poem of golden harvests, autumn quiet, and smoke of campfires. With gentle sympathy, Longfellow sang of love and sorrow and parting. He did not, like Emerson, strive for any philosophy. He only put into words of wonderful, flowing music the stories of his country, of John Alden and Priscilla, Evangeline, and Hiawatha.

But, with the Civil War, that great New England period of American literature ended. Longfellow, Emerson, and Hawthorne still lived on, but a new note was to be struck in the writing that came later; for, great as these men were, they wrote in the manner of English and European writers. None of them, save Emerson, who had traveled in the West, had had a glimpse of the vast America stretching, over plains and mountains, away to the Pacific. They were of one section only: they all belonged to New England. But, one day, Thoreau remarked, "I have heard an alarm or a trumpet note ringing through the American camp!" Thoreau had met a new poet, a man who lived in Brooklyn, a friend of bus drivers and pilots, who shouted his words to the sea as he raced along the sands. This man was Walt Whitman, born in 1819, on a Long Island farm. No single section, but the whole vast America was in Walt Whitman's heart.

"Great poetry," he cried, "is the result of a national spirit and not the privilege of the select and polished few!" He sang, not of knights and heroes, but of the common man, the working man and working woman. "The commonplace I sing," he said, "the common day and night—the common earth and waters—your farm, your work, trade, occupation, the democratic wisdom underneath, like solid ground for all." His vision was so huge, so tumultuous, he could hardly get it into words, and he wrote, with no care for old forms of rhyme or rhythm, in a kind of poetical prose that was new in the world of letters. His poems in *Leaves of Grass* were full of the mighty thrill of universal life.

H A L L S O F F A M E

They burst forth without the restraint New England poets knew. America's distinctive contribution to the world, he said, would be to carve out from the common man something new and uncommon.

Writers did not know what to make of Whitman. Emerson admired him, but Whittier destroyed his book, and Thoreau both admired and disliked him. "Well, he looks like a MAN!" Abraham Lincoln said.

But, whatever was thought of Whitman, he had, indeed, sounded a trumpet that ended the type of writing for which the New England group was famous. After the Civil War, different parts of the country began all at once to be heard from. Joaquin Miller and Bret Harte wrote of the West; James Lane Allen, of Kentucky; Joel Chandler Harris, of the South; James Whitcomb Riley, of the Middle West; and, greatest of them all, from the banks of the Mississippi, came the voice of a young river pilot, Samuel Clemens, who wrote under the name Mark Twain. *Tom Sawyer* and *Huckleberry Finn* breathed wholly of American life and the outlook and feelings of the ordinary, everyday American.

The way was paved, too, by Whitman's independence in casting old verse forms aside, for the modern American poets, Carl Sandburg, Vachel Lindsay, Amy Lowell, and others who are wholly American in their feeling and manner of expression. Recent years have brought us, in the United States, a great desire for a distinctive expression of our own native genius with a growing interest in our own language and all our own colorful folk tales like the lumberman's *Paul Bunyan*, the cowboy's *Pecos Bill*, and the Yankee sailor's *Old Stormalong*.

But, in the days of Longfellow, life at Cambridge was pleasant and peaceful. It looked out across the Atlantic, always facing Europe and keeping its back well-turned to the vast, almost unknown America which lay to the west of New England. So Longfellow, in his day, sang his songs in peace and quiet, stirred by none of the thrill, the tumult, and vitality of the poets of today.

'Way Down South in Dixie

JOEL CHANDLER HARRIS (*American*, 1848-1908)

A LITTLE, red-haired, freckle-faced midget of a boy dashing down the main street of a sleepy Georgia town behind a team of powerful horses and handling the reins with all the confidence of a six-foot hostler! Joel Chandler Harris, you mischievous little monkey! Whose horses have you borrowed? Come down off that box at once! Your mother is horrified.

H A L L S   O F   F A M E

It was well for Joel that he did not distress that good mother of his too often, for all her hopes were centered on him. Long years ago the boy's father had deserted the two, and his mother had shouldered with splendid courage the burden of their support. She took in sewing and the two lived in a tiny cottage behind the great house of a friend.

Eatonton was a typical little Southern town of the days before the Civil War. It had a courthouse and a town square, a tavern and several wide streets shaded by rows of fine old trees. On either side of the road, behind the trim boxwood hedges, rose stately colonial houses, the white pillars of their piazzas glinting here and there through the screen of odorous cedars, brightly blossoming myrtles and oleanders around them.

A fun-loving, rough-and-tumble lad on the surface was Joel, playing all sorts of pranks with his friends and rolling in the white mud gullies or munching ginger-cakes with the little Negro children. But he was a tender-hearted boy at bottom and never forgot a kindness. See him now behind the old school house, showing a wren's nest to three little girls with such delight in the tiny, fragile thing. And how gentle and kind the little girls are to the lad. A simple thing, but he never forgot it!

One day Joel found these words in a newspaper, "Boy Wanted to Learn the Printer's Trade." Here was his opportunity. He was only fourteen years old but he put away his tops and marbles, packed up his little belongings in an old-fashioned trunk, kissed his mother good-bye and was off. He went to work for Mr. Joseph Addison Turner of Turnwold, a fine old plantation, with cotton-fields white as snow in the season, and a group of Negro cabins hid in a grove of oak trees behind the house. Mr. Turner published a paper called *The Countryman*, and the little printing office where the boy worked was a primitive place on the roof of which the squirrels scampered and the bluejays cracked their acorns. Not twenty steps from the office door a partridge had built her nest and was raising a brood of young, while more than once a red fox went loping stealthily by to the woods.

It was hard to say whether Joel enjoyed most the out-of-door life on the plantation, tramping about with a boy just his age who knew every path in the countryside, or browsing in Mr. Turner's fine library, for he dearly loved to read. But when the work and play of the day were ended, and the glow of the light-wood knot could be seen in the Negro cabins, Joel and the Turner children would steal away from the house and visit their friends in the slave quarters. Tucked away in the nook of a chimney corner, Joel listened with eager interest while Old Harbert and Uncle George Terrell, their black faces a-gleam in the firelight, told their precious tales of Brer Rabbit and all the other lore of beasts and birds handed down from their African forefathers. And sometimes, while the yellow yam baked in the ashes, or a hoe-cake browned on the shovel, the Negroes would croon a camp-meeting hymn, or sing a corn-shucking melody.

So passed months and years at Turnwold. And then the Civil War! Joel Harris, a youth, with all the fire and passionate prejudices of boyhood, sitting up on a fence and watching the victorious Northern troops pass by, ploughing ankle-deep through the mud! The defeat of the South meant the end of *The Countryman* and the ruin of Mr. Turner. Joel had to start life anew. One paper after another gave him employment, and then, at last, he began to write for the *Atlanta Constitution* all those lively Negro folk tales impressed so vividly on his mind in the old days at Turnwold —the stories of Uncle Remus. To Joel's immense surprise, Uncle Remus made him famous. And so it happened that the little red-haired boy, now grown a man with a wife and children of his own, could offer his mother a real home, and as his fame grew with the passing years, he brought her increasing happiness and fulfilled all her early dreams.

UNCLE REMUS, HIS SONGS AND SAYINGS　　　DADDY JAKE, THE RUNAWAY　　　THE TAR BABY

The Hoosier Poet

JAMES WHITCOMB RILEY (*American*, 1853-1916)

BUDDY RILEY was a sturdy, flaxen-haired little boy with wide-open blue eyes. Greenfield, Indiana, where he lived was a region of cornfields, meadows, woodlands, and orchards, and the people there spoke that racy Hoosier dialect of the pioneer days of the Middle West. Hard work and ragged clothes were Buddy's daily companions and his chief delight was a plunge in the "old swimmin' hole."

When he was twenty-two Buddy was seized with the spirit of adventure. He could not go off on a voyage in search of the Golden Fleece, but he went away in a wagon behind a pair of glossy sorrel horses in the company of a traveling doctor who sold patent medicines, a queer old faker with breezy, long, white whiskers. How delightful it was to bowl over the country. Miles and miles of somber landscape were made bright with merry song, and while the sun shone and all the golden summer lay spread out before him, it was glorious.

It was Buddy's business to write "catchy" songs and to act

in funny little plays to draw a crowd around while the doctor sold his wares. Sometimes he took a soap box and pretended it was a hand organ. Again, he wrapped a companion in buffalo robes, led him about on all fours and with a series of alarming "Woo-ahs" told the story of the *Little Boy Who Went Into the Woods to Shoot a Bear!* But when the first thrill of adventure wore off, the business seemed shabby enough and Riley soon left it to give performances of his own.

His first public appearance was in the little town of Monroeville, Indiana, and his audience was composed chiefly of the "rag-tags" of the neighborhood, a gang of rough fellows. The response to his selections was a sickening jumble of cat-calls and hisses, but he kept a stiff upper lip and finished his program. As he sat down, the village blacksmith, one of the few serious people in his audience, rose and said abruptly, "You fellows have had your fun with this young man and I think you have hurt his feelings. He has done his best to please you and has given us a pretty good show. I move we pass the hat." He dropped in two quarters for luck and passed the hat himself. When it had been the rounds and came back to Riley, it was found to contain beans, pebbles, nails, screws, tobacco quids, buttons, pieces of iron, a doorknob, a wishbone and 58 cents in money!

Thus for two years Riley went about to small towns reciting in schools and churches and generally losing money, happy and astonished if he earned enough to purchase a feast of gingerbread. For these entertainments he wrote his own poems, chiefly in the Hoosier dialect with a warmth of tender sympathy, like *Little Orphant Annie*, till at last the tide turned for him and he met with a huge success. During his later days he gave up wandering and settled down to write in his home in Indiana, one of the few gifted Americans who have created a distinctly native literature.

RHYMES OF CHILDHOOD   A CHILD WORLD   A HOST OF CHILDREN

The Poet of the Sierras

JOAQUIN (Cincinnatus Heine) MILLER (*American*, 1841-1913)

MOUNTED on a little spotted pony, Cincinnatus Miller rode along the trail toward the mining camp. He had run away from his home in Oregon to seek his fortune mining gold beneath the snowy peak of Mt. Shasta in California.

One night a sailor-man from San Francisco drifted into camp and helped himself to the sluice boxes. The miners caught him in the act, tied him to a tree and told him to dig his grave. The digging proceeded but slowly, so Cincinnatus was called in to help. After they had dug a few feet the sailor-man announced

143

mournfully that his sudden departure from this life would be a hard blow for his wife.

"Have you a wife?" asked the lad with interest.

"Yes, she's in Yrebe," a town a day distant from camp.

"You keep on digging," said Cincinnatus. "I'll tell the men."

The miners heard the story and decided to send for the woman. They told the condemned man that if his tale was true and his wife was brought to camp, his life would be spared on condition that they two should remain and do the cooking for the miners. The sailor-man meekly agreed. He preferred to cook rather than be hanged; and so the woman was brought to camp, a cabin was built for her, and to make sure that she was really the sluice-robber's wife, the miners decided to have them married before their eyes. Opportunity now knocked at the door of young Cincinnatus. There was need of a song for the miners to sing to celebrate the wedding. The only books Cincinnatus knew were Shakespeare and the Bible, but various ringle-jingles kept running in his head. Finally he ground out several yards like the following:

> Samson, he was a mighty man,
> Oh, a mighty man was he-e,
> But he lost his beard and he lost his hair,
> Likewise his liber-tee-ee;
> For a woman she can
> Do more than a man,
> Than a King and his whole ar-mee-ee.

The sailor provided the music and the song was yelled at the torchlight wedding by a sturdy chorus of miners.

Now Cincinnatus made no glittering fortune at mining of gold but he managed to earn a living until he was eighteen years old, when he went back home to Oregon to get a little "book learning." Confinement in a schoolroom, however, was more than he could bear, and the next year found him enjoying life by driving the pony express. This was dangerous business enough, for he carried

H A L L S   O F   F A M E

Uncle Sam's mail, an alluring bait in those days for white or redskin highwaymen. Somewhere about this time, too, Cincinnatus made the acquaintance of a famous Mexican bandit named Joaquin (Walkeen) Murietta. This boy he regarded with pity as a brave and ill-used young fellow who had been driven to desperation by wrongs inflicted in his own country too brutal to be told. His sympathy was aroused, his love of daring and romance, and he cast away his burdensome appellation of Cincinnatus, replacing it forever with the far more picturesque name of Joaquin. Henceforth, when he contributed poems to the Eugene City Review, he always signed them Joaquin.

It was in a little cabin which he had built with his own hands on land given him by the Shasta Chief, Blackfoot, that Joaquin first began serious writing. By and by he had saved enough money to cross the ocean to London. Think of him now, coming from the land of far distances and great sweeps, shut up in narrow London lodgings. Whenever he stopped work he saw in place of the fog and smoke the snow peaks of Oregon looming clear against the sky. Imprisoned as he was, he yearned as never before for America's great plains, where there is "room, room to turn round in, to breathe and be free."

"And to east and to west, to the north and the sun,
Blue skies and brown grasses are welded as one,
And the buffalo come like a cloud on the plain,
Pouring on like the tide of a storm-driven main,
And the lodge of the hunter to friend and to foe
Offers rest; and unquestioned you come and you go."

Presently he caused to be printed with his own hard-earned dollars a thin little volume of poems which fortunately attracted the attention of the famous Rossetti family and their literary friends. They were struck by the breezy freedom of the poet from the west and with their help he brought out a book called *Songs of the Sierras*. Suddenly Miller awakened to find himself famous.

Henceforth, he was feasted and dined and entertained everywhere.

One evening he was invited to a grand reception to meet Lily Langtry, the celebrated actress, who had been reciting his poem *Columbus*. When the time came and the guests stood about all well groomed in their evening clothes, Joaquin appeared, to their astonishment, in a red flannel shirt with blue overalls tucked into tall miner's boots and a high crowned broad-brimmed sombrero. Led by his hostess, he advanced to meet Miss Langtry and lifting his hands to his sombrero, he dexterously showered from it a profusion of beautiful rose leaves. At the same time he exclaimed to the delighted lady: "The tribute of the California miners—California, the land of poetry and romance and flowers—to the Jersey Lily."

So it was England which first recognized Joaquin Miller's genius and he returned to America in the full noontide of his glory, to remain the most unique and picturesque figure in all the field of American letters—tall, broad-shouldered, long-haired and bearded like a pard, always in his big sombrero, his high-top boots and coat to match.

At last he settled down with his wife and daughter in a home called "The Heights," high up in the mountains overlooking San Francisco Bay. When a stranger once asked him where he lived he said: "Three miles east and one mile perpendicular." Indeed, he lived nearer the sun than most men and his normal dwelling place was always one mile perpendicular.

The poet who could picture California, "where the plants are as trees and the trees are as towers," had need of a wide canvas and a generous hand when it came to laying on color. These Joaquin Miller possessed; his poetry breathes of the pine-clad slopes of the Sierras. He was as typically Californian as a giant redwood, and it is due to him, more than any other American, that California literature has impressed itself on the world.

COLUMBUS   SONGS OF THE SIERRAS   TRUE BEAR STORIES

*A Tramp of the Middle West

NICHOLAS VACHEL LINDSAY (*American* 1879-1931)

AROUND the cliff, with a boom and a bang, rattled a gypsy wagon. On the front seat sat a man and a woman, laughing and showing white teeth, and appearing to think this the gayest morning the sun had ever shone on. The woman was covered with bangles and more bedecked than Carmen. Suddenly, at her suggestion, the horses were pulled up short. Before them appeared a fellow tramp, a tall and sunburned young man in yellow corduroy trousers, sombrero and scarlet tie. At his back he carried a pack which seemed to Mrs. Gypsy to contain some delightful mystery connected with the tramping profession.

"What you sellin', boy?" she asked.

Obligingly the Tramp took down his pack and opened it. First he gave Mrs. Gypsy a pamphlet called the *Gospel of Beauty*, then

*Told chiefly from Lindsay's own book, ADVENTURES WHILE PREACHING THE GOSPEL OF BEAUTY.

he handed her a booklet named *Rhymes to be Traded for Bread*. Was that what he was selling? Mrs. Gypsy was quite dumbfounded. Strange wares indeed for a tramp! Clucking to the horses, she vanished, smiling, down the road.

Vachel Lindsay had started from his home town, Springfield, Illinois, to walk across Illinois, Missouri and Kansas, up and down Colorado and into New Mexico. He had vowed to take with him neither baggage nor money, but to trade the rhymes he wrote for bread, and so to preach his Gospel of Beauty. Surely, he thought, the common man, the farmer of the Middle West had his secret dreams and visions. Vachel would coax these forth; he would urge a flowering of beauty on lonely prairie farms or in ugly little prairie villages.

Though he was a man and a poet he was still a boy at heart. At any moment he might break out strong and enthusiastic, making the heavens ring with a rousing cry of "Rah for Bryan!" or waking the sleeping echoes by shouting, "Liberty and union, one and inseparable, now and forever-r-r!" When he was back home reciting his poems on a stage he would go through extravagant antics, roaming up and down, shouting, gesticulating. He was nothing if not original. Fancy a poet who could end the reciting of a poem on Daniel in the Lion's Den, as if he were leading a football yell, by insisting that his hearers join in the roar with the lions!

> *We want Daniel, Daniel, Daniel,*
> *We want Daniel, Daniel, Daniel.*
> *Grrrrrrrrrrrrrrrrrrr,*
> *Grrrrrrrrrrrrrrrrrrr!*

Or imagine the great Lord Tennyson shouting like Vachel Lindsay:

> *Black cats, gray cats, green cats, mi-au,*
> *Chasing the deacon who stole the cow!*

But the very important fact was that Lindsay was not English; he was thoroughly American, a native of the Middle West. New rhythms ran in his soul. Something strong and vivid, vital, crude and different had to get out in his poems. If his verses had football rhythms, both he and his country were young, at an age when that was their natural boisterous outlet for expression. Why should he write in the finished, staid, sedate and time-worn cadences of Old England, a land two thousand years old? A poet must shadow forth the spirit of his native land. So had the English done and so must Lindsay do. He was a Voice from the Middle West. The youth of a very young country was in the things he wrote. But the beauty of prairie and wheat-field, of farms and simple farmers, was in his poems, too. He was most sincerely in earnest; he dreamed of beauty and loved it and where American towns were ugly, drab and colorless, the people bound down by labor and blind to the vision of beauty, he wanted to wake them up, to make them love beauty as he did, so that they might express it by making more beautiful villages, more charming and interesting buildings, a lovelier countryside. As he tramped he handed the country folk such poems as the *Proud Farmer*, *The Illinois Village* and *The Building of Springfield*, or he pasted up on their walls in some conspicuous place where everyone must see it, his poster with startling drawings called, *The Village Improvement Parade*.

Now he was off to Kansas because Kansas was to him the ideal American state, a state of tremendous crops, of hardy, simple devout, and supremely natural men, all ruled by the crossroads church. In eastern Kansas he tramped past rich fields with neat little hedges, past picturesque orchards and gardens till he came to the vast stretch of prairie, treeless yet beautifully green, and patterned like a carpet with the shadows of the clouds. On and on he walked over unbroken prairie sod, where half-wild cattle grazed. Then came alfalfa fields with lavender haze of blossoms and music of gorging bees. Later he marched for days with wheat waving all around him as yellow as the sun.

149

Many a night he slept in the hay-loft of a barn, with the wide loft-door rolled open and the golden moon for his friend. It was Romance itself for him, sleeping in a hay-mow. The alfalfa was soft and fragrant, the wind blew clear and clean and the stars shone through the cottonwoods. Before he knew it, it was morning and the birds in the mulberry trees were singing, "Shivaree, Shivaree, Rachel Jane, Rachel Jane!" After a little walk he bargained for his breakfast at a farm house and was on his way again. Sometimes he hoed corn all morning in order to earn his dinner and as he worked, he talked about his Gospel of Beauty. Then when dinner time came, he entertained the farmer's children by telling them a thrilling tale concerning Grandpa Mouse. Using the ketchup bottle to represent Grandpa Mouse, the salts and peppers for little mice and an old black hat for the owls that came swooping down from the moon to eat unfortunate mice, he acted out the story he told till the children around the table were all quite breathless with interest. The moon was the Queen of the Night-owls and Grandpa Mouse bade the little mice beware of the dread Owl-Queen.

She pours the owls upon us!
They hoot with horrid noise,
And eat the naughty mousie-girls
And wicked mousie-boys.

So climb the moon-vine every night
And to the owl-queen pray!
Leave good green cheese by moonlit trees
For her to take away.

And never squeak, my children,
Nor gnaw the smoke-house door:
The owl-queen then will love us
And send her birds no more!

150

Sometimes Vachel traveled with section gangs on their hand-cars, but usually he walked, tramping the railroad track or striking out over the prairies as they stretched off flat before him.

"Goin' west harvestin'?" the farmers asked of him.

At first he answered no. He had not intended to harvest. But when he saw how the good folk toiled happy and ungrudging he presently answered yes!

And so he tramped on and on till at last he found himself harvesting at the home of a Mennonite farmer. Fine people and deeply religious were these Pennsylvania Dutchmen, Mennonites by faith, who had come out and settled in Kansas. On Sunday morning Vachel went with them to their meeting. There sat all the women on one side of the aisle. The most pious were down in front wearing little black scoop bonnets, but towards the middle of the church their bonnets gained in color. Here was a cream-colored satin, a soft gray or dull moon-yellow, and when the children trooped in, the little girls were wearing headgear of every hue, yet the same scoop pattern still. Opposite the women sat the men, and not a few of these had piously left off their neckties as a particular sign of their doctrines.

Tillie, the farmer's daughter, like all other Mennonite women, had a pretty way of covering her head with a dainty little lace prayer-cap before Bible lessons were read or grace was said at table, and after supper all the family went about in clean bare feet. They had no profane hour in that family. When not at work, they sang hymns. Their religion was always with them.

Out in the fields Vachel worked beside a Mennonite lad, the sturdy son of the household. Together they followed the reaper and built the sheaves into shocks, so stacked that they could not be shaken by any ordinary Kansas wind. And as they worked the boy sang: "The Day Star Hath Risen," while Vachel, catching the spirit that pervaded all work at the farm, sang every hymn he knew. At noon the Mennonite maid came to the field with their dinner. Then they unhitched the mules, Tillie or one of the men offered a prayer of thanksgiving, and they ate in the shade of the thorn-trees.

When in the afternoon they went back to work in the fields, the sun was a roaring lion. Now the men wrestled with the sheaves as though they had the sun by the beard. It was one long struggle with the heat. But at last, after hours of labor, the sun acknowledged defeat. He shone through the hedge as a blur, as a mist-wrapped golden mountain that some fairy traveler might climb wearing enchanted shoes, no longer an enemy, but a fantasy, a vision and a dream!

Those wide-stretching open spaces where the armies of wheat sheaves were marshalled were magic places for the poet despite their sweat and dust. It was all on so vast a scale. There was nothing small in the whole panorama. Vachel thought of the Bible, of the beautiful Book of Ruth and the Jewish feast of the ingathering and he was happy indeed that he had the strength

to bear his part in the harvest of a noble and devout household
as well as in the feeding of the world.

O, I have walked in Kansas
Through many a harvest field,
And piled the sheaves of glory there
And down the wild rows reeled!

Yet it was gay in Kansas,
A-fighting that strong sun:
And I and many a fellow-tramp
Defied that wind and won.

And we felt free in Kansas,
From any sort of fear,
For thirty thousand tramps like us
There harvest every year.

Our beds were sweet alfalfa hay
Within the barn-loft wide,
The loft doors opened out upon
The endless wheat-field tide.

I loved to watch the windmills spin
And watch the big moon rise.
I dreamed and dreamed with lids half shut,
The moonlight in my eyes.

When Vachel came home to Springfield after that long tramp,
the moonlight was still in his eyes. As he had seen the wheat
harvest rich and ripe before him, he dreamed of another harvest,
a harvest of art and beauty to be gathered there in Kansas. The
children now born in the west should be not only farmers, laborers
and workers. They should be poets, artists, actors, musicians,
gardeners, architects, classic dancers. They should have the vision
of beauty deep within their souls and live for the joy of expressing
all that beauty to the world. So dreamed the poet-tramp.

Lindsay's unique individuality and indifference to old verse forms is characteristically modern. It goes back
to Walt Whitman and that quiet little spinster, Emily Dickinson, singing her songs as she pleased. When Japan
was opened to the West in the 19th Century, acquaintance with Japanese poetry revealed to Americans the beauty
of simplicity as opposed to Victorian elaborateness. See Vol. VI, page 196.

Pioneer in Surgery
The Story of Daniel Hale Williams
By Louis Haber

"Sewed Up His Heart" shouted the headline of the Chicago *Daily Inter-Ocean*. History had just been made. In a time when few surgeons dared to operate on the abdomen, let alone on the heart, Dr. Williams had successfully operated on a dying man who had been stabbed in the heart. The man not only survived but he lived for fifty years afterward. It was the first time in the history of medicine that this kind of surgery was attempted, and it was performed successfully! What was the background of this great pioneering surgeon?

Born in Hollidaysburg, Pennsylvania, on January 18, 1856, Dan was the fifth of a family of seven children. His father, of mixed Negro and white ancestry, had learned the practice of barbering from his father. Very active in the Abolitionist cause, he was a prominent member of the Equal Rights League. His mother's family included Negro, white, and Indian ancestors.

At the age of forty-seven Dan's father died of consumption, leaving his wife and seven children in financial difficulties. Dan, who was ten years old at the time, was apprenticed to a shoemaker in Baltimore, and his mother left Pennsylvania and went to Rockford, Illinois. Unhappy with his lot, Dan managed to run away and rejoin his mother in Illinois. A few months later, however, his mother returned east without him. Left on his own, Dan worked on lake steamers and learned the barber's trade. When his oldest sister, Sally, wrote asking him to join her in Edgerton, Wisconsin, Dan jumped at the chance. Opportunities for the Negro were greater in the West than in the South and he soon opened his own barbershop in Edgerton at the age of seventeen. But Janesville, a few miles away, had schools, an opera

house, and flourishing industries, so Sally and Dan moved there, and Dan got a job in the barbershop of Harry Anderson. After Dan's sister married and left Janesville, Anderson took Dan into his home and treated him as one of the family.

Dan began to attend Haire's Classical Academy, which was the equivalent of the present high school. After graduating, he clerked and read the law in a lawyer's office for about one year, no doubt influenced by his older brother, who was already a successful practicing lawyer. However, he soon realized that the law was not for him.

In Janesville everybody stood in awe of Dr. Henry Palmer, a local physician. Dr. Palmer was an excellent surgeon who had been the director of the largest military hospital during the Civil War and surgeon general of Wisconsin for ten years. News of Dr. Palmer's exciting work was often in the local newspaper, and when Dan read of it, he was determined that medicine was going to be his life's work. At the age of twenty-two he became an apprentice in Dr. Palmer's office. He stayed there for two years reading medicine, learning to practice, and scrubbing up the office at the end of the day.

In those days it was customary for a person to open his own private practice of medicine at the end of two years of apprenticeship in a doctor's office. Few physicians at that time had gone to medical college. Dan, however, under Dr. Palmer's influence, was determined to obtain the best medical training available. In 1880, with a one-hundred-dollar bank loan in his pocket, Dan went off to Chicago Medical College (later to become Northwestern University Medical School). At that time, Chicago Medical College was one of the best medical schools in the country and had the "heroically high standard" of an eighteen-months' course. Although standards were very high, laboratory work was virtually nonexistent, and the staff lectured, and operated also, in stiff collars and black swallow-tails. Dan graduated from medical school in 1883 and opened an office at Thirty-first Street and Michigan Avenue in Chicago.

Dan Williams' true place in medicine must be measured against the background of his times. A new era in surgery began in the eighties. As a graduate in 1883, he belonged to a group of young men not bound by the prejudices of the previous generation and receptive to new thoughts and practices in surgery. A revolution was taking place in the field because of the work of Louis Pasteur in France and Joseph Lister in England. In the late seventies, Pasteur had laid the foundations of bacteriology. He had proven the relationship between certain microorganisms and specific diseases. He set forth his "Germ Theory of Disease" that was to sweep the medical world. Lister applied Pasteur's theory and revolutionized surgery by demonstrating the effectiveness of antiseptics (germ-killing chemicals) in the treatment of wounds. A furor was created, although it was difficult for the doctrine of antisepsis to gain acceptance among the older men of that day.

Many explanations of disease were offered before Pasteur. It was thought that illness was caused by demons inhabiting the body. The art of healing was dominated by superstition, witchcraft, and misinformation. Surgery was practiced by barbers. It was held that a sick person was filled with bad blood and for a cure should be bled. In many cases, patients who should have been given blood had blood taken from them instead. More patients died from the treatment than from the disease.

It remained for Pasteur to prove that disease was caused by harmful microorganisms or germs within the body. His work was to result in the virtual elimination of many diseases caused by germs. This knowledge was just beginning to be known in Williams' day. Abdominal and chest surgery was rarely if ever attempted, because even if successful the infection that invariably followed caused the death of the patient.

Ether was given as an anesthetic to a human being for the first time in 1842, during an operation by Dr. Long of Georgia. Today we have a choice of many anesthetics, both general and local. We also have sulfa drugs and antibiotics to help fight infection.

When Williams began to practice medicine, Pasteur's germ theory of disease, Lister's antiseptic surgery, and the availability of anesthetics opened new vistas for the surgeon, and Williams was in a position to take advantage of the "new" advances. Operations could be attempted now that were previously out of the question.

In his practice of medicine, "Dr. Dan," as his patients and friends came to call him, turned more and more to surgery. In those days operations in private homes were common. Not only did people distrust hospitals but Negroes could not gain admission except in the city's charity wards, where they were either neglected or used for experimentation. Furthermore, Negro doctors could not get hospital appointments because of racial prejudice, and therefore could not get their patients into hospitals. It was even impossible for Negro women to get training as nurses since training schools would not accept them.

Williams' first operation took place in Mrs. LeBeau's dining room where he performed minor surgery. He went on to do more and more surgery in the kitchens and dining rooms of patients' homes. In each case he applied Lister's principles of antiseptic surgery conscientiously and meticulously. He scrubbed the entire room with soap and water. He then sprayed carbolic acid, a strong germ killer, all over the room and followed that by sterilizing all the instruments to be used in the operation in a wash boiler filled with steam. Hands and clothing were also included in the cleaning and sterilizing process. His results were excellent. Infection, the feared and dangerous aftermath of surgery, was avoided.

H A L L S   O F   F A M E

Soon Dr. Dan's reputation as a successful surgeon spread and he was appointed to the surgical staff of the South Side Dispensary in Chicago. He also became clinical instructor and demonstrator in anatomy at the Chicago Medical College, where one of his students was Charlie Mayo of the famous Mayo Brothers. Later still he became surgeon to the City Railway Company, a position never previously held by a Negro physician. His appointment to the Illinois State Board of Health in 1889 was indicative of the kind of recognition he was shown. While the position carried no salary, it carried tremendous prestige.

In describing Williams' surgical skill, Dr. U. G. Dailey, a former student of his, said, "His surgical work was marked by profound anatomical knowledge, a thorough understanding of physiology—normal and pathological—and an uncanny surgical judgment. As an operator, his attention to technical detail was meticulous."

It was a cold, wintry day in 1890. Dr. Dan was sitting in the warm, comfortable parlor of his friend, the Reverend Louis Reynolds, pastor of St. Stephen's African Methodist Church. The Reverend Reynolds had just asked him to use his influence to have Reynold's sister admitted to a training course for nurses in one of the Chicago hospitals normally closed to Negro applicants. Williams thought for a moment and then said, "No. I don't think I'll try to get your sister into one of these training courses. We'll do something better. We'll start a hospital of our own and we'll train dozens and dozens of nurses." He went on, "There must be a hospital for Negroes but not a Negro hospital." Williams had been thinking of it for some time. He was well established in private practice by 1890 and was famed for his surgical skill, but still as a Negro he lacked a hospital appointment. This lack, and his indignation that all Negro patients were thrown into the city's charity wards, made him determined to start a new kind of hospital—one to be owned, staffed, and

159

managed by blacks and whites together. Here Negro sick and poor would receive the best of care, ambitious young Negro doctors would have their chance, and young black women, not admitted to white schools, would be trained for the nursing the times demanded.

Williams threw himself into this new effort with enthusiasm. He formed committees of black and white people. He spoke at churches, street corners, club meetings, and anywhere else he was permitted to speak. He got the cooperation of many people, rich and poor, black and white. The idea of a hospital run by Negroes where Negroes would be received on an equal basis was very appealing to the black community.

On January 23, 1891, medical history was made. The first interracial hospital in the United States was founded. Articles of incorporation were drawn up in the name of the Provident Hospital and Training School Association. The trustees, executive committee, and finance committee were all black. The hospital itself opened its doors in May, 1891—a three-story building at Twenty-ninth Street and Dearborn, with room for twelve beds. The first year, out of 175 applicants for nurse training, Dr. Dan accepted seven, the sister of the Reverend Reynolds among them. All were high-school graduates. The training period was for eighteen months.

The staff of Provident Hospital was made up of Negro and white doctors carefully selected for their qualifications. George Hall was one of the Negro doctors whose application was rejected by Dr. Dan. Hall's medical training was very poor and his medical diploma came from the Eclectic School in Chicago, a dubious institution. Hall accused Williams of discrimination and succeeded in convincing the trustees to appoint him to the staff. He was given an unimportant appointment in the children's clinic. From that time Hall became the lifelong enemy of Williams and sought to discredit him whenever he could.

H A L L S   O F   F A M E

At the end of the first year, of 189 sick and injured treated at the Provident Hospital, twenty-three had improved, three had not, twenty-two had died, and 141 recovered entirely—a remarkable record when only desperate cases were taken to a hospital. However, the economic depression of 1893 began to threaten Provident's existence. At that time help came in the form of Frederick Douglass, one of the most important Negro leaders in the country. It was the year of the Chicago World's Fair and Douglass came as the Haitian commissioner. At the Fair he urged Negroes to contribute to Provident Hospital, the type of interracial organization of which he highly approved. Money began to come in and things became easier for the hospital after the Fair.

July 9, 1893, was a hot and humid day in Chicago and tempers were short. A fight in a saloon ended in the stabbing of a young Negro expressman, James Cornish. He was rushed to Provident Hospital with a one-inch knife wound in the chest near the heart. The call went out for Dr. Dan. By the time he arrived Cornish had collapsed from loss of blood and shock and it was obvious that he would soon die if nothing was done. But what could be done? Opening the chest cavity in those days was an invitation to death. Nobody would have criticized Williams if he had followed the standard treatment in this case of "absolute rest, cold, and opium" after which the patient invariably died. Why should he risk his surgical reputation? If he did not operate and the patient died, nobody would blame him. If he did operate and the patient died, he would be condemned by the medical profession. X-rays had not as yet been discovered to help him, blood transfusions were unknown at that time, sulfa drugs and antibiotics to fight infection were also unknown. What to do? The patient was sinking. Dr. Dan decided to operate.

Six physicians—four white and two black—witnessed the operation. Dr. Dan worked swiftly. He opened the chest cavity and saw that the knife used in the stabbing had penetrated the heart about one-tenth of an inch, and had cut the pericardium (the sac surrounding the heart) one and one-quarter inches in length. He decided that the heart muscle did not need any suturing (sewing up), but he did suture the pericardium. The atmosphere was tense as he worked and continued to be so until he finally closed up the wound. It was a daring operation—the first time a surgeon had entered the chest cavity. Would it work? Would the dread infection set in and kill the patient? On August 30, fifty-one days after Cornish had entered the hospital a dying man, he was discharged completely recovered. He lived for fifty years afterwards and died in 1943, having outlived his surgeon by twelve years!

Although Dr. Dan did not make an official report of this operation until three and a half years later, the newspaper headlines sent the news around the world. "Sewed Up His Heart" read the headlines of the Chicago *Daily Inter-Ocean*. Williams was acclaimed as the first man in the world to "sew up the heart." Of course, his great contribution was the successful entrance of the chest and surgical exploration of the heart. His aseptic surgery was so perfect that no sign of infection appeared in the patient after the operation. His results were miraculous when one considers that he had very few of the advantages modern surgeons have today in their open-heart surgery.

Not long after his precedent-making heart operation, Williams learned that the position of chief surgeon at the Freedmen's Hospital in Washington, D.C., was open. This hospital with its two hundred beds as compared to the twelve beds at Provident Hospital offered new opportunities and broader challenges. Here he could help advance medical opportunities for Negroes on a national rather than a local scale. On September 17, 1893, he wrote to the Secretary of the Interior, Hoke Smith, applying for the position.

HALLS OF FAME

The Freedmen's Bureau was created in March, 1865, to help emancipated slaves adjust themselves to their new conditions. The Bureau turned to the pressing problems of Negro health and gave medical assistance to at least a million Negro patients. It established more than one hundred hospitals and dispensaries; among them the Freedmen's Hospital in Washington, D.C., erected on the grounds of Howard University. The first surgeon-in-chief was Dr. Robert Reyburn, who took over in 1868. In 1881 Dr. Charles B. Purvis was appointed surgeon-in-chief, the first Negro civilian in the United States to head a hospital under civilian auspices. He served for almost twelve years and was about to be replaced by the incoming Democratic administration.

Dr. Williams' application was endorsed by top medical men. It was also supported by Walter Gresham, the newly appointed Secretary of State. The author was surprised to come across a letter in the National Archives in Washington written by Frederick Douglass (supposedly a friend of Williams) urging the retention of Dr. Purvis in Freedmen's Hospital as an "honest and able physician and a good and true man."[1] Nevertheless, Williams was appointed chief surgeon of Freedmen's Hospital in February, 1894.

To understand the situation at the time Williams took over at Freedmen's, it must be pointed out that the liberal period of Reconstruction was over and reaction had begun to set in. The Negro gradually began to lose his voting rights in the South and in parts of the North as well. Only the Freedmen's Hospital remained as a remnant of the liberal period and even that was threatened by indifference and neglect. Dr. Purvis, who had been in charge for the past twelve years, had been inefficient,

[1] Douglass was the Haitian Commissioner at that time under a Republican administration. Dr. Purvis was also a Republican. Douglass's letter supporting Dr. Purvis could well have had political motivation as well as personal loyalty to the man. It was in favor of Dr. Purvis but not against Dr. Williams.

medically behind the times, and had let things deteriorate badly.

Williams went to work. He reorganized the hospital into seven separate medical and surgical departments. He set up pathological and bacteriological departments in recognition of the new and more modern methods then being practiced. He set up a biracial staff of twenty of Washington's most competent specialists, who were willing to serve in the hospital without salary. He opened Freedmen's to outside white and black doctors. This was the first opportunity for many Negro doctors in Washington to gain hospital affiliation. He also set up the first internship program at Freedmen's Hospital, giving black internes an opportunity not afforded them at white hospitals.

Dr. Williams himself demonstrated and lectured in surgery, and while surgical cases increased almost two hundred per cent, the mortality rate dropped lower than three per cent. By 1896 Freedmen's was admitting five hundred surgical cases per year and doctors from Johns Hopkins and the University of Pennsylvania were coming to watch Williams operate at clinics.

As he had done at Provident Hospital, Williams set up a training program for nurses, which had high standards and requirements. Of five hundred applicants, fifty-nine were accepted, and by the end of the first month thirteen had been eliminated as unsatisfactory. The eighteen-month training course included instruction in diet, disinfection, antisepsis, and massage. Again, as at Provident, the program was a huge success.

Within the first year of Williams' arrival there was a profound change in Freedmen's Hospital. New order and efficiency was apparent everywhere and the mortality rate went to an unprecedented low. The change was aptly described by Dr. William A. Warfield, one of the men whom Dr. Williams trained (later himself surgeon-in-chief of Freedmen's Hospital), who said, "Before Dr. Williams came to the hospital in 1894 there was no real surgical department. I was at the hospital three years before

Dr. Williams and witnessed most of the surgical work, such as amputations of the thigh, leg, foot and toes. It can be said that with the arrival of Dr. Williams surgical development began in all forms, especially abdominal. That is where I got my start and inspiration. Dr. Williams established a training school for nurses, replacing the old red-bandanna nurse. He appointed the first internes and brought into existence a horse ambulance. He was laying the foundation for more and better surgical work. By the time he left the hospital, a great impetus had been given to all branches of surgery."

Dr. Dan's political troubles began in 1896, when the Democrats lost the presidential election and the Republicans swept into power. Dr. Purvis, his Republican predecessor, instigated a Congressional investigation, hoping to oust Williams and replace him. Williams was completely exonerated. However, political harassment followed, which was difficult for a man of Williams' temperament to endure, and on February 1, 1898, he tendered his resignation.

While in Washington Williams met and fell in love with Alice Johnson, the daughter of an ex-slave and the famous sculptor Moses Jacob Ezekiel. A few days after he resigned from Freedmen's Hospital, Dr. Dan, at the age of forty-two, married Alice Johnson. Paul L. Dunbar, Negro poet and friend of Dr. Dan, wrote a poem to commemorate the occasion. It reads in part:

> *'Tis no time for things unsightly,*
> *Life's the day and life goes lightly*
> *Science lays aside her sway*
> *Love rules Dr. Dan today*
>
> *Diagnosis, cease your squalling*
> *Check that scalpel's senseless bawling*
> *Put that ugly knife away*
> *Doctor Dan doth wed today*

After their marriage Williams and his wife returned to Chicago, where he resumed his place as chief surgeon at Provident Hospital, now enlarged from twelve to sixty-five beds. As soon as they heard of his return, his former patients, black and white, flocked back. He became very active in his practice not only at Provident but at St. Luke's and Mercy hospitals as well. Because of his growing reputation as an outstanding surgeon he was frequently called to distant places—to North Dakota to perform surgery on a mining millionaire and to New York to attend a bishop of the Episcopal Church. On one occasion he was called to Tuskegee Institute by Booker T. Washington to perform an appendectomy on Washington's personal secretary.

In 1899 Dr. George W. Hubbard, president of Meharry Medical College, invited Williams to hold surgical clinics one week each year at Meharry. The annual Williams Clinics at Meharry were continued for many years and each was considered the great event of the school year. At Williams' urging, Nashville opened its own interracial hospital and thereby opened the whole field of modern surgery to Meharry students and doctors.

It was in Atlanta that Williams met Booker T. Washington, president of Tuskegee Institute and the most influential Negro leader at the time. Williams had come to Atlanta to meet with other Negro physicians from all over the country to organize the National Medical Association. Because of racial prejudice, it was virtually impossible for Negro physicians to join the American Medical Association. Williams was elected vice-president of the newly organized National Medical Association. Booker T. Washington had just made his famous Atlanta speech which alienated many Negro intellectuals because of its emphasis upon vocational rather than academic training for Negro youth. Williams urged Washington to build a medical and surgical center at Tuskegee that would serve the blacks of the South. He kept up a lively correspondence with Washington on this and other subjects concerning the medical care of the Negro. All of it came to naught. Washington was not interested.

Years after Williams had returned to Chicago, the Freedmen's Hospital was finally to be reorganized. Williams saw a great opportunity to build a really excellent hospital that would benefit Negroes all over the nation. He appealed to Booker T. Washington for help. At Washington's request, Williams submitted a list of several outstanding Negro physicians who, he felt, could run Freedmen's Hospital so as to make it a real contribution to Negro medicine. But in the meantime, Dr. Hall, his old enemy, had ingratiated himself with Booker Washington by means of political favors, and Washington asked Williams why he had left Dr. Hall's name off his list. Williams explained why he felt that Dr. Hall was not qualified. At that point Washington lost interest in Freedmen's Hospital and its reorganization and nothing was ever done.

Many Negro leaders felt that Booker T. Washington overemphasized industrial training and thereby neglected cultural education for the "Talented Tenth" (the ten per cent of Negro youth who were talented). They felt that Washington should push harder for the political rights of the Negro. While Williams felt that he had to work with Booker Washington, his heart and intelligence were with the protestors; those who, like his friend W. E. B. Du Bois, called and organized the Niagara Movement in 1905—the first formal organization to demand political and civil rights and the abolition of unequal economic opportunity for the Negro. Williams argued that "the ignorant and naturally suspicious will have to be gradually induced to relinquish their unquestioning faith in the infallible skill and judgment of the white man." He spoke like the militants in the Niagara Movement and its successor, the National Association for the Advancement of Colored People, when he said, "Those who toil get too little of the benefits of their labor, hence the power of the state should be used to regulate economic conditions and raise the living standards of the poor." Williams felt that political and social equality must arise from economic emancipation.

Dr. Hall had taken advantage of Dr. Williams' absence in Washington to advance himself at Provident Hospital by trickery and threats. Upon Williams' return, Hall made life unpleasant for him. The operating room would not be ready for him, nurses would not be detailed to him, his patients would be shown discourtesies. When in 1908 Negro physicians from all over the country gathered at a banquet in Chicago to celebrate Dr. Dan's twenty-fifth year in medicine, a silver bowl engraved with the names of thirty-seven Chicago doctors, black and white, was presented to Williams. Hall's name was not among them.

In 1912 Williams received the unprecedented honor of being appointed associate attending surgeon at St. Luke's Hospital in Chicago, an honor that no other member of his race would attain for twenty-five years after his death. St. Luke's was the largest, wealthiest, and most important hospital in Chicago at that time. Hall claimed that Williams' acceptance of this post was "an act of disloyalty to the Negro race" and succeeded in prevailing upon the Provident Hospital board to order Williams to bring all his patients to Provident. The order was absurd! Furthermore, it was insulting. Sorrowfully, Williams resigned from Provident.

Williams served at St. Luke's Hospital from his appointment in 1912 until his retirement from medicine. He ran one of the largest gynecological services in Chicago. His success at St. Luke's was so great that the hospital planned to name a ward after him. Wilberforce and Howard Universities conferred honorary degrees upon him. With the founding of the American College of Surgeons in 1913, Williams was among the charter members, the only Negro so honored. For many years he was a member of the exclusive Chicago Surgical Society and read papers before the organization and, by invitation, before numerous state and national scientific bodies.

In 1920 Williams built a summer home in beautiful Idlewild in the north Michigan woods. There he engaged in his favorite sports — swimming, fishing, and hunting. But it was not long before misfortune struck. One year after he built the summer home his wife, Alice, died of Parkinson's disease. Five years after his wife's death, Williams suffered a stroke which partially paralyzed him and effectively ended his medical career. Other strokes followed, complicated by the development of diabetes. Williams rallied and lived five years more, but his life was spent, and on August 4, 1931, he died at his summer home in Idlewild at the age of seventy-five.

In his will, Williams left his medical books to Mercy Hospital in Philadelphia, provision for his sisters, his brother's widow, his housekeeper, and his secretary, $2,000 for the colored YWCA in Washington, $2,000 for the operating room of a new interracial hospital on the South Side of Chicago, $5,000 each to Meharry and Howard Medical Schools to assist poor medical students, and $8,000 to the National Association for the Advancement of Colored People.

The world will remember Dr. Williams as a great American surgeon accorded top rank by his contemporary colleagues, white and black; as the founder of Provident Hospital, the first interracial hospital in the United States and forerunner of a hundred such institutions; as the first surgeon in the world to successfully enter the chest cavity; as the one who introduced the training of Negro nurses and internes in the United States; as a charter member of the American College of Surgeons; and finally, as one of the founders and first vice-president of the National Medical Association.

The Lone Star Team of Texas
THE STORY OF BABE DIDRIKSON
BY GEORGE VASS

The taxicab raced from a Chicago hotel toward Dyche Stadium in suburban Evanston, Illinois. The woman sitting beside the teen-age girl in the back seat glanced at her watch.

"Babe, you're not going to have time to get into your uniform when we get to the stadium," said Mrs. Henry Wood to Babe Didrikson. "I'll hold a blanket around you while you change."

As the cab struggled through heavy traffic, Babe hurriedly changed into her track suit while Mrs. Wood shielded her with the blanket. They arrived at Dyche Stadium just moments before the announcer began to introduce the teams entered in the United States women's track and field championship and Olympic trials of 1932.

When the announcer called for the team from Texas, Babe ran out on the field, waving her arms. The crowd jamming the stadium hesitated momentarily, as if wondering what had happened to the rest of the Texas team. Then, realizing Babe was the entire squad, the fans let out a mighty roar.

The cheers raised goose bumps all over the slender girl, who was to hear the roar of the crowd reverberate in countless sports arenas and playing fields for the next twenty years.

More than 200 girls were entered in the competition in July, 1932. Most of the teams had ten or more girls; the largest, the Illinois Women's Athletic Club, had twenty-two.

Texas, the Lone Star State, had only Babe, who was sponsored by the Employers Casualty Company of Dallas. But Texas didn't need anyone else. One skinny girl, standing 5'6" and weighing 110 pounds, was enough.

Babe had short, sand-colored hair and green eyes. She was feminine, with a fondness for pretty clothes, boys and dancing. She had the grace of a girl moving into womanhood at eighteen.

But Babe wasn't a little girl made only of sugar and spice. She was constructed of steel springs and whipcord, wrapped in rawhide, with the competitive drive and determination of a tigress.

She proved it that day at Dyche Stadium.

Babe, the team from Texas, entered eight of the ten scheduled events, including two in which she seldom competed, the discus throw and the shot put. The other six events she entered were the 100-meter dash, 80-meter hurdles, high jump, broad jump, javelin toss and baseball throw.

It was an exhausting two-and-a-half hour test of endurance and determination for Babe. Most of the other girls competed in only one event; just a few entered two or three. But Babe was all over the place, one moment running the 100-meter dash, the next tossing the 8-pound shot put, then hurling the javelin.

When it was all over, Babe had won five events, tied for first in another and finished fourth in the seventh. She missed picking up a team point only in the 100-meter dash, although she made the semifinals in that before bowing out.

The team from Texas scored thirty points and won the national championship. The twenty-two girls of the Illinois Women's Athletic Club finished second with twenty-two points.

Mrs. Wood was so happy and excited, she was crying.

"You did it! You did it! You won the championship all by yourself," she said, hugging Babe.

George Kirksey, a reporter for the United Press, called it "the most amazing series of performances ever accomplished by any individual, male or female, in track history."

Paul Gallico, a famous sportswriter and novelist who later became Babe's close friend, wrote, "I cannot think of any male athlete with the possible exception of old Jim Thorpe who had come even close to spread-eagling a track meet all by himself."

Babe had not only won five events and tied for first in the high jump but also set four world records. She threw a baseball 272'2". She hurled the javelin 139'3". She won an 80-meter hurdles heat in 11.9 seconds. She and Jean Shiley, a specialist in the high jump, tied for the record at 5'33-3/16".

It was a full day's work, but Babe wasn't as worn out as one might think. Friends took her and Mrs. Wood out that night, and they danced until three o'clock in the morning. The next day, just to make sure her muscles didn't tighten up, Babe worked out, already thinking of the Olympic Games to be held in Los Angeles two weeks later.

From Chicago, Babe took a train to Los Angeles with the other girls who had made the Olympic team. Unlike the other girls, who spent their time looking at the scenery or just talking, Babe worked out even on the train. She jogged the full length of the train and back, exercised and did her hurdle bends in the aisles.

"Why don't you take it easy for a while?" the other girls would ask.

"I can't," replied Babe. "I've had my heart set on the Olympic Games for a long time. I want to make sure I'll be in shape when I get there."

When she arrived in Los Angeles, she noticed a big girl wearing an Olympic jacket in the hotel lobby.

"Ah'm gonna whup you tomorrow," Babe told her.

Babe was a cocky youngster, as she later admitted, but she was truthful. If she said she was going to "whup" somebody, she did.

If Babe had been permitted, she would have entered all five events for women in the Olympic Games. But an individual was limited to three, so she chose the javelin, 80-meter hurdles and high jump.

First came the javelin throw. A little German flag was set in the ground 130' 0" from the release point to show the distance for the Olympic record, held by a German girl. Babe's throw sailed 13' 4" past the flag for a new Olympic and world record of 143' 4".

Then came the 80-meter hurdles. The Olympic record was 12.2 seconds, and Babe had set the world record of 11.9 seconds two weeks before. She beat both records, winning her qualifying heat in 11.8 seconds. In the finals she cut the record to 11.7 seconds to win her second gold medal.

Still, when competitors and newsmen crowded about to congratulate and interview her, she seemed sad. There was only one event left for her to compete in and only one record to set, when there could have been three if she had been allowed to enter all five events.

She almost shrugged off the congratulations on having set two records.

"I'd break them all if they'd let me," she said.

In the high jump finals Babe again competed against Jean Shiley, with whom she had set a world record at Evanston. They both went over 5' 5", almost 2 inches higher than their former mark.

In a final effort to break the tie, the bar was set at 5' 5¼". Jean cleared the bar first. Then Babe went over it. It appeared that the tie would stand and that the girls would share the medal.

But the judges disallowed Babe's jump. They ruled that her head had gone over the bar before her feet, which constituted a "dive" and was against the rules. She used what is called a Western roll, kicking up and over. She had always used it.

"If you were diving before, we didn't see it," said the judges. "We just saw it this time."

Despite Babe's protests, she placed second in the high jump. It was unfair. A picture showed that she had gone over the bar feet first. Later the Western roll was legalized; it is used today by many high jumpers.

But even if the decision of the judges cost Babe an Olympic gold medal, it was the luckiest break of her life. Grantland Rice, then the nation's best-known sportswriter, sympathized with the young girl. Her great athletic skill had captivated him. "I think you've been given a raw deal, Babe," Rice told her.

"But there's nothing we can do about it. Let's forget it. Why don't you join me and some friends for a round of golf tomorrow?"

Babe had been on a driving range once and had played five holes of golf another time. That was her entire experience as a golfer when Rice issued the invitation. But she wouldn't have dreamed of saying no to such a famous writer, who had featured her in all his Olympic stories.

She was eagerly waiting at her hotel the next morning when Rice came around to take her to the Brentwood Country Club. His friends turned out to be Paul Gallico, Westbrook Pegler and Braven Dyer, also famous sportswriters. It almost seemed as if they were in a conspiracy to test how good a natural athlete Babe was. They wanted to see how she would do in a sport that was new to her.

Babe didn't disappoint them. Her drive off the first tee sailed 240 yards straight down the fairway. None of the men could match it. They could scarcely believe she wasn't an experienced golfer.

That golf drive was the beginning of something important — a golf career that was to make Babe wealthy and one of the most famous woman athletes in history. It also was another step in Babe's contribution toward elevating the position of women in sports.

For a time girl athletes were viewed in almost the same light as carnival sideshow freaks. But when Babe appeared, with her unequaled versatility and skill, respect rose for women athletes. She was better at many sports than most men and good enough at some to compete with the best males.

Babe gave girl athletes dignity. She proved females could compete successfully in many sports. Babe went all out to win, to be the best at everything she attempted.

"All my life I've always had the urge to do things better than anybody else." she later said.

She was able to achieve her goals because she had great natural athletic talent. But that's not enough in sports, whether the athlete is male or female. There also has to be a competitive spirit and an indomitable will to win.

This spirit and will produced the patience and strength of character expressed in Babe's ability to practice for endless hours. Even as a child she recognized that with all her natural ability she could reach the top and stay there only by means of incessant drill and hard work.

It never occurred to her that because she was a girl she couldn't excel in athletics.

"I think every girl should go in for athletics of some sort," she later said. "Those who are not strong at the start can build up gradually."

Mildred Ella Didrikson was born on June 26, 1914, in Port Arthur, Texas. She was the sixth child of seven in the family of Ole Didrikson, an immigrant Norwegian ship's carpenter and cabinetmaker. The family called her "Baby" until she went to grade school in Beaumont, Texas, where the Didriksons moved in 1918.

"Baby" became "Babe" because Mildred started hitting home runs in playground ball games and the children's hero at the time was Babe Ruth, the great slugger of the New York Yankees.

Father Didrikson, like many Norwegians, firmly believed in physical conditioning, especially gymnastics. He set up a regular gymnasium in the backyard, with bars for jumping, rings for swinging and all the rest.

"I am not rich," he said. "I cannot give my children many fine things, but I can build good bodies for them."

Babe played football, baseball and basketball with her brothers, her older sister, Lillie, and the other children in the neighborhood. She also loved to jump over hedges. It was her way of practicing for the hurdles.

HALLS OF FAME

By the time she was fourteen, she was already thinking of becoming an Olympic athlete. It was 1928, the year the Olympics were held in Amsterdam, The Netherlands. Father Didrikson was very interested in sports and often read the sports pages of the newspapers aloud to Babe. One day he was reading about the Olympic Games.

"Next year I'm going to be in the Olympics myself," announced Babe.

"Babe, you can't," laughed Father Didrikson. "You'll have to wait another four years."

Not until then did Babe realize that the Olympics were held only every fourth year and that the next games would be in Los Angeles in 1932. Still, she was right. She was going to be in those games.

First, though, she had a lot of learning to do, in sports as well as school. Possibly the most important lesson she learned was that nothing comes easily; you have to work for everything

Babe played basketball on the girls' team at South End Junior High School in Beaumont. But when she got to Beaumont Senior High, she wasn't able to make the team because she was too small.

Babe was furious. More importantly, her competitive spirit was aroused. She went to Lil Dimmitt, coach of the boys' basketball team.

"Coach, I want to learn to play the game right," Babe told Dimmitt. "How about watching me for a while and helping me out?"

Coach Dimmitt showed Babe how to pivot properly, how to shoot free throws, how to play defense. He was very patient with her because she seemed so eager to do well and had natural ability. He let her watch the boys practice so she could pick up additional pointers.

At last she was permitted to join the girls' team. She became their best scorer from the start. The Beaumont team was unbeatable, and little stories began to appear in the newspapers about Babe Didrikson.

"Beaumont Girl Stars in Basketball Game," said one headline, and Babe had her first taste of fame. She was selected all-city, then all-state champion in basketball.

Colonel M. J. McCombs, an executive with the Employers Casualty Company, a Dallas insurance firm, heard about Babe. The colonel directed the firm's athletic program for women. He came to Beaumont to see Babe play basketball and was impressed.

Colonel McCombs persuaded Babe's parents to let her play for the company team, the Golden Cyclones, promising her a job for the summer and after she finished high school. Babe went to Dallas and was just as successful with her new team as she had been in high school.

Babe was chosen All-American three years in a row, 1930, 1931, 1932, and the Employers Casualty Company team won the national championship in 1931. Babe scored 108 points in one game.

Eventually, the colonel decided to form a girls' track team to represent the company when the basketball season ended. Babe was eager to join the team and was on hand when the colonel asked the candidates what events they wanted to compete in.

"I'm going to run the 100-yard dash," said one girl.

"I'd like to throw the javelin," said another.

"Colonel, how many events are there in this track and field?" asked Babe. When the colonel replied that there were ten, Babe said, "Well, I'm going to do them all."

The other girls couldn't help laughing at the earnest sixteen-year-old. But Babe was serious. What's more, she proved she could do it. In a Texas State meet soon afterward she entered all ten events and won eight of them.

HALLS OF FAME

Then came the 1930 national Amateur Athletic Union meet in Dallas, in which she won the javelin toss and baseball throw. A year later the national meet was held in Jersey City, New Jersey. Babe led the competition with three first places.

Yet Babe's interests weren't confined to basketball, track and field. For example, she also made a blue silk dress with pleats, which won her a prize at the Texas State fair.

A 1931 newspaper clipping describes another interest:

"An exhibition of fancy diving and swimming stunts will be given at White Rock municipal pool Sunday afternoon from 3 until 5 o'clock by Mildred Didrikson and her Employers Casualty girls. In addition the Babe will drive a motor speedboat in some

fancy area and later will show the populace how to handle the bounding and treacherous aquaplane."

Those who saw her said that Babe would have been good enough to qualify for the Olympic diving team if she had concentrated on diving. But track and field was her consuming interest in 1932.

Colonel McCombs knew what Babe wanted. He had a grand idea. He called her into the office to tell her he was going to send her to the national meet at Evanston.

"Babe, if you enter enough events and give your regular performance," said Colonel McCombs, "you can do something that's never been done before. You can win the national championship for us single-handed."

Just a few days later Babe found herself on that wild cab ride to Dyche Stadium. And she did what Colonel McCombs had predicted she could do.

Then followed her triumph in the Olympics of 1932. For that and her performance in the national meet she was selected Woman Athlete of the Year for 1932 by an Associated Press poll of sportswriters.

When she returned to Dallas, she was greeted by Mom and Dad Didrikson and a ticker tape parade. She was a national celebrity, and for a time she was too busy earning money to pursue the interest in golf aroused by Grantland Rice.

First, she turned to the stage and did a song and dance act. She tired of that and played a billiard exhibition series with Ruth McGinnis, a woman professional, in New York. But, having earned some money, she returned to Dallas to work for the Employers Casualty Company in 1933.

Golf was still on her mind, so she decided to move to Los Angeles to learn the game. When she arrived, she was interviewed by reporters.

"I have enough money to last for three years and I intend to win a women's golf championship before those three years and my bankroll are gone," she told them.

She started taking lessons with Stan Kertes, a young professional golfer. But she ran out of money sooner than she expected and had to return to her job in Dallas.

In 1934 a promoter named Ray Doan persuaded her to form a girls' basketball team, Babe Didrikson's All-Americans, to tour the country. Doan also had a baseball team of bearded men called the House of David. He persuaded Babe to pitch an inning of each game for the bearded men.

Her greatest moment as a baseball pitcher came in 1934, when she visited the training camp of the St. Louis Cardinals at Bradenton, Florida. The Cardinals were to play the Philadelphia Athletics in an exhibition game that day.

Dizzy Dean, the great Cardinal pitcher, was joking with Jimmy Foxx, the marvelous home run hitter of the Athletics.

"We'll pitch Babe against you, and I'll bet that Paul [his brother] and Babe and I can beat you," Dean told Foxx.

Babe pitched the first inning. The Athletics loaded the bases against her on three hits, but she got the fourth batter to hit into a double play without anyone's scoring. The fifth batter was Foxx. She got him to fly out to end the inning.

It wasn't a spectacular performance, but Babe had shown she could survive against baseball's best.

There was hardly any sport she didn't attempt in those days and none in which she didn't show some skill. She bowled for a time, played lacrosse, fenced, played tennis, appeared on a polo pony, passed and kicked footballs and tried her hand at volley ball.

But golf was still on her mind. She never forgot the vow she had made to win a women's championship by 1936. Once again, in the summer of 1934, she began taking lessons, this time with

George Aulbach, the pro at the Dallas Country Club.

By November she felt ready to enter a tournament, the Fort Worth Women's Open. She showed up for the qualifying round.

"What do you think you'll shoot, Babe?" asked a reporter.

"I think I'll shoot a 77," she replied.

The amazing fact is that she did just that; she became medalist, having the lowest score in the qualifying round.

"Wonder Girl Makes Her Debut in Tournament Golf; Turns in 77 Score," said the headline in the Fort Worth newspaper.

Babe was eliminated in an early round of the match play that followed but had satisfied herself that she could become a fine golfer with practice. And practice she did.

This was her schedule: up at 5:00 a.m., practice 5:30 to 8:30, report to work at 9:00. During the lunch hour she putted on the carpet in her boss's office and chipped balls onto his leather chair. When she left work, she dashed out to the golf course, hitting balls until dark. First, she had an hour's lesson from Aulbach; then, she practiced all her shots. She worked so hard and long that she got blisters on her hands. She taped the blisters, and often the tape was covered with blood. When it got too dark to practice, she read the rule book and memorized it.

In April, 1935, she felt ready to enter her second tournament. This was the Texas Women's Golf Championship. She won it two up, beating Peggy Chandler, a veteran player, in the finals. She had made good her pledge to the Los Angeles sportswriters with a year to spare.

But once again she was to face disappointment. Just two weeks later, in May, 1935, the United States Golf Association ruled her ineligible for further competition in women's amateur tournaments because she had been a professional in other sports.

Not in golf, in other sports! It didn't make sense to Babe or to her friends, but there was nothing to be done. She turned professional. She began touring the country in exhibition matches with famous golfers such as Gene Sarazen.

The fans loved to watch her. The galleries followed her around the course, enjoying her jokes as much as her golf.

"Boy! Don't you men wish you could hit a ball like that?" she'd tell them after whacking a drive 300 yards. Then she would add: "Ladies and gentlemen, whatever I say today can't be held against me, because it's for your entertainment."

She was paid well for the exhibition matches and also for endorsing golf clubs and sports clothes. But it was just as important to her to improve her game by learning from Sarazen and the other fine men she met.

The 1938 Los Angeles Open was even more important for Babe. She had little hope of beating the men in the tournament. She thought, however, that by entering the competition she could establish herself as a champion woman golfer.

Babe was to have two partners on the course. One was a minister; the other was George Zaharias, a professional wrestler known as "The Crying Greek from Cripple Creek," who was in the tournament just for fun.

A photographer wanting to pose the wrestler, famous as a ring "villain," with the greatest girl athlete ran up to Babe and George, an enormously strong young man of twenty-nine.

"Do you mind my taking a picture of you together?" the photographer asked. "Put your arm around her," he instructed George.

Zaharias was embarrassed, but Babe smiled encouragingly. "Sure, put your arm around me."

Then they played their round of golf.

They began to see each other regularly and to think about getting married. Some people thought Babe was a tomboy because she was so athletic. It wasn't true. She liked nice clothes, cooking and housekeeping as much as the next girl.

She loved to dance and often went out with young men. But no one seriously interested her until she met Zaharias.

They were married in St. Louis on December 23, 1938. Leo Durocher, later manager of the Brooklyn Dodgers, New York Giants and Chicago Cubs, was George's best man. It was a happy marriage. George was proud of his wife's athletic skill. He wanted her to become the greatest woman golfer in the world. But in those days most of the major women's tournaments were amateur, and she had been banned from competing in them.

"Babe, you can regain your amateur standing if you quit now as a professional," George said. "It'll take three years of sitting out all professional events, but you will be an amateur again. I know you want to compete and win championships."

Babe was delighted. That's what she truly wanted. The time of the professional woman golfer hadn't yet arrived. Babe was to make that possible. But if she wanted to be a champion, she had to compete in amateur tournaments.

Fortunately, George was wealthy, having made money by wrestling and from good investments, so Babe no longer needed the income from exhibition matches. She could turn down all the prize money and become strictly an amateur.

It took three long years, but on January 21, 1943, Babe was restored to amateur standing. She was able to play again. And she began the road back by winning the mid-winter women's golf championship at the Los Angeles Country Club.

Babe Didrikson Zaharias was a champion once more.

In the years to come she was to prove herself over and over. She was selected Woman Athlete of the Year by the Associated Press in 1945 and again in 1946, 1947 and 1950. In 1950 she was the recipient of an even greater honor. She was voted Woman Athlete of the Half Century.

She deserved the award for many reasons, among them an unprecedented streak of seventeen major victories in a row, including victories in the National Women's Amateur, the All-American Open, the North and South and, most impressively, the British Women's Amateur Open.

An Athlete, particularly a golfer, would appreciate such success more than anyone else. It is proof not only of skill but also of nerve, gumption, courage and determination.

An athlete understands the terrible pressures exerted on his nerves and body in competition against the best at his particular sport. Babe faced these pressures, tournament after tournament, yet her iron will sustained her for seventeen straight events.

The most memorable triumph was her victory in the 1947 British Women's Amateur at Gullane, Scotland. No American had won the tournament before.

"Aren't you afraid you'll be jinxed in this tournament like all the other American girls before you?" one of her competitors asked before the tournament opened.

Babe just laughed. "I didn't come over here to lose."

Her competitor kept reminding her of the fate of previous American contenders each time she met her. "Don't forget about the jinx," she'd tease.

Nothing was further from Babe's mind. Still, she was a little superstitious. She began the final match against England's little Jacqueline Gordon wearing what she termed "some refined clothes"—a gray flannel skirt, wool sweater and a yellow and white blouse.

When she was no better than even after eighteen holes, she changed to a pair of old slacks. Then she went out and beat her foe, five holes up with only four left to play.

"My lucky pants did it," she laughed.

After that great triumph, Babe turned professional again and proceeded to win every major title open to women golfers. Three times she won the world championship at Tam O'Shanter, near

Chicago. In 1952 she set a record for woman golfers by winning the Tampa Open in 288 strokes.

By this time Babe and George had built a beautiful house in Tampa, Florida. He was prospering as a sports promoter and real estate developer. She was making one hundred thousand dollars a year from her sports activities and endorsements. Even if young girls were coming along every year to challenge her skill, she was still the champ.

But in April, 1953, a new and more dangerous challenger appeared—cancer. Babe had to undergo a serious operation. Her life, not to mention her golfing career, was in danger. The operation was performed and appeared successful. Yet it seemed that Babe would never golf again. She was lucky to be alive.

Then, one day, after spending seventy days in the hospital and another month recuperating at the house in Tampa, she sneaked out of the house to the Tampa golf course. She shot 37 for the first nine holes. George found out what she had done and was frightened.

"Take it easy, dear," he said. "It has only been three months."

"I feel fine, just fine," replied Babe. "I can play again. I'm going to go back."

She resumed tournament play, and soon she was winning again. She was still the champ and was awarded the Ben Hogan Trophy for the Greatest Comeback of the Year in 1953.

In 1954 she won the National Open and All-American Open, and in 1955 she won two more tournaments. Then it was discovered that the cancer had reappeared.

This time there was no reprieve. Babe Didrikson Zaharias died in 1956 at the age of forty-two.

To the end, in every aspect of life, she displayed the extraordinary courage and determination of the truly great.

As Grantland Rice said: "The Babe is without any question the athletic phenomenon of all time, man or woman."

The Negro Speaks of Rivers
By Langston Hughes

I've known rivers:
I've known rivers ancient as the world and older than the
flow of human blood in human veins.

My soul has grown deep like the rivers.

I bathed in the Euphrates when dawns were young.
I built my hut near the Congo and it lulled me to sleep.
I looked upon the Nile and raised the pyramids above it.
I heard the singing of the Mississippi when Abe Lincoln
went down to New Orleans, and I've seen its muddy
bosom turn all golden in the sunset.

I've known rivers:
Ancient, dusky rivers.

My soul has grown deep like the rivers.

A Boy in Russia
Leo N. Tolstoy (*Russian*, 1828-1910)

Leo Tolstoy lived with his three brothers at Yasnaya Polyana, the beautiful country estate of his father, Count Nicolay Tolstoy. They were a merry group of youngsters, always up to something interesting. One day Nicolay, the oldest of the brothers, said to Sergey, Dmitri and Leo, who was five, "I know a secret which will make all men happy when it is discovered. There will be no more dieases and no more troubles. No one will be angry with anyone else, all will love each other, and all will become Ant-brothers."

Doubtless Nicolay meant Moravian-brothers, for he had read of the Moravian brotherhood and their ideals of peace and brotherly love; but, in Russian, the word for Moravia is the same as the word for ant, so they became to Nicolay the Ant-brothers. Nicolay said he had written the great secret of happiness on a green stick, which he had buried by the road on the edge of a certain ravine. He then organized a game called Ant-brothers wherein all the children lay down under a chair, sheltered behind boxes and screened with handkerchiefs.

HALLS OF FAME

Thus, crouching together in the dark, they pressed close against each other. Leo remembered experiencing a special feeling of love for his brothers in playing that game. But, though the Ant-brotherhood was thus revealed to the children, the chief secret still remained hidden. They were never able to find the green stick on which was written the way for all men to cease suffering, leave off quarreling, and become continuously happy. Nevertheless, as Leo grew older, that was the secret he was ceaselessly striving to find, that he might disclose it to men.

Leo was only eight years old when the family moved to Moscow. They drove away from the old house, leaving behind them a crowd of staring, bare-footed children; menservants in coats and kaftans; and women in striped petticoats with babies in their arms.

Moscow was a very large and beautiful city, the Mother of all
the Russias, for it was from Mother Moscow that the whole
great Russian empire had grown. The children admired the city
greatly—its crooked old streets; its great open spaces and boule-
vards; the scores of white churches, each crowned with a dome
of brilliant color—gold, green, or blue with silver stars. They
loved to see the white palaces that overhung the narrow, winding
banks of the Moskva River; the ancient monasteries with their
high walls and round towers; and, best of all, the historic old
fort of the Kremlin, sacred in Russian history. When they were
not in school, they visited these places of interest. At such
times, they rode in a carriage drawn by four bay horses harnessed
abreast, according to the custom of the time and country.

They had only been a few months in Moscow, however, when
their father suddenly died. And, as their mother was already
dead, they were now orphans with their Aunt Alexandra as
their guardian. Count Nicolay disappeared so suddenly from
Leo's life that the boy could not believe he was gone, but would
scan the faces of passersby, thinking to see him again somewhere in the streets of Moscow.

For a time, the children lived with their grandmother, a very
grand old lady who dwelt in considerable state and maintained
the strictest etiquette in all the affairs of life.

But, soon after the death of Count Nicolay, Grandmother also
died. Henceforth, the boys stayed in Moscow winters to go to
school and went to Yasnaya Polyana for the summers. It was
during those days that Leo learned for the first time that cor-
poral punishment was being inflicted on the serfs at Yasnaya
Polyana, a thing which had never been heard of when his father
was alive. He and his brothers were returning from a walk with
their tutor when they met near the barn the fat steward, Andrey
Flyin. He was followed by the coachman's assistant, Squinting
Koozma, as he was called. Koozma was a married man no longer

young, and he wore just then a piteous face. One of the children asked Andrey where he was going, and the steward quietly answered:

"We are going to the barn where Koozma must be punished."

This meant that Koozma was to be whipped, and it was a terrible feeling that came upon Leo at sight of the good-natured, crestfallen fellow on the way to such a punishment. In the evening he told his Aunt Tatiana what had happened. She was deeply moved and said to the boy: "And why did you not stop it?"

And why had he not stopped it? He had not even dreamed before that he could interfere in such an affair. Could he have stopped it? He never forgot the incident.

In 1841, when Leo was thirteen years old, Aunt Alexandra died, and now the children fell to the care of another of their father's sisters, Aunt Pelageya, the wife of Yushkoff, a rich land owner of Kazan. Aunt Pelageya came almost at once and took her niece and nephews from Yasnaya Polyana to Kazan. Ordering some boats, she loaded them with everything which it was possible for her to take away from her brother's estate. All the servants had to follow her, too—carpenters, tailors, blacksmiths, chefs, upholsterers. Moreover, she gave to each of the four brothers a serf of about his own age, to be forever attached to him as a man-servant.

When all was ready, Leo and his sister and brothers bade farewell to their beloved Aunt Tatiana, who went to live with a sister, and set out in numerous carriages and other vehicles for Kazan. It was a long journey and they crept along very slowly, but the time of year was autumn, the weather was fine, and they often camped out in the fields or the woods, bathing when they came to streams of water. Thus they traveled for four hundred miles eastward.

They found Kazan a half barbaric city, one of the most interesting in Russia. It was the busy gateway to the East, and from

its quays they saw ships floating out on the mighty waters of the
river Volga, bound for the distant Caspian Sea. They saw its
marts crowded with picturesque caravans, arriving from Bok-
hara and other cities of Persia, or departing perhaps for India,
while its streets were thronged with Greeks, Tartars, Persians,
dark-skinned Armenians and wayfarers from the Caucasus, a
motley multitude indeed.

At the house of his uncle Yushkoff in Kazan Leo grew to manhood, and he and his brothers attended the university of Kazan.
It was a rich, exciting life they lived, for they were members of a
high-born family. Leo was not sure it was the life for him, however. He enjoyed it, but he was ashamed of the time he wasted.
He felt he should do something useful in life.

In this mood he left the university at Kazan and went back
to Yasnaya Polyana. He was filled with a great desire to improve
the lives of the peasants there. Unfortunately, his attempts to
help them were met with suspicion and distrust. The serfs

wanted to continue living as they always had; they did not like new ideas in farming, education, or housekeeping. When their master worked in the fields along with them, they lost respect for him.

At last Leo gave up and went to join his brother Nicolay, who was in the Russian army in the Caucasus mountains. Here the army was helping the Cossack people defend themselves from the raids of the nomadic Tartars. In the mountains Leo lived a simple outdoor life, very different from the well-to-do life he was used to. The majestic beauty of the mountains, the spirit and courage of the Cossacks, and the primitive way of life, so close

to nature, were things he had been searching for all his life. He began to write, to express the emotions he felt while living in that wild and beautiful place.

In 1853 Russia became involved in the Crimean War. Tolstoy had himself transferred so that he could take part in the defense of the city of Sebastopol. There he wrote of the tremendous heroism he saw around him. But in spite of the courage of the Russian soldiers, the city was lost after a long siege, and soon after that the war ended. Tired of battles, Tolstoy went home again to Yasnaya Polyana. Now older and wiser than before, he was more successful in helping the peasants to a better way of life. His farm prospered and the workers prospered with it. Tolstoy had come to believe that all men should be equal, that no one was entitled to enjoy wealth while others remained poor. He wanted nothing more than to find a way for all men to have equal wealth and happiness, the secret of the green stick he had sought as a little boy.

At the age of thirty-five Leo Tolstoy married Sofiya Behrs and began raising a family. His children enjoyed life on the farm

MAUD-MISKA
PETERSHAM

as he had. Tolstoy, too, was happy, for, besides enjoying the companionship of wife and children and the bounty of his land, he had become a respected author, honored throughout Russia for his novels. As he grew to be an old man, he became still more deeply concerned with living a life that was not wasteful or selfish. He did not want his standard of living to be higher than anyone else's. He wanted to be as poor as the poorest man, rather than rich. He lived like the peasants on his farm, dressing as they did, eating as they did, and working at the hardest manual labor. He gave all his possessions to his wife and children because he did not want to own property anymore.

As an old man he liked to leave the farm and travel among the poor people of Russia. Only by leaving the comfortable farm could he feel completely without wealth. When he was eighty-two years old he left Yasnaya Polyana for the last time. While traveling he fell ill and died in the humble home of a railroad station master.

All over Russia the common people mourned his death, for they had great respect for this man who valued equality more than wealth. They came from the nearby villages in their long overcoats to stand in groups around the doorstep, weeping and embracing one another, and one was heard to comfort the others, saying:

"Fear not for him; he loved the people so."

Old man though he lived to be, Tolstoy never forgot the game of Ant-brothers which he had played as a child, and when he was over seventy, he wrote:

"The ideal of Ant-brothers, lovingly clinging to one another, though not under two arm chairs curtained by handkerchiefs, but of all mankind under the wide dome of heaven, has remained the same for me. As I then believed that there existed a little green stick, whereon was written the message that could destroy all evil in men and give them universal welfare, so I now believe that such truth exists and will be revealed to men and will give them all it promises."

Learning to be Free
THE STORY OF FREDERICK DOUGLASS
BY MILDRED BARGER HERSCHLER

Gray winter skies replaced the deep blue of autumn, and cold and hunger stalked like wolves. All kinds of food were there, but beyond Frederick's reach. He peeked into the dairy, the finest on the Eastern Shore of Maryland, but he never tasted milk. Clothing was made from fine cloth in the sewing room, but Frederick shivered with the cold. The nights were hardest to bear, and he often got down the bag used for carrying corn to the mill and crawled into it head first, his feet sticking out.

After one such frosty night, Frederick woke to a day cold but clear. He slapped his numb feet, rubbing the deeply cracked flesh until blood began to tingle through. Then out into the yard he ran. But the bright day only made him more aware of his stomach, and he stood a moment, blinking at the sun. Then he took a deep breath of the nippy air and began to sing. He knew that "make a noise there" was an overseer's constant cry, but now he realized that warbling a tune was balsam for his gloom.

Frederick Douglass escaped slavery in the South and was one of the first black Americans to fight for justice and equality for all blacks. He founded an anti-slavery newspaper and during the Civil War was a trusted advisor to President Abraham Lincoln. Through his newspaper editorials he helped stir action against slavery. He helped other blacks escape the slave states and often risked his life to speak openly against the inhumanity of slavery.

In this episode, at a time when it was unlawful to teach slaves to read and write, Frederick dared to defy his master and learn. Learning to read and write enabled Frederick Douglass to free himself from slavery and enabled him to crusade for the freedom of all blacks.

As the days wore on, Frederick sang whenever hunger threatened to dominate his life. Then one day he stood under the window where Miss Lucretia sat with her sewing. He was valiantly belting forth a melody, his stomach muscles as tense as the strings on a violin.

He heard a window open. "Freddy," called Miss Lucretia, "come to the window."

He walked slowly, not knowing what to expect, though as usual her voice was soft and gentle.

"How about a piece of bread and butter?"

Frederick took it eagerly from her outstretched hand. "Thank you," he murmured.

"We wouldn't want such a lovely song to go unpaid for, would we? I do enjoy singing."

Somehow Miss Lucretia had understood. And he suspected that when his ration of food was narrow and the space beneath his ribs wide, he could sing at her window and count on her reward. Such rare favors stood out as shining moments in a dark expanse of time.

Another summer, another winter came and went, and Frederick still looked to the blackbirds with a wistful envy. The sight of the windmill always sent his thoughts soaring, and now he knew in his heart that to regard God as "Our Father" branded slavery as wrong.

Then one day when the weather was balmy and the children were laughing and chasing each other near the house, Miss Lucretia called to him. "Come. I have good news for you." She led him into the parlor. "In three days you'll be on your way to Baltimore. My father is going to send you to live with my brother-in-law, Mr. Hugh Auld. His little son needs a fine boy like you to take care of him."

Frederick shifted from foot to foot.

"You're going on the *Sally Lloyd*, Freddy. Isn't it exciting?

Now, you must scrub all the dead skin off your feet and knees, for we wouldn't want people laughing at you, would we? Besides, I'm going to give you trousers, and you can't put them on over dirt. Run along now, and don't come back until you're all ready for the trousers."

He walked solemnly out of the parlor, but when he was a safe distance from the house, he gave such a loud whoop that the children stopped playing and stared.

"I'm going to Baltimore to live," he cried, jumping up and down. "I'm leaving here in three days!"

He did not notice the sudden smile on Eliza's face or the look of envy on Perry's, for it was Tom who came forward. "Oh, you'll l-l-like Baltimore!" he said, with authority. "You'll see s-soldiers and hear shooting-crackers and b-bells ringing . . ."

Frederick smiled. "Tell me all about it when I get back from the creek, Tom."

"The cr-creek?"

"I have to scrub. I'm going to have trousers!" His eyes widened and he whooped again.

"Everyb-body wears t-trousers in B-baltimore," said Tom, as Frederick went leaping toward the creek.

He spent most of the next three days in the bubbling water, scrubbing furiously. Every evening he made sure the *Sally Lloyd* was still at anchor in the swash, and every morning he made sure she was not yet ready to sail.

Then came the trousers. "You've done a good job, Freddy," said Miss Lucretia. "Put these on first thing in the morning, and go down to the dock. You'll be leaving early, so I'll say good-bye now."

Frederick held them to him and looked at the floor. "Thank you, Miss Lucretia." He turned to go.

"Oh, Freddy, please tell Master Hugh that you are eight, going on nine, and you were born in February. And remember, don't get into any nasty fights."

He could not sleep that night. He tossed about, thinking of wonderful Baltimore, certain that his new home would be much better than this one. He was glad he knew his age, though he had no knowledge of the months of the year or the years themselves, since slaves measured the ages of their children by planting-time, summertime, harvest-time, or wintertime. Masters said that questions concerning birth-dates were "impudent curiosity," and so if a slave had a yen to know when he was born, it was better forgotten.

But Frederick did know the days of the week, and it was early on a Saturday morning that he sailed out of the Mills River. Many years later he found out from the dates of other events that it was in the spring of 1825 that he put on his first trousers and climbed aboard the *Sally Lloyd*.

On setting sail, he walked aft and saw the stately chimneys of the Great House moving slowly away. He surveyed the plantation with no mixed emotion. He clearly hoped he would never see it or any place like it again.

Then he made his way to the bow of the boat and spent the rest of the day looking ahead. In the distance were other vessels sweeping the broad bay, which opened before his hungry eyes like a sea without end.

Frederick went to sleep that night thinking about his view of Annapolis, the dome of the State House rising from a forest of structures new to his eye. He slept soundly, for the roll of the boat was a lullabye, and nothing could change his destination now.

The next morning, Baltimore stood waiting. They docked at Smith's wharf, and Frederick was all eyes and ears until a ship-hand led him to his new home. He skipped beside the sternly

quiet man, despite a temptation to stop and stare at the ship-
yards and buildings. At last they reached the house on Alliciana
Street near Fells Point.

"Hello, there, Rich!" said the pretty lady inside, and Frederick glanced at his companion, who had replaced his grim mask
with a broad smile.

"Good mornin', Miss Sophia!"

"And this is Freddy! What a fine-looking boy!"

"Tell my brother we are pleased," said a sourlooking man at
her side.

"Yes, Master Hugh."

A rosy-cheeked little boy peeked out from behind his mother's
skirts. He kept trying to wink at Frederick, but it came out a
blink every time. When Frederick smiled, the boy stepped forward.

"Dear, here is your Freddy," said Miss Sophia to her son.
"He's going to take care of you. This is little Tommy. Be kind
to him, won't you?"

Frederick nodded. It was a foolish question. The bright-eyed
lad aroused instant affection.

"Tommy will show you your bed and where to freshen up.
Then come and get some bread."

"Yes, ma'am." His eyes were properly lowered.

Suddenly she reached out to him, and placing her hand gently
under his chin, raised his face to hers. "You mustn't be afraid,
child. We're going to be good friends. Now hurry and change
your clothes."

Tommy took his hand and together they climbed to the
kitchen loft. There before him was a straw bed well-furnished
with covers, and a change of clothes hung on a nearby nail.

"Will you play with me?" asked Tommy, flashing an impish
grin. "I'll wait for you downstairs."

Frederick sat down on the bed wonderingly.

"Hurry up, Freddy," came a small voice from the kitchen, and he felt he'd found a family at last. Soon he caught a strange new glimpse of himself, for whenever he approached Miss Sophia, she seemed to say, "Look up, child, look up." Different from any other mistress in the world, she thought it altogether fitting and proper for him to look her in the eye. This was hard for him at first, but Frederick remembered that his mother had held her head high, and Grandmamma had bowed to no one.

His main duty was the care of Tommy, keeping him out of the way of carriages and any other danger in the streets where they played. He ran errands for his mistress, whose affection for him grew as time went by. But a boy of the open country-side, he felt walled in by the towering buildings around him.

The first time he ventured out alone to explore the neighborhood, he met a group of boys. They stared at him and one of them growled, "Where are you from?"

"From Colonel Lloyd's."

The boys became as one enormous boy, advancing on him. He began to run.

"Eastern-Shore man," they yelled, at his heels.

He was glad to reach Alliciana Street. Still panting, he stood inside the door of the house.

"Freddy, is that you?" Miss Sophia called, sharply.

"Yes, ma'am."

"Where have you been? We've been looking for you!" There she stood, a deep frown on her face.

"I won't go out without asking ever again!"

Tommy took his hand. "It's all right, Freddy. I still love you."

Miss Sophia broke into a smile. "You and Tommy run along now."

"Yes, ma'am. Come on, Tommy. Let's go watch them build that frigate down the street."

As they left the house and skipped along together, Frederick realized something: no cuffing from Aunt Katy ever hurt as much as his new mistress's frown. He guessed he could get used to the closed-in feeling of a town where he had a home.

He had no way of knowing that in three short years he would be in grave danger of losing that home! After the sudden death of Old Master, Frederick found himself back on the Lloyd plantation, waiting to be divided with the rest of Captain Anthony's property. The question was whether he would go to Andrew, the son who had grown to be mean and worthless, or to Miss Lucretia. When the time came, he would have no more choice than the pigs.

Tommy had run to him sobbing, "Don't leave us, Freddy! Please don't go!"

But he had had to go, and now he stood with cattle and oxen and men, sheep and women and children, all waiting to be inspected by men called "appraisers," valued in silver and gold, and divided.

The older slaves kept a protective silence, but they dreaded the prospect of falling into the hands of Master Andrew, who had already spent a fortune. They believed that his slaves would in time be sold at public auction to the cotton fields and rice swamps of the Deep South—that far-off, dreaded place of no return. And they mourned the coming separation from friends or family. So again Frederick saw change in the shape of a threat, and he met it, as the others did, with fear.

A month of suspense passed, and then he was told that he belonged to Miss Lucretia. He sighed with relief. He did not know to whom his brother and sisters had gone, and time moved so fast now that he could not find out. Captain Auld and his wife Lucretia immediately decided on the boy's return to Baltimore. He didn't look back when he left.

Soon after Frederick's reunion with Tommy and Miss Sophia,

Master Hugh received a letter edged in black. Frederick was in the parlor when it came.

"It's Thomas's wife. She has passed away."

"Lucretia? How sad!" exclaimed Miss Sophia. "She was in poor health a long time, wasn't she?" She glanced at Frederick. "Why, Freddy, what's wrong? You look as if you had lost your best friend!"

His lips trembled, and he could not speak into the great silence. He ran from the room and upstairs to his straw bed. Great sobs came from his throat, sobs without tears. What would he do without his kind friend to plead for him when the wind of change might blow again?

"The Lord is my shepherd; I shall not want . . ."

Miss Sophia's voice came from her room, and Frederick knew she was reading the Bible. Sometimes she let him listen at her side, and he looked at the words curiously. These words his mother had somehow mastered; she was the only slave in Tuckahoe to leap to the knowledge of reading.

He waited until Miss Sophia appeared, and then he gulped. "Miss Sophia, would—would you teach me to read?"

She cocked her head, and her reply was instant. "Why, Freddy, how sweet. Of course I'll teach you."

He almost jumped with joy! He was not allowed to attend school, but he had found a teacher.

He was an apt pupil, and Miss Sophia was so proud of him that she bubbled over one evening. "Oh, Hugh, you would be surprised at how well Freddy reads after so few lessons!"

"You're teaching him to read?" Master Hugh put down his newspaper and looked toward Frederick, who sat playing with Tommy on the floor. "Freddy?"

"You seem surprised. I thought you knew. Why, his progress has been so rapid, you'd be as proud—"

"Sophia!" He cleared his throat, as if to prepare for a long speech, and his voice was strained. "You should never teach a slave to read, my dear."

"But Hugh, isn't it my duty to teach him to read the Bible?"

"Your duty! It is not only against the law, but unsafe! Give a slave an inch and he will take an ell. Learning will ruin him, make him unfit to be a slave! I thought you knew that Freddy should know nothing but our will, and learn only to obey it!"

Miss Sophia was pale. "But he wants to learn—"

"It's for his own good as well as ours. Learning will only make him discontented. Why, first thing you know, he'll want to learn to write, and then what! You have to start early to keep them in their place. A slave should learn only the will of his master, I say! I forbid you to give him further instruction!"

"I'm sorry, Hugh, I—I didn't know." She looked at Frederick, who was looking intently at the floor. She got up and left the room.

Frederick climbed to the kitchen loft and fell into his straw bed without undressing. Master Hugh's words rang in his ears like a funeral knell, and sank into his heart like lead.

Then as he lay in the darkness, he realized that a question had been answered for him tonight. He had always wanted to know how the slave system could exist, what power the slave-holder held over the slave, why men were masters of men! Master Hugh had made it very clear. Knowledge was the answer! Learning makes a child unfit to be a slave, he had said, right before Frederick's very ears!

He suddenly smiled out the tiny attic window at the moon. From that moment on, he held tight to the knowledge that ignorance fostered slavery, and education was the pathway to freedom.

The cloud that hung over the household became darker with

time. Frederick was determined to read, and a change was taking place in Miss Sophia's attitude toward him. The kind lady who used to feel his love and know him to be human now struggled in her mind with the principles of the slave system, which denied human rights. Now she complained that he was sullen and secretive, and she watched his every move. Her heart and mind surrendered to the rules set down by her husband. Slaveholder she was not, but slaveholder she became.

One day Frederick picked up a newspaper and sat down in a corner of the parlor. A sudden movement at the door made him look up to see Miss Sophia rushing at him. She snatched the newspaper from him, and there was fury in her voice. "Don't let me ever catch you reading again!"

Frederick tried to take that advice, though he was caught on other occasions, when the intensity of her wrath surprised even Master Hugh.

If only he could explain to her how he felt, try to make her understand his need of knowledge! But when he looked at her, he saw that it was no use. Her aim was to keep him a slave, and now her smile was for a "good" slaveboy.

He climbed slowly to his loft. He felt little and alone again— alone on a long, dusty road. But he was impelled to take that "ell"—he'd find a way!

Now Tommy went to school, and Frederick ambled along, a discarded copy of Webster's Spelling Book in his pocket and a terrible truth torturing his mind: "I am a slave for life!"

Tommy skipped merrily at his side. "Look, Freddy," he said, suddenly bending over. "What is it?"

Frederick looked at the sidewalk. A bug was struggling to emerge from a crack between the bricks.

"Looks like a beetle," he said.

"Let's help him," cried Tommy, loosening one of the bricks. He laughed when the creature walked unsteadily away. "I'll bet he's glad to get out!"

"Yeah," said Frederick. He envied the bug.

He sat down on the schoolhouse steps to wait for Tommy. Sometimes he salvaged school papers here.

Two boys walked up the steps. "What are you going to learn for the exhibition?" asked one.

The other one frowned. "Something from the *Columbian Orator*. Maybe the one about liberty or death."

Frederick's ears strained to hear more, but the boys were on the other side of the doors that kept him out. Well, he had time on his hands. He would go down to Thames Street while the conversation was fresh in his mind.

Mr. Knight's store had many books, but it was not hard to

find the one he wanted. He picked it up and began to leaf through it. What had the boy said? Liberty or death?

"That costs fifty cents," Mr. Knight said over his shoulder. "Do you have the money to pay for it?"

Frederick shook his head. "But I will, soon."

Mr. Knight motioned him to the door. "What would your sort want with a book, anyway!"

Frederick spent all his spare time blacking boots until he had enough money to buy the book. He was thirteen now, and read fairly well. The *Columbian Orator* was a treasure. Besides Patrick Henry's cry of "Give me liberty, or give me death!" he found speeches by William Pitt and Lord Chatham who wrote of the American Revolution, and Sheridan's powerful defense of the rights of man. Over and over he read a piece which was a conversation between a master and his slave, whose valiant argument against slavery resulted in his emancipation, or being set free.

The book increased Frederick's vocabulary, giving him words to express thoughts that had been locked in his mind. He felt he could win any argument with slavery's defenders, who claimed that God was on their side. How angry that made him!

Now he was really sullen and gloomy. "Giving me good clothing and food can't excuse taking my liberty away from me," he told the moon from his attic window. "Slaveholders are wicked robbers."

And so the condition of unhappiness described by Master Hugh was upon him. He was indeed unfit to be a slave!

And what had happened to his childhood? He had left it where the windmill whirled, where the blackbird sang, where men fashioned wood into a frigate, ready for the open sea . . .

"Those abolitionists cause a lot of trouble in this country," said Master Hugh.

A visitor slammed down his fist on the arm of a chair. "They should all be deported!"

"I agree, but it's a free country, you know."

Frederick was walking past the parlor when he overhead those words. It wasn't the first time he had heard of the abolitionists, who seemed to be feared as well as hated. He went to the bookcase and got down the dictionary.

"Let's see," he said, "it says to abolish is to do away with, but to do away with what?" He was more puzzled than ever. Now he searched through the *Baltimore American*, a city newspaper. Here it was! A vast number of petitions had been sent to Congress asking for the *abolition* of slavery in the District of Columbia, and for the *abolition* of slave trade between the states. So that was it! No wonder slaveholders spoke angrily against abolitionists!

Though slavery was defended in local newspapers, the quoted words of abolitionists now brought hope. If he was too young to think of escape, he would do the next-best thing—learn to write!

Soon he was put to work in Master Hugh's shipyard. His job was to keep a fire under the steambox and watch the yard while the carpenters went to dinner. Whenever it was deserted, he copied the letters written on the wood to show the section of the ship where it belonged. And during his spare time, he often played spelling and writing games with white schoolboy friends.

Then one day when he was left alone in the house, he carried a chair and a flour barrel to his loft. The room was seldom visited by the family anymore, and here he could bring his bits of paper and books from which to copy. After that he often sat by candlelight until late at night, perfecting his handwriting at his makeshift desk.

He was busy teaching other slaveboys to read when the next swift wind of change blew.

Captain Auld had married again two years after the death of Miss Lucretia. He and his wife were living in St. Michaels on Maryland's Eastern Shore when a bitter family feud broke out.

Soon Master Hugh called Frederick into the parlor to break
vital news to him.

"Fred, I've been ordered to send you back to Captain Auld,"
he said, fingering a letter in his lap. "I have no choice, because
you are still his legal property, you know."

Frederick looked at Miss Sophia, sitting in a chair near her
husband. "We'll be sorry to see you go, Freddy," she said.
"Tommy's gone to bed, but he knows you are leaving and he is
sorry, too."

"Yes, ma'am." Frederick felt hot and cold at the same time.
"When do I sail?"

"The *Amanda* docks with its cargo at dawn. It will take you
back when it sails."

"Is that all, Master Hugh?"

"Yes, except to say good-bye and good luck."

The Coin
By Sara Teasdale

Into my heart's treasury
   I slipped a coin
That time cannot take
   Nor thief purloin.
Oh, better than the minting
   Of a gold-crowned king
Is the safe-kept memory
   Of a lovely thing.

The Interesting History of Old Mother Goose

THE most remarkable dame in all history who was born gray-headed and yet never grows old, who perennially keeps her charm, who is ever, forever, calling out the spirit of childhood in the human heart to go gamboling with her over the green, turning somersaults, kicking up its heels, and yet learning, too, at her knee from her quaint store of sage and precious nonsense, is that beloved old creature, Old Mother Goose. Who she was, nobody knows. Her personality remains enshrouded in the most delightful mystery. But, if the truth were known, she has doubtless dwelt forever in the human heart; for her rhymes and jingles are nothing more nor less than the spontaneous bubblings of the eternal spirit of childhood, that delicious, joyous, nonsensical wisdom which is foolishness only to men.

The rhymes and jingles of Old Mother Goose are a gradual growth like the folk tales, composed at no one time by no one individual, but springing up all down through the ages, who knows how?—naturally, spontaneously, joyously, like the droll little Jack-in-the-Pulpits and Dutchmen's-Breeches of the woodland. They need no other claim to a reason for being than the pure joy of expressing that bubbling spirit (albeit sometimes by means of well

nigh meaningless words) and the everlasting delight of man in
rhyme and rhythm and musical arrangement of sounds. What
other excuse for existence, save its beautiful arrangement of s's,
is needed by that immortal line—"Sing a Song of Sixpence!"

There have been many interesting theories as to the origin of
the name Mother Goose. But the one most stoutly maintained was
advanced in the quaint little volume published at Boston in the
year 1833 by the firm of Munroe and Frances, under the title,
*The Only True Mother Goose, without addition or abridgment, em-
bracing also a reliable Life of the Goose Family never before published.*

According to this story a certain Thomas Fleet, born in England and brought up in a printing office in the city of Bristol,
came to Boston in the year 1712 when that city was little more
than an over-grown village with its narrow, crooked streets still
bespeaking the cow-paths from which they sprang. Here Thomas
Fleet established a printing office in that street of the delectable
name, Pudding Lane, where he published small books, pamphlets
and such matter as came to hand. It was not long before he
became acquainted with a well-to-do family of the name of Goose,
and he grew exceedingly fond of the pretty young daughter,
Elizabeth Goose. Under the date June 8, 1715, there appears
in the record of marriages still preserved in the historic old town
hall of Boston, an entry recording the wedding by the famous
Reverend Cotton Mather, of Thomas Fleet, "now residing in
Pudding Lane of this city, to Elizabeth Goose."

The happy couple took up their residence in the same quaint
little house with the small paned windows where the printing
office was situated in Pudding Lane, and Elizabeth's mother, Old
Mother Goose, went to live with them. Here various children
were born to the Fleets, and Old Mother Goose, being a most
devoted grandmother, was so over-joyed that she spent the greater
part of her time in the nursery, pouring out to the little ones the
songs and ditties which she had learned in her childhood.

The industrious father Fleet, having these ditties constantly dinned into his ears, shrewdly conceived the idea of collecting the songs and publishing them. This he did under the title, *Songs for the Nursery or Mother Goose's Melodies*, and he sold the same from the Pudding Lane shop for the price of two coppers apiece. The story further goes on to relate how a goose with a very long neck and a wide open mouth flew across the title page of the book; and Munroe and Frances solemnly announced that they had merely reprinted these wonderful original verses.

This interesting, picturesque, and delightful tale may or may not be true. Certainly the grave of Old Mother Goose remains to this very day carefully marked in one of Boston's old church-yards, where it is visited by many devoted pilgrims each year; but unfortunately, no scrap of the original book has ever been found to corroborate the claim of Messrs. Munroe and Frances. Moreover, whether the tale be true or not, it still in no way explains the origin of the name Mother Goose; for in the very childhood of Thomas Fleet, more than twenty years before his supposed publication of *Mother Goose's Melodies*, there appeared in France a little prose collection of the best known fairy tales, *Cinderella, Little Red Riding Hood, Toads and Diamonds, Bluebeard, Sleeping Beauty*, etc. These were written by a most distinguished French writer, Charles Perrault, were published in Paris in the year 1697, and were called *Contes de ma Mere, l'Oye*, or, *Tales of My Mother, the Goose*. On the frontispiece of his book is an old woman spinning and telling tales to a man, a girl, a boy, and a cat. It is not even known whether Perrault originated the name Mother Goose, for it is said, that long before his time, the goose had been given the reputation for story telling. Instead of saying of stories the origin of which they did not care to disclose, "A little bird told me!" people used to say, "Oh, a goose told me!" And so, after all, perhaps even the name Mother Goose belongs to the people and not to any one individual.

These tales of Perrault's, however, were all in prose while it is through her rhymes and jingles that Mother Goose has won her best-deserved fame. The first known collection of rhymes under her name was published in London about 1765, having been gathered together by John Newbery, the famous publisher of St. Paul's Churchyard, and the first publisher in the world to give special attention to children's books. It was he who published *Little Goody Two Shoes*, the story generally attributed to that prime friend of childhood, Oliver Goldsmith, who undoubtedly edited the *Mother Goose Melodies* for Newbery. In Welsh's *Life of Goldsmith* we are told that Goldsmith taught a certain little maid "Jack and Jill by two bits of paper on his fingers," and that after the successful production of his play *The Good-natured Man*, Mr. Goldsmith was so overjoyed that he sang lustily for his friends his favorite song, "about an old woman tossed in a blanket seventeen times as high as the moon."

In 1785 Newbery's edition of Mother Goose was reprinted in Worcester, Massachusetts, by Isaiah Thomas, who had married one of the grand-daughters of Thomas Fleet, and a great-grand-daughter of old Dame Goose. A very beautiful copy of this book is to be found in the Boston Library, and since the story of Thomas Fleet's edition cannot be proved, John Newbery must be accepted as the first publisher, and Isaiah Thomas as the first American publisher, of our best beloved nursery classic.

Some twenty years after the Thomas edition, another collection of nursery rhymes appeared, called *Gammer Gurton's Garland*, which contained all of the *Mother Goose Melodies* and a great many more besides, but much of this material was taken from old jest books, and was worthless and coarse, and *Gammer Gurton's Garland* never attained the popularity of Mother Goose.

In 1842, James Halliwell, a man of fine scholarship, made a careful study of the nursery rhymes of England, collected principally from oral tradition. He writes that these nonsense scraps "have come down in England to us in such numbers that in the short space of three years the author has collected considerably more than a thousand." Besides Halliwell, many other men of the highest literary ability have edited Mother Goose.

It is intensely interesting to know how very old some of our best known rhymes are. In the preface to the Newbery edition, the writer, probably Oliver Goldsmith, says, "The custom of singing these songs and lullabies to children is of very great antiquity. It is even as old as the time of the ancient Druids. Charactacus, King of the Britons, was rocked in his cradle in the Isle of Mona, now called Anglesea, and tuned to sleep by some of these soporiferous sonnets." Old King Cole was certainly an ancient Celtic king of about the third century A. D., an original Briton, who lived even before the Angles and Saxons had come to conquer England. Dim and far away seem those days in the dawn of English history when the Druids still held sway with the dark mysteries of their religion in the dusky oak forests of England, but the whole flashes suddenly into light and life when we realize that those were the very days when

Old King Cole
  Was a merry old soul
And a merry old soul was he;
  Old King Cole
  He sat in his hole,
And called for his fiddlers three.
And every fiddler, he had a fine fiddle,
And a very fine fiddle had he,
  "Tweedledee, tweedledee," said the fiddlers three.

The Gentle Genius
THE STORY OF ALBERT EINSTEIN
BY TAMSIN MURPHY

Albert Einstein was one of the greatest thinkers who ever lived. All over the world scientists and non-scientists alike remember him for his brilliant and original ideas. He was not only a great scientist, he was a great man. Although acclaimed as a genius, he remained humble. He wanted no greater reward than to help mankind to understand the nature of the universe.

When Albert Einstein was a child, he seemed different from other children. He did not learn to talk as quickly as most children do. As he grew older, he remained a quiet child who would rather sit and daydream than play games with other children. He liked to think instead of being active. Einstein was born in Ulm, Germany in 1879. Soon afterward his family moved to Munich, where young Albert grew up. His father, Hermann Einstein, managed a small factory there with the aid of his brother, James.

When he was only a young boy, Albert showed an interest in science and mathematics. His Uncle James, who was an engineer, shared Albert's interest. He encouraged the boy by teaching him algebra. Another person who encouraged Albert's interest in science was Max Talmey, a young medical student who often came to dinner at the Einstein home. He introduced Albert to books on physical and natural science. One of Albert's favorite books, however, was a geometry book. He loved geometry because of its logic and systematic rules.

In contrast to the ease with which Albert learned at home, he did not do well in school. German schools at that time were very strict, and the teaching was dull and boring. Although Albert was greatly interested in science, he did not care for most of the other things he had to study. In class he was silent and aloof, and the other children teased him for being so quiet.

As Albert grew up his dislike for school continued. He often received low grades and his teachers were rarely pleased with him. With difficulty he managed to graduate from the German equivalent of high school. He was a very happy graduate because it meant that he could go to college and study science and mathematics instead of the other things that bored him so. He chose the finest engineering school in Europe as the place to receive his higher education: The Federal Polytechnic School in Zurich, Switzerland.

In the summer of 1895 Albert moved to Zurich and took the entrance examination for the great school. To his astonishment, he failed it. Although he was far above average in mathematics and science, he did not know enough Latin and Greek. Swallowing his disappointment, the boy enrolled at a small technical school at Aarau, twenty miles from Zurich. He was surprisingly happy there. It was a school in which students were encouraged to think for themselves instead of being told what to do. Albert loved this freedom and he made many friends at Aarau. After a year there he earned a diploma which enabled him to enter the Federal Polytechnic School without taking an entrance examination. With great expectations he did so, and he was not disappointed. There were boring lessons to be learned there, but he was also able to study his favorite subject, theoretical physics.

After four years at the Polytechnic, Albert graduated and applied for an assistant teaching position there. A professor of physics was what he had decided to be, and this was the first step to it. His application was rejected, however, so he had to take a temporary job as a high school science teacher. In hope of working with some of the finest thinkers in Europe, Albert wrote letters to several renowned men of science. None of them even bothered to reply. When his temporary teaching job ended, Albert took another position as a schoolteacher. This job soon ended when Albert was fired over a disagreement with the principal. Albert's friend, Marcel Grossman, was the one who finally helped find the young scientist a job. Through Marcel's father, Albert was hired as a patent officer in Bern, Switzerland. Glad to have steady employment, Albert settled down in Bern. In 1901 he married a former classmate, Mileva Marec.

In his spare time Albert pursued his scientific career. He was interested in formulating the basic laws by which time, motion and space were governed. An earlier thinker, Isaac Newton, had said that there was only one kind of space, one kind of time, and one kind of motion, everywhere in the universe. Albert Einstein thought that space, time, and motion interacted with each other and influenced each other, and thus must be relative, not absolute as Newton had stated. This was his Special Theory of Relativity, and it was published in 1905 in a magazine called *The Annals of Physics.* When other scientists read Einstein's article they were impressed. They hurried to contact him and were shocked to learn that the originator of the theory was a patent officer. They arranged to have the young man made a professor as soon as possible.

Once Einstein came to the attention of the scientific world, he had no more difficulty in obtaining employment. From a position of professor of theoretical physics at the University of Zurich he moved to another professorship in Prague, Czechoslovakia. From there he went to the Federal Polytechnic School in Zurich, where he had received his education. During these years as a professor he continued developing his Theory of Relativity. His fame grew as more people learned of his ideas and he was soon regarded as one of the world's most brilliant

scientists. Yet in the classroom he tried to communicate his ideas in a simple and interesting manner. Remembering his difficulties in school as a child, he did not try to impress his listeners with the complexity of his ideas. Instead he tried to communicate his enthusiasm for physics.

In 1913 Einstein moved to the University of Berlin, where he joined the Royal Prussian Academy of Science. His wife, who had never been happy married to the great scientist, remained in Zurich, and some time afterward they were divorced. In addition to his teaching at the University of Berlin, Einstein traveled all over Europe, sharing his ideas with students of other universities. He grew tired of always explaining his scientific theories and began to talk about his ideas on other subjects. Europe was moving toward World War I and he found many things to speak out about. He had devoted his life to the study of universal laws and he saw the earth as only a small part of the universe. To him the conflict between nations over property and ideas seemed unimportant. He thought men should live in peace.

Soon after his arrival in Berlin, Einstein renewed his acquaintance with his cousin Elsa, who was a widow. In the absence of his wife she was a great help to him. She attended to the details of his personal life that he had no time for, in addition to cooking occasional meals and nursing him when he was ill. A simple, motherly woman, Elsa knew nothing about his scientific work, yet she understood him very well. In 1916 they decided to marry.

Despite the events of World War I, Einstein continued his work. After the war ended he traveled more than ever. In addition to lecturing throughout Europe he toured the Orient and, in 1921, he made his first visit to the United States. This visit was meant to promote the new Hebrew University in Israel, but the American people were more interested in the great scientist than in his cause. Unaware of his popularity in America, Einstein did not expect the large crowds and enthusiastic publicity that awaited him there. Americans were fascinated not only by the Theory of Relativity, but also by the man who formulated it. They wanted to know everything about Albert Einstein.

Whenever Einstein returned to Germany from his travels to other countries, he was distressed by the contrasting conditions in Germany. Poverty was widespread and the German people were getting increasingly restless because of their deprivation. The political situation was changing. The people were beginning to adopt the ideas of Adolf Hitler, including the hatred of Jews. Einstein's friends warned him of the dangers of appearing publicly, but he ignored them. His scientific work continued as always. He was now working on his Unified Field Theory. Convinced that there was a similarity among the forces of gravity, electricity, and magnetism, he hoped to formulate a mathematical law to unite them. When he could spare time from his theoretical work he often answered some of the many letters he received. His wife answered most of the mail, but Einstein wished to consider many of the letters personally. He tried to answer all of the scientific questions that were asked of him. And he often composed rhymes to send to the children who wrote to him. The Einsteins received many invitations to meetings, receptions, and various social events. The great scientist did not enjoy such things, but he went when he felt he should. He never accepted invitations when he thought he had been invited only to lend prestige to the gathering.

As the political situation in Germany grew worse, the pressure on Jews to leave the country intensified. Yet Einstein was still reluctant to flee because he and Elsa loved their home in Berlin.

In the winters of 1931 and 1932 Einstein came to America again, this time to do research at the California Institute of

Technology. While in California he was invited to join the Institute for Advanced Study, a school being established for promising graduate students in Princeton, New Jersey. At first he turned down the invitation, as he had so many others. But when Hitler came to power in Germany, Einstein knew that as a scientist and a Jew he could not live there any longer. In 1933 he moved his family to Princeton and began his work at the Institute.

The Americans, who had always loved and revered the great scientist, were happy to have him in their country. His theories and opinions made headlines and his popularity increased as the Americans got to know him better. He was a kind and gentle man with strange habits that pleased the American sense of individuality. Because his work was so important to him, he lacked interest in other things, most notably his personal appearance. He wore tattered old sweaters and baggy pants most of the time, and when required to dress up he often appeared in a suit that needed pressing. Often he wore no socks. When thinking hard, he twisted the ends of his long hair with his fingers so that it usually stuck out in all directions. Although he could have been wealthy, he chose to live a very simple life because he had no use for luxuries. For entertainment he liked nothing better than to play his violin or go sailing.

During World War II Einstein helped the American scientists who were trying to make an atomic bomb. Over thirty years before this, Einstein had formulated an equation, $E = mc^2$, which expressed his idea that mass could be converted to energy. At that time there had been no known way to split an atom to see if the equation were true. But by the time of World War II scientists knew it was true. They sought Einstein's advice in creating a weapon that could utilize the splitting of atoms to create energy. Einstein was much more in favor of peaceful uses of atomic power than destructive uses, but he gave his advice when it was needed. Although opposed to war, he was more opposed to Nazi policies of coercion and extermination of Jews.

After the bomb had been used and the war was over, Einstein continued campaigning for a ban on military use of atomic power. Now an old man, he wisely foresaw how the revolutionary new source of power could destroy man's civilization. When asked what weapons he thought might be used in a possible third world war, he replied, "I don't know. But I can tell you what they'll use in the fourth. They'll use rocks."

These words have meant more to us as the years pass, as have many of the things that Einstein said. One proof of his genius is that he was far ahead of his time. Although he died in 1955, his theories remain with us, and they have become more significant as we move into the space age. Einstein helped us to visualize space in a new way and to understand more fully the forces that affect objects in space. He did not explore strange new worlds out in space, but his explorations in the realm of ideas made it possible for others to do so. He had no means of proving some of his points, but he seemed to know intuitively that they were right. Years after his death, scientists were still discovering new evidence of the correctness of his theories.

In addition to his scientific contribution, he served as an admirable example of true human goodness. A gentle, humble man, he was kind and generous to all. Fame gave him many opportunities to become conceited, but he never did. In fact, he did not even think he was a genius. He only thought he was more dedicated to his work than most scientists. He loved physics, but he also loved people, and the object of his work was to help mankind. Certainly he did this, and the world will always be grateful for his achievements.

Index to My Book House

MY BOOK HOUSE has been indexed to make the material quickly and easily accessible. Selections have been classified into three categories so that specific stories may be located quickly and related material on various subjects easily found, according to the purpose or object of search. Thus, the index is divided into *three parts:* first, *Authors, Titles, and Leading Characters;* second, *Special Subjects;* and third, *Character Building.* Preceding each index are explanations and suggestions which clarify and simplify its use so that the greatest amount of value may be gained from MY BOOK HOUSE.

Authors, Titles, and Leading Characters Index

This index will enable either parent or child to locate quickly a specific selection, either by the title, by the name of the author, or by the leading characters.

All titles of stories, poems, biographical sketches, etcetera, are listed in large type in order that they be distinguished, at a glance, from the names of authors and leading characters which also appear in this index.

Names of authors appear in small type, directly *above* the titles of their respective writings.

The name of each leading character listed, either real or fictional as the case may be, is followed on the same line by the title—*in italics*—of the story or poem in which the character appears. All listings are alphabetical, except those following the names of individual authors where the selections of each author are given in the numerical order of the volumes.

A

	VOL.	PAGE
A, B, C, KITTY'S IN THE SNOW I SEE! —*German Rhyme*	I	120
ABRAHAM LINCOLN—*A poem by Rosemary and Stephen Vincent Benét...*	V	132
See also Lincoln, Abraham		
ACORN AND THE PUMPKIN, THE— *Jean de La Fontaine*	VII	132
Adoniram—*The King's Cream*	VI	209
ADVENTURES OF ALEXANDER SELKIRK, THE—*Basis of Defoe's Robinson Crusoe*	IX	41
ADVENTURES OF A WATER BABY —*Told from Water Babies by Charles Kingsley*	III	211
ADVENTURES OF GENERAL TOM THUMB, THE—*Phineas T. Barnum*	VIII	155
ADVENTURES OF PERSEUS, THE— *Greek Myth*	IX	140
Aeneas—*The Wanderings of Aeneas*	X	203
Aesop—*Greek* (About 620-560 B.C.)		
The Two Crabs*	II	33
Belling the Cat*	II	35
The Donkey and the Lap Dog*	II	50
The City Mouse and the Country Mouse*	II	84
The Dancing Monkeys*	II	92
The Hare and the Tortoise*	II	106
The Lion and the Mouse*	II	108
The Boaster*	III	175
The Wind and the Sun*	III	196
The Dog in the Manger*	III	197
AFAR IN THE DESERT—*Thomas Pringle*	VIII	36
AIRPLANE, THE—*Olive Beaupré Miller*	I	194
Alcott, Louisa May—*American* (1833-1888)		
Little Gulliver	V	103
Biog. Sketch (Life in Concord)	XII	122
Alden, Raymond MacDonald—*American* (1873-1924)		

	VOL.	PAGE
The Knights of the Silver Shield	VII	173
Aldrin, Buzz—*The First Moon Landing*	XII	30
Alighieri, Dante *See Dante Alighieri*		
ALL ABOUT COLUMBUS	V	112
ALL AROUND THE COBBLER'S BENCH—*American Rhyme*	I	107
ALL THE CATS CONSULTED— *American Rhyme*	I	85
AMERICAN MINER'S SONG, AN— *"Giant" O'Neill*	II	23
Anders—*The Cap That Mother Made*	III	12
Andersen, Hans Christian—*Danish* (1805-1875)		
The Little Girl and the New Dress	I	168
The Children and the Bear*	I	206
Ole Shut-Eyes, the Sandman*	II	26
The Ugly Duckling—*Retold*	II	131
The Snow-Queen	VII	48
Andromeda—*The Adventures of Perseus*	IX	140
Angelica—*The Rose and the Ring*	IX	177
ANIMAL CRACKERS—*Christopher Morley*	I	162
ANNIE GOES TO THE CABBAGE FIELD—*Czechoslovakian Rhyme*	I	129
ANSWER TO A CHILD'S QUESTION— *Samuel Taylor Coleridge*	II	142
Apollo—*Phaeton*	VII	90
Appleseed, Johnny *See Johnny Appleseed*		
APRIL—*John Galsworthy*	VI	97
Aram—*My Name Is Aram*	VII	156
Archimago—*Una and the Red Cross Knight*	XI	8
Ariel—*The Tempest*	VIII	18
Aristophanes—*Greek* (455-375 B.C.)		
The Birds' Convention	II	142

227

* *Adapted*

	VOL.	PAGE
Armstrong, Neil—*The First Moon Landing*	XII	30
Arthur, King		
See King Arthur		
ARUMAN, A HERO OF JAVA.........	VI	202
AS I WENT TO BONNER—*English Rhyme*	I	29
AS IT FELL UPON A DAY—*William Shakespeare*	I	148
AS TOMMY SNOOKS AND BESSIE BROOKS—*English Rhyme*	I	46
AS YOU LIKE IT—*Told from the play by William Shakespeare*	X	165
Asbjörnsen, Peter Christen—*Norwegian (1812-1885)*		
The Squire's Bride	VI	98
Ashiepattle—*Doll i' the Grass*............	IV	24
Aspinwall, Alicia—*American*		
A Quick-Running Squash	III	104
ASSEMBLING OF THE FAYS, THE— *Joseph Rodman Drake*	VI	17
AT CHRISTMAS PLAY AND MAKE GOOD CHEER—*From the Farmers' Daily Diet by Thomas Tusser*..........	II	217
AT THE WEDDING OF MISS JENNY WREN—*French Rhyme*	I	125
Athenaeus—*Greek (Second Century)*		
Where Are My Roses?..............	I	205
A-TISKET, A-TASKET—*American Rhyme*	I	89
August—*The Nuremberg Stove*	V	162
AUNTIE, WHERE ARE YOU GOING? —*Czechoslovakian Rhyme*	I	128
AWAKE, O NORTH WIND—*From the Bible—(Song of Solomon)*	II	79

B

BAA, BAA, BLACK SHEEP—*English Rhyme*	I	29
BABE MOSES, THE—*Retold from the Bible*	III	156
BABE RUTH, THE HOME-RUN KING OF BASEBALL	VII	144a
BABY BYE, HERE'S A FLY—*American Rhyme*	I	90
Bacon, Josephine Daskam—*American*		
The Sleepy Song	I	119
Bailey, Carolyn Sherwin—*American*		
The Little Rabbit Who Wanted Red Wings—*Retold*	II	87
The Story of Li'l Hannibal— *Transcribed*	III	116
The Nutcracker and Sugardolly Stories	IV	83
BALLAD OF EAST AND WEST, THE —*Rudyard Kipling*	IX	129
BANG-WHANG-WHANG—*Robert Browning*	I	185
BANNOCKBURN—*Robert Bruce's address to his army (By Robert Burns)*........	X	29
Barney, Joshua—*A Boy on the High Seas*..	VIII	8
Barnum, Phineas T. *(1810-1891)*		
Note	I	105
Biog. Sketch (The Circus Man)......	VIII	144

	VOL.	PAGE
The Greatest Show on Earth *(Poem about Barnum's Circus)*....	VIII	149
The Adventures of General Tom Thumb	VIII	155
BARNYARD, THE—*American Rhyme*...	I	114
Baron Münchausen—*The Strange Adventure of Baron Münchausen*.......	II	182
Baroness Jane van Lawick-Goodall—*Jane and the Wild Chimps*..................	XII	70
Barn, Mathias—*Scottish* Moon, So Round and Yellow........	II	40
Baruch, Dorothy—*American* The Elevator	I	183
Basho—*Japanese (1643-1694)* Off We'll Go	VI	196
BAT, BAT, COME UNDER MY HAT— *English Rhyme*	I	45
BATS- -*Effie Lee Newsome*	I	211
BATTLE OF THE FIREFLY AND THE APES, THE—*Filipino Tale*	III	59
BATTLE OF THE FROGS AND THE MICE, THE—*Retold from a classic Greek poem*	IV	104
BATTLE TACTICS—*Farley Mowat*......	VII	165
Baum, L. Frank—*American* The Wizard of Oz....................	VI	62
Beate—*The Doll Under the Briar Rosebush*	III	204
Beatrice—*Dante's Voyage to the Inferno, Purgatory, and Paradise*.........	XI	156
BEE, THE MOUSE, AND THE BUM-CLOCK, THE—*Irish Tale*	II	155
BEHOLD THE FIG TREE—*From the Bible—(Jesus of Nazareth)*	II	78
BELGIAN MORNING, A—*Emile Cammaerts*	II	141
BELLING THE CAT—*Adapted from Aesop*	II	35
BELLS, THE—*Edgar Allan Poe*.........	VII	71
Benét, Stephen Vincent—*American (1898-1943), and Rosemary, his wife* Wilbur Wright and Orville Wright....	V	66
Abraham Lincoln	V	132
Beowulf—*How Beowulf Delivered Heorot.*	X	80
Bharat—*The Exile of Rama*............	X	175
BIG BUS, STOP!—*Olive Beaupré Miller*..	I	173
BIG CLOCK—TICK, TOCK!—*Polish Rhyme*	I	72
BIG ENGINE, THE....................	I	179
BIG STREET IN THE BIG CITY, THE —*Lucy Sprague Mitchell*..............	I	170
BIG UMBRELLA AND THE LITTLE RUBBERS, THE	I	190
BILLY, BILLY, COME AND PLAY— *English Rhyme*	I	47
BIRDS' CONVENTION, THE— *Aristophanes*	II	142
BIRDS OF A FEATHER—*English Rhyme*	I	55
BIRDS' ST. VALENTINE'S DAY, THE— *Retold from the Parlement of Foules by Geoffrey Chaucer*	III	198
BITING MARION—*Lucy Sprague Mitchell*	I	174

	VOL.	PAGE
Björnson, Björnstjerne—*Norwegian* (1832-1910)		
Oeyvind and Marit	III	137
BLACKSMITH, THE—*A story of the song by Johannes Brahms*	IV	159
Blake, William—*English* (1757-1827)		
Laughing Song	II	75
Nurse's Song	II	152
BLESSINGS ON THEE, DOG OF MINE —*Elizabeth Barrett Browning*	I	143
BLOW, WIND, BLOW, AND GO, MILL, GO!—*English Rhyme*	I	31
BOASTER, THE—*Adapted from Aesop*	III	175
BOATMAN HE'S A LUCKY MAN!, THE —*American Rhyme*	I	97
BOBBY SHAFTO'S GONE TO SEA— *English Rhyme*	I	44
BOHEMIAN EVENING, A—*Czecho-slovakian Rhyme*	II	140
Boone, Daniel		
Boots—*The Princess on the Glass Hill*	VI	80
See Daniel Boone		
BOOTS AND HIS BROTHERS—*Sir George Webbe Dasent*	V	157
Bottom—*A Midsummer Night's Dream*	VI	38
BOW THAT BRIDGES HEAVEN, THE —*Christina Rossetti*	II	105
"BOW-WOW," SAYS THE DOG— *English Rhyme*	I	21
BOW, WOW, WOW, WHOSE DOG ART THOU?—*English Rhyme*	I	23
BOY HERO OF HARLEM, THE— *Legend of Holland*	IV	57
BOY IN RUSSIA, A—*Biog. Sketch of Leo N. Tolstoy*	XII	190
BOY IN THE ISLAND OF BALI, A	II	176
BOY ON THE HIGH SEAS, A—*Biog. Sketch of Joshua Barney*	VIII	8
BOY SAMUEL, THE—*Retold from the Bible*	IV	80
BOY WHO MADE HAY, THE—*Norse Rhyme*	I	134
BOYS AND GIRLS, COME OUT TO PLAY—*English Rhyme*	I	39
BOY'S SONG, A	VI	96
BOY WHO SAVED THE WORLD, THE —*Roland A. Martone*	VI	170
BRIDGE, THE—*Olive Beaupré Miller*	I	210
BRING THE COMB AND PLAY UPON IT!—*Robert Louis Stevenson*	I	159
BROOK SONG, THE—*James Whitcomb Riley*	III	161
Brotherton, Alice Williams—*American*		
Give Praise *from* The First Thanksgiving Day	V	117
BROWNIES IN THE TOY SHOP, THE— *Palmer Cox*	III	40
Browning, Elizabeth Barrett—*English* (1806-1861)		
Blessings on Thee, Dog of Mine	I	143
Go Out, Children	I	185
Two Children—*Translated*	II	138
Browning, Robert—*English* (1812-1889)		
Bang-Whang-Whang	I	185
Note	VII	73
A Cavalier Tune	X	19
Bruce, Robert—*Robert Bruce, Scotland's Hero* (Biog. Sketch)	X	21
Brunhilda—*The Tale of the Rhine-Gold*	XI	73
Buck, Pearl S.—*American*		
What the Children Do in Summer (Story and Note)	I	212
BUCKY, THE BIG, BOLD FAWN	III	85
BUFFALO BILL—*James Daugherty*	IX	27
Comment in Poem	IV	192a
BUGLE SONG, THE—*Alfred Tennyson*	XI	7
BUILDING THE BRIDGE—*Adapted from a Russian folk song*	II	149
BUILDING WITH BLOCKS	I	164
Bunyan, Paul		
See Paul Bunyan		
Burgess, Gelett—*American* (1866-1951)		
The Purple Cow	II	163
The Pert Fire Engine	IV	218
The Steamboat and the Locomotive	V	96
Burgess, Thornton W.—*American*		
Peter Rabbit Decides to Change His Name	III	49
Burns, Robert—*Scottish* (1759-1796)		
O Lady Mary Ann	I	153
O Rattlin', Roarin' Willie	I	153
The Ploughman He's a Bonnie Lad	I	153
Wee Robin's Christmas Song	II	209
Bannockburn	X	29
Burroughs, Margaret Taylor—*American*		
Jasper the Drummin' Boy	VI	108
BUTTERFLIES, BUTTERFLIES— *American Indian Song*	I	81
BUTTERFLY'S BALL, THE—*English Rhyme*	III	162
BYE-LO, BUBBELI, SLEEP— *Pennsylvania Dutch Rhyme*	I	117
BYE-O! BYE-O!—*American Rhyme*	I	90
Byron, George Gordon, Lord—*English* (1788-1824)		
Solitude	IX	65

C

	VOL.	PAGE
Caliban—*The Tempest*	VIII	18
Cammaerts, Emile—*Belgian* (1878-1953)		
A Belgian Morning	II	141
CAP THAT MOTHER MADE, THE —*Swedish Tale*	III	12
Carey, Henry—*English*		
Of All the Girls That Are So Smart	I	169
Carnegie, Andrew—*Telegraph Boy*	XII	60
Carroll, Lewis (Pen Name of Charles Lutwidge Dodgson)—*English* (1832-1898)		
The Mock Turtle's Song	III	170
CASEY AT THE BAT—*Ernest Lawrence Thayer*	VII	144c
CASEY JONES—*A Song of Railroad Men*	V	64

	VOL.	PAGE
CASEY'S COMEBACK—*James Wilson*..	VII	144f
CATARACT OF LODORE, THE—*Robert Southey*	VII	47
CATHERINE, MY DEARIE—*French Rhyme*	I	124
CAVALIER TUNE, A—*Robert Browning*.	X	19
Cawein, Madison—*American* (1865-1914) The Twilight	II	41
Cervantes, Miguel de—*Spanish* (1547-1616) The Surprising Adventures of Don Quixote of La Mancha—*Edited by Frances Jenkins Olcott*............	XI	90
Chamisso, Albert von—*French* (1781-1838) A Tragic Story....................	IV	136
CHANTICLEER AND PARTLET—*Retold from the Nun's Priest's Tale by Chaucer*	III	176
Chapman, John (Johnny Appleseed) *See Johnny Appleseed*		
Charlemagne—*The Song of Roland*.......	X	38
Charles VII (The Dauphin)—*Joan of Arc*	X	98
CHARLEY, BARLEY, BUCK AND RYE —*American Rhyme*	I	94
CHARLEY'S NEAT AND CHARLEY'S SWEET—*American Rhyme*	I	99
CHARLOTTE'S WEB—*E. B. White*......	V	54
Chaucer, Geoffrey—*English* (1340-1400) Chanticleer and Partlet—*Retold from the Nun's Priest's Tale*.............	III	176
The Birds' St. Valentine's Day—*Retold from the Parlement of Foules*	III	198
A Perfect Knight....................	X	7
Biog. Sketch (The Royal Page)......	XII	11
Cherry—*The King's Cream*..............	VI	209
Chet'l—*How Yehl, the Hero, Freed the Beaming Maiden*	VI	102
Chief Villager—*Old Pipes and the Dryad*..	VI	18
CHILD, I MUST SWEEP THE HUT TODAY—*African Rhyme*	I	147
CHILD, I SEE THEE!—*John Keats*.....	I	152
CHILD IN A MEXICAN GARDEN, A—*Grace H. Conkling*..................	IV	103
Child, Lydia Maria—*American* (1802-1880) Over the River and Through the Woods	I	87
CHILDREN AND THE BEAR, THE—*Adapted from Hans Christian Andersen*.	I	206
CHILDREN'S CRUSADE, THE.........	X	30
CHILDREN'S SONGS OF ANCIENT GREECE	I	204
CHIMNEY SWEEP—*Swiss Rhyme*.......	I	67
CHINK, CHINK, CHOCKET—*Mexican Rhyme*	I	70
Chocolate—*The King's Cream*...........	VI	209
CHRISTENING THE BABY IN RUSSIA—*Arthur Ransome*	IV	63
CHRISTMAS SONG AT SEA, A—*Alfred Noyes*	VIII	187
Christopher Robin—*Winnie-the-Pooh*	V	68
CHRONICLE OF KIEV, A.............	X	118

	VOL.	PAGE
Cid, The (Ruy Diaz) *See Diaz, Ruy*		
CINDERELLA—*Adapted from Charles Perrault*	IV	12
CINDERELLA DRESSED IN GREEN—*American Rhyme*	I	83
CIRCUS MAN, THE—*Biog. Sketch of Phineas T. Barnum*....................	VIII	144
CIRCUS PARADE, THE—*Olive Beaupré Miller*	III	46
CITY MOUSE AND THE COUNTRY MOUSE, THE—*Adapted from Aesop*...	II	84
Clark, George Rogers—*George Rogers Clark and the Conquest of the Northwest*....	IX	66
Clark, William—*Pushing Westward with Lewis and Clark*..................	IX	25
CLOUD, THE—*Percy Bysshe Shelley*.....	VII	95
CLOUDS	III	48
CLUCKING HEN, THE—*From Aunt Effie's Rhymes*	I	214
CLYTIE—*Flora J. Cooke*..............	III	151
COCK IS CROWING, THE—*William Wordsworth*	I	208
COCK, THE MOUSE, AND THE LITTLE RED HEN, THE—*Félicité Le Fèvre*....	II	192
COCK-A-DOODLE-DOO!—*English Rhyme*	I	32
COCK'S ON THE HOUSETOP, THE—*English Rhyme*	I	42
Cody, William Frederick *See Buffalo Bill*		
COIN, THE—*Sara Teasdale*.............	XII	212
COLD, SON OF WIND AND SNOW—*Finnish Rhyme*	I	145
Coleridge, Samuel Taylor—*English* (1772-1834) Answer to a Child's Question........	II	142
Collins, Mike—*The First Moon Landing*..	XII	30
COLUMBINE AND HER PLAY-FELLOWS OF THE ITALIAN PANTOMIME	VII	119
Columbus—*All About Columbus*.........	V	112
COME, LET'S GO TO SANT' ANITA—*Mexican Rhyme*	I	70
COME, LITTLE LEAVES—*George Cooper*	II	70
Conkling, Grace H.—*American* (1878-1958) A Child in a Mexican Garden.......	IV	103
CONVERSATION—*Rose Fyleman*	I	163
Cook, Royal *See Royal Cook*		
Cooke, Flora J.—*American* (1865-1953) Clytie	III	151
Cooper, George—*American* (1840-1927) Come, Little Leaves	II	70
Corn-Planter, Chief *See Chief Corn-Planter*		
Cowardly Lion—*The Wizard of Oz*.......	VI	62
COWBOY'S LIFE, THE—*American Cowboy Song*	IV	193

VOL. PAGE

Cox, Palmer—*Canadian-American*
(1840-1924)
    The Brownies in the Toy Shop (*Poem
    and note*) .... III 40
Craik, Dinah M. Muloch—*English*
(1826-1887)
    The Shaking of the Pear Tree....... III 146
CROCUS FLOWERS BLOOM LIKE
    FIRE—*Meleager* .... I 205
Crossette, George—*American*
    Jane and the Wild Chimps.......... XII 70
CUCKOO AND THE DONKEY, THE—
    German Rhyme .... I 122
CUCULAIN, THE IRISH HOUND—
*Retold from tales of the ancient Gaelic
bards* .... X 188

D

Da Rimini, Francesca
    See Francesca Da Rimini
DAFFY-DOWN-DILLY—*English Rhyme*. I 25
DAINTY LITTLE MAIDEN—*Alfred
Tennyson* .... I 155
DAME DURDEN—*Welsh Rhyme* .... I 58
DAME WIGGINS OF LEE—*Mary E.
Sharpe and John Ruskin*.............. II 188
Dan, Old
    See Old Dan
DANCE, LITTLE BABY, DANCE UP
    HIGH!—*English Rhyme* .... I 18
DANCE TO YOUR DADDIE—*Scottish
Rhyme* .... I 58
DANCING MONKEYS, THE—*Adapted
from Aesop* .... II 92
Daniel Boone—*Exploring the Wilderness*
    (*Biog. Sketch*) .... IX 9
Dante Alighieri—*Italian* (1265-1321)
    The Man Who Lived in the World of
    Dreams—*A story about Dante*..... XI 152
    Dante's Voyage to the Inferno, Purga-
    tory, and Paradise—*Retold from The
    Divine Comedy* .... XI 156
DANTE'S VOYAGE TO THE
    INFERNO, PURGATORY, AND
    PARADISE—*Retold from The Divine
    Comedy* .... XI 156
DARING PRINCE, THE—*James
Whitcomb Riley* .... III 127
Darius, King
    See King Darius
Dasent, Sir George Webbe—*English-
Norwegian* (1817-1896)
    Boots and His Brothers............. V 157
    The Princess on the Glass Hill....... VI 80
Daugherty, James—*American*
    Buffalo Bill .... IX 27
DAVID COPPERFIELD AND LITTLE
    EM'LY—*Adapted from Charles Dickens* VII 182
DAVID, THE SHEPHERD BOY—
    Arranged from the Bible.............. VII 73
Davy—*Little Gulliver* .... V 103
DAWLISH FAIR—*John Keats*........... II 67

VOL. PAGE

De La Mare, Walter—*English* (1873-1956)
    Old Shellover .... II 185
Diaz, Ruy—*The Story of the Cid*........ X 108
DICK WHITTINGTON AND HIS
    CAT—*English Legend* .... V 33
Dickens, Charles—*English* (1812-1870)
    David Copperfield and Little Em'ly—
    Arranged from David Copperfield .. VII 182
    Biog. Sketch (London Streets)....... XII 102
DICKERY, DICKERY, DARE—*English
Rhyme* .... I 24
Dickinson, Emily—*American* (1830-1886)
    The Sea .... III 155
    Note .... XII 153
DIDDLE, DIDDLE, DUMPLING—
    English Rhyme .... I 37
DIDDLE, DIDDLE ON A BASS
    FIDDLE—*Polish Rhyme* .... I 73
Dido, Queen
    See Queen Dido
Didrikson, Babe—*The Lone Star Team of
Texas* .... XII 170
DIVINE COMEDY, THE—*Biog. Sketch
of Dante Alighieri*................... XII 154
Doctor Dolittle—*The Rarest Animal of All* IV 113
Dodge, Mary Mapes—*American*
(1831-1905)
    What They Say .... I 207
    Snow .... II 208
    Who Can Crack Nuts?............. IV 82
Dodgson, Charles Lutwidge (Lewis
Carroll—Pen Name)
    See Carroll, Lewis
DOG IN THE MANGER, THE—
    Adapted from Aesop .... III 197
DOG OF POMPEII, THE—*Louis
Untermeyer* .... VII 145
Dolittle, Doctor
    See Doctor Dolittle
DOLL I' THE GRASS—*Norse Folk Tale*. IV 24
DOLL UNDER THE BRIAR ROSE-
    BUSH, THE—*Translated from the
    Norwegian by Gudrun Thorne-Thomsen*. III 204
Don Quixote—*The Surprising Adventures of
Don Quixote of La Mancha*.......... XI 90
DONKEY AND THE LAP DOG,
    THE—*Adapted from Aesop* .... II 50
DON'T RUN AWAY MY KITTY—
    Russian Rhyme .... I 132
Dorothy—*The Wizard of Oz*............. VI 62
Douglass, Frederick—*Learning To Be Free* XII 198
DOWN BY THE RIVER AVON—
    Biog. Sketch of William Shakespeare.... XII 15
DOWN IN A COTTAGE—*Irish Rhyme*.. I 59
Drake, Joseph Rodman—*American*
(1795-1820)
    The Assembling of the Fays......... VI 17
DREAMLAND OPENS HERE—
    American Rhyme .... I 91
DRUMS CALL THE VILLAGE TO
    DANCE, THE—*African Rhyme* .... I 147

	VOL.	PAGE
Dryad—*Old Pipes and the Dryad*........	VI	18
DUCKS' DITTY—*Kenneth Grahame*	III	62
Dunbar, Paul Laurence—*American Negro* (1872-1906)		
The Knight	IV	129

E

	VOL.	PAGE
EAST O' THE SUN AND WEST O' THE MOON—*Norse Folk Tale*........	VII	31
Echo-dwarf—*Old Pipes and the Dryad*....	VI	18
Eells, Elsie Spicer—*American* How the Brazilian Beetles Got Their Gorgeous Coats	III	172
Einstein, Albert—*The Gentle Genius*......	XII	218
ELEVATOR, THE—*Dorothy Baruch*	I	183
ELF AND THE DORMOUSE, THE— *Oliver Herford*	III	39
Eliot, George (Pen Name of Mary Ann Evans)—*English* (1819-1880) Maggie Tulliver Goes to Live with the Gypsies—*Arranged from The Mill on the Floss*	VIII	189
ELSA AND THE TEN ELVES— *Swedish Fairy Tale*	IV	45
Emerson, Ralph Waldo—*American* (1803-1882)		
We Thank Thee	V	117
Comments (Life in Concord)........	XII	122
Comments (The Harvard Professor)..	XII	135
Em'ly, Little *See Little Em'ly*		
ENCHANTED ISLAND, THE—*Howard Pyle*	VIII	134
ENGINE, ENGINE NUMBER NINE— *American Rhyme*	I	85
Evans, Mary Ann (George Eliot—Pen Name) *See Eliot, George*		
EVE OF THE WISE MEN—*Santo Domingo Rhyme*	I	224
EVENING AT THE FARM—*John Townsend Trowbridge*	X	79
EVERYONE'S GLAD IN OUR CITY TODAY—*Swedish Rhyme*	I	75
Ewing, Juliana Horatia—*English* (1841-1885) The Owl's Answer to Tommy.......	III	29
EXILE OF RAMA, THE—*Retold from the Ramayana, the sacred poem of India*	X	175
EXPLANATION OF THE GRASS-HOPPER, AN—*Vachel Lindsay*	II	77
EXPLORING THE WILDERNESS— *Biog. Sketch of Daniel Boone*..........	IX	9

F

	VOL.	PAGE
Fabre, Jean Henri—*The Fairyland of Science* (Biog. Sketch)	VI	184
FAIRY AND CHILD—*Eugene Field*.....	III	25
FAIRY FORESTS—*Alfred Noyes*	VI	190

	VOL.	PAGE
FAIRYLAND OF SCIENCE, THE— *Biog. Sketch of Jean Henri Fabre*.......	VI	184
Fanny—*A Musical Visit to Fairyland*.....	VI	59
FARMER IN THE DELL, THE— *American Rhyme*	I	102
FARMER'S BOY, THE—*American Rhyme*	I	108
Farragut, David—*Young Midshipman David Farragut* (Biog. Sketch).........	VIII	84
FATHER AND I WENT DOWN TO CAMP—*American Rhyme*	I	101
Ferdinand—*The Tempest*	VIII	18
Fern—*Charlotte's Web*	V	54
Field, Eugene—*American* (1850-1895) Wynken, Blynken, and Nod (*Poem and note*)	II	24
The Sugar-Plum Tree	II	223
Fairy and Child	III	25
Firdusi (Pen Name of Abul Kasim Mansur)—*Persian* (940-1020) A Story of Rustem, the Hero of Persia—*Retold from the Shah-Nameh*	X	228
Firouz Schah, Prince *See Prince Firouz Schah*		
FIRST ADVENTURES	I	160
FIRST MOON LANDING, THE— *Margaret Waldorf*	XII	30
FIRST THANKSGIVING DAY, THE— *Olive Beaupré Miller*	V	113
FISHERMAN WHO CAUGHT THE SUN, THE—*Hawaiian Legend*	VI	198
FIVE LITTLE CHICKS—*Spanish Rhyme*	I	64
FOG, THE—*Carl Sandburg*	I	184
FOOLISH, TIMID, LITTLE HARE, THE—*East Indian Fable*	III	76
FOUR-AND-TWENTY TAILORS— *English Rhyme*	I	39
FOURTH OF JULY, THE—*Olive Beaupré Miller*	V	129
Francesca Da Rimini—*Dante's Voyage to the Inferno, Purgatory, and Paradise*..	XI	156
Friar Tuck—*Ye Merry Doinges of Robin Hood* ..:.....................	XI	49
FREDDY, THE PAD DOG— *T. Beverly Kelly*	V	214
FRIENDLY COW ALL RED AND WHITE, THE—*Robert Louis Stevenson*.	I	159
FRITHJOF, THE VIKING—*Retold from the Norse saga of Frithjof*.............	X	130
Fröding, Gustaf—*Swedish* (1860-1911) A Swedish Evening	II	141
FROGGIE GOES A-COURTING— *American Rhyme*	I	111
Frost, Robert—*American* Stopping By Woods on a Snowy Evening	VII	172
Fulton, Robert—How Robert Fulton Harnessed the Giant (Biog. Sketch).......	V	48
Fyleman, Rose—*English* (1877-1957) Conversation	I	163

G

	VOL.	PAGE
Galsworthy, John—*English* (1867-1933)		
April	VI	97
Ganelon—*The Song of Roland*	X	38
Gareth—*Sir Beaumains, the Kitchen Knight*	X	8
GATHERING SONG OF DONUIL DHU —*Sir Walter Scott*	X	20
GAY GO UP AND GAY GO DOWN— *English Rhyme*	I	54
General Tom Thumb—(Charles E. Stratton)—*The Adventures of General Tom Thumb*	VIII	155
GENTLE GENIUS, THE—*Tamsin Murphy*	XII	218
GEORGE ROGERS CLARK AND THE CONQUEST OF THE NORTHWEST —*Theodore Roosevelt*	IX	66
GEORGE WASHINGTON AND THE FIRST AMERICAN FLAG	V	118
Gerda—*The Snow-Queen*	VII	48
GERMAN EVENING, A—*Wilhelm Schiller*	II	140
Gessler—*The Legend of William Tell*	X	44
GET OUT OF THE WAY—*American Rhyme*	I	93
GET UP, LITTLE HORSEY—*Spanish Rhyme*	I	65
GIDEON, THE WARRIOR—*From the Bible*—(*Book of Judges*)	IX	134
GIGI AND THE MAGIC RING— *Italian Fairy Tale*	VII	199
Giglio—*The Rose and the Ring*	IX	177
GINGERBREAD MAN, THE—*New England Tale*	II	58
Giovanni—*The Wonderland of an Artist's Workshop*	VI	164
Gipson, Fred—*American*		
Old Yeller	IX	98
GIRL WHO USED HER WITS, THE— *Chinese Folk Tale*	IV	137
GIUSEPPI, THE COBBLER—*Italian Rhyme*	I	63
GIVE PRAISE—*Alice Williams Brotherton*	V	117
GO ASK YOUR MOTHER FOR FIFTY CENTS—*American Rhyme*	I	104
GO OUT, CHILDREN—*Elizabeth Barrett Browning*	I	185
GO TO SLEEPY, LITTLE BABY— *American Negro Rhyme*	I	90
GOAT ONE DAY WAS FEELING FINE, A—*American Negro Rhyme*	I	106
GOD HATH MADE ME TO LAUGH —*From the Bible*	I	217
GOLDEN BIRD, THE—*German Fairy Tale*	VII	134
GOLDEN TOUCH, THE—*Nathaniel Hawthorne*	VII	210
GOLDFINCH, THE—*Odell Shepard*	II	45
GOLDILOCKS AND THE THREE BEARS—*English Folk Tale*	III	20
Goliath—*David, the Shepherd Boy*	VII	73

	VOL.	PAGE
GOOD MORNING, PETER	I	165
GOOD MORROW, 'TIS SAINT VALENTINE'S DAY—*William Shakespeare*	I	209
GOOSEY, GOOSEY, GANDER—*English Rhyme*	I	22
Grahame, Kenneth—*English* (1859-1932)		
Ducks' Ditty	III	62
GRASSHOPPER GREEN	II	76
GREAT A, LITTLE A, BOUNCING B—*English Rhyme*	I	52
GREATEST SHOW ON EARTH, THE—	VIII	149
Greenaway, Kate—*English* (1846-1901)		
Tommy Was a Silly Boy (*Poem and note*)	I	150
Higgledy, Piggledy! See How They Run! (*Poem and note*)	I	151
Yes, That's the Girl That Struts About (*Poem and note*)	III	26
School Is Over (*Poem and note*)	III	27
Grethel—*Hansel and Grethel*	IV	73
Griffis, William Elliot—*American* (1843-1928)		
Pigling and Her Proud Sister	VI	191
Grimm, Wilhelm (1786-1859) and Jacob (1785-1863)—*German*		
The Little Girl and the Hare— *Adapted*	III	111
Snow-white and Rose-red—(*Story and note*)	IV	34
GROCERIES—*James S. Tippett*	I	182
GULLIVER'S TRAVELS TO LILLIPUT—*Jonathan Swift*	VIII	38
GURGLE, WATER, GURGLE—*Polish Rhyme*	I	72

H

	VOL.	PAGE
Haber, Louis—*American*		
Pioneer in Surgery	XII	154
HALLOWE'EN—*Olive Beaupré Miller*	IV	142
HANDY-SPANDY—*English Rhyme*	I	33
Hans—*The Boy Hero of Harlem*	IV	57
HANSEL AND GRETHEL— *Humperdinck Version*	IV	73
Hansworst—*Little Hansworst*	II	164
HAPPY DAY IN THE CITY, A— *Olive Beaupré Miller*	III	181
HARBOR, THE	I	184
HARE AND THE TORTOISE, THE— *Adapted from Aesop*	II	106
HARK, HARK! BOW-WOW!—*William Shakespeare*	I	149
HARK, THE CHRISTMAS BELLS ARE RINGING—*Russian Rhyme*	I	133
Harlequin—*Columbine and Her Playfellows of the Italian Pantomime*	VII	119
Harris, Joel Chandler—*American* (1848-1908)		
A Story About the Little Rabbits	III	123
Comment (The Harvard Professor)	XII	135
Biog. Sketch ('Way Down South in Dixie)	XII	138

	VOL.	PAGE
HARVARD PROFESSOR, THE—*Biog.* *Sketch of Henry Wadsworth Longfellow*.	XII	135
Hawthorne, Nathaniel—*American* (1804-1864)		
The Golden Touch	VII	210
Comments (Life in Concord)	XII	122
Comments (The Harvard Professor)	XII	135
HEAP ON MORE WOOD—*Sir Walter Scott*	II	217
HEAR HOW THE BIRDS—*Alexander Pope*	I	208
HECTOR PROTECTOR—*English Rhyme*.	I	45
HEI, JIM ALONG JOSEY— *Pennsylvania Dutch Rhyme*	I	117
HEIDI IN THE ALPINE PASTURE— *Johanna Spyri*	V	146
Heine, Heinrich—*German* (1797-1856)		
Two Children—*Translated from the German by Elizabeth Barrett Browning*	II	138
Helena—*Vladimir's Adventures in Search of Fortune*	VII	102
Hepburn, Thomas N. (Gabriel Setoun— Pen Name)		
See Setoun, Gabriel		
Hercules—*The Labors of Hercules*	IX	151
HERE AM I, LITTLE JUMPING JOAN—*English Rhyme*	I	32
HERE COME THREE JOLLY, JOLLY SAILOR BOYS—*American Rhyme*	I	96
HERE IS THE KEY—*Dutch Rhyme*	I	127
HERE WE COME, WE CHILDREN COME—*Theognis*	I	204
HERE WE SAIL SO FAST AND FREE— *American Rhyme*	I	96
HERE'S THE CHURCH—*American Rhyme*	I	83
Herford, Oliver—*American* (1863-1935)		
The Elf and the Dormouse	III	39
Hermia—*A Midsummer Night's Dream*	VI	38
Herrick, Robert—*English* (1591-1674)		
There's Not a Budding Boy	I	208
Note	XII	29
Herschler, Mildred Barger—*American*		
Learning To Be Free	XII	198
HEY DIDDLE DIDDLE—*English Rhyme*	I	22
HIAWATHA'S CHILDHOOD—*Henry Wadsworth Longfellow*	V	222
HIAWATHA'S FASTING—*Legend of the First Indian Corn*	IX	89
HICKETY, PICKETY, MY BLACK HEN—*English Rhyme*	I	24
HICKORY, DICKORY, DOCK!— *English Rhyme*	I	22
HIE AWAY, HIE AWAY—*Sir Walter Scott*	VI	70
HIGGLEDY, PIGGLEDY! SEE HOW THEY RUN!—*Kate Greenaway*	I	151
Hine Moa—*The Trial by Fire*	VII	26
HIPPETY HOP TO THE BARBER SHOP—*English Rhyme*	I	28
HI-YI, HI-YI, HYTOLA—*Finnish Rhyme*.	I	144
Hogg, James—*Scottish* (1770-1835)		
A Boy's Song	VI	96
HOME-COMING OF ODYSSEUS, THE —*Retold from the Greek Epic, the Odyssey by Homer*	X	217
Homer—*Greek* (About 900 B.C.)		
Note	IV	104
The Home-Coming of Odysseus— Retold	X	217
HONEST WOODMAN, THE—*Adapted from Jean de La Fontaine*	III	114
Hood, Robin		
See Robin Hood		
Hood, Thomas—*English* (1799-1845)		
Precocious Piggy	I	196
HOOSIER POET, THE—*Biog. Sketch of James Whitcomb Riley*	XII	141
HOP, MOTHER ANNIKA!—*Swedish Rhyme*	I	74
HOP, MY HORSEY, LEAP AND SPRING—*German Rhyme*	I	123
HOW BEOWULF DELIVERED HEOROT—*Retold from the old English Epic, Beowulf*	X	80
HOW BRER RABBIT MET BRER TAR-BABY	IV	130
HOW DOTH THE LITTLE BUSY BEE—*Isaac Watts*	I	143
HOW JACK SOUGHT THE GOLDEN APPLES—*English Folk Tale*	V	76
HOW MANY DAYS HAS MY BABY TO PLAY?—*English Rhyme*	I	19
HOW MANY MILES TO BABYLON?— *English Rhyme*	I	55
HOW PEARY REACHED THE NORTH POLE	IX	127
HOW ROBERT FULTON HARNESSED THE GIANT	V	48
HOW STRONG, HOW STRONG A BRIDGE HAVE YOU?— *Czechoslovakian Rhyme*	I	129
HOW THE BRAZILIAN BEETLES GOT THEIR GORGEOUS COATS— *Elsie Spicer Eells*	III	172
HOW THE FINCH GOT HER COLORS —*Flemish Legend*	II	143
HOW THE GODDESS OF SPRING CAME TO SCORING—*Charles Kingsley*	IX	176
HOW YEHL, THE HERO, FREED THE BEAMING MAIDEN— *Alaskan Legend*	VI	102
Howells, William Dean—*American* (1837-1920)		
The Pony Engine and the Pacific Express	V	54

	VOL.	PAGE
Howitt, Mary—*English* (1799-1888)		
The Sea Gull	V	111
Hughes, Langston—*American*		
The Negro Speaks of Rivers	XII	188
HUMPTY DUMPTY—*English Rhyme*	I	46
HURRY UP, ENGINE—*American Rhyme*	I	92

I

I HAD A LITTLE DOG—*American Negro Rhyme*	I	106
I HAD A LITTLE HUSBAND—*English*.	I	27
I HAD A LITTLE MULE—*American Negro Rhyme*	I	106
I HAD A LITTLE NUT TREE—*English*.	I	37
I HAD A PIECE OF PIE—*American*....	I	98
I HEARD THE BELLS ON CHRISTMAS DAY—*Henry Wadsworth Longfellow*	II	217
I LOVE LITTLE PUSSY—*Jane Taylor*...	I	143
I SAW A CROW A-FLYING LOW—*American Rhyme*	I	107
I SAW A SHIP A-SAILING—*English Rhyme*	I	35
I SHOULD LIKE TO PLOUGH—*Hungarian Rhyme*	I	136
I STAND IN THE PULPIT AND PREACH—*Pennsylvania Dutch Rhyme*	I	117
I TOOK A WALK ONE EVENING—*Swedish Rhyme*	I	75
I WENT TO THE ANIMAL FAIR—*American Rhyme*	I	104
Ibsen, Henrik—*Norwegian* (1828-1906)		
Peer Gynt—*Told from the play*	IX	98
ICE-COLD LEMONADE—*American Rhyme*	I	88
Iduna—*The Stealing of Iduna*	IX	172
IF I COULD WALK—*Italian Rhyme*....	I	62
Igor—*The Word of Igor's Armament*	X	119
IHI! IHI! IHI!—*American Indian Song*...	I	80
Ilmarinen—*Kalevala, Land of Heroes*	X	151
I'M A BUTCHER—*Czechoslovakian Rhyme*	I	128
I'M A LITTLE INDIAN—*Mexican Rhyme*	I	71
I'M A PEDDLER—*American Rhyme*....	I	94
I'M CAPTAIN JINKS—*American Rhyme*	I	93
I'M GOING TO LADY WASHINGTON'S —*American Rhyme*	I	82
IN COLUMBUS' TIME—*Annette Wynne*.	V	112
IN SPRING THE BIRDS DO SING—*English Rhyme*	I	57
IN THE SPRINGTIME—*William Shakespeare*	I	148
INDIAN CHILDREN—*Annette Wynne*...	III	93
Ingeborg—*Frithjof, the Viking*	X	130
INTERESTING HISTORY OF OLD MOTHER GOOSE, THE	XII	213
Irving, Washington—*American* (1783-1859)		
Wolfert Webber, or Golden Dreams..	XI	107
Biog. Sketch (A Rover in the Catskills)	XII	99

"IT"—*James Whitcomb Riley*	VI	131
IT IS GOD THAT HATH MADE US—*From the Bible*	I	216
IT SNOWS AND IT BLOWS—*American Rhyme*	I	87
IT'S RAINING!—*Swiss Rhyme*	I	67
IT'S SPRING	I	208
Ivan—*The Little-Man-As-Big-As-Your-Thumb-With-Mustaches-Seven-Miles-Long*	VII	112
I-YAY! I-YAY! I-YAY!—*Eskimo Song*...	I	131

J

JACK AND JILL—*English Rhyme*	I	40
JACK AND THE BEANSTALK—*English Folk Tale*	V	20
JACK, BE NIMBLE—*English Rhyme*....	I	39
JACK FROST—*Gabriel Setoun*	II	186
JACK THE GIANT-KILLER—*English Folk Tale*	VI	140
Jacob—*Joseph and His Brethren*	X	48
Jacobs, Joseph—*English, born in Australia* (1854-1916)		
Master of All Masters	III	148
Note	V	156
Jacoby, Arnold—*Norwegian*		
Señor Kon-Tiki	XII	45
JAMIE WATT and the GIANT in the TEAKETTLE	V	45
JANE AND THE WILD CHIMPS—*George Crossette*	XII	70
Jane van Lawick-Goodall—*Jane and the Wild Chimps*	XII	70
JAPANESE LULLABY, A	I	78
JASPER THE DRUMMIN' BOY—*Margaret Taylor Burroughs*	VI	108
JINGLE BELLS, JINGLE BELLS—*American Rhyme*	I	87
JOAN OF ARC—*(Biog. Sketch)*	X	98
Joanna—*The Three Wishes*	VI	92
JOG ON, JOG ON—*William Shakespeare*.	I	148
JOHN BROWN HAD A LITTLE INDIAN—*American Rhyme*	I	100
JOHN HENRY, THE BIG STEEL-DRIVIN' MAN—*From American Popular Ballads*	V	139
JOHN PAUL JONES, THE FIRST AMERICAN NAVAL HERO	VIII	82
JOHNNY AND THE THREE GOATS—*Norse Tale*	II	47
Johnny Appleseed—*Old Johnny Appleseed*	IV	213
JOHNNY SHALL HAVE A NEW BONNET—*English Rhyme*	I	20
JOKELI—*Swiss Rhyme*	I	66
JOSEPH AND HIS BRETHREN—*From the Bible (Book of Genesis)*	X	48
Judson, Clara Ingram—*American*		
Telegraph Boy	XII	60

	VOL.	PAGE
JUMBO WAS AN ELEPHANT—*American Rhyme*	I	105

K

	VOL.	PAGE
KALEVALA, LAND OF HEROES—*Retold from the Kalevala, national epic of Finland*	X	151
Kay—*The Snow-Queen*	VII	48
Keats, John—*English (1795-1821)*		
Child, I See Thee!	I	152
There Was a Naughty Boy	I	152
Where Be You Going, You Devon Maid?	I	152
Dawlish Fair	II	67
Meg Merrilies	VIII	188
Kelley, F. Beverly—*American (1905-)*		
Freddy, The Pad Dog	V	214
King Arthur—*Sir Beaumains, the Kitchen Knight*	X	8
KING DAGOBERT—*French Rhyme*	I	124
KING HILARY AND THE BEGGARMAN—*A. A. Milne*	III	70
King Midas—*The Golden Touch*	VII	210
KING OF FRANCE WENT UP THE HILL, THE—*English Rhyme*	I	41
KING'S CREAM, THE—*Frances R. Sterrett*	VI	209
KING STEPHEN WAS A WORTHY PEER—*William Shakespeare*	I	149
Kingsley, Charles—*English (1819-1875)*		
Adventures of a Water Baby, The	III	211
How the Goddess of Spring Came to Scoring	IX	176
Kipling, Rudyard—*English (1865-1936)*		
The Ballad of East and West	IX	129
Mowgli's Brothers	V	182
KITTEN AND FALLING LEAVES, THE—*William Wordsworth*	III	133
KNIGHT, THE—*Paul Laurence Dunbar*	IV	129
KNIGHTS OF THE SILVER SHIELD, THE—*Raymond MacDonald Alden*	VII	173
KNITTING STILL—*Czechoslovakian*	I	128
KON-TIKI, SEÑOR—*Arnold Jacoby*	XII	45
KRAZY KAT—*Story of the pantomime by John Alden Carpenter*	II	172

L

	VOL.	PAGE
La Fontaine, Jean de—*French (1621-1695)*		
The Honest Woodman—*Adapted*	III	114
The Acorn and the Pumpkin	VII	132
LABORS OF HERCULES, THE—*Greek Myth*	IX	151
LAST OF THE DRAGONS, THE—*E. Nesbit*	X	89
LATE—*Josephine Preston Peabody*	II	153
LAUGHING SONG—*William Blake*	II	75
LAVENDER'S BLUE—*English Rhyme*	I	56
Lazarus, Emma—*American (1849-1887)*		
The New Colossus	XI	172
LAZY OLD MARY—*American Rhyme*	I	98
Le Fèvre, Félicité—*French*		
The Cock, the Mouse, and the Little Red Hen	II	192

	VOL.	PAGE
Lear, Edward—*English (1812-1888)*		
Please Give Me a Ride on Your Back	II	154
There Was an Old Man with a Beard	II	154
The Owl and the Pussy-Cat	II	180
LEARNING TO BE FREE—*Mildred Barger Herschler*	XII	198
Lee, Robert E.—*See Robert E. Lee*	XI	170
Lemon—*The King's Cream*	VI	209
Lewis, Meriwether—*Pushing Westward with Lewis and Clark*	IX	25
LIE A-BED—*Christina Rossetti*	I	157
LIFE IN CONCORD—*Biog. Sketch of Louisa May Alcott*	XII	122
Lincoln, Abraham—*A Story About Abe Lincoln*	V	133
LINCOLN, ABRAHAM—*Rosemary and Stephen Vincent Benét*	V	132
LINCOLN'S GETTYSBERG ADDRESS.	XI	170a
Lindsay, Maud—*American (1874-1941)*		
The Little Gray Pony	II	17
Mrs. Tabby Gray	III	129
Lindsay, Nicholas Vachel—*American (1879-1931)*		
The Little Turtle	I	162
An Explanation of the Grasshopper	II	77
Biog. Sketch (A Tramp of the Middle West)	XII	147
LINES FOR A CITY CHILD—*Robert and Elizabeth Barrett Browning*	I	185
LION AND THE MOUSE, THE—*Aesop*.	II	108
LITTLE BELLS, PRETTY FLOWERS OF THE STEPPES—*Russian Rhyme*	I	133
LITTLE BEPPO PIPPO—*Italian Rhyme*	I	63
LITTLE BIRD SITS IN THE WILLOW, A—*Polish Rhyme*	I	73
LITTLE BLUE APRON	III	210
LITTLE BO-PEEP—*English Rhyme*	I	32
LITTLE BOY BLUE—*English Rhyme*	I	33
LITTLE COCK SPARROW, A—*English Rhyme*	I	52
LITTLE DIAMOND AND THE NORTH WIND—*George MacDonald*	IV	119
LITTLE DOG WALTZ, THE—*A story of the musician, Frederic Chopin*	II	150
Little Em'ly—*David Copperfield and Little Em'ly*	VII	182
LITTLE ENGINE THAT COULD, THE	II	200
LITTLE GIRL AND THE HARE, THE—*Adapted from Wilhelm and Jacob Grimm*	III	111
LITTLE GIRL AND THE NEW DRESS, THE—*Adapted from Hans Christian Andersen*	I	168
LITTLE GIRL, LITTLE GIRL—*English Rhyme*	I	56
LITTLE GOOD BABY—*American Indian Song*	I	80
LITTLE GRAY PONY, THE—*Maud Lindsay*	II	17
LITTLE GULLIVER—*Louisa May Alcott*	V	103
LITTLE GUSTAVA—*Celia Thaxter*	II	30

236

	VOL.	PAGE
LITTLE HANSWORST—*Story of the Dutch puppet show*	II	164
LITTLE HOUSE IN THE BIG WOODS—*Laura Ingalls Wilder*	IX	119
LITTLE JACK HORNER—*English Rhyme*	I	48
Little John—*Ye Merry Doinges of Robin Hood*	XI	49
LITTLE KING BOGGIN—*English Rhyme*	I	40
LITTLE LIESE COMES A-RUNNING—*German Rhyme*	I	121
LITTLE MAID OF FAR JAPAN—*Annette Wynne*	III	164
LITTLE MAID, PRETTY MAID—*English Rhyme*	I	56
LITTLE-MAN-AS-BIG-AS-YOUR-THUMB-WITH-MUSTACHES-SEVEN-MILES-LONG, THE—*Russian Tale*	VII	112
LITTLE MISS MUFFET—*English Rhyme*	I	40
LITTLE NANNY ETTICOAT—*English Rhyme*	I	41
LITTLE PEPPINO—*Italian Rhyme*	I	62
LITTLE PICTURES FROM FAR JAPAN	VI	196
LITTLE PIG, THE	I	198
LITTLE RABBIT WHO WANTED RED WINGS, THE—*Negro Folk Tale*	II	87
LITTLE RED HEN AND THE GRAIN OF WHEAT, THE—*English Folk Tale*	II	13
LITTLE ROBIN REDBREAST—*English Rhyme*	I	23
LITTLE ROOSTER AND THE LITTLE HEN, THE—*Czechoslovakian Folk Tale*	II	71
LITTLE TOMMY TUCKER—*English Rhyme*	I	42
LITTLE TOY LAND OF THE DUTCH, THE—*Olive Beaupré Miller*	IV	56
LITTLE TURTLE, THE—*Vachel Lindsay*	I	162
Lofting, Hugh—*English* (1886-1947) The Rarest Animal of All	IV	113
LOHENGRIN—*Retold from the opera by Richard Wagner*	X	89
LONDON STREETS—*Biog. Sketch of Charles Dickens*	XII	102
LONELIEST BATTLER, THE—*George Vass*	XII	79
LONE STAR TEAM OF TEXAS, THE—*George Vass*	XII	170
Longfellow, Henry Wadsworth—*American* (1807-1882)		
I Heard the Bells on Christmas Day	II	217
Hiawatha's Childhood	V	222
Hiawatha's Fasting	IX	89
Thor	IX	171
Biog. Sketch (The Harvard Professor)	XII	135
LOOK, SEE THE BOAT!—*Olive Beaupré Miller*	I	184
LOST SPEAR, THE—*South African Tale*	VI	132
Lotus-blossom—*The Girl Who Used Her Wits*	IV	137
Lowell, Amy—*American* (1874-1925)		
The Sea Shell	III	150
Comment (The Harvard Professor)	XII	135
Lowell, James Russell—*American* (1819-1891)		
Comment (Life in Concord)	XII	122
Comment (The Harvard Professor)	XII	135
Lucy—*Maggie Tulliver Goes to Live with the Gypsies*	VIII	189
LUCY LOCKET LOST HER POCKET—*English Rhyme*	I	26
Lynette—*Sir Beaumains, the Kitchen Knight*	X	8
Lysander—*A Midsummer Night's Dream*	VI	36

M

	VOL.	PAGE
MacDonald, George—*Scottish* (1824-1905) Little Diamond and the North Wind	IV	119
Macdonell, Anne—*English* Gigi and the Magic Ring	VII	199
MAD DOG, THE—*Based on the poem by Oliver Goldsmith and on the illustrations for that poem done by Randolph Caldecott*	III	63
MAGGIE TULLIVER GOES TO LIVE WITH THE GYPSIES—*Arranged from The Mill on the Floss*	VIII	189
MAGIC HORSE, THE—*The Arabian Nights*	VIII	92
MAGPIE'S NEST, THE—*English Folk Tale*	II	42
Maid Marian—*Ye Merry Doinges of Robin Hood*	XI	49
MAIDEN, THE KNIGHT, AND THE WATERFALL, THE—*Roumanian Fairy Tale*	VII	40
MAN WHO HAS PLENTY OF GOOD PEANUTS, THE—*American Rhyme*	I	95
MAN WHO LIVED IN THE WORLD OF DREAMS, THE—*A story about Dante Alighieri*	XI	152
MAN WHO LOVED HAI QUAI, THE—*Indian Tale of Mt. Tacoma*	VI	127
MAN WHO MADE ADOLF HITLER RUN, THE—*George Vass*	XII	104
Mansur, Abul Kasim (Firdusi—Pen Name) See Firdusi		
MANY, MANY STARS ARE IN THE SKIES—*American Rhyme*	I	86
Marian, Maid See Maid Marian		
Marie—*The Tale of Nutcracker*	II	218
MARIO, MARIETTA, AND VANNO—*Italian Rhyme*	I	63
Marit—*Oeyvind and Marit*	III	137
MARKO, THE CHAMPION OF SERBIAN LIBERTY—*Tale of the 14th century from ballads of the Yugoslavs*	XI	29
Maroosia—*Christening the Baby in Russia*	IV	63
Martone, Roland A.—*American* The Boy Who Saved the World	VI	170

	VOL.	PAGE
MARY AND THE CHRIST-CHILD— *Olive Beaupré Miller*...................	I	218
MARY HAD A LITTLE LAMB— *American Rhyme*	I	88
MARY, MARY, QUITE CONTRARY— *English Rhyme*	I	25
MARY MILKS THE COW—*Norse Rhyme*	I	135
Marygold—*The Golden Touch*...........	VII	210
Masefield, John—*English*		
Sea-Fever	VIII	35
A Wanderer's Song................	VIII	91
Mr. Hampden's Shipwreck...........	VIII	172
MASTER OF ALL MASTERS—*Joseph Jacobs*	III	148
Mave, Queen *See Queen Mave*		
Medusa—*The Adventures of Perseus*......	IX	140
MEG MERRILIES—*John Keats*.........	VIII	188
Meleager—*Greek*—(About 50 B.C.) Crocus Flowers Bloom Like Fire.....	I	205
MELTING POT, THE—*Retold from the play by Israel Zangwill*................	XI	173
Mendelssohn, Felix—*A Musical Visit to Fairyland*	VI	59
Mercury—*The Adventures of Perseus*.....	IX	140
Meredith, George—*English* (1828-1909) Richard Feverel and the Hay-Rick— *Arranged from The Ordeal of Richard Feverel*	X	54
MERMAN, THE—*Alfred Tennyson*......	VI	182
MERRY CHRISTMAS	II	217
MICE, THE—*Winnebago Fable*..........	VI	131
Midas, King *See King Midas*		
MIDSUMMER NIGHT'S DREAM, A— *Told from the play by William Shakespeare*	VI	38
MILKWEED AND A BUTTERCUP, A—*Peter Newell*	IV	118
Miller, Joaquin—*The Poet of the Sierras* (Biog. Sketch)	XII	143
Miller, Olive Beaupré—*American* O I'll Build a Square with My Pretty Red Blocks	I	164
Big, Bus, Stop!....................	I	173
Policeman Joe	I	173
Mister Postman	I	182
Look, See the Boat!...............	I	184
The Airplane	I	194
Thunder and Lightning..............	I	195
The Bridge	I	210
Mary and the Christ-Child...........	I	218
A Song for Easter..................	II	80
The Road to China.................	III	19
New Year's Day....................	III	45
The Circus Parade.................	III	46
The Mad Dog.....................	III	63
A Happy Day in the City...........	III	181
The Little Toy Land of the Dutch....	VI	56
Hallowe'en	IV	142

	VOL.	PAGE
Tippity Witchit's Hallowe'en.........	IV	145
The First Thanksgiving Day........	V	113
The Fourth of July.................	V	129
The Yankee Peddler...............	V	130
A Boy on the High Seas...........	VIII	8
Milne, A. A.—*English* (1882-1956) King Hilary and the Beggarman......	III	70
Winnie-the-Pooh	V	68
Milton, John—*English* (1608-1674) Note	VII	122
Note	XII	29
MINNIE AND MATTIE—*Christina Rossetti*	I	156
MISKA AND THE MAN-WITH-THE-IRON-HEAD—*Hungarian Fairy Tale*...	VII	11
MISTER POSTMAN—*Olive Beaupré Miller*	I	182
Mitchell, Lucy Sprague—*American* The Big Street in the Big City.......	I	170
Biting Marion	I	174
MIX A PANCAKE—*Christina Rossetti*...	I	157
MOCK TURTLE'S SONG, THE—*Lewis Carroll*	III	170
Moe, Jorgen—*Norwegian* (1813-1882) The Doll Under the Briar Rosebush..	III	204
MONKEYS—*James Whitcomb Riley*.....	I	142
MOON, SO ROUND AND YELLOW— *Mathias Barr*	II	40
MOON-MAIDEN, THE—*Japanese Fairy Tale*	VI	222
Moore, Clement—*American* (1779-1863) The Night Before Christmas........	II	213
Morley, Christopher—*American* (1890-1957) Animal Crackers	I	162
Moses—*The Babe Moses*................	III	156
Mourad—*My Name Is Aram*............	VII	156
MOUSE CLIMBED UP THE CANDLE-STICK, THE—*Chinese Rhyme*.........	I	77
Mowat, Farley—*Canadian* Battle Tactics	VII	165
MOWGLI'S BROTHERS —*Rudyard Kipling* from the Jungle Book	V	182
MR. HAMPDEN'S SHIPWRECK— *John Masefield*	VIII	172
MR. TOAD SET OUT ON A JOURNEY— *South American Rhyme*..............	I	68
MRS. TABBY GRAY—*Maud Lindsay*...	III	129
Münchausen, Baron *See Baron Münchausen*		
Murphy, Tamsin—*American* Snowflake the Gorilla...............	VI	159
The Gentle Genius.................	XII	218
MUSICAL VISIT TO FAIRYLAND, A— *A Story about Felix Mendelssohn*......	VI	59
MY BELOVED IS GONE DOWN INTO HIS GARDEN—*From the Bible* (Song of Solomon)....................	II	78
MY BOAT	I	163
MY LADY WIND—*English Rhyme*......	I	46
MY MAID MARY—*English Rhyme*.....	I	51
MY NAME IS ARAM—*William Saroyan*.	VII	156

N

	VOL.	PAGE
Ned—*A Happy Day in the City*	III	181
NEGRO SPEAKS OF RIVERS, THE—*Langston Hughes*	XII	188
Nesbit, E.—*English* The Last of the Dragons	X	89
NEW COLOSSUS, THE—*Emma Lazarus*.	XI	172
NEW HEROES	VII	144
NEW YEAR'S DAY—*Olive Beaupré Miller*	III	45
Newell, Peter—*American* (1862-1924) A Milkweed and a Buttercup	IV	118
Wild Flowers	VI	69
Newsome, Effie Lee—*American* Bats	I	211
NIGHT BEFORE CHRISTMAS, THE—*Clement Moore*	II	213
NOAH'S ARK—*Retold from the Bible*...	II	101
Nokomis—*Hiawatha's Childhood*	V	222
Nokomis—*Hiawatha's Fasting*	IX	89
NONSENSE RHYMES	II	154
Nottingham, Sheriff of *See Sheriff of Nottingham*		
Noyes, Alfred—*English* (1880-1942) Fairy Forests	VI	190
A Song of Drake's Men	VIII	7
A Christmas Song at Sea	VIII	187
NUREMBERG STOVE, THE—*Louise de la Ramée*	V	162
NURSE'S SONG—*William Blake*	II	152
NUTCRACKER AND SUGARDOLLY STORIES, THE—*Carolyn Sherwin Bailey*	IV	83

O

	VOL.	PAGE
O IF MY TOP WOULD ONLY SPIN—*Canadia Song*	I	130
O I'LL BUILD A SQUARE WITH MY PRETTY RED BLOCKS—*Olive Beaupré Miller*	I	164
O I'M A JOLLY OLD COWBOY—*American Rhyme*	I	100
O LADY MARY ANN—*Robert Burns*...	I	153
O MY DAME HAD A LAME TAME CRANE—*American Rhyme*	I	95
O RATTLIN', ROARIN' WILLIE—*Robert Burns*	I	153
O SAILOR, COME ASHORE—*Christina Rossetti*	I	157
O 'TWAS ON A BRIGHT MORNIN' IN SUMMER—*Irish Rhyme*	I	59
O WELL FOR THE FISHERMAN'S BOY—*Alfred Tennyson*	I	154
O WILL YOU SHOE OUR PONY, PRAY?—*Swiss Rhyme*	I	66
Oberon—*A Midsummer Night's Dream*...	VI	38
Odysseus—*The Home-Coming of Odysseus*	X	217
OEYVIND AND MARIT—*A Story of Norway*	III	137

	VOL.	PAGE
OF A TAILOR AND A BEAR—*From the music by Edward MacDowell*	III	134
OF ALL THE BEASTS THAT ROAM THE WOODS—*American Negro Rhyme*	I	106
OF ALL THE GIRLS THAT ARE SO SMART—*Henry Carey*	I	169
OF SPECKLED EGGS THE BIRDIE SINGS—*Robert Louis Stevenson*	I	158
OF WE'LL GO—*Basho*	VI	196
OH, HERE'S A LEG FOR A STOCKING—*English Rhyme*	I	20
Old Dan—*Little Gulliver*	V	103
OLD JOHNNY APPLESEED—*Legend of the Middle West*	IV	213
OLD KING COLE—*English Rhyme*	I	44
OLD MOTHER GOOSE—*English Rhyme*	I	23
OLD MOTHER HUBBARD—*English Rhyme*	I	38
OLD MOTHER WIND—*Chinese Rhyme*.	I	76
OLD NOAH—*American Rhyme*	I	112
Old Peter—*Christening the Baby in Russia*.	IV	63
OLD PIPES AND THE DRYAD—*Frank R. Stockton*	VI	18
OLD SHELLOVER—*Walter de la Mare*..	II	185
OLD STORMALONG—*Yarn of American Sailors*	IV	183
OLD YELLER—*Fred Gipson*	IX	98
OLE SHUT-EYES, THE SANDMAN—*Adapted from Hans Christian Andersen*.	II	26
Oliver—*The Song of Roland*	X	38
Oliver—*As You Like It*	X	165
ONCE I SAW A LITTLE BIRD—*English Rhyme*	I	25
ONE MISTY, MOISTY MORNING—*English Rhyme*	I	42
ONE, TWO, THREE, FOUR—*American Rhyme*	I	99
O'Neill, "Giant" An American Miner's Song (*Poem and note*)	II	23
OPEN YOUR BEAK, MY LITTLE BIRD—*African Rhyme*	I	146
OPPORTUNITY—*Edward Rowland Sill*..	X	18
ORCHESTRA, THE	I	187
Orlando—*As You Like It*	X	165
OTTO WOULD A-RIDING GO—*Swedish Rhyme*	I	75
Ouida (Pen Name of Louise de la Ramée) *See Ramée, Louise de la*		
OVER IN THE MEADOW—*Olive A. Wadsworth*	I	138
OVER THE HILL TO FEED MY SHEEP—*American Rhyme*	I	99
OVER THE RIVER AND THROUGH THE WOODS—*American Rhyme*	I	87
Owens, Jesse—*The Man Who Made Adolf Hitler Run*	XII	104

	VOL.	PAGE
OWL AND THE PUSSY-CAT, THE—*Edward Lear*	II	180
OWL, THE—*Alfred Tennyson*	III	28
OWL'S ANSWER TO TOMMY, THE—*Juliana Horatia Ewing*	III	29

P

	VOL.	PAGE
Pantaloon—*Columbine and Her Playfellows of the Italian Pantomine*	VII	119
Panza, Sancho *See Sancho Panza*		
Paolo—*Dante's Voyage to the Inferno, Purgatory, and Paradise*	XI	156
PAPER BOATS—*Rabindranath Tagore*	II	139
Parizade—*The Story of the Talking Bird*	VIII	109
PARK PLAY—*James S. Tippett*	I	189
PAT-A-CAKE, PAT-A-CAKE, BAKER'S MAN!—*English Rhyme*	I	19
Paul Bunyan—*The Story of Big Paul Bunyan*	IV	161
Peabody, Josephine Preston—*American (1874-1922)* Late	II	153
Peach—*The King's Cream*	VI	209
Peary, Robert—*How Peary Reached the North Pole*	IX	127
PEASE-PORRIDGE HOT—*English Rhyme*	I	47
PECOS BILL, THE COWBOY—*A Tall Tale of American Cowboys*	IV	195
PEDDLER'S CARAVAN, THE—*William Brighty Rands*	IV	11
PEDDLER'S SONG, THE—*William Shakespeare*	VII	145
Pedro—*The Three Wishes*	VI	92
PEEKABOO, I SEE YOU!—*Swedish Rhyme*	I	74
PEER GYNT—*Told from the play by Henrik Ibsen*	IX	98
Peggotty—*David Copperfield and Little Em'ly*	VII	182
PERFECT KNIGHT, A—*Geoffrey Chaucer*	X	7
Perrault, Charles—*French (1628-1703)* Cinderella—*Adapted*	IV	12
Comments (The Interesting History of Old Mother Goose)	XII	213
PERT FIRE ENGINE, THE—*Gelett Burgess*	IV	218
Perviz—*The Story of the Talking Bird*	VIII	109
Peter—*The Little Snow Maiden*	IV	119
Peter—*Heidi in the Alpine Pasture*	V	147
Peter, Old *See Old Peter*		
PETER, PETER, PUMPKIN EATER—*English Rhyme*	I	36
Peter Rabbit *See the Tale of Peter Rabbit*		
PETER RABBIT DECIDES TO CHANGE HIS NAME—*Thornton W. Burgess*	III	49
PHAETON—*Greek Myth*	VII	90
Pharaoh—*The Babe Moses*	III	156
Pharaoh—*Rhodopis and Her Gilded Sandals*	VII	84
Phebe—*As You Like It*	X	165
PIE SAT ON A PEAR TREE, A—*English Rhyme*	I	27
Pierrot—*Columbine and Her Playfellows of the Italian Pantomime*	VII	119
PIGLING AND HER PROUD SISTER—*Korean Cinderella Tale*	VI	191
PINNY, PINNY, POPPY SHOW!—*American Rhyme*	I	88
PIONEER IN SURGERY—*Louis Haber*	XII	154
PLEASE GIVE ME A RIDE ON YOUR BACK—*Edward Lear*	II	154
PLOUGHMAN HE'S A BONNIE LAD, THE—*Robert Burns*	I	153
Poe, Edgar Allen—*American (1809-1849)* The Bells	VII	71
Note	XII	135
POET OF THE SIERRAS, THE—*Biog. Sketch of Joaquin Miller*	XII	143
POLICEMAN JOE—*Olive Beaupré Miller*	I	173
POLLY, PUT THE KETTLE ON—*English Rhyme*	I	31
Pombo, Rafael—*Colombian (1833-1912)* Reen-Reen-Reeny-Croak-Frog	II	37
The Poor Old Lady	II	68
POOR OLD LADY, THE—*Rafael Pombo*	II	68
POP! GOES THE WEASEL!—*American Rhyme*	I	107
Pope, Alexander—*English (1688-1744)* Hear How the Birds	I	108
Potiphar—*Joseph and His Brethren*	X	48
Potter, Beatrix—*English* The Tale of Peter Rabbit	II	112
PRECOCIOUS PIGGY—*Thomas Hood*	I	196
PRETTY, SEE THE CLOUD APPEAR!—*American Indian Song*	I	81
PRINCE WHO RODE THROUGH A MOUSEHOLE, THE—*Czech Folk Tale*	VII	96
Princess Moonbeam—*The Moon-Maiden*	VI	222
PRINCESS NELLY AND THE SENECA CHIEF	IX	78
PRINCESS ON THE GLASS HILL, THE—*Sir George Webbe Dasent*	VI	80
Pringle, Thomas—*Scottish (1789-1834)* Afar in the Desert	VIII	36
Puck—*A Midsummer Night's Dream*	VI	38
PUMPKIN, THE—*John Greenleaf Whittier*	IV	23
Punch and Judy—*The Renowned and World-Famous Adventures of Punch and Judy*	VII	160
PURPLE COW, THE—*Gelett Burgess*	II	163
PUSHING WESTWARD WITH LEWIS AND CLARK	IX	25
PUSSY CAT, PUSSY CAT—*English Rhyme*	I	44
PUSSY, KITTIE—*Spanish Rhyme*	I	64
PUSSY, PUSSY, DEAR PUSSY—*Polish Rhyme*	I	72

	VOL.	PAGE

PUSSY SITS BESIDE THE FIRE—
English Rhyme .... I 36

Pyle, Howard—*American* (1853-1911)
The Enchanted Island.............. VIII 134

Q

QUAKER, QUAKER, HOW IS THEE?
—*American Rhyme* .... I 82

Queen Dido—*The Wanderings of Aeneas*.. X 203

Queen Mave—*Cuculain, the Irish Hound*.. X 188

QUICK-RUNNING SQUASH, A—
Alicia Aspinwall .... III 104

Quixano, David—*The Melting Pot* .... XI 173

Quixote, Don
See Don Quixote

R

Rabbit—*Winnie-the-Pooh* .... V 68

RAIN—*Robert Louis Stevenson*.......... I 191

RAJAH WENT TO DELHI, THE—
East Indian Rhyme................... I 79

Rama—*The Exile of Rama*.............. X 175

RAMA AND THE TIGERS............ II 118

Ramée, Louise de la (Ouida—Pen Name)
English (1839-1908)
The Nuremberg Stove............... V 162

Rands, William Brighty—*English*
(1823-1882)
The Wonderful World .... III 11
The Peddler's Caravan.............. IV 11

Ransetsu—*Japanese* (1654-1707)
Snow .... VI 196

Ransome, Arthur—*English*
Christening the Baby in Russia....... IV 63

RAREST ANIMAL OF ALL, THE—
Hugh Lofting .... IV 113

Raspberry—*The King's Cream* ...... VI 209

Raspe, Rudolph Erich—*German* (1737-1794)
The Strange Adventure of Baron
Münchausen (*Story and note*)..... II 182

RECOLLECTIONS OF THE ARABIAN
NIGHTS—*Alfred Tennyson* .... VIII 108

Red Cross Knight—*Una and the Red Cross
Knight* .... XI 8

RED ETTIN, THE—*A tale told in England
and Scotland* .... V 90

REEN-REEN-REENY-CROAK-FROG—
South American Tale .... II 37

REINAR WAS WATCHING HIS COWS
—*Norse Rhyme* .... I 61

RENOWNED AND WORLD-FAMOUS
ADVENTURES OF PUNCH AND
JUDY, THE .... VII 160

Restrepo, Don Antonio José—*Colombian*
(1855-1933)
The Toads in the Lake.............. I 68
Mr. Toad Set Out on a Journey..... I 68
When Mrs. Bird Wants Mr. Bird..... I 68
Right Out in Our Barnyard.......... I 69
When I See a Lady................. I 69

RHODOPIS AND HER GILDED
SANDALS—*First Cinderella story*...... VII 84

RICHARD FEVEREL AND THE HAY-
RICK—*Arranged from The Ordeal of
Richard Feverel* .... X 54

Richards, Laura E.—*American* (1850-1943)
Rosy Posy .... III 128

RIDE A COCK-HORSE TO BANBURY
CROSS—*English Rhyme* .... I 28

RIDE AWAY, RIDE AWAY—*English
Rhyme* .... I 24

RIDE, RIDE A HORSEY—*Pennsylvania
Dutch Rhyme* .... I 116

RIDE, RIDE AWAY—*Norse Rhyme*..... I 60

RIGHT OUT IN OUR BARNYARD—
South American Rhyme............... I 69

RIGHT TIME TO LAUGH, THE—
Australian Tale .... III 81

Riley, James Whitcomb—*American*
(1853-1916)
Monkeys .... I 142
A Sea-Song from the Shore.......... I 202
A Winkey-Tooden Song............. I 215
The Daring Prince.................. III 127
The Brook Song.................... III 161
"It" .... VI 131
Comment (The Harvard Professor)... XII 135
Biog. Sketch (The Hoosier Poet) .... XII 141

RING AROUND A ROSY—*American
Rhyme* .... I 84

ROAD TO CHINA, THE—*Olive Beaupré
Miller* .... III 19

ROBERT BRUCE, SCOTLAND'S HERO
—*Biog. Sketch* .... X 21

ROBERT E. LEE, A HERO IN WAR
AND IN PEACE.................... XI 170c

ROBIN AND A ROBIN'S SON, A—
English Rhyme .... I 36

ROBIN AND RICHARD WERE TWO
PRETTY MEN—*English Rhyme*....... I 26

Robin Hood—*Ye Merry Doinges of Robin
Hood* .... XI 49

Robinson, Jackie—*The Loneliest Battler*... XII 79

ROCK-A-BYE, BABY—*English Rhyme*... I 18

Roland, Sir
See Sir Roland

Roland—*The Song of Roland*........... X 38

ROLL IT, BOWL IT—*Canadian Song*.... I 130

Roosevelt, Theodore—*American*
(1858-1919)
George Rogers Clark and the Conquest
of the Northwest.................. IX 66
Biog. Sketch (The Rough Rider)..... IX 72

ROOSTER AND THE SULTAN, THE—
Hungarian Fairy Tale................ II 52

ROOSTERS AT THE OLD CROWN INN,
THE—*Swiss Rhyme* .... I 67

Rosalba—*The Rose and the Ring*........ IX 177

Rosalind—*As You Like It*.............. X 165

	VOL.	PAGE
ROSE AND THE RING, THE— *William Makepeace Thackeray*	IX	177
ROSE IS RED, THE—*American Rhyme*	I	86
Rose-red—*Snow-white and Rose-red*	IV	34
Rossetti, Christina—*English (1830-1894)*		
A White Hen Sitting	I	156
Minnie and Mattie	I	156
Lie a-Bed	I	157
Mix a Pancake	I	157
O Sailor, Come Ashore	I	157
Who Has Seen the Wind?	I	201
The Bow That Bridges Heaven	II	105
ROSY POSY—*Laura E. Richards*	III	128
ROUGH RIDER, THE—*Biog. Sketch of Theodore Roosevelt*	IX	72
ROUMANIAN LULLABY, A	I	137
ROUND IS MY BUN—*Hungarian Rhyme*	I	136
ROVER IN THE CATSKILLS, A— *Biog. Sketch of Washington Irving*	XII	99
ROW, ROW! A-FISHING WE'LL GO! —*Norse Rhyme*	I	61
Royal Cook—*The King's Cream*	VI	209
ROYAL PAGE, THE—*Biog. Sketch of Geoffrey Chaucer*	XII	11
RUB-A-DUB-DUB—*English Rhyme*	I	48
Ruskin, John—*English (1819-1900)*		
Dame Wiggins of Lee (*In collaboration with Mary E. Sharpe*)	II	188
Note	III	26
Rustem—*A Story of Rustem, the Hero of Persia*	X	228
Ruth—*A Happy Day in the City*	III	181

S

	VOL.	PAGE
SALLY'S BLUE BALL—*Marian Walker*	I	188
Samuel—*The Boy Samuel*	IV	80
Sancho Panza—*The Surprising Adventures of Don Quixote of La Mancha*	XI	90
Sandburg, Carl—*American*		
The Fog	I	184
The Village of Cream Puffs	II	124
Comment (The Harvard Professor)	XII	135
Saroyan, William—*American*		
My Name Is Aram	VII	156
Saul—*David, the Shepherd Boy*	VII	73
Scarecrow—*The Wizard of Oz*	VI	62
Schiller, Wilhelm—*German*		
A German Evening	II	140
SCHOOL IS OVER—*Kate Greenaway*	III	27
Scott, Sir Walter—*Scottish (1771-1832)*		
Heap on More Wood	II	217
Hie Away, Hie Away	VI	70
Gathering Song of Donuil Dhu	X	20
SEA, THE—*Emily Dickinson*	III	155
SEA-FEVER—*John Masefield*	VIII	35
SEA GULL, THE—*Mary Howitt*	V	111
SEA SHELL, THE—*Amy Lowell*	III	150
SEA-SONG FROM THE SHORE, A—		

	VOL.	PAGE
James Whitcomb Riley	I	202
SEE-SAW, MARGERY DAW—*English Rhyme*	I	51
SEE-SAW, SACARADOWN—*English Rhyme*	I	18
SELFISH GIANT, THE—*Oscar Wilde*	IV	50
Selim, the Baker—*The Enchanted Island*	VIII	132
Selim, the Fisherman—*The Enchanted Island*	VIII	132
Selkirk, Alexander—*The Adventures of Alexander Selkirk*	IX	41
SEÑOR KON-TIKI—*Arnold Jacoby*	XII	45
Setoun, Gabriel (Pen Name of Thomas N. Hepburn)—*Scottish (1861-1930)*		
Jack Frost	II	186
Sevolod—*The Word of Igor's Armament*	X	119
Shakespeare, William—*English (1564-1616)*		
As It Fell Upon a Day	I	148
In the Springtime	I	148
Jog On, Jog On	I	148
Hark, Hark! Bow-wow!	I	149
King Stephen Was a Worthy Peer	I	149
When That I Was But a Little Tiny Boy	I	149
Good Morrow, 'Tis Saint Valentine's Day	I	209
A Midsummer Night's Dream—*Told from the play*	VI	38
The Tempest—*Told from the play*	VIII	18
As You Like It—*Told from the play*	X	165
Under the Greenwood Tree	XI	72
Biog. Sketch (Down by the River Avon)	XII	15
SHAKING OF THE PEAR TREE, THE— *Dinah M. Muloch Craik*	III	146
Sharpe, Mary E.		
Dame Wiggins of Lee (*In collaboration with John Ruskin*)	II	188
SHEEP AND THE PIG THAT MADE A HOME, THE—*Norse Folk Tale*	II	145
Shelley, Percy Bysshe—*English (1792-1822)*		
The Cloud	VII	95
Shepard, Odell—*American*		
The Goldfinch	II	45
Sheriff of Nottingham—*Ye Merry Doinges of Robin Hood*	XI	49
SHINGEBISS—*Chippewa Indian Tale*	II	96
SHOEMAKER AND THE ELVES, THE —*German Folk Tale*	III	95
Siegfried—*The Tale of the Rhine-Gold*	XI	73
Sieglinda—*The Tale of the Rhine-Gold*	XI	73
Siegmund—*The Tale of the Rhine-Gold*	XI	73
Sill, Edward Rowland—*American (1841-1888)*		
A Tropical Morning at Sea	VI	201
Opportunity	X	18
Silvius—*As You Like It*	X	165
SIMPLE SIMON—*English Rhyme*	I	50
SING A SONG OF SIXPENCE—*English Rhyme*	I	49

	VOL.	PAGE
SING, SING!—WHAT SHALL I SING? *English Rhyme*	I	31
SIR BEAUMAINS, THE KITCHEN KNIGHT—*Legend of the Round Table.*	X	8
Sir Roland—*The Knights of the Silver Shield*	VII	173
Sita—*The Exile of Rama*	X	175
SIX SWANS, THE—*German Fairy Tale*	VII	126
SKY AT NIGHT, THE—*From the Bible*	VII	72
SLEEP, BABY, SLEEP—*English Rhyme*	I	20
SLEEP, MY BABY, SLEEP AN HOUR— *Roumanian Lullaby*	I	137
SLEEP, MY BABY! SLEEP MY BABY!— *Japanese Lullaby*	I	78
SLEEP, SLEEP, MY LITTLE ONE!— *African Rhyme*	I	146
SLEEP, SLEEP, SLEEP!—*American Indian Song*	I	80
SLEEPING BEAUTY, THE	VI	11
SLEEPY SONG, THE—*Josephine Daskam Bacon*	I	119
SMILING GIRLS, ROSY BOYS—*English Rhyme*	I	30
SNAIL, SNAIL—*Russian Rhyme*	I	132
SNOW—*Mary Mapes Dodge*	II	208
SNOW—*Ransetsu*	VI	196
SNOW BLOSSOMS	VI	197
SNOWFLAKE THE GORILLA—*Tamsin Murphy*	VI	159
SNOW MAN, THE	I	192
SNOW-QUEEN, THE—*Hans Christian Andersen*	VII	48
SNOW-WHITE AND ROSE-RED— *Wilhelm and Jacob Grimm*	IV	34
SOLITUDE—*Lord Byron*	IX	65
Solveig—*Peer Gynt*	IX	98
SONG FOR EASTER, A—*Olive Beaupré Miller*	II	80
SONG OF DRAKE'S MEN, A—*Alfred Noyes*	VIII	7
SONG OF ROLAND, THE—*French Epic, retold from the Chanson de Roland*	X	38
SONG OF SOLOMON, THE—*From the Bible*	III	136
SONG OF THE BEE, THE—*Old Jingle*	II	163
SONG OF THE CANADIAN LUMBER-JACK, A—*Canadian Folk Song*	IV	180
SONG OF THE FLEA, THE—*From the opera on Faust*	II	185
SONG OF THE RAILROAD MEN, A	I	181
SONGS OF JOY FROM THE BIBLE	I	216
Southey, Robert—*English (1774-1843)* The Cataract of Lodore	VII	47
Spencer, Edmund—*English (1552-1599)* Una and the Red Cross Knight—*Retold from Book I of The Faerie Queene.*	XI	8
SPRING SONGS FROM THE BIBLE	II	78
Spyri, Johanna—*Swiss (1827-1901)* Heidi in the Alpine Pasture	V	146
SQUIRE'S BRIDE, THE—*Peter Christen Asbjörnsen*	VI	98
SQUIRREL WENT OUT TO CUT THE HAY, THE—*Norse Rhyme*	I	60
STAR LIGHT, STAR BRIGHT— *American Rhyme*	I	86
STAR, THE—*Jane Taylor*	II	83
STEALING OF IDUNA, THE—*Norse Myth*	IX	172
STEAMBOAT AND THE LOCOMOTIVE, THE—*Gelett Burgess*	V	96
Stephen—*The Children's Crusade*	X	30
Stephens, James—*Irish (1882-1950)* White Fields	I	193
Sterrett, Frances R.—*American* The King's Cream	VI	209
Stevenson, Robert Louis—*Scottish (1850-1894)*		
The World Is So Full	I	17
Of Speckled Eggs the Birdie Sings	I	158
Bring the Comb and Play Upon It!	I	159
The Friendly Cow All Red and White	I	159
When I Was Down Beside the Sea	I	159
What Are You Able to Build with Your Blocks?	I	164
Rain	I	191
Where Go the Boats?	III	94
Stockton, Frank R.—*American* Old Pipes and the Dryad	VI	18
STOPPING BY WOODS ON A SNOWY EVENING—*Robert Frost*	VII	172
Stormy—*Old Stormalong*	IV	183
STORY ABOUT ABE LINCOLN, A	V	133
STORY ABOUT THE LITTLE RABBITS, A—*Joel Chandler Harris*	III	123
STORY OF BIG PAUL BUNYAN, THE— *Tale of American Lumber Camps*	IV	161
STORY OF LI'L HANNIBAL, THE— *Transcribed by Carolyn Sherwin Bailey*	III	116
STORY OF RUSTEM, THE HERO OF PERSIA, A—*Retold from the Shah-Nameh (Book of Kings) by Firdusi*	X	228
STORY OF THE CID, THE—*A Spanish Epic, retold from the ancient Poem of the Cid*	X	108
STORY OF THE TALKING BIRD, THE—*From The Arabian Nights*	VIII	109
STORY OF THE WIND, A	I	200
STORY OF TOM THUMB, THE— *English Folk Tale*	V	11
STRANGE ADVENTURE OF BARON MÜNCHAUSEN, THE	II	182
Stratton, Charles E. (General Tom Thumb) *See General Tom Thumb*		
Strawberry—*The King's Cream*	VI	209
STRONG BOY, THE—*Canadian Tale*	VI	71
Sugardolly—*The Nutcracker and Sugardolly Stories*	IV	83

243

	VOL.	PAGE
SUGAR-PLUM TREE, THE—*Eugene Field*	II	223
SUM-M, SUM-M, SUM-M!—*German Rhyme*	I	122
SURPRISING ADVENTURES OF DON QUIXOTE OF LA MANCHA, THE—*Miguel de Cervantes*	XI	90
SWEDISH EVENING, A—*Gustaf Fröding*	II	141
SWEET AND LOW—*Alfred Tennyson*	I	118
Swift, Jonathan—*Irish* (1667-1745)		
Gulliver's Travels to Lilliput	VIII	38

T

	VOL.	PAGE
Tagore, Rabindranath—*Bengali* (1861-1941)		
Paper Boats	II	139
TALE OF NUTCRACKER, THE—*Basis of the ballet by Peter Tchaikovsky*	II	218
TALE OF PETER RABBIT, THE—*Beatrix Potter*	II	112
TALE OF THE RHINE-GOLD, THE—*Germanic Epic, retold from the operas of Richard Wagner*	XI	73
Taylor, Jane—*English* (1783-1824)		
I Love Little Pussy	I	143
The Star	II	83
Teasdale, Sara—*American*		
The Coin	XII	212
TEDDY BEAR, TEDDY BEAR—*American Rhyme*	I	91
TEDDY BEARS' PICNIC, THE—*From the musical composition by John W. Bratton*	II	57
TEENY-TINY—*English Folk Tale*	IV	143
TELEGRAPH BOY—*Clara Ingram Judson*	XII	60
Tell, William		
See William Tell		
Telramund—*Lohengrin*	X	89
TEMPEST, THE—*Told from the play by William Shakespeare*	VIII	18
Templeton—*Charlotte's Web*	V	54
TEN LITTLE INDIANS	II	94
Tennyson, Alfred, Lord—*English* (1809-1892)		
Sweet and Low	I	118
O Well for the Fisherman's Boy	I	154
What Does Little Birdie Say?	I	154
Dainty Little Maiden	I	155
The Owl	III	28
The Merman	VI	182
Recollections of The Arabian Nights	VIII	108
Note	X	10
The Bugle Song	XI	7
Thackeray, William Makepeace—*English* (1811-1863)		
A Tragic Story—*Translated by*	IV	136
The Rose and the Ring (*Story and note*)	IX	177
Thaxter, Celia—*American* (1836-1894)		
Little Gustava	II	30
Thayer, Ernest Lawrence—*American* (1863-1940)		
Casey at the Bat	VII	144c
Theognis—*Greek* (About 500 B.C.)		
Here We Come, We Children Come	I	204

	VOL.	PAGE
THERE ARE TWELVE MONTHS—*Old English Ballad*	I	57
THERE GOES A SCOUT	IV	194
THERE WAS A CROW—*English Rhyme*	I	54
THERE WAS A FARMER HAD A DOG—*American Rhyme*	I	85
THERE WAS A HORSE—*English Rhyme*	I	54
THERE WAS A LITTLE BOY—*Chinese*	I	77
THERE WAS A LITTLE BOY—*English*	I	199
THERE WAS A LITTLE MAN AND HIS NAME WAS GICE—*Dutch Rhyme*	I	126
THERE WAS A MONKEY—*English*	I	52
THERE WAS A NAUGHTY BOY—*John Keats*	I	152
THERE WAS A PIPER HAD A COW—*English Rhyme*	I	29
THERE WAS AN OLD DAME CALLED TARTINE—*French Rhyme*	I	124
THERE WAS AN OLD MAN—*English Rhyme*	I	30
THERE WAS AN OLD MAN WITH A BEARD—*Edward Lear*	II	154
THERE WAS AN OLD, OLD INDIAN—*Canadian Song*	I	131
THERE WAS AN OLD PIG—*American Rhyme*	I	107
THERE WAS AN OLD WOMAN—*English Rhyme*	I	27
THERE WAS AN OLD WOMAN—*Chinese Rhyme*	I	76
THERE WAS AN OLD WOMAN OF HARROW—*English Rhyme*	I	26
THERE WAS AN OLD WOMAN TOSSED UP IN A BASKET—*English Rhyme*	I	41
THERE WAS AN OLD WOMAN WHO LIVED IN A SHOE—*English Rhyme*	I	43
THERE WAS AN OWL—*English Rhyme*	I	50
THERE WERE THREE DUCKIES—*Dutch Rhyme*	I	127
THERE WERE TWO BLACKBIRDS—*English Rhyme*	I	51
THERE WERE TWO LITTLE BOYS—*Swedish Rhyme*	I	74
THERE'S NOT A BUDDING BOY—*Robert Herrick*	I	208
THIS LITTLE ANT WORKED WITH MIGHT AND MAIN—*Mexican Rhyme*	I	71
THIS LITTLE PIG WENT TO MARKET—*English Rhyme*	I	19
THIS ONE STOLE AN EGG—*Mexican Rhyme*	I	71
THOR—*From the saga of King Olaf by Henry Wadsworth Longfellow*	IX	171
Thorne-Thomsen, Gudrun—*Norwegian*		
The Doll Under the Briar Rosebush—*Translated by*	III	204
Why the Sea Is Salt	V	144

	VOL.	PAGE

THOR'S JOURNEY TO JOTUN-HEIM—
Norse Myth .... IX 164

THREE JOVIAL HUNTSMEN........ III 110

THREE LITTLE KITTENS—*English
Rhyme* .... I 53

THREE OLD MAIDS A-SKATING
WENT—*American Rhyme* .... I 110

THREE TRUCKS, THE—*Adapted from
The Three Autos by Lucy Sprague Mitchell* I 177

THREE WISHES, THE—*Spanish Fairy
Tale* .... VI 92

THROUGH THE JUNGLE—*East Indian
Rhyme* .... I 79

Thumb, Tom
See Tom Thumb

THUNDER AND LIGHTNING—*Olive
Beaupré Miller* .... I 195

THUS I GUARD MY MOTHER'S
LAMBKINS—*Finnish Rhyme* .... I 144

TING-A-LING-LING—*American Rhyme*. I 84

Tin Woodman—*The Wizard of Oz*....... VI 62

Tippett, James S.—*American*
Groceries .... I 182
Park Play .... I 189

TIPPITY WITCHIT'S HALLOWE'EN
—*Olive Beaupré Miller* .... IV 145

Titania—*A Midsummer Night's Dream*.... VI 38

TO MARKET, TO MARKET—*English
Rhyme* .... I 33

TOADS IN THE LAKE, THE—*South
American Rhyme* .... I 68

Tolstoy, Leo N.—*Russian (1828-1910)*
Uncle Mitya's Horse................ II 46
Biog. Sketch (A Boy in Russia)...... XII 190

Tom—*Maggie Tulliver Goes to Live with
the Gypsies* .... VIII 189

Tom Thumb—*The Story of Tom Thumb*.. V 11

Tom Thumb, General (Charles Stratton)—
See General Tom Thumb

TOM, TOM, THE PIPER'S SON—*English
Rhyme* .... I 34

TOMMY WAS A SILLY BOY—*Kate
Greenaway* .... I 150

TONGUE-CUT SPARROW, THE—
Teresa Peirce Williston................ III 165

Toto—*The Wizard of Oz*............... VI 62

TRAGIC STORY, A—*Translated by
William Makepeace Thackeray*........ IV 136

TRAMP OF THE MIDDLE WEST, A—
*Biographical Sketch of
Nicholas Vachel Lindsay*.............. XII 147

TRIAL BY FIRE, THE—
*Maorian Folk Tale
from New Zealand* .... VII 26

TROPICAL MORNING AT SEA, A—
Edward Rowland Sill .... VI 201

Trowbridge, John Townsend—*American
(1827-1916)*
Evening at the Farm............... X 79

	VOL.	PAGE

TRUMPET OF THE SWAN, THE—
E. B. White .... IX 106

Tsuru—*Japanese*
Willows in the Snow.............. VI 197

Tuck, Friar
See Friar Tuck

Tudur ap Einion—*The Youth Who Wanted
Some Fun* .... VII 20

TURKEY IN THE STRAW—*American
Rhyme* .... I 113

TURTLE WHO COULD NOT STOP
TALKING, THE—*East Indian Fable*... II 178

Tusser, Thomas—*English (1524-1580)*
At Christmas Play and Make Good
Cheer—*From the Farmer's Daily Diet* II 217

TWELVE DANCING PRINCESSES,
THE—*German Folk Tale* .... IV 28

TWILIGHT, THE—*Madison Cawein*..... II 41

TWINKLING BUGS .... III 61

TWO BIRDS AND THEIR NEST—
Walt Whitman .... II 45

TWO CHILDREN—*Translated by Elizabeth
Barrett Browning from the German of
Heinrich Heine* .... II 138

TWO CRABS, THE—*Adapted from Aesop* II 33

U

UGLY DUCKLING, THE—*Retold from
Hans Christian Andersen*.............. II 131

UNA AND THE RED CROSS KNIGHT
—*Retold from Book I of The Faerie
Queene by Edmund Spenser*.......... XI 8

UNCLE MITYA'S HORSE—*Leo N.
Tolstoy* .... II 46

Uncle Remus—*A Story About the Little
Rabbits* .... III 123

UNDER THE GREENWOOD TREE—
William Shakespeare .... XI 72

Untermeyer, Louis—*American*
The Dog of Pompeii............... VII 145

UP IN THE GREEN ORCHARD—
English Rhyme .... I 30

V

Vanilla—*The King's Cream* .... VI 209

Vanya—*Christening the Baby in Russia*... IV 63

Vass, George—*American*
The Loneliest Battler .... XII 79
The Lone Star Team of Texas........ XII 170
The Man Who Made Adolf Hitler Run XII 104

Vera—*The Melting Pot*................ XI 173

VILLAGE OF CREAM PUFFS, THE—
Carl Sandburg .... II 124

Vinci, Leonardo da—*The Wonderland of
an Artist's Workshop* .... VI 164

Violet—*Pigling and Her Proud Sister*..... VI 191

Virgil—*Roman (70-19 B.C.)*
The Wanderings of Aeneas—*Retold
from the Latin* .... X 203
Comments (Dante's Voyage to the
Inferno, Purgatory, and Paradise).. XI 156

VOL. PAGE

VLADIMIR'S ADVENTURES IN SEARCH OF FORTUNE—*Yugoslavian Tale from Serbia* .... VII 102

W

Wadsworth, Olive A.—*American*
Over in the Meadow .... I 138
Wainamoinen—*Kalevala, Land of Heroes* .. X 151
WAKE UP, JACOB—*American Rhyme* ... I 84
Waldorf, Margaret—*American*
The First Moon Landing .... XII 30
Walker, Marian—*American*
Sally's Blue Ball .... I 188
WANDERER'S SONG, A—*John Masefield* VIII 91
WANDERINGS OF AENEAS, THE—*An epic of the Romans, retold from the Latin of Virgil* .... X 203
Washington, George—*George Washington and the First American Flag* .... V 118
WATER BABY, THE ADVENTURES OF A—*told from Water Babies by Charles Kingsley* .... III 211
Watts, Isaac—*English (1674-1748)*
How Doth the Little Busy Bee .... I 143
'WAY DOWN SOUTH IN DIXIE—*Biog. Sketch of Joel Chandler Harris* .... XII 138
WE THANK THEE—*Ralph Waldo Emerson* .... V 117
WEE ROBIN'S CHRISTMAS SONG—*Scottish Folk Tale* .... II 209
WEE, WEE MANNIE AND THE BIG, BIG COO, THE—*Scottish Folk Tale* ... III 99
WEE WILLIE WINKIE—*English Rhyme* . I 28
WE'VE COME TO SEE MISS JENNY JONES—*American Rhyme* .... I 89
WHALING ADVENTURE, A .... VIII 132
WHAT ARE YOU ABLE TO BUILD WITH YOUR BLOCKS?—*Robert Louis Stevenson* .... I 164
WHAT DOES LITTLE BIRDIE SAY?—*Alfred Tennyson* .... I 154
WHAT THE CHILDREN DO IN SUMMER—*Pearl S. Buck* .... I 212
WHAT THEY SAY—*Mary Mapes Dodge* . I 207
WHAT'S THE NEWS OF THE DAY—*English Rhyme* .... I 37
WHAT'S YOUR NAME?—*American Rhyme* .... I 95
WHEN I GO A-COURTING—*American Rhyme* .... I 92
WHEN I SEE A LADY—*South American Rhyme* .... I 69
WHEN I WAS A BABY—*Estonian Folk Song* .... I 145
WHEN I WAS DOWN BESIDE THE SEA —*Robert Louis Stevenson* .... I 159
WHEN MRS. BIRD WANTS MR. BIRD —*South American Rhyme* .... I 68

VOL. PAGE

WHEN THAT I WAS BUT A LITTLE TINY BOY—*William Shakespeare* ..... I 149
WHEN UNCLE HENRY WAS A LITTLE TINY BOY—*American Rhyme* .... I 97
WHEN WOODS AWAKE—*Old English Ballad* .... I 57
WHERE ARE MY ROSES?—*Athenaeus* .. I 205
WHERE BE YOU GOING, YOU DEVON MAID?—*John Keats* .... I 152
WHERE GO THE BOATS?—*Robert Louis Stevenson* .... III 94
WHERE, O WHERE HAS MY LITTLE DOG GONE—*German-American Rhyme* I 107
WHISKY FRISKY .... II 82
White, E. B.—*American*
Charlotte's Web .... V 54
The Trumpet of the Swan........... IX 106
WHITE FIELDS—*James Stephens*....... I 193
WHITE HEN SITTING, A—*Christina Rossetti* .... I 156
Whitman, Walt—*American (1819-1892)*
Two Birds and Their Nest........... II 45
Comments (The Harvard Professor).. XII 135
Whittier, John Greenleaf—*American (1807-1892)*
The Pumpkin .... IV 23
WHO CAN CRACK NUTS?—*Mary Mapes Dodge* .... IV 82
WHO HAS SEEN THE WIND?—*Christina Rossetti* .... I 201
WHO'S ON THE ROOF?—*Spanish Rhyme* I 64
WHY THE SEA IS SALT—*Norse Folk Tale* .... V 144
Wilbur—*Charlotte's Web* .... V 54
WILBUR WRIGHT AND ORVILLE WRIGHT—*Rosemary and Stephen Vincent Benét* .... V 66
WILD FLOWERS—*Peter Newell*........ VI 69
Wilde, Oscar—*English, born in Ireland (1856-1900)*
The Selfish Giant.................. IV 50
Wilder, Laura Ingalls—*American*
Little House in the Big Woods....... IX 119
Will Scarlet—*Ye Merry Doinges of Robin Hood* .... XI 49
Williams, Daniel Hale—*Pioneer in Surgery* XII 154
WILLIAM T. TRINITY—*American Rhyme* .... I 98
William Tell—*The Legend of William Tell* X 44
WILLIE BOY, WILLIE BOY—*English* ... I 45
Williston, Teresa Peirce—*American*
The Tongue-Cut Sparrow........... III 165
WILLOWS IN THE SNOW—*Tsuru* ...... VI 197
Wilson, James—*American*
Casey's Comeback .... VII 144f
Wilson, T. Woodrow—*American (1856-1924)*
Your America—*An address to new-made citizens* .... XI 216

	VOL.	PAGE
WIND AND THE SUN, THE—*Aesop*...	III	196
WIND BLOWETH WHERE IT LIST-ETH, THE—*From the Bible (Jesus of Nazareth)*	II	79
Wing Tip, the Spick—*The Village of Cream Puffs*	II	124
WINKY-TOODEN SONG, A—*James Whitcomb Riley*	I	215
WINNIE-THE-POOH—*A. A. Milne*	V	68
WINTER'S TALE, THE—*Charles and Mary Lamb*	VII	146
WIZARD OF OZ, THE—*L. Frank Baum*	VI	62
WOLFERT WEBBER, OR GOLDEN DREAMS—*Tale of old New York*	XI	107
WOMAN HAD A ROOSTER, A—*Polish Rhyme*	I	73
WONDERFUL WORLD, THE—*William Brighty Rands*	III	11
WONDERLAND OF AN ARTIST'S WORKSHOP, THE—*A story about Leonardo da Vinci*	VI	164
WORD OF IGOR'S ARMAMENT, THE —*Retold from an old Russian epic of the 12th Century*	X	119
Wordsworth, William—*English (1770-1850)*		
The Cock Is Crowing	I	208
The Kitten and Falling Leaves	III	133
WORLD IS SO FULL, THE—*Robert Louis Stevenson*	I	17
Wotan—*The Tale of the Rhine-Gold*	XI	73
WOULD YOU LIKE TO SEE GOATS DANCE ON STILTS?—*German Rhyme*	I	121
WYNKEN, BLYNKEN, AND NOD—*Eugene Field*	II	24

	VOL.	PAGE
Wynne, Annette—*American*		
Indian Children	III	93
Little Maid of Far Japan	III	164
In Columbus' Time	V	112

Y

	VOL.	PAGE
YANKEE DOODLE—*American Rhyme*	I	101
YANKEE PEDDLER, THE—*Olive Beaupré Miller*	V	130
Yarmil—*The Prince Who Rode Through a Mousehole*	VII	96
Yaroslavna—*The Word of Igor's Armament*	X	119
YE MERRY DOINGES OF ROBIN HOOD	XI	49
Yehl—*How Yehl, the Hero, Freed the Beaming Maiden*	VI	102
YES, THAT'S THE GIRL THAT STRUTS ABOUT—*Kate Greenaway*...	III	26
Yevrosima—*Marko, the Champion of Serbian Liberty*	XI	29
YOUNG MIDSHIPMAN DAVID FARRAGUT—*Biog. Sketch*	VIII	84
YOUR AMERICA—*An address to new-made citizens by T. Woodrow Wilson*...	XI	216
YOUTH WHO WANTED SOME FUN, THE—*Welsh Fairy Tale*	VII	20

Z

	VOL.	PAGE
Zandilli—*The Lost Spear*	VI	132
Zangwill, Israel—*English (1864-1926)*		
The Melting Pot	XI	173
Note	XI	216
ZOO IN THE PARK, THE	I	186

Special Subjects Index

This index groups together under topical headings all *related* material in MY BOOK HOUSE pertaining to, or illustrating, a specific subject. If a parent or child wishes to find stories having reference to a certain country, for example, he will find such stories listed under the name of that country, under the general heading, *Countries of the World*. If the special interest is in birds, he will find all selections referring to them under the heading, *Nature—Birds*. Likewise, boat or train selections are listed alphabetically under *Transportation—Boat* or *Train*. This index will be especially helpful to the school child in finding special reference material or supplementary reading.

This index also includes a listing of Famous People who are referred to *only* in notes and comments. Among these are authors whose names are *not* included in the Index of Authors, Titles, and Leading Characters.

	VOL.	PAGE
ACTION RHYMES		
See IN YOUR HANDS—Chaper IV		
ADVENTURE STORIES		
A Song of Drake's Men—(*Poem*)	VIII	7
A Boy on the High Seas—*Biog.*		
Sketch of Joshua Barney	VIII	8
Gulliver's Travels to Lilliput	VIII	38
Young Midshipman David Farragut—		
Biog. Sketch	VIII	84
John Paul Jones—*Biog. Sketch*	VIII	82
A Whaling Adventure	VIII	142a
Mr. Hampden's Shipwreck	VIII	172
Pushing Westward with Lewis and		
Clark	IX	25
Exploring the Wilderness—*Biog.*		
Sketch of Daniel Boone	IX	9
Buffalo Bill—*James Daugherty*	IX	27
The Adventures of Alexander Selkirk	IX	41
George Rogers Clark and the Conquest		
of the Northwest	IX	66
The Rough Rider—*Biog. Sketch of*		
Theodore Roosevelt	IX	72
How Peary Reached the North Pole	IX	127
Wolfert Webber, or Golden Dreams	XI	107
The First Moon Landing	XII	30
Señor Kon-Tiki	XII	45
AFRICA		
See COUNTRIES OF THE WORLD—		
Africa		
AIRPLANE		
See TRANSPORTATION—Airplane		
ALASKA		
See COUNTRIES OF THE WORLD—		
Alaska		
AMERICA		
See COUNTRIES OF THE WORLD—		
United States of America		

	VOL.	PAGE
ANIMALS		
See NATURE—Animals		
ARABIA		
See COUNTRIES OF THE WORLD—		
Arabia		
ARBOR DAY		
See NATURE—Trees		
ARMENIA		
See COUNTRIES OF THE WORLD—		
Armenia		
ARTISTS AND ILLUSTRATORS IN MY BOOK HOUSE		
ENDPAPERS—Ray Naylor—*American*		
VOLUME ONE		
COVER PICTURE—RICARDO		
MAGNI—*Italian*		
Angelico, Fra—*Italian* (1387-1455)		
(*Pictures suggested by his paintings*		
—see note on page 218)		
Breuer, Matilda—*American*		
Crane, Donn P.—*American* (1878-		
1944)		
Enright, Maginel Wright—*American*		
Ferring, Cyril P.—*American*		
Greenaway, Kate—*English* (1846-		
1901)		
(*Author and Illustrator—see notes*		
on pages 150, 151)		
Heath, Gordon—*American*		
Hollings, The—*American*		
Hurford, Miriam Story—*American*		
Martin, Mary—*American*		
Moran, Constance—*American*		
Nelson, Don—*American*		
Petersham, Maud—*American*		
Petersham, Miska—*Hungarian*		
Turner, Mariel Wilhoite—*American*		
Ward, Keith—*American*		

ARTISTS AND ILLUSTRATORS (*Continued*)

VOLUME TWO
  COVER PICTURE—MILO
    WINTER—*American*
  Breuer, Matilda
  Brown, Hazel—*American*
  Collier, Corina M.—*American*
  Crane, Donn P.
  Enright, Maginel Wright
  Farnam, Nellie H.—*American*
  Ferring, Cyril P.
  Heath, Gordon
  Hollings, The
  Horton, Elizabeth—*American*
  Hurford, Miriam Story
  Martin, Mary
  Moran, Constance
  Nelson, Don
  Turner, Mariel Wilhoite
  Ward, Keith

VOLUME THREE
  COVER PICTURE—LILIAN
    WESTCOTT HALE—*American*
    (*Daughter of Edward Everett Hale.*
    The little girl on cover is grand-
    daughter of Edward Everett Hale.)
  Bianco, Pamela—*English*
  Breuer, Matilda
  Caldecott, Randolph—*English*
    (1846-1886)
    (*See notes on pages 63, 197*)
  Chamberlin, Helen—*American*
  Cheney, Garnett—*American*
  Cox, Palmer—*Canadian-American*
    (1840-1924)
    (*Author and Illustrator—see note on*
    page 40)
  Crane, Donn P.
  Crane, Walter—*English* (1845-1915)
    (*Pictures modeled on his illustra-*
    tions—see notes on pages 196, 197)
  Davis, Marguerite—*American*
  Dodge, Katharine Sturges—
    American
  Elliott, Bertram R.—*American*
  Enright, Maginel Wright
  Greenaway, Kate
    (*Author and Illustrator—see notes*
    on pages 26, 27, 197)
  Gruelle, Johnny—*American*
    (1880-1938)
  Hetherington, Mildred Lyon—
    American
  Kemble, E. W.—*American*
    (1861-1933)
  Ketchum, Glen—*American*
  McBarron, H. C.—*American*
  Martin, Mary
  Miller, Martha E.—*American*
  Nelson, Don
  Parks, Billie—*American*
  Petersham, Maud and Miska
  Reynolds, K.—*American*

Rudeen, Herbert N.—*American*
Shepard, E. H.—*English*
  (*See note on page 70*)
Simpson, Salter—*American*
Todd, Dorothy—*American*
Turner, Mariel Wilhoite
Wuerfel, Lilian B.—*American*

VOLUME FOUR
  COVER PICTURE—JOSEPH
    CHENOWETH—*American*
  Birch, Reginald—*English*
    (1856-1943)
  Breuer, Matilda
  Brown, Hazel
  Crane, Donn P.
  Davis, Marguerite
  Ferring, Cyril P.
  Hetherington, Mildred Lyon
  Horton, Elizabeth
  Laufer, Anna
  Lofting, Hugh—*English* (1886-1947)
    (*Author and Illustrator—see note on*
    page 114)
  McBarron, H. C.
  Martin, Mary
  Nelson, Don
  Newell, Peter—*American*
    (1862-1924)
    (*Author and Illustrator*)
  Parks, Billie
  Petersham, Maud and Miska
  Pogany, Willy—*Hungarian*
    (1882-1955)
  Turner, Mariel Wilhoite

VOLUME FIVE
  COVER PICTURE—J. ALLEN
    ST. JOHN—*American*
  Brown, Hazel
  Crane, Donn P.
  Cruikshank, George—*English*
    (1792-1878)
    (*See note on page 20*)
  Currier and Ives—*American*
    (*See notes on pages 116, 117*)
  Elliott, Bertram R.
  Hetherington, Mildred Lyon
  Lee, Doris—*American*
  McAnnelly, Florence M.—*American*
  McBarron, H. C.
  Moran, Constance
  Naylor, Ray
  Rossiter, T. P.—*American*
    (1818-1871)
    (*See note on page 125*)
  Rudeen, Herbert N.
  Shepard, E. H.—*English*
  Todd, Dorothy
  Trumbull, John—*American*
    (1756-1843)
    (*See note on page 120*)
  Turner, Mariel Wilhoite
  Williams, Garth—*American*

ARTISTS AND ILLUSTRATORS (*Continued*)
  VOLUME SIX
    COVER PICTURE—ALICE
      BEARD—*American*
    Adams, Pauline B.—*American*
    Armstrong, George D., Jr.—*American*
    Crane, Donn P.
    Denslow, W. W.—*American*
    Dodge, Katharine Sturges
    Gruelle, Johnny
    Hetherington, Mildred Lyon
    Horton, Elizabeth
    Hurford, Miriam Story
    Lewin, Ted
    McAfee, Ida—*American*
    McBarron, H. C.
    Michelangelo—*Italian* (1475-1564)
      (*Note on page 164*)
    Miller, Martha E.
    Nelson, Don
    Newell, Peter
      (*Author and Illustrator*)
    Oughten, Taylor
    Rudeen, Herbert N.
    Sampson, Larry D.—*American*
    Turpin, Fay—*American*
    Vinci, Leonardo da—*Italian*
      (1452-1519)
      (*For story about, see page 164, notes
      on pages 164, 165*)
  VOLUME SEVEN
    COVER PICTURE—J. ALLEN
      ST. JOHN
    Collier, Corina M.
    Crane, Donn P.
    Gauguin, Paul—*French* (1848-1903)
      (*Note on page 26*)
    Greene, Hamilton
    Horton, Elizabeth
    Ketchum, Glen
    Laufer, Anna
    McBarron, H. C.
    Miller, Martha E.
    Naylor, Ray
    Petersham, Maud and Miska
    Riley, Garada C.—*American*
    Sarg, Tony—*American* (1882-1942)
    Savitt, Sam
    Turner, Mariel Wilhoite
    Winter, Milo
    Zavada, Emerich
  VOLUME EIGHT
    COVER PICTURE—J. ALLEN
      ST. JOHN
    Charleson, Malcolm D.
    Crane, Donn P.
    Elliott, Bertram R.
    Laufer, Anna
    Petersham, Maud and Miska
    Pyle, Howard—*American*
      (1853-1911)
      (*Author and Illustrator—see note on
      page 142*)
    Turner, Mariel Wilhoite
  VOLUME NINE
    COVER PICTURE—N. C.
      WYETH—*American* (1882-1945)
    Burger, Carl

    Charleson, Malcolm D.
    Daugherty, James
    Elliott, Bertram R.
    Frascino, Edward
    Horton, Elizabeth
    Moran, Constance
    Pogany, Willy
    Sheffer, Glen C.—*American*
    Thackeray, William Makepeace—
      English (1811-1863)
      (*Author and Illustrator—see note on
      page 177*)
    Westland, C. O.—*American*
    Williams, Garth
  VOLUME TEN
    COVER PICTURE—MALCOLM
      D. CHARLESON—*American*
    Armstrong, George
    Brown, Hazel
    Charleson, Malcolm D.
    Crane, Donn P.
    Hurford, Miriam Story
    Martin, Mary
    Petersham, Maud and Miska
    Pogany, Willy
    Shatte, Fern—*American*
    Simpson, Walter
  VOLUME ELEVEN
    COVER PICTURE—J. ALLEN
      ST. JOHN
    Charleson, Malcolm D.
    Crane, Donn P.
    Turner, Mariel Wilhoite
    Ward, Keith
  VOLUME TWELVE
    COVER PICTURE—J. ALLEN
      ST. JOHN
    Crane, Donn P.
    Downs, John
    Grifalconi, Ann
    Ketchum, Glen
    Kohn, Arnie
    Petersham, Maud and Miska
    Savage, Steele
    Wood, Chuck

AUSTRALIA
  See COUNTRIES OF THE WORLD—
  Australia

AUSTRIA
  See COUNTRIES OF THE WORLD—
  Austria

AUTHORS IN MY BOOK HOUSE
  See COUNTRIES OF THE WORLD
  for listings according to nationality.
  See also AUTHORS, TITLES, AND
  LEADING CHARACTERS INDEX
  for alphabetical listings.

AUTOMOBILE
  See TRANSPORTATION—Automobile

BAGPIPE
  See MUSICAL INSTRUMENTS—
  Bagpipe

BAKER
  See OCCUPATIONS—Baker

BALI
  See COUNTRIES OF THE WORLD—
  Bali

VOL. PAGE

BALLOON
See TRANSPORTATION—Balloon

BASEBALL HEROES
Babe Ruth, the Home-Run King
of Baseball .... VII 144a
Casey at the Bat.................... VII 144c
Casey's Comeback .... VII 144f
The Loneliest Battler .... XII 79

BELGIUM
See COUNTRIES OF THE WORLD—
Belgium

BELLS
See MUSICAL INSTRUMENTS—
Gongs and Bells

BIBLE SELECTIONS
Old Noah (*New England Song*)....... I 112
Songs of Joy from the Bible.......... I 216
Mary and the Christ-Child—*Based on
the story of the Nativity*............ I 218
Spring Songs from the Bible.......... II 78
Noah's Ark (*Retold*)................ II 101
The Song of Solomon............... III 136
The Babe Moses (*Retold*).......... III 156
The Boy Samuel (*Retold*)........... IV 80
Daniel in the Lions' Den............. VI 180
The Sky at Night.................... VII 72
David, the Shepherd Boy............ VII 73
Gideon, the Warrior................. IX 134
Joseph and His Brethren............ X 48

BIOGRAPHICAL SKETCHES
Alcott, Louisa May.................. XII 122
Barney, Joshua .... VIII 8
Barnum, Phineas T................. VIII 144
Boone, Daniel .... IX 9
Bruce, Robert .... X 21
Carnegie, Andrew .... XII 60
Chaucer, Geoffrey .... XII 11
Clark, George Rogers............... IX 66
Clark, William .... IX 25
Cody, William (Buffalo Bill)......... IX 27
Dickens, Charles .... XII 102
Didrikson, Babe .... XII 170
Douglass, Frederick .... XII 198
Einstein, Albert .... XII 218
Fabre, Jean Henri.................. VI 184
Farragut, David .... VIII 84
Fulton, Robert .... V 48
Goodall, Jane (Baroness van Lawick-
Goodall) .... XII 70
Harris, Joel Chandler............... XII 138
Heyerdahl, Thor .... XII 45
Irving, Washington .... XII 99
Joan of Arc........................ X 98
Jones, John Paul................... VIII 82
Lawick-Goodall, Baroness Jane van.... XII 70
Lee, Robert E...................... XI 170c
Lewis, Meriwether .... IX 25
Lincoln, Abraham .... V 129
Lindsay, Nicholas Vachel........... XII 147
Longfellow, Henry Wadsworth........ XII 135
Mendelssohn, Felix .... VI 58
Miller, Cincinnatus Heine
(Joaquin Miller) .... XII 143
Owens, Jesse .... XII 104
Peary, Robert Edwin .... IX 127

VOL. PAGE

Riley, James Whitcomb .... XII 141
Robinson, Jackie .... XII 79
Roosevelt, Theodore .... IX 72
Ruth, George Herman (Babe) .... VII 144a
Selkirk, Alexander .... IX 41
Shakespeare, William .... XII 15
Tolstoy, Leo N..................... XII 190
Vinci, Leonardo da................. III 148
Washington, George .... V 116
Watt, James .... V 45
Williams, Daniel Hale............... VII 154

BIRDS
See NATURE—Birds

BIRD CALLS
See NATURE—Bird Calls

BLACKS
Famous People
Learning To Be Free............... XII 198
The Loneliest Battler.............. XII 79
The Man Who Made Adolf Hitler Run XII 104
Pioneer in Surgery................. XII 154
Stories and Poems
Jasper the Drummin' Boy.......... VI 108
The Negro Speaks of Rivers........ XII 188

BLACKSMITH
See OCCUPATIONS—Blacksmith

BOATS
See TRANSPORTATION—Boats;
TOYS—Boat

BRAZIL
See COUNTRIES OF THE WORLD—
Brazil

BRIDGE
Illustration .... I 65
How Strong, How Strong a Bridge
Have You? .... I 129
Illustration .... I 150
Trip: San Francisco .... I 210
Building the Bridge................. II 149
A Happy Day in the City........... III 181

BROOK
See NATURE—Brook

BROWNIES
See ELVES AND BROWNIES

BUGLE
See MUSICAL INSTRUMENTS—
Bugle

BUILDER
See OCCUPATIONS—Builder

BUS
See TRANSPORTATION—Bus

BUTCHER
See OCCUPATIONS—Butcher

CALLIOPE
See MUSICAL INSTRUMENTS—
Calliope

CANADA
See COUNTRIES OF THE WORLD—
Canada

CAR
See TRANSPORTATION—
Automobile

VOL. PAGE

CARAVAN
See TRANSPORTATION—Caravan

CARRIAGE
See TRANSPORTATION—Carriage

CART
See TRANSPORTATION—Cart

CATARACT
See NATURE—Cataract

CHARIOT
See TRANSPORTATION—Chariot

CHINA
See COUNTRIES OF THE WORLD—
China

CHRISTMAS
See HOLIDAYS—Christmas

CIRCUS
Go Ask Your Mother for Fifty Cents.. I 104
Jumbo Was an Elephant .... I 105
The Circus Parade.................. III 46
The Circus Man..................... VIII 144
The Greatest Show on Earth......... VIII 149

CITIZENSHIP
The First Thanksgiving Day .... V 113
George Washington and the First
   American Flag .... V 118
Robert E. Lee...................... XI 170c
Lincoln's Gettysburg Address .... XI 170a
The Melting Pot.................... XI 173
Your America .... XI 216

CITY
Lines for a City Child.............. I 185
A Happy Day in the City........... III 181

CLOUDS
See NATURE—Clouds

COBBLER
See OCCUPATIONS—Cobbler

COLOMBIA
See COUNTRIES OF THE WORLD—
Colombia

COLUMBUS DAY
See HOLIDAYS—Columbus Day

COMPOSERS IN MY BOOK HOUSE
See MUSIC—Composers for
   alphabetical listings
See also COUNTRIES OF
   THE WORLD for listings
   according to nationality

COOK
See OCCUPATIONS—Cook

COSTUMES (Illustrations)
See also IN YOUR HANDS—
   Chapter XX
AFRICAN .... I 146,
   147
   Moroccan .... IX 114
AMERICAN
   Colonial .... I 82,
   83, 101
   V 117-
   123
   Cowboy .... I 100
   IV 193

VOL. PAGE

   Indian .... I 80,
   81
   III 93
   V 222,
   VI 71
   VIII 148
   IX 88-
   97
   Pennsylvania Dutch .... I 116,
   117
   Pilgrim .... V 113,
   114
   Quaker .... I 82
   Revolutionary War Uniforms .... I 101
   V 116-
   125

BALINESE .... II 176,
   177

BELGIAN .... II 141
BIBLICAL .... I 218-
   223
   II 78,
   79, 101-104
   III 156-
   159
   IV 80
   VII 73-
   83
   IX 134-
   139

CANADIAN .... I 130
   IV 180-
   182

CHINESE .... I 76,
   77
   III 19
   IV 139

CZECHOSLOVAKIAN .... I 128,
   129
   II 72-
   74, 140

DUTCH .... I 126,
   127
   II 164-
   171
   IV 56-
   62

EAST INDIAN .... II 179
   Hindustani .... I 79
   Javanese .... VI 202-
   207

EGYPTIAN
   Ancient .... VII 86,
   87
   Biblical .... III 159
ENGLISH .... I 45,
   150, 151, 155, 185, 208
   II 67,
   75, 152
   III 26,
   27, 63-68
   Court .... III 70,
   71, 75

VOL. PAGE

COSTUMES (Illustrations)
ENGLISH (*Continued*)

Elizabethan   I   44,
49

Medieval   I   57
V   33-
44, 86, 87
XI   53,
57, 61
XII   11

Shakespearean   I   148,
149, 209
X   166,
170
XII   15,
18, 19, 27

ESKIMO   I   131
IV   186

FRENCH   I   124

Medieval   X   98,
107

GERMAN   I   121
II   140
IV   34-
44
V   162-
179

GRECIAN (Ancient)   I   204,
205
X   203-
227

HUNGARIAN   I   136
VII   11-
19

IRISH   I   59
II   155-
162

Medieval   X   195,
198

ITALIAN   I   62,
63

Medieval   XI   152,
153

JAPANESE   III   164-
167

KOREAN   VI   191,
193

MEXICAN   I   70,
71

NEW ZEALAND (Maorian).........   VII   26-
30

NORWEGIAN   I   60,
61
III   140-
145
IV   27
V   140-
145
VII   48-
70
IX   102,
104

POLISH   I   72,
73

ROMAN
See COSTUMES—Italian

ROUMANIAN   I   137
VII   41-
46

RUSSIAN   I   132,
133
II   218-
222
IV   65,
68, 72
XII   190-
197

Medieval   X   118,
125, 127

SCOTTISH   I   29,
58, 153
X   20

Medieval   X   25,
29

SOUTH AMERICAN (Colombian)...   I   69

SPANISH   I   64,
65

Medieval   V   112
X   110-
115

SWEDISH   I   74,
75
II   141
III   12-
18
IV   46-
49

SWISS   I   66,
67

TURKISH   II   52-
56

WELSH   I   58

YUGOSLAVIAN (Serbian)   VII   106

COUNTING RHYMES
See also IN YOUR HANDS—
Chapter X

Baa, Baa, Black Sheep..............   I   29
Diddle, Diddle, Dumpling............   I   37
Old King Cole.....................   I   44
Rub-a-Dub-Dub   I   48
There Were Two Blackbirds..........   I   51
Three Little Kittens................   I   53
Dame Durden   I   58
Row! Row! A-Fishing We'll Go!......   I   61
Five Little Chicks.................   I   64
There Were Two Little Boys..........   I   74
Engine, Engine Number Nine........   I   85
Here Come Three Jolly, Jolly Sailor
Boys   I   96
One, Two, Three, Four..............   I   99
John Brown Had a Little Indian.......   I   100
Three Old Maids a-Skating Went......   I   110
There Were Three Duckies   I   127
Mary Milks the Cow.................   I   135
Over in the Meadow.................   I   138
Ten Little Indians..................   II   94

COUNTRIES OF THE WORLD
AFRICA (Continent)
African Child Rhymes   I   146

COUNTRIES OF THE WORLD

AFRICA (Continued)

	VOL.	PAGE
The Babe Moses (*Egyptian*)........	III	156
The Lost Spear (*South African*)....	VI	132
Snowflake the Gorilla..............	VI	159
Rhodopis and Her Gilded Sandals (*Egyptian*)	VII	84
Afar in the Desert (*South African*)..	VIII	36
Joseph and His Brethren (*Egyptian*).	X	48
Jane and the Wild Chimps (*Tanzania*).	XII	70

ALASKA (Forty-ninth State of the United States)

	VOL.	PAGE
How Yehl, the Hero, Freed the Beaming Maiden	VI	102

AMERICA
See COUNTRIES OF THE WORLD—United States of America

ARABIA

	VOL.	PAGE
The Magic Horse—*From The Arabian Nights*—(*Story and note*)	VIII	92
Recollections of The Arabian Nights.	VIII	108
The Story of the Talking Bird—*From The Arabian Nights*........	VIII	109

ARMENIA

	VOL.	PAGE
My Name Is Aram.................	VII	156

AUSTRALIA (Continent)

	VOL.	PAGE
The Right Time to Laugh..........	III	81

Composers
See MUSIC—Composers—Grainger

AUSTRIA

	VOL.	PAGE
The Nuremberg Stove..............	V	162

Composers
See MUSIC—Composers—Haydn; Franz Schubert; Johann Strauss

BALI (Island—Indonesia)

	VOL.	PAGE
A Boy in the Island of Bali (*Poem and notes*)	II	176

BELGIUM

	VOL.	PAGE
A Belgian Morning	II	141
How the Finch Got Her Colors.....	II	143

Authors
See AUTHORS, TITLES, AND LEADING CHARACTERS IN-DEX—Cammaerts

BRAZIL (South America)

	VOL.	PAGE
How the Brazilian Beetles Got Their Gorgeous Coats	III	172

CANADA

	VOL.	PAGE
Canadian Songs	I	130
The Story of Big Paul Bunyan (*Story and note*)...............	IV	161
A Song of the Canadian Lumber-jack	IV	180
The Strong Boy...................	VI	71
Battle Tactics	VII	165

Authors
See AUTHORS, TITLES, AND LEADING CHARACTERS IN-DEX—Carman, Mowat

CHINA

	VOL.	PAGE
Chinese Nursery Rhymes...........	I	76
The Road to China................	III	19
The Girl Who Used Her Wits.......	IV	137

COLOMBIA (South America)

	VOL.	PAGE
South American Rhymes...........	I	68

	VOL.	PAGE
Reen-Reen-Reeny-Croak-Frog	II	37
The Poor Old Lady...............	II	68

Authors
See AUTHORS, TITLES, AND LEADING CHARACTERS IN-DEX—Pombo; Restrepo

CZECHOSLOVAKIA

	VOL.	PAGE
Czechoslovakain Rhymes	I	128
The Little Rooster and the Little Hen	II	71
A Bohemian Evening..............	II	140
The Prince Who Rode Through a Mousehole	VII	96

Composers
See MUSIC—Composers—Dvorak; Friml

DENMARK
See AUTHORS, TITLES, AND LEADING CHARACTERS IN-DEX—Hans Christian Andersen

EGYPT
See COUNTRIES OF THE WORLD—Africa

ENGLAND

	VOL.	PAGE
English Nursery Rhymes............	I	18
The Little Red Hen and the Grain of Wheat	II	13
The Magpie's Nest	II	42
Goldilocks and the Three Bears.....	III	20
King Hilary and the Beggarman.....	III	70
The Butterfly's Ball................	III	162
Teeny-Tiny	IV	143
The Story of Tom Thumb..........	V	11
Jack and the Beanstalk............	V	20
Dick Whittington and His Cat......	V	33
How Jack Sought the Golden Apples	V	76
The Red Ettin....................	V	90
Jack the Giant-Killer...............	VI	140
The Adventures of General Tom Thumb	VIII	155
Sir Beaumains, the Kitchen Knight..	X	8
How Beowulf Delivered Heorot.....	X	80
Ye Merry Doinges of Robin Hood..	XI	49
The Interesting History of Old Mother Goose..................	XII	213

Artists and Illustrators
See ARTISTS AND ILLUSTRA-TORS for listings according to volumes—Birch; Caldecott; Walter Crane; Cruikshank; Greenaway; Lofting; Shepard; Thackeray

Authors
See AUTHORS, TITLES, AND LEADING CHARACTERS IN-DEX—Addison; Blake; Elizabeth Browning; Robert Browning; Byron; Carey; Carroll; Chaucer; Coleridge; Craik; Dasent; De la Mare; Dickens; Eliot; Ewing; Fyleman; Galsworthy; Grahame; Greenaway; Herrick; Hood; Howitt; Jacobs; Keats; Kingsley; Kipling; Charles Lamb; Mary Lamb; Lear; Lofting; Macdonell; Masefield; Meredith; Milne; Milton; Noyes; Pope; Potter; Louise de la Ramée; Rands; Ransome; Rossetti; Ruskin;

COUNTRIES OF THE WORLD

ENGLAND—Authors (*Continued*)
Shakespeare; Shelley; Southey;
Spenser; Taylor; Tennyson; Thackeray; Tusser; Watts; Wilde; Wadsworth; Zangwill

Composers
See MUSIC—Composers—Arne;
Bishop; Coleridge-Taylor; Purcell

Famous People referred to in Notes
and Comments
See FAMOUS PEOPLE—Queen
Anne; Austin; Bennett; Bronte;
Bunyan; Burke; Conrad; Cromwell;
Defoe; Edward I; Edward III;
Queen Elizabeth I; Garrick; Geof-
frey of Monmouth; Hardy; Hatha-
away; Hunt; Samuel Johnson; Ben
Jonson; Lovelace; Malory; Mar-
lowe; Newbery; Sir Walter Raleigh;
Charles Edward Stuart; Queen Vic-
toria; Wells.

ESTONIA
When I Was a Baby..............   I   145

FINLAND
Rhymes from Finland..............   I   144
Kalevala, Land of Heroes..........   X   151

Composers
See MUSIC—Composers—
Sibelius

FRANCE
French Nursery Rhymes...........   I   124
Cinderella   IV   12
The Sleeping Beauty..............   VI   11
The Fairyland of Science—*Biog.
Sketch of Jean Henri Fabre*........   VI   184
The Adventures of General Tom
Thumb   VIII   155
The Song of Roland..............   X   38
Joan of Arc—*Biog. Sketch*..........   X   98

Artists and Illustrators
See ARTISTS AND ILLUSTRA-
TORS for listings according to vol-
umes—Gauguin

Authors
See AUTHORS, TITLES, AND
LEADING CHARACTERS IN-
DEX—Chamisso; La Fontaine; Le
Fèvre; Perrault

Composers
See MUSIC—Composers—Berlioz;
Coucy; Damare; David; Debussy;
Gounod; Massenet; Ravel; Saint-
Saens; Thomas

Famous People referred to in Notes
and Comments
See FAMOUS PEOPLE—Lafay-
ette; George Sand

GERMANY
German Nursery Rhymes..........   I   120
A German Evening...............   II   140

The Shoemaker and the Elves.......   III   95
The Little Girl and the Hare.......   III   111
The Twelve Dancing Princesses......   IV   28
Snow-white and Rose-red..........   IV   34
Hansel and Grethel (*Story and note*)   IV   73
The Nuremberg Stove..............   V   162
A Musical Visit to Fairyland—*A
story of Felix Mendelssohn*.......   VI   59
The Six Swans...................   VII   126
The Golden Bird.................   VII   134

Authors
See AUTHORS, TITLES, AND
LEADING CHARACTERS IN-
DEX—Goethe; Jacob Grimm;
Wilhelm Grimm; Heine; Raspe;
Wilhelm Schiller

Composers
See MUSIC—Composers—Bach;
Beethoven; Brahms; Gluck; Han-
del; Humperdinck; Jessel; Krantz;
Mendelssohn; François Schubert;
Schumann; Richard Strauss; Wag-
ner; Weber

Famous People referred to in Notes
and Comments
See FAMOUS PEOPLE—Johann
Schiller

GREECE
Children's Songs of Ancient Greece
(*Songs and notes*)..............   I   204
The Battle of the Frogs and the
Mice (*Story and note*)..........   IV   104
Phaeton   VII   90
The Adventures of Perseus.........   IX   140
The Labors of Hercules............   IX   151
The Home-Coming of Odysseus.....   X   217

Authors
See AUTHORS, TITLES, AND
LEADING CHARACTERS IN-
DEX—Aesop; Aristophanes; Ath-
enaeus; Homer; Meleager; Theognis

HAWAII (Fiftieth State of the United
States)
The Fisherman Who Caught the Sun
(*Story and note*)................   VI   198

HOLLAND
Dutch Nursery Rhymes...........   I   126
Little Hansworst   II   164
The Little Toy Land of the Dutch...   IV   56
The Boy Hero of Harlem..........   IV   57

HUNGARY
Hungarian Rhymes   I   136
The Rooster and the Sultan.........   II   52
Miska and the Man-With-The-Iron-
Head (*Story and note*)..........   VII   11

Artists and Illustrators
See ARTISTS AND ILLUSTRA-
TORS for listings according to vol-
umes—Miska Petersham; Pogany

Composers
See MUSIC—Composers—Liszt;
Poldini

VOL. PAGE

COUNTRIES OF THE WORLD (*Continued*)
INDIA

East Indian Rhymes..............	I	79
Rama and the Tigers..............	II	118
Mowgli's Brothers	V	182
Paper Boats	II	139
The Turtle Who Could Not Stop Talking	II	178
The Foolish, Timid, Little Hare.....	III	76
The Ballad of East and West........	IX	129
The Exile of Rama...............	X	175

Authors
See AUTHORS, TITLES, AND LEADING CHARACTERS INDEX—Tagore

IRAN
See COUNTRIES OF THE WORLD—Persia

IRELAND

Rhymes from Ireland..............	I	59
The Bee, the Mouse, and the Bum-Clock	II	155
Cuculain, the Irish Hound..........	X	188

Authors
See AUTHORS, TITLES, AND LEADING CHARACTERS INDEX—Stephens; Swift

Composers
See MUSIC—Composers—Balfe

ITALY

Italian Nursery Rhymes............	I	62
The Wonderland of an Artist's Workshop—*A story about Leonardo da Vinci*	VI	164
Columbine and Her Playfellows of the Italian Pantomime	VII	119
The Dog of Pompeii...............	VII	145
Gigi and the Magic Ring...........	VII	199
The Wanderings of Aeneas (*Roman*)	X	203
The Man Who Lived in the World of Dreams—*A story about Dante Alighieri*	XI	152

Artists and Illustrators
See ARTISTS AND ILLUSTRATORS for listings according to volumes—Fra Angelico; Magni; Michelangelo; Leonardo da Vinci

Authors
See AUTHORS, TITLES, AND LEADING CHARACTERS INDEX—Dante Alighieri; Virgil

Composers
See MUSIC—Composers—Bazzini; Boito; Leoncavallo; Rossini; Verdi

VOL. PAGE

JAPAN

A Japanese Lullaby................	I	78
Little Pictures from Far Japan......	VI	196
The Moon-Maiden	VI	222
Note	XII	153

Authors
See AUTHORS, TITLES, AND LEADING CHARACTERS INDEX—Basho; Ransetsu; Tsuru

JAVA (Island—Indonesia)

Aruman, a Hero of Java...........	VI	202

KOREA

Pigling and Her Proud Sister.......	VI	191

MEXICO

Mexican Rhymes	I	70
A Child in a Mexican Garden......	IV	103

NEW ZEALAND

The Trial by Fire (*Maorian*).......	VII	26

NORWAY

Norse Nursery Rhymes...........	I	60, 134
Johnny and the Three Goats........	II	47
The Sheep and the Pig That Made a Home	II	145
Oeyvind and Marit—*A story of Norway*	III	137
Doll i' the Grass..................	IV	24
East o' the Sun and West o' the Moon	VII	31
Peer Gynt	IX	98
Thor's Journey to Jotun-heim.......	IX	164
Thor	IX	171
The Stealing of Iduna.............	IX	172
Frithjof, the Viking...............	X	130

Authors
See AUTHORS, TITLES, AND LEADING CHARACTERS INDEX—Asbjörnsen; Björnson; Ibsen; Jacoby; Moe; Thorne-Thomson

Composers
See MUSIC—Composers—Grieg

PALESTINE
See also BIBLE SELECTIONS

Get Up, Little Horsey (*Bethlehem*)..	I	65
Mary and the Christ-Child (*Bethlehem*)	I	218

PERSIA

A Story of Rustem, the Hero of Persia—*Retold from the Shah-Nameh* (*Book of Kings*).........	X	228

Authors
See AUTHORS, TITLES, AND LEADING CHARACTERS INDEX—Firdusi

PHILIPPINE ISLANDS

The Battle of the Firefly and the Apes	III	59

	VOL.	PAGE
COUNTRIES OF THE WORLD		
(*Continued*)		
POLAND		
Polish Rhymes	I	72
Composers		
See MUSIC—Composers—Chopin		
ROUMANIA		
A Roumanian Lullaby.............	I	137
The Maiden, the Knight, and the		
Waterfall	VII	40
RUSSIA		
Russian Rhymes	I	132
Building the Bridge...............	II	149
Christening the Baby in Russia......	IV	63
The Little-Man-As-Big-As-Your-		
Thumb-With-Mustaches-Seven-		
Miles-Long	VII	112
A Chronicle of Kiev...............	X	118
The Word of Igor's Armament......	X	119
The Melting Pot..................	XI	173
A Boy in Russia—*Biog. Sketch of*		
Leo N. Tolstoy..................	XII	190
Authors		
See AUTHORS, TITLES, AND		
LEADING CHARACTERS IN-		
DEX—Tolstoy		
Composers		
See MUSIC—Composers—Borodin;		
Rimski-Korsakov; Rubinstein;		
Tchaikovsky		
SCOTLAND		
Dance to Your Daddie.............	I	58
Wee Robin's Christmas Song........	II	209
The Wee, Wee Mannie and the Big,		
Big Coo	III	99
Jamie Watt and the Giant in the		
Teakettle	V	45
The Red Ettin	V	90
Gathering Song of Donuil Dhu......	X	20
Robert Bruce, Scotland's Hero		
(*Story and note*)...............	X	21
Bannockburn (*Address and note*) ...	X	29
Authors		
See AUTHORS, TITLES AND		
LEADING CHARACTERS IN-		
DEX— Bannerman; Barr; Burns;		
Hendry; MacDonald; Pringle; Scott;		
Setoun, Stevenson		
Famous People referred to in Notes		
and Comments		
See FAMOUS PEOPLE—James		
Boswell		
SPAIN		
Spanish Nursery Rhymes...........	I	64
The Three Wishes	VI	92
The Song of Roland...............	X	38
The Story of the Cid..............	X	108
The Surprising Adventures of Don		
Quixote of La Mancha..........	XI	90
Authors		
See AUTHORS, TITLES, AND		
LEADING CHARACTERS IN-		
DEX—Miguel de Cervantes		

	VOL.	PAGE
SWEDEN		
Swedish Rhymes	I	74
A Swedish Evening	II	141
The Cap That Mother Made........	III	12
Elsa and the Ten Elves............	IV	45
Authors		
See AUTHORS, TITLES, AND		
LEADING CHARACTERS IN-		
DEX—Fröding		
Famous People referred to in Notes		
and Comments		
See FAMOUS PEOPLE—Jenny		
Lind		
SWITZERLAND		
Swiss Nursery Rhymes	I	66
Heidi in the Alpine Pasture........	V	146
The Legend of William Tell (*Story*		
and notes)	X	44
Authors		
See AUTHORS, TITLES, AND		
LEADING CHARACTERS IN-		
DEX—Spyri		
UNITED STATES OF AMERICA		
American Indian Songs.............	I	80
American Rhymes	I	82-115
Pennsylvania Dutch Rhymes	I	116
A Song of the Railroad Men (*New*		
Mexico)	I	181
An American Miner's Song		
(*Pennsylvania*)	II	23
The Gingerbread Man (*New*		
England)	II	58
The Little Rabbit Who Wanted		
Red Wings (*Negro*)	II	87
Ten Little Indians.................	II	94
Shingebiss (*Chippewa Indian*).......	II	96
Indian Children	III	93
The Story of Li'l Hannibal (*Negro*).	III	116
A Story About the Little Rabbits		
(*Negro*)	III	123
How Brer Rabbit Met Brer Tar-Baby		
(*Negro*)	IV	130
The Story of Big Paul Bunyan......	IV	161
Old Stormalong	IV	183
There Goes A Scout...............	IV	194
The Cowboy's Life	IV	193
Pecos Bill, the Cowboy............	IV	195
Old Johnny Appleseed (*Story and*		
note)	IV	213
How Robert Fulton Harnessed the		
Giant	V	48
Casey Jones	V	64
Wilbur Wright and Orville Wright...	V	66
All About Columbus...............	V	112
The First Thanksgiving Day (*New*		
England)	V	113
George Washington and the First		
American Flag (*Story and notes*)..	V	118
The Yankee Peddler	V	130
The Fourth of July...............	V	129
Abraham Lincoln	V	132
A Story About Abe Lincoln (*Story*		
and notes)....................	V	133
John Henry, the Big Steel-Drivin'		
Man	V	139
The Man Who Loved Hai Quai		
(*Indian Tale of Mt. Tacoma*)	VI	127

COUNTRIES OF THE WORLD

UNITED STATES OF AMERICA—(*Continued*)

	VOL.	PAGE
The Mice (*Winnebago Fable*)	VI	131
Babe Ruth	VII	144a
Casey at the Bat	VII	144c
Casey's Comeback	VII	144f
A Boy on the High Seas— *Biog. Sketch*	VIII	8
Young Midshipman David Farragut— *Biog. Sketch*	VIII	84
The Circus Man (*Story and note*)	VIII	144
The Greatest Show on Earth	VIII	149
The Adventures of General Tom Thumb	VIII	155
Pushing Westward with Lewis and Clark—*Biog. Sketch*	IX	25
Exploring the Wilderness—*Biog. Sketch*	IX	9
Buffalo Bill	IX	27
George Rogers Clark and the Conquest of the Northwest	IX	66
The Rough Rider—*Biog. Sketch*	IX	72
Princess Nelly and the Seneca Chief	IX	78
How Peary Reached the North Pole	IX	127
Wolfert Webber, or Golden Dreams	XI	107
Robert E. Lee	XI	170c
Lincoln's Gettysburg Address	XI	170a
The New Colossus	XI	172
The Melting Pot	XI	173
Your America	XI	216
A Rover in the Catskills—*Biog. Sketch*	XII	99
Life in Concord—*Biog. Sketch*	XII	122
The Harvard Professor—*Biog. Sketch*	XII	135

Artists and Illustrators

See ARTISTS AND ILLUSTRA-
TORS for listings according to vol-
umes—Adams; Armstrong; Burger;
Beard; Breuer; Brown; Chamber-
lain; Charleson; Cheney; Cheno-
weth; Collier; Cox; Crane; Currier
and Ives; Davis; Denslow, Dodge;
Downs; Elliott; Enright; Farnam;
Ferring; Frascino; Greene; Grifal-
coni; Gruelle; Hale; Heath; Hether-
ington; The Hollings; Horton;
Hurford; Kemble; Ketchum; Kohn;
Lee; Lewin; McAfee; McAnnelly;
Martin; Miller; Moran; Naylor;
Nelson; Newell; O'Malley; Oughten;
Parks; Petersham; Pyle; Reynolds;
Riley; Rossiter; Rudeen; St. John;
Sampson; Sarg; Savage; Savitt;
Shatte; Simpson; Todd; Trumbull;
Turner; Turpin; Ward; Westland;
Williams; Winter; Wood; Wuerfel;
Wyeth; Zavada

Authors

See AUTHORS, TITLES, AND
LEADING CHARACTERS IN-
DEX—Alcott; Alden; Aspinwall;
Bacon; Bailey; Barnum; Baruch;
Baum; Benét; Brotherton; Bryant;
Buck; Burgess; Burroughs; Cather;
Cawein; Chapman; Child; Conkling;
Cooke; Cooper; Cox; Crossette;
Daugherty; Dickinson; Dodge;
Drake; Dunbar; Eaton; Eells, Emer-
son; Field; Frost; Gipson; Griffis;
Haber; Harris; Hawthorne; Herford;
Herschler; Hughes; Irving; Jacoby;
Judson; Lazarus; Lindsay; Long-
fellow; Lowell; Martone; Miller;
Mitchell; Murphy; Nesbit; O'Neill;
Peabody; Percy; Poe; Pyle; Rich-
ards; Riley; Roosevelt; Sandburg;
Saroyan; Shepard; Sill; Sterrett;
Stockton; Teasdale; Thaxter;
Thayer; Tippett; Trowbridge, Under-
wood; Untermeyer; Vass; Waldorf;
Walker; White; Whitman; Whittier;
Wilder; Williston; Wilson; Wynne

Composers

See MUSIC—Composers—Bratton;
Cadman; Carpenter; DeKoven;
Gershwin; Hanson; Herbert; Lieur-
ance; MacDowell; Nevin; Sousa;
Taylor

Famous People referred to in Notes
and Comments

See FAMOUS PEOPLE—Gov.
Bradford; Kit Carson; Cooper; Gen.
Custer; Garrison; Harte; Patrick
Henry; "Wild Bill" Hickok; Holmes;
Mrs. Kinzie; Nancy Hanks Lincoln;
McKinley; Betsy Ross; Thoreau;
Mark Twain; Martha Washington;
Brigham Young

WALES

	VOL.	PAGE
Dame Durden	I	58
Three Jovial Huntsmen	III	110
The Youth Who Wanted Some Fun (*Story and note*)	VII	20

WEST INDIES

	VOL.	PAGE
A Rhyme from Santo Domingo	I	224

YUGOSLAVIA

	VOL.	PAGE
Vladimir's Adventures in Search of Fortune	VII	102
Marko, the Champion of Serbian Liberty	XI	29

COUNTRY
See FARM AND COUNTRY

COWBOY
See OCCUPATIONS—Cowboy

CREATIVE ACTIVITIES
See IN YOUR HANDS—Chapters
XVII; XVIII; XIX; XX

CREEK
See NATURE—River or Creek

CRWTH
See MUSICAL INSTRUMENTS—
Crwth

VOL. PAGE

CYMBALS
See MUSICAL INSTRUMENTS—
Cymbals

CZECHOSLOVAKIA
See COUNTRIES OF THE WORLD—
Czechoslovakia

DENMARK
See AUTHORS, TITLES, AND LEAD-
ING CHARACTERS INDEX—Hans
Christian Andersen

DESERT
See NATURE—Desert

DOLL
See TOYS—Doll

DRAGONS
How Jack Sought the Golden Apples.. V 76
(*Illustration on page 82*)
Jack the Giant-Killer.................. VI 140
(*Illustration on page 151*)
The Adventures of Perseus........... IX 140
(*Illustration on page 147*)
The Last of the Dragons............. X 89
Una and the Red Cross Knight....... XI 8
(*Illustration on page 27*)
The Tale of the Rhine-Gold.......... XI 73
(*Illustration on page 85*)

DRAMATIZATION
See also COSTUMES; FESTIVALS;
and IN YOUR HANDS—Chapter
XX
Pease-Porridge Hot .... I 47
Teddy Bear, Teddy Bear............. I 91
The Barnyard .... I 114
Policeman Joe .... I 173
The Zoo in the Park................. I 186
The Little Red Hen and the Grain of
Wheat .... II 13
Rama and the Tigers................. II 118
The Sheep and the Pig That Made a
Home .... II 145
The Cock, the Mouse, and the Little
Red Hen .... II 192
The Little Engine That Could........ II 200
Goldilocks and the Three Bears....... III 20
Hansel and Grethel.................. IV 73
Columbine and Her Playfellows of the
Italian Pantomime .... VII 119
Down by the River Avon—*Biog. Sketch
of William Shakespeare* .... XII 15
Life in Concord—*Biog. Sketch of
Louisa May Alcott*................. XII 122

DRIVER
(Bus, Taxi, Truck)
See OCCUPATIONS—Driver

DRUM
See MUSICAL INSTRUMENTS—
Drum; and TOYS—Drum

DWARFS
See also ELVES AND BROWNIES
Snow-white and Rose-red............. IV 34
Old Pipes and the Dryad............. VI 18
The Adventures of General Tom Thumb VIII 155
The Tale of the Rhine-Gold.......... XI 73

VOL. PAGE

EASTER
See HOLIDAYS—Easter

EGYPT
See COUNTRIES OF THE WORLD—
Africa

ELEVATOR OPERATOR
See OCCUPATIONS—Elevator
Operator

ELVES AND BROWNIES
An Explanation of the Grasshopper.... II 77
The Owl's Answer to Tommy......... III 29
The Elf and the Dormouse........... III 39
The Brownies in the Toy Shop........ III 40
The Shoemaker and the Elves......... III 95
Elsa and the Ten Elves.............. IV 45
The Youth Who Wanted Some Fun.... VII 20

ENGLAND
See COUNTRIES OF THE WORLD—
England

EPICS
EAST INDIAN
The Exile of Rama—*From the
Ramayana* .... X 175
ENGLISH
Sir Beaumains, the Kitchen Knight
—*A legend of the Round Table*... X 8
How Beowulf Delivered Heorot—
From Beowulf .... X 80
Una and the Red Cross Knight—
From The Faerie Queene by Spenser XI 8
FINNISH
Kalevala, Land of Heroes—*From
the Kalevala* .... X 151
FRENCH
The Song of Roland—*From the
Chanson de Roland*.............. X 38
GERMAN
The Tale of the Rhine-Gold—*From
the operas of Richard Wagner*.... XI 73
GREEK
The Home-Coming of Odysseus—
From the Odyssey by Homer...... X 217
IRISH
Cuculain, the Irish Hound—*From
tales of the ancient Gaelic bards*... X 188
NORSE
Frithjof, the Viking—*From the saga
of Frithjof* .... X 130
PERSIAN
A Story of Rustem, the Hero of
Persia—*From the Shah-Nameh
by Firdusi* .... X 228
ROMAN
The Wanderings of Aeneas—*From
the Latin of Virgil*.............. X 203
RUSSIAN
The Word of Igor's Armament...... X 119
SPANISH
The Story of the Cid—*From the
ancient Poem of the Cid*.......... X 108

	VOL.	PAGE
EPICS (*Continued*)		
YUGOSLAVIAN		
Marko, the Champion of Serbian Liberty—*From the ballads of the Yugoslavs*	XI	29
ESTONIA		
See COUNTRIES OF THE WORLD— Estonia		
EXPERIENCE STORIES AND POEMS		
Monkeys	I	142
Building with Blocks	I	164
Good Morning, Peter	I	165
The Little Girl and the New Dress	I	168
The Big Street in the Big City	I	170
Big Bus, Stop!	I	173
Policeman Joe	I	173
Biting Marion	I	174
The Three Trucks	I	177
The Big Engine	I	179
Groceries	I	182
Mister Postman	I	182
The Elevator	I	183
The Zoo in the Park	I	186
The Orchestra	I	187
Sally's Blue Ball	I	188
Park Play	I	189
The Big Umbrella and the Little Rubbers	I	190
The Snow Man	I	192
White Fields	I	193
Thunder and Lightning	I	195
The Little Pig	I	198
A Story of the Wind	I	200
Trip: San Francisco	I	210
What the Children Do in Summer	I	212
Little Gustava	II	30
Moon, So Round and Yellow	II	40
Two Birds and Their Nest	II	45
The Star	II	83
Two Children	II	138
Paper Boats	II	139
Late	II	153
Jack Frost	II	186
Snow	II	208
The Night Before Christmas	II	213
The Circus Parade	III	46
The Shaking of the Pear Tree	III	146
A Happy Day in the City	III	181
The Knight	IV	129
FABLES		
The Two Crabs*	II	33
Belling the Cat*	II	35
The Donkey and the Lap Dog*	II	50
The City Mouse and the Country Mouse*	II	84
The Dancing Monkeys*	II	92
The Hare and the Tortoise*	II	106
The Lion and the Mouse*	II	108
The Turtle Who Could Not Stop Talking (*East Indian*)	II	178
The Foolish, Timid, Little Hare (*East Indian*)	III	76
The Honest Woodman—*Adapted from La Fontaine* (Fable and note)	III	114
The Boaster*	III	175

	VOL.	PAGE
The Wind and the Sun*	III	196
The Dog in the Manger*	III	197
The Mice (*Winnebago*)	VI	131
The Acorn and the Pumpkin (*La Fontaine*)	VII	132
FAIRS		
Simple Simon	I	50
Mario, Marietta, and Vanno	I	63
Dawlish Fair	II	67
The Bee, the Mouse, and the Bum-Clock	II	155
Down by the River Avon	XII	15
FAIRY TALES AND POEMS		
See also FOLK LORE AND LEGENDS		
The Rooster and the Sultan (*Hungarian*)	II	52
An Explanation of the Grasshopper	II	77
The Village of Cream Puffs	II	124
The Tale of Nutcracker	II	218
Fairy and Child	III	25
The Owl's Answer to Tommy	III	29
The Elf and the Dormouse	III	39
The Brownies in the Toy Shop	III	40
The Tongue-Cut Sparrow (*Japanese*)	III	165
Elsa and the Ten Elves (*Swedish*)	IV	45
The Selfish Giant	IV	50
The Nutcracker and Sugardolly Stories	IV	83
The Red Ettin (*English and Scottish*)	V	90
Little Diamond and the North Wind	IV	119
The Assembling of the Fays	VI	17
Hie Away, Hie Away	VI	70
The Three Wishes (*Spanish*)	VI	92
The Strong Boy (*Canadian*)	VI	71
The Merman	VI	182
The Moon-Maiden	VI	222
Miska and the Man-With-The-Iron-Head (*Hungarian*)	VII	11
The Youth Who Wanted Some Fun (*Welsh*)	VII	20
The Maiden, the Knight, and the Waterfall (*Roumanian*)	VII	40
The Snow-Queen	VII	48
The Little-Man-As-Big-As-Your-Thumb-With-Mustaches-Seven-Miles-Long (*Russian*)	VII	112
The Six Swans (*German*)	VII	126
The Golden Bird (*German*)	VII	134
The Knights of the Silver Shield	VII	173
Gigi and the Magic Ring (*Italian*)	VII	199
The Golden Touch	VII	210
The Enchanted Island	VIII	134
The Last of the Dragons	X	89

FAMOUS PEOPLE IN MY BOOK HOUSE
(Referred to in Notes and Comments)
This list does not include names of artists and illustrators which appear under the heading, ARTISTS AND ILLUSTRATORS, nor does it include composers whose names appear under the heading, MUSIC—Composers.
All BOOK HOUSE authors, whether or not referred to in notes and comments, will be found listed in AUTHORS, TITLES, AND LEADING CHARACTERS INDEX.

*Adapted from Aesop

	VOL.	PAGE
FAMOUS PEOPLE (*Continued*)		
Bradford, William—*American* (1590-1657) (Governor of Plymouth Colony)		
Comment	V	113
Carson, Kit—*American* (1809-1868)		
Comment	IX	29
Cromwell, Oliver—*English* (1599-1658)		
Note	I	45
Note	XII	29
Custer, Gen. George Armstrong— *American* (1839-1876)		
Comments	IX	38e,
73		
Edward I, King of England (Edward Longshanks) (1239-1307)		
Comments	X	21
Edward III, King of England (1312-1377)		
Comment	XII	12
Elizabeth I, Queen of England (1533-1603)		
Note	I	44
Geoffrey of Monmouth—*English* (1100-1154)		
Note	X	10
Harte, Bret—*American* (1836-1902)		
Comment	XII	137
Hathaway, Anne—*English*		
Comment	XII	25
Henry, Patrick—*American* (1736-1799)		
Comment	IX	67
Hickok, "Wild Bill"—*American*		
Comment	IX	38d
Holmes, Oliver Wendell—*American* (1809-1894)		
Comment	XII	135
Hunt, Leigh—*English* (1784-1859)		
Comments	XII	91
Jonson, Ben—*English* (1573-1637)		
Note	XII	26
Kinzie, Mrs. John—*American*		
Note	IX	78
Lafayette, Marquis de—*French* (1757-1834)		
Note and picture	V	125
Lincoln, Nancy Hanks—*American*		
Comment	V	129
Lind, Jenny—*Swedish* (1820-1887)		
Comment	VIII	150
Lovelace, Richard—*English* (1618-1658)		
Note	XII	29
Malory, Sir Thomas—*English* (15th Century)		
Note	X	10
Marlowe, Christopher—*English* (1564-1593)		
Note	XII	171
	VOL.	PAGE
McKinley, William—*American* (1843-1901)		
Comments	IX	77
Newbery, John—*English* (1713-1763)		
Comments	XII	216
Ross, Betsy—*American* (1752-1836)		
Comments	V	121,
122, 123, 124		
Sand, George (Pen Name of Madame Amantine L. Dudevant)—*French* (1804-1876)		
Note	II	150
Schiller, Johann—*German* (1759-1805)		
Note	X	44
Stuart, Charles Edward (Bonnie Prince Charley)—*English* (1720-1788)		
Note	I	34
Note	I	99
Thoreau, Henry—*American* (1817-1862)		
Comments	XII	123,
129, 135, 136		
Twain, Mark (Pen Name of Samuel Clemens)—*American* (1835-1910)		
Comment	VII	137
Victoria, Queen of Great Britain and Ireland and Empress of India— (1819-1901)		
Comments	VIII	157-
162		
Washington, Martha—*American* (1732-1799)		
Comment	V	118
FARM AND COUNTRY		
Willie Boy	I	45
My Maid Mary	I	51
Dame Durden	I	58
O 'Twas on a Bright Mornin' in Summer	I	59
Over the River and Through the Woods	I	87
The Farmer in the Dell	I	102
The Farmer's Boy	I	108
Turkey in the Straw	I	113
The Barnyard	I	114
I Stand in the Pulpit and Preach	I	117
The Boy Who Made Hay	I	134
I Should Like to Plough	I	136
When I Was a Baby	I	145
The Ploughman He's a Bonnie Lad	I	153
Minnie and Mattie	I	156
White Fields	I	193
The Little Pig	I	198
There Was a Little Boy	I	199
The Clucking Hen	I	214
The Gingerbread Man	II	58
The Ugly Duckling	II	131
A Swedish Evening	II	141
The Shaking of the Pear Tree	III	146
Elsa and the Ten Elves	IV	45
Charlotte's Web	V	54
Maggie Tulliver Goes to Live with the Gypsies	VIII	189
Evening at the Farm	X	79
A Boy in Russia	XII	190

VOL. PAGE

FARMER
    See OCCUPATIONS—Farmer

FATHER'S DAY
    See HOLIDAYS—Father's Day

FESTIVALS
    See also HOLIDAYS
    BETHLEHEM, FEAST OF
      Get Up, Little Horsey.............. I   65
    CORN, FESTIVAL OF THE
      Princess Nelly and the Seneca Chief. IX 78
    NEW YEAR, FESTIVAL OF THE
      The Magic Horse.................. VIII 92
    PURIM
      The Melting Pot.................. XI 173
    SPRING, FESTIVAL OF
      Here We Come, We Children Come
      (*Poem and note*)................. I 204

FIDDLE
    See MUSICAL INSTRUMENTS—
    Violin

FIELD
    See NATURE—Field and Meadow

FIFE
    See MUSICAL INSTRUMENTS—
    Fife

FINLAND
    See COUNTRIES OF THE WORLD—
    Finland

FISH
    See NATURE—Fish

FISHERMAN
    See OCCUPATIONS—Fisherman

FLAG DAY
    See HOLIDAYS—Flag Day

FLOWERS
    See NATURE—Flowers

FLUTE
    See MUSICAL INSTRUMENTS—
    Flute

FOG
    See NATURE—Fog

FOLKLORE AND LEGENDS
    See also FAIRY TALES AND POEMS

    AFRICAN
      The Lost Spear .... VI 132

    ALASKAN
      How Yehl, the Hero, Freed the
      Beaming Maiden .... VI 102

    AMERICAN
      The Gingerbread Man (*New
      England*) .... II 58
      The Little Rabbit Who Wanted Red
      Wings (*Negro*) .... II 87
      Shingebiss (*Indian*) .... II 96
      The Story of Li'l Hannibal (*Negro*). III 116

VOL. PAGE

      A Story About the Little Rabbits....
      (*Negro*) .... III 123
      How Brer Rabbit Met Brer Tar-Baby
      (*Negro*) .... IV 130
      The Story of Big Paul Bunyan...... IV 161
      Old Stormalong .... IV 183
      Pecos Bill, the Cowboy............ IV 195
      Old Johnny Appleseed .... IV 213
      John Henry, the Big Steel-Drivin' Man V 139
      The Man Who Loved Hai Quai
      (*Indian*) .... VI 127
      Hiawatha's Fasting (*Indian*)........ IX 89

    ARABIAN
      The Magic Horse—*From The
      Arabian Nights* .... VIII 92
      The Story of the Talking Bird—*From
      the Arabian Nights* .... VIII 109

    AUSTRALIAN
      The Right Time to Laugh.......... III 81

    BRAZILIAN
      How the Brazilian Beetles Got Their
      Gorgeous Coats .... III 172

    CHINESE
      The Girl Who Used Her Wits....... IV 137

    CZECHOSLOVAKIAN
      The Little Rooster and the Little Hen II 71
      The Prince Who Rode Through a
      Mousehole .... VII 96

    DUTCH
      The Boy Hero of Harlem.......... IV 57

    EGYPTIAN
      Rhodopis and Her Gilded Sandals... VII 84

    ENGLISH
      The Little Red Hen and the Grain of
      Wheat .... II 13
      The Magpie's Nest .... II 42
      Goldilocks and the Three Bears..... III 20
      Master of All Masters............. III 148
      Teeny-Tiny .... IV 143
      The Story of Tom Thumb.......... V 11
      Jack and the Beanstalk............. V 20
      Dick Whittington and His Cat...... V 33
      How Jack Sought the Golden Apples V 76
      Jack the Giant-Killer .... VI 140
      Sir Beaumains, the Kitchen Knight.. X 8
      Ye Merry Doinges of Robin Hood... XI 49

    FILIPINO
      The Battle of the Firefly and the Apes III 59

    FLEMISH
      How the Finch Got Her Colors.... II 143

    FRENCH
      Cinderella .... IV 12
      The Sleeping Beauty.............. VI 11

    GERMAN
      The Shoemaker and the Elves....... III 95
      The Little Girl and the Hare....... III 111
      The Twelve Dancing Princesses...... IV 28
      Snow-white and Rose-red.......... IV 34
      Hansel and Grethel................ IV 73

	VOL.	PAGE

FOLKLORE AND LEGENDS (*Continued*)

HAWAIIAN
The Fisherman Who Caught the Sun   VI   198

IRISH
The Bee, the Mouse, and the Bum-
    Clock II   155
Cuculain, the Irish Hound.......... X   188

JAVANESE
Aruman, a Hero of Java............ VI   202

KOREAN
Pigling and Her Proud Sister....... VI   191

MAORIAN (New Zealand)
The Trial by Fire.................. VII   26

NORSE
Johnny and the Three Goats........ II   47
The Sheep and the Pig That Made a
    Home II   145
Doll i' the Grass.................. IV   24
Why the Sea Is Salt............... V   144
Boots and His Brothers............ V   157
The Princess on the Glass Hill...... VI   80
The Squire's Bride................ VI   98
East o' the Sun and West o' the Moon   VII   31

RUSSIAN
Building the Bridge............... II   149

SCOTTISH
Wee Robin's Christmas Song........ II   209
The Wee, Wee Mannie and the Big,
    Big Coo III   99

SWEDISH
The Cap That Mother Made........ III   12

SWISS
The Legend of William Tell........ X   44

YUGOSLAVIAN
Vladimir's Adventures in Search of
    Fortune VII   102

FOLK MUSIC AND SONGS
See MUSIC—Folk Music and Songs

FOREST
See NATURE—Forest or Jungle

FOURTH OF JULY
See HOLIDAYS—Independence Day

FRANCE
See COUNTRIES OF THE WORLD—
France

GAMES AND RHYTHMS
See also IN YOUR HANDS—
    Chapter IV
Once I Saw a Little Bird............ I   25
Lucy Locket Lost Her Pocket........ I   26
Hippety Hop to the Barber Shop...... I   28
Baa, Baa, Black Sheep............... I   29
Handy-Spandy I   33

	VOL.	PAGE

Jack, Be Nimble I   39
Pease-Porridge Hot I   47
Three Little Kittens................. I   53
Peekaboo, I See You!............... I   74
Quaker, Quaker, How Is Thee?...... I   82
Ring Around a Rosy I   84
It Snows and It Blows.............. I   87
A-Tisket, A-Tasket................. I   89
We've Come to See Miss Jenny Jones.. I   89
Teddy Bear, Teddy Bear............. I   91
Lazy Old Mary I   98
John Brown Had a Little Indian...... I   100
The Farmer in the Dell............. I   102
Pop! Goes the Weasel!............... I   107
Three Old Maids a-Skating Went...... I   110
Hop, My Horsey, Leap and Spring.... I   123
Bring the Comb and Play Upon It!.... I   159
The Zoo in the Park................ I   186
The Orchestra I   187
Where Are My Roses............... I   205
The Little Gray Pony.............. II   17
Ten Little Indians.................. II   94

GARDEN
See NATURE—Garden

GERMANY
See COUNTRIES OF THE WORLD—
Germany

GIANTS
The Selfish Giant IV   50
Jack and the Beanstalk............. V   20
The Strong Boy.................... VI   71
Jack the Giant-Killer (*Cormoran,*
    Blunderbore, Thunderdell,—
    Gailigantua) VI   140
David, the Shepherd Boy (*Goliath*)... VII   73
The Knights of the Silver Shield...... VII   173
The Labors of Hercules (*Atlas,*
    Antaeus, Geryon) IX   151
Thor's Journey to Jotun-heim
    (*Skrymir*) IX   164
Una and the Red Cross Knight
    (*Orgoglio*) XI   8
The Tale of the Rhine-Gold
    (*Fasolt and Fafner*).............. XI   73

GODS AND GODDESSES
See also MYTHS

GREEK
Phaeton (*Apollo*) VII   90
Note (*Orpheus*) IX   140
The Labors of Hercules (*Iris*)....... IX   151
The Home-Coming of Odysseus
    (*Athene, Hermes, Poseidon, Zeus*). X   217
Una and the Red Cross Knight
    (*Morpheus*) XI   8

INDIAN
The Man Who Loved Hai Quai
    (*Tootah*) VI   127

NORSE
Thor's Journey to Jotun-heim
    (*Loki, Thor*) IX   164

263

VOL. PAGE

GODS AND GODDESSES (*Continued*)

Thor (*Thor*) .... IX 171
The Stealing of Iduna (*Bragi, Freya, Hoenir, Iduna, Loki, Odin, Thor*). IX 172
Frithjof, the Viking (*Balder, Freya, Odin, Thor*) .... X 130
The Tale of the Rhine-Gold (*Freya, Loki, Wotan*) .... XI 73

ROMAN

Phaeton (*Jupiter*) .... VII 90
The Adventures of Perseus (*Mercury, Minerva*) .... IX 140
The Labors of Hercules (*Diana, Mercury, Pluto*) .... IX 151
The Wanderings of Aeneas (*Aeolus, Aurora, Ceres, Diana, Juno, Mercury, Neptune, Venus*) .... X 203
The Home-Coming of Odysseus (*Aurora*) .... X 217

RUSSIAN

A Chronicle of Kiev (*Perun*)....... X 118

GONGS

See MUSICAL INSTRUMENTS—
Gongs and Bells

GREECE

See COUNTRIES OF THE WORLD—
Greece

GUITAR

See MUSICAL INSTRUMENTS—
Guitar

GYPSIES

Meg Merrilies (*Poem and note*)....... VIII 188
Maggie Tulliver Goes to Live with the Gypsies .... VIII 189
A Tramp of the Middle West........ XII 147

HALLOWE'EN

See HOLIDAYS—Hallowe'en

HAND ORGAN

See MUSICAL INSTRUMENTS—
Hand Organ

HARP

See MUSICAL INSTRUMENTS—
Harp

HAWAII

See COUNTRIES OF THE WORLD—
Hawaii

HERO AND HEROINE STORIES

TRUE

George Washington and the First American Flag .... V 118
Abraham Lincoln (*Poem*).......... V 132
A Story About Abe Lincoln........ V 133
David, the Shepherd Boy........... VII 73
A Boy on the High Seas—*Biog. Sketch of Joshua Barney*......... VIII 8

VOL. PAGE

Young Midshipman David Farragut.. VIII 84
John Paul Jones................... VIII 82
Princess Nelly and the Seneca Chief. IX 78
How Peary Reached the North Pole. IX 127
Gideon, the Warrior .... IX 134
Robert Bruce, Scotland's Hero—*Biog. Sketch* .... X 21
Joan of Arc—*Biog. Sketch*......... X 98
Marko, the Champion of Serbian Liberty .... XI 29
Robert E. Lee.................... XI 170c
Lincoln's Gettysburg Address .... XI 170a

PARTLY TRUE AND PARTLY IMAGINATIVE

The Boy Hero of Harlem.......... IV 57
The Song of Roland............... X 38
The Legend of William Tell........ X 44
The Story of the Cid.............. X 108
The Word of Igor's Armament...... X 119
A Story of Rustem, the Hero of Persia X 228

IMAGINATIVE

See also FAIRY TALES AND POEMS
The Knight (*Poem*) .... IV 129
How Yehl, the Hero, Freed the Beaming Maiden .... VI 102
Aruman, a Hero of Java........... VI 202
The Adventures of Perseus.......... IX 140
The Labors of Hercules............ IX 151
Sir Beaumains, the Kitchen Knight .. X 8
How Beowulf Delivered Heorot..... X 80
Frithjof, the Viking............... X 130
Kalevala, Land of Heroes.......... X 151
Cuculain, the Irish Hound.......... X 188
The Wanderings of Aeneas.......... X 203
The Home-Coming of Odysseus ..... X 217
Ye Merry Doinges of Robin Hood... XI 49

HILL

See NATURE—Mountain or Hill

HOLIDAYS

See also FESTIVALS

ARBOR DAY

See NATURE—Trees

CHRISTMAS

Little Jack Horner................. I 48
Get Up, Little Horsey............. I 65
Jingle Bells, Jingle Bells........... I 87
Hark, the Christmas Bells Are Ringing I 133
A Rhyme from Santo Domingo..... I 224
The Little Engine That Could....... II 200
Wee Robin's Christmas Song........ II 209
The Night Before Christmas (*Poem and note*) .... II 213
The Tale of Nutcracker............ II 218
The Brownies in the Toy Shop...... III 40
The Shoemaker and the Elves....... III 95
The Nutcracker and Sugardolly Stories .... IV 83
Why the Sea Is Salt............... V 144
A Christmas Song at Sea.......... VIII 187
Note .... IX 177
Down by the River Avon.......... XII 15

264

	VOL.	PAGE

HOLIDAYS (*Continued*)

COLUMBUS DAY

	VOL.	PAGE
All About Columbus...............	V	112
In Columbus' Time	V	112

EASTER

See also NATURE—Seasons—*Spring;*
 NATURE—Animals—*Rabbit;*
 NATURE—Birds—*Chickens;*
 NATURE—Flowers

A Song for Easter.................	II	80

FATHER'S DAY

An American Miner's Song.........	II	23
Late	II	153
The Legend of William Tell........	X	44
Joseph and His Brethren	X	48
The Exile of Rama................	X	175
The Home-Coming of Odysseus.....	X	217

FLAG DAY

Note	III	46
George Washington and the First American Flag	V	118
Robert E. Lee.....................	XI	170c
Your America	XI	216

FOURTH OF JULY

See HOLIDAYS—Independence Day

HALLOWE'EN

Hallowe'en	IV	142
Tippity Witchit's Hallowe'en	IV	145

INDEPENDENCE DAY

Yankee Doodle	I	101
Go Ask Your Mother for Fifty Cents	I	104
How Robert Fulton Harnessed the Giant	V	48
George Washington and the First American Flag	V	118
The Fourth of July...............	V	129

LINCOLN'S BIRTHDAY

Abraham Lincoln (*Poem*)..........	V	132
A Story About Abe Lincoln........	V	133
Lincoln's Gettysburg Address.......	XI	170a

MAY DAY

There Are Twelve Months.........	I	57
The Cuckoo and the Donkey........	I	122
Catherine, My Dearie.............	I	124
Little Bells, Pretty Flowers of the Steppes	I	133
As It Fell Upon a Day.............	I	148
There's Not a Budding Boy (*Rhyme and note*)...............	I	208
Ye Merry Doinges of Robin Hood (*Story and note*)	XI	49
Down by the River Avon...........	XII	15

MOTHER'S DAY

Chink, Chink, Chocket.............	I	70
A Roumanian Lullaby..............	I	137
Over in the Meadow..............	I	138
Thus I Guard My Mother's Lambkins	I	144
The Cap That Mother Made........	III	12

	VOL.	PAGE
Mrs. Tabby Gray..................	III	129
The Babe Moses...................	III	156
The Strong Boy	VI	118
Princess Nelly and the Seneca Chief..	IX	78
The Adventures of Perseus.........	IX	140
The Exile of Rama...............	X	175
Life in Concord—*Biog. Sketch of Louisa M. Alcott*	XII	122

NEW YEAR'S DAY

New Year's Day	III	45
The Magic Horse (*Persian*).........	VIII	92

ST. PATRICK'S DAY

See COUNTRIES OF THE WORLD—Ireland

ST. VALENTINE'S DAY

The Rose Is Red..................	I	86
Good Morrow, 'Tis Saint Valentine's Day	I	209
The Birds' St. Valentine's Day.......	III	198

THANKSGIVING DAY

Over the River and Through the Woods	I	87
Songs of Joy from the Bible........	I	216
The First Thanksgiving Day.........	V	113
Give Praise	V	117
We Thank Thee...................	V	117
The Sky at Night.................	VII	72

WASHINGTON'S BIRTHDAY

I'm Going to Lady Washington's....	I	82
George Washington and the First American Flag	V	118

HOLLAND

See COUNTRIES OF THE WORLD— Holland

HORN

See MUSICAL INSTRUMENTS—Horn

HOUSEWIFE

See OCCUPATIONS—Housewife

HUMOROUS RHYMES AND STORIES

Hey Diddle Diddle..................	I	22
Little Robin Redbreast	I	23
Dickery, Dickery Dare...............	I	24
Wee Willie Winkie	I	28
As I Went to Bonner...............	I	29
Here Am I, Little Jumping Joan......	I	32
Peter, Peter, Pumpkin Eater.........	I	36
A Robin and a Robin's Son...........	I	36
Diddle, Diddle, Dumpling	I	37
The King of France Went Up the Hill.	I	41
There Was an Old Woman Tossed Up in a Basket	I	41
Humpty Dumpty	I	46
Rub-a-Dub-Dub	I	48
Little Jack Horner..................	I	48
Sing a Song of Sixpence..............	I	49
Simple Simon	I	50
There Was an Owl..................	I	50
Great A, Little A, Bouncing B........	I	52
There Was a Monkey...............	I	52
There Was a Crow	I	54

HUMOROUS RHYMES AND STORIES (*Continued*)

There Was a Horse...................	I	54
The Roosters at the Old Crown Inn...	I	67
Mr. Toad Set Out on a Journey.......	I	68
Come, Let's Go to Sant' Anita.......	I	70
Otto Would a-Riding Go.............	I	75
There Was an Old Woman...........	I	76
The Mouse Climbed Up the Candlestick	I	77
There Was a Little Boy..............	I	77
Through the Jungle.................	I	79
All the Cats Consulted...............	I	85
Go Ask Your Mother for Fifty Cents..	I	104
I Went to the Animal Fair...........	I	104
A Goat One Day Was Feeling Fine....	I	106
I Had a Little Mule.................	I	106
Pop! Goes the Weasel!...............	I	107
Where, O Where Has My Little Dog Gone	I	107
Three Old Maids a-Skating Went......	I	110
Would You Like to See Goats Dance on Stilts?	I	121
King Dagobert	I	124
There Was an Old Dame Called Tartine	I	124
Precocious Piggy	I	196
A Story of the Wind.................	I	200
A Winky-Tooden Song...............	I	215
Reen-Reen-Reeny-Croak-Frog	II	37
Johnny and the Three Goats..........	II	47
The Rooster and the Sultan...........	II	52
The Poor Old Lady..................	II	68
Rama and the Tigers................	II	118
Nonsense Rhymes	II	154
The Bee, the Mouse, and the Bum-Clock	II	155
The Purple Cow....................	II	163
Krazy Kat	II	172
The Owl and the Pussy-Cat...........	II	180
The Strange Adventure of Baron Münchausen	II	182
The Song of the Flea................	II	185
Dame Wiggins of Lee................	II	188
The Mad Dog	III	63
King Hilary and the Beggarman.......	III	70
The Wee, Wee Mannie and the Big, Big Coo	III	99
A Quick-Running Squash.............	III	104
Three Jovial Huntsmen..............	III	110
The Daring Prince..................	III	127
The Mock Turtle's Song.............	III	170
The Battle of the Frogs and the Mice..	IV	104
The Rarest Animal of All.............	IV	113
How Brer Rabbit Met Brer Tar-Baby..	IV	130
Master of All Masters	III	148
A Tragic Story.....................	IV	136
Teeny-Tiny	IV	143
The Story of Big Paul Bunyan........	IV	161
Old Stormalong	IV	183
Pecos Bill, the Cowboy..............	IV	195
The Pert Fire Engine................	IV	218
Charlotte's Web	V	54
Winnie-the-Pooh	V	68
The Steamboat and the Locomotive....	V	96
Wild Flowers	VI	69
The Squire's Bride.................	VI	98
The Acorn and the Pumpkin..........	VII	132
Battle Tactics	VII	165
The Rose and the Ring.............	IX	177
The Last of the Dragons.............	X	89
The Surprising Adventures of Don Quixote of La Mancha.............	XI	90

HUNGARY
See COUNTRIES OF THE WORLD—Hungary

IMAGINATIVE STORIES
See FAIRY TALES AND POEMS; FOLKLORE AND LEGENDS; also HERO AND HEROINE STORIES—Imaginative

INDEPENDENCE DAY
See HOLIDAYS—Independence Day

INDIA
See COUNTRIES OF THE WORLD—India

INDIANS
(North American)

I'm a Little Indian (*Mexican*).........	I	71
American Indian Songs (*Cheyenne, Hopi, Nootka*)	I	80
John Brown Had a Little Indian.......	I	100
There Was an Old, Old Indian........	I	131
Ten Little Indians..................	II	94
Shingebiss (*Chippewa*)	II	96
Indian Children	III	93
Pecos Bill, the Cowboy..............	IV	195
The First Thanksgiving Day..........	V	113
Hiawatha's Childhood (*Ojibway*)......	V	222
How Yehl, the Hero, Freed the Beaming Maiden	VI	102
The Strong Boy	VI	71
The Man Who Loved Hai Quai.......	VI	127
Pushing Westward with Lewis and Clark	IX	39
Exploring the Wilderness (*Cherokee, Shawnee*)	IX	9
Buffalo Bill (*Cheyenne, Choctaw, Delaware, Kickapoo, Pottawatomie, Sioux*)	IX	27
George Rogers Clark and the Conquest of the Northwest.................	IX	66
Princess Nelly and the Seneca Chief (*Delaware, Iroquois, Seneca*).......	IX	78
Hiawatha's Fasting (*Ojibway*)........	IX	89

INSECTS
See NATURE—Insects

INVENTIONS

Jamie Watt and the Giant in the Tea-kettle	V	45
How Robert Fulton Harnessed the Giant	V	48
Wilbur Wright and Orville Wright.....	V	66
The Wonderland of an Artist's Workshop	VI	164
The King's Cream...................	VI	209

IRAN
See COUNTRIES OF THE WORLD—Persia

IRELAND
See COUNTRIES OF THE WORLD—Ireland

ITALY
See COUNTRIES OF THE WORLD—Italy

JAPAN
See COUNTRIES OF THE WORLD—
Japan

JAVA
See COUNTRIES OF THE WORLD—
Java

JUNGLE
See NATURE—Forest or Jungle

KOREA
See COUNTRIES OF THE WORLD—
Korea

LAKE
See NATURE—Lake

LEADING CHARACTERS
See AUTHORS, TITLES, AND LEAD-
ING CHARACTERS INDEX

LIGHTNING
See NATURE—Lightning

LINCOLN'S BIRTHDAY
See HOLIDAYS—Lincoln's Birthday

LITERATURE
See listings according to individual sub-
jects. See also AUTHORS, TITLES,
AND LEADING CHARACTERS
INDEX

LULLABIES
Rock-a-Bye, Baby I   18
Sleep, Baby, Sleep.................. I   20
Old Mother Wind I   76
A Japanese Lullaby................. I   78
American Indian Songs.............. I   80
Go to Sleepy, Little Baby............. I   90
Bye-O! Bye-O! I   90
Dreamland Opens Here I   91
Bye-Lo, Bubbeli, Sleep.............. I   117
Sweet and Low I   118
The Sleepy Song.................... I   119
A Roumanian Lullaby I   137
Sleep, Sleep, My Little One.......... I   146
Lie a-Bed, Sleepy Head.............. I   157
Wynken, Blynken, and Nod.......... II   24
Fairy and Child.................... III   25
A Midsummer Night's Dream
(Lullaby for Titania) VI   38

LUMBERJACK
See OCCUPATIONS—Lumberjack

LUTE
See MUSICAL INSTRUMENTS—
Lute

MAILMAN
See OCCUPATIONS—Mailman

MARIONETTES
See PUPPETS, MARIONETTES, AND
SHADOW PLAYS

MAY DAY
See HOLIDAYS—May Day

MEADOW
See NATURE—Field and Meadow

MEXICO
See COUNTRIES OF THE WORLD—
Mexico

MILKMAID or MILKMAN
See OCCUPATIONS—Milkmaid or
Milkman

MILLER
See OCCUPATIONS—Miller

MINER
See OCCUPATIONS—Miner

MOON
See NATURE—Moon

MOTHER GOOSE RHYMES
See also IN YOUR HANDS—
Chapter II
Nursery Rhymes I   18-
                                          56
The Interesting History of Old
Mother Goose XII   213

MOTHER'S DAY
See HOLIDAYS—Mother's Day

MOTORCYCLE
See TRANSPORTATION—
Motorcycle

MOUNTAIN
See NATURE—Mountain or Hill

MUSIC
See also IN YOUR HANDS—
Chapters II, XXI
(Where there is a direct connection
between a story or poem in MY
BOOK HOUSE and a musical com-
position, the title of the composition
is listed below the composer's name)

COMPOSERS
Arne, Thomas—English (1710-1778)
Note X   165
Bach, Johann Sebastian—German
(1685-1750)
Note IX   134
Balfe, Michael—Irish (1808-1870)
Note VIII   188
Bazzini, Antonio—Italian
(1818-1897)
Note IV   149
Beethoven, Ludwig van—German
(1770-1827)
Note II   40
Berlioz, Hector—French (1803-1869)
The Song of the Flea—From the
opera on Faust................. II   185
Note IV   147
Bishop, Sir Henry—English
(1786-1855)
Note X   165
Borodin, Alexander—Russian
(1834-1887)
Prince Igor (Note).............. X   119
Brahms, Johannes—German
(1833-1897)
Note II   26
The Smith (Note)............... IV   159
Note VII   11

MUSIC

COMPOSERS (*Continued*)

Bratton, John W.—*American*
The Teddy Bears' Picnic (*Note*)...   II   57

Cadman, Charles Wakefield—
American (1881-1946)
Note   III   61

Carpenter, John Alden—*American*
(1876-1951)
Krazy Kat (*Note*)...............   II   172
Notes   III   182,
                           183, 185

Chopin, Frederic—*French-Polish*
(1810-1849)
The Little Dog Waltz (*Note*).....   II   150

Coleridge-Taylor, Samuel—*English*
(1875-1912)
Note   IX   92

Coucy, Chatelain de—*French*
(1157-1192)
Crusader's Hymn (*Note*).........   X   32

Damare, E.—*French*
Note   II   212

David, Félicien—*French* (1810-1876)
Note   III   173

Debussy, Claude—*French*
(1862-1918)
Note   III   151

DeKoven, Reginald—*American*
(1861-1920)
Robin Hood (*Note*).............   XI   60

Dvořák, Antonin—*Bohemian*
(1841-1904)
New World Symphony (*Note*)....   XI   215

Gershwin, George—*American*
(1898-1937)
Note   III   185

Gluck, Christoph—*German*
(1714-1787)
Note   IX   140

Grieg, Edvard—*Norwegian*
(1843-1907)
Note   III   95
Peer Gynt Suite (*Notes*)..........   IX   98,
                      100, 110, 114, 115

Handel, George Frederick—*German*
(1685-1759)
Saul (*Note*)   VII   73

Hanson, Howard—*American*
Lament for Beowulf (*Note*)......   X   81

Haydn, Joseph—*Austrian*
(1732-1809)
Note   III   42

Herbert, Victor—*American*
(1859-1924)
Note   VI   111
Note   IX   172

Humperdinck, Engelbert—*German*
(1854-1921)
Hansel and Grethel (*Notes*)......   IV   73,
                      75, 78

Jessel, Leon—*German*
Note   VI   111

Krantz, Eugen—*German* (1844-1898)
Note   II   70

Leoncavallo, Ruggiero—*Italian*
(1858-1919)
Note   II   143

Lieurance, Thurlow—*American*
Note   IX   93

Liszt, Franz—*Hungarian* (1811-1886)
Note   VII   11
Symphony After Dante's Divina
Commedia (*Note*)   XI   163

MacDowell, Edward—*American*
(1861-1908)
Of a Tailor and a Bear (*Note*)....   III   134
Note   X   11
Note   XI   58

Massenet, Jules—*French* (1842-1912)
The Cid (*Note*).................   X   109

Mendelssohn, Felix—*German*
(1809-1847)
Note   II   81
Note   III   151
A Midsummer Night's Dream.....   VI   38
(*For story about composition, see
page 59*)
Note   XI   58

Nevin, Ethelbert—*American*
(1862-1901)
Note   IX   140
Note   X   11

Poldini, Eduard—*Hungarian*
Note   III   43

Purcell, Henry—*English* (1658-1695)
Dido and Aeneas (*Note*).........   X   203

Ravel, Maurice—*French* (1875-1937)
Note   VI   224

Rimski-Korsakov, Nikolai—*Russian*
(1844-1908)
The Snow Maiden (*Note*)........   IV   119
Note   VII   91
Note   VIII   93

Rossini, Gioacchino—*Italian*
(1792-1868)
William Tell (*Note*).............   X   45

Rubinstein, Anton—*Russian*
(1829-1894)
Note   II   81

Saint-Saëns, Camille—*French*
(1835-1921)
Note   II   137
Phaeton (*Note*)   VII   90
Note   IX   121
The Youth of Hercules (*Note*)....   IX   151

Schubert, François—*German*
(1808-1878)
Note   II   163

	VOL.	PAGE

MUSIC

COMPOSERS (*Continued*)

Schubert, Franz Peter—*Austrian*
(1797-1828)
	VOL.	PAGE
Note	II	26

Schumann, Robert—*German*
(1810-1856)
Notes	II	18,
	40, 41	
Note	IX	172

Sibelius, Jean—*Finnish* (1865-1957)
Note	X	154

Sousa, John Philip—*American*
(1854-1932)
Note	III	46

Strauss, Johann—*Austrian*
(1825-1899)
Note	IX	172

Strauss, Richard—*German*
(1864-1949)
Don Quixote (*Note*).............	XI	90

Taylor, Deems—*American*
Note	III	171

Tchaikovsky, Peter—*Russian*
(1840-1893)
Nutcracker Suite (*Notes*)........	II	218,
	222	
Notes	IV	65,
	145	
Sleeping Beauty Waltz (*Note*).....	VI	11
The Tempest (*Note*).............	VIII	18
Jeanne d'Arc (*Note*)...........	X	98
Francesca Da Rimini (*Note*)......	XI	162

Thomas, Ambroise—*French*
(1811-1896)
Note	VIII	188

Verdi, Giuseppe—*Italian*
(1813-1901)
Note	IV	160

Wagner, Richard—*German*
(1813-1883)
Note	IV	192
Notes	V	162,
	179	
Note	VII	72
Note	X	11
The Rhine-Gold (*Note*)..........	XI	73

Weber, Carl Maria von—*German*
(1786-1826)
Note	III	110

FOLK MUSIC AND SONGS

American
	VOL.	PAGE
American Indian Songs.............	I	80
Jingle Bells, Jingle Bells...........	I	87
A-Tisket, A-Tasket	I	89
Get Out of the Way...............	I	93
I'm Captain Jinks..................	I	93
The Man Who Has Plenty of Good Peanuts	I	95
When Uncle Henry Was a Little Tiny Boy	I	97
The Boatman He's a Lucky Man!...	I	97
Lazy Old Mary....................	I	98
John Brown Had a Little Indian....	I	100
O I'm a Jolly Old Cowboy.........	I	100
Yankee Doodle	I	101

	VOL.	PAGE
The Farmer in the Dell............	I	102
I Went to the Animal Fair.........	I	104
Note	I	106
Pop! Goes the Weasel!.............	I	107
Where, O Where Has My Little Dog Gone	I	107
Froggie Goes a-Courting...........	I	111
Old Noah	I	112
Turkey in the Straw..............	I	113
The Barnyard	I	114
A Song of the Railroad Men.......	I	181
An American Miner's Song.........	II	23
Wynken, Blynken, and Nod........	II	24
The Cowboy's Life................	IV	193
Casey Jones	V	64
John Henry, the Big Steel-Drivin' Man	V	139

Canadian
Canadian Songs	I	130

English
Sing a Song of Sixpence............	I	49
Note	III	110

Estonian
When I Was a Baby...............	I	145

Hawaiian
Note	VI	198

Russian
Building the Bridge...............	II	149

Scottish
Note	X	21
Note	X	29

Welsh
Note	VII	20

MUSICAL INSTRUMENTS
See also IN YOUR HANDS—
Chapter XXI

BAGPIPE
There Was a Piper Had a Cow.....	I	29
Old Pipes and the Dryad..........	VI	18
Illustration	VI	61
Note	X	21

BASSOON
A Musical Visit to Fairyland.......	VI	59

BUGLE
The Bugle Song..................	XI	7
Illustration	III	46

CALLIOPE
The Circus Parade................	III	46

CRWTH (Welsh)
Note	VII	20

CYMBALS
Illustration	I	187
Illustration	I	215

DRUMS
Illustration	I	101
Bang-Whang-Whang	I	185
The Orchestra	I	187
Illustration	I	215
Jasper the Drummin' Boy..........	VI	108

FIDDLE
See MUSICAL INSTRUMENTS—
Violin

FIFE
Bang-Whang-Whang	I	185

FLUTE
The Orchestra	I	187

	VOL.	PAGE
MUSICAL INSTRUMENTS (*Continued*)		
GONGS AND BELLS		
Note	II	177
GUITAR		
The Owl and the Pussy-Cat	II	180
HAND ORGAN		
Of Speckled Eggs the Birdie Sings	I	158
HARP		
The Bee, the Mouse, and the Bum-		
Clock	II	155
Jack and the Beanstalk	V	20
HORN		
The Orchestra	I	187
Illustration	I	215
LUTE		
Columbine and Her Playfellows of		
the Italian Pantomime	VII	119
Illustration	X	170
PIANO		
The Little Dog Waltz	II	150
A Musical Visit to Fairyland	VI	59
SAXOPHONE		
Illustration	I	215
TRUMPET		
The Trumpet of the Swan	IX	106
VIOLIN (Fiddle)		
Hey Diddle Diddle	I	22
Old King Cole	I	44
Diddle, Diddle on a Bass Fiddle	I	73
The Orchestra	I	187
Illustration (*Bass violin*)	I	215
Of a Tailor and a Bear	III	134
A Musical Visit to Fairyland	VI	59
The Youth Who Wanted Some Fun	VII	20
MYTHS		
GREEK		
Clytie	III	151
Phaeton	VII	90
The Golden Touch	VII	210
The Adventures of Perseus	IX	140
The Labors of Hercules	IX	151
NORSE		
Thor's Journey to Jotun-heim	IX	164
The Stealing of Iduna	IX	172
NATURE		
ANIMALS		
Amphibian		
See NATURE—Animals—*Frog; Salamander;*		
Toad		
Anteater		
The Right Time to Laugh	III	81
Antelope		
Afar in the Desert (*Eland, Gazelle,*		
Gnu, Hartébeest, Kudu, Oribi)	VIII	36
Ape		
The Battle of the Firefly and the Apes	III	59
Snowflake the Gorilla	VI	159
Jane and the Wild Chimps	XII	70
Ass		
See also NATURE—Animals—*Don-*		
key; Mule		
A Midsummer Night's Dream	VI	38
Afar in the Desert (*Quagga*)	VIII	36
Una and the Red Cross Knight	XI	8
The Surprising Adventures of Don		
Quixote of La Mancha	XI	90
Baboon		
I Went to the Animal Fair	I	104
Old Noah	I	112
Bat		
Bat, Bat, Come Under My Hat	I	45
Bats	I	211
The Right Time to Laugh	III	81
Tippity Witchit's Hallowe'en	IV	145
Illustration (*Ariel's Song*)	VIII	35
Bear		
The Children and the Bear	I	206
Illustration	I	215
Uncle Mitya's Horse	II	46
The Teddy Bears' Picnic	II	57
Goldilocks and the Three Bears	III	20
Of a Tailor and a Bear	III	134
Snow-white and Rose-red	IV	34
How Brer Rabbit Met Brer Tar-Baby	IV	130
Pecos Bill, the Cowboy	IV	195
Old Johnny Appleseed	IV	213
Winnie-the-Pooh	V	68
Mowgli's Brothers	V	182
The Strong Boy	VI	71
East o' the Sun and West o' the Moon	VII	31
The Snow-Queen	VII	48
Beaver		
Hiawatha's Childhood	V	222
Boar		
The Labors of Hercules	IX	151
Buffalo		
The Girl Who Used Her Wits	IV	137
Pecos Bill, the Cowboy	IV	195
Buffalo Bill	IX	27
Bull		
Right Out in Our Barnyard	I	69
The Red Ettin	V	90
The Labors of Hercules	IX	151
Cuculain, the Irish Hound	X	188
Calf		
There Was an Old Man	I	30
I Stand in the Pulpit and Preach	I	117
Little Liese Comes a-Running	I	121
There Was a Little Man and His		
Name Was Gice	I	126
There Was a Little Boy	I	199
A Song for Easter	II	80
Illustration	II	163
Camel		
Mary and the Christ-Child	I	218
The Circus Parade	III	46
Illustration	XII	194
Cat		
"Bow-Wow," Says the Dog	I	21
Hey Diddle Diddle	I	22
Ride Away, Ride Away	I	24
Sing, Sing!—What Shall I Sing?	I	31
Pussy Sits Beside the Fire	I	36
Pussy Cat, Pussy Cat	I	44

NATURE

ANIMALS—Cat (*Continued*)

	VOL.	PAGE
Great A, Little A, Bouncing B......	I	52
Three Little Kittens................	I	53
The Squirrel Went Out to Cut the Hay	I	60
Pussy, Kittie	I	64
Who's on the Roof?...............	I	64
Pussy, Pussy, Dear Pussy...........	I	72
Diddle, Diddle on a Bass Fiddle.....	I	73
The Rajah Went to Delhi...........	I	79
All the Cats Consulted.............	I	85
The Rose Is Red	I	86
Bye-O! Bye-O!	I	90
The Farmer in the Dell...........	I	102
I Saw a Crow a-Flying Low........	I	107
The Barnyard	I	114
I Stand in the Pulpit and Preach....	I	117
A, B, C, Kitty's in the Snow I See!..	I	120
Don't Run Away My Kitty.........	I	132
I Love Little Pussy................	I	143
First Adventures	I	160
Conversation	I	163
The Little Girl and the New Dress...	I	168
Little Gustava	II	30
Belling the Cat...................	II	35
Reen-Reen-Reeny-Croak-Frog	II	37
The Poor Old Lady...............	II	68
The City Mouse and the Country Mouse	II	84
The Tale of Peter Rabbit..........	II	112
The Ugly Duckling	II	131
Two Children	II	138
Krazy Kat	II	172
The Owl and the Pussy-Cat........	II	180
Dame Wiggins of Lee.............	II	188
Wee Robin's Christmas Song	II	209
Mrs. Tabby Gray..................	III	129
The Kitten and Falling Leaves......	III	133
Christening the Baby in Russia......	IV	63
Tippity Witchit's Hallowe'en	IV	145
Dick Whittington and His Cat.......	V	33
Gigi and the Magic Ring...........	VII	199
The Adventures of Alexander Selkirk	IX	41

Cow

	VOL.	PAGE
There Was a Piper Had a Cow......	I	29
Little Maid, Pretty Maid	I	56
O 'Twas on a Bright Mornin' in Summer	I	59
Reinar Was Watching His Cows.....	I	61
The Farmer's Boy	I	108
The Barnyard	I	114
Bye-Lo, Bubbeli, Sleep	I	117
I Stand in the Pulpit and Preach....	I	117
Would You Like to See Goats Dance on Stilts?..................	I	121
There Was a Little Man and His Name Was Gice.................	I	126
I'm a Butcher....................	I	128
The Boy Who Made Hay...........	I	134
Mary Milks the Cow..............	I	135
The Friendly Cow All Red and White	I	159
Mary and the Christ-Child.........	I	218
The Gingerbread Man..............	II	58
Illustration	II	102
A German Evening................	II	140
The Bee, the Mouse, and the Bum-Clock	II	155

	VOL.	PAGE
The Purple Cow....................	II	163
The Wee, Wee Mannie and the Big, Big Coo	III	99
The Dog in the Manger...........	III	197
The Cowboy's Life	IV	192b
The Story of Tom Thumb.........	V	11
Jack and the Beanstalk............	V	20
Old Pipes and the Dryad..........	VI	18

Coyote

	VOL.	PAGE
Pecos Bill, the Cowboy.............	IV	195

Crab

	VOL.	PAGE
The Two Crabs	II	33

Deer

See also NATURE—Animals— *Reindeer*

	VOL.	PAGE
The Foolish, Timid, Little Hare.....	III	76
The First Thanksgiving Day.........	V	113
Bucky, the Big, Bold Fawn.........	III	85
Jack the Giant-Killer (*Doe*)........	VI	140
Hiawatha's Fasting...............	IX	89
The Labors of Hercules (*Stag*)......	IX	151

Dog

	VOL.	PAGE
"Bow-Wow," Says the Dog....	I	21
Hey Diddle Diddle	I	22
Bow, Wow, Wow, Whose Dog Art Thou?	I	23
Ride Away, Ride Away.............	I	24
Pussy Sits Beside the Fire.........	I	36
Old Mother Hubbard	I	38
Ride, Ride Away	I	60
Little Peppino	I	62
There Was a Farmer Had a Dog....	I	85
I Had a Little Dog...............	I	106
Where, O Where Has My Little Dog Gone	I	107
The Farmer's Boy	I	108
The Barnyard	I	114
Would You Like to See Goats Dance on Stilts?..................	I	121
Blessings on Thee, Dog of Mine.....	I	143
Hi-Yi, Hi-Yi, Hytola...............	I	144
Thus I Guard My Mother's Lambkins	I	144
Hark, Hark! Bow-wow!.............	I	149
First Adventures	I	160
The Little Girl and the New Dress...	I	168
Illustration	I	215
Little Gustava	II	30
The Donkey and the Lap Dog......	II	50
The Ugly Duckling................	II	131
A Belgian Morning................	II	141
The Little Dog Waltz..............	II	150
Krazy Kat	II	172
Dame Wiggins of Lee.............	II	188
The Mad Dog....................	III	63
Chanticleer and Partlet............	III	176
The Dog in the Manger...........	III	197
The Boy Hero of Harlem..........	IV	57
Christening the Baby in Russia......	IV	63
Little Gulliver	V	103
Freddy the Pad Dog..............	V	214
The Wizard of Oz.................	VI	62
The Dog of Pompeii..............	VII	145
Battle Tactics	VII	165
Gigi and the Magic Ring...........	VII	199
Old Yeller	IX	98
Cuculain, the Irish Hound..........	X	188

Dolphin

	VOL.	PAGE
The Adventures of Perseus..........	IX	140

NATURE

ANIMALS (*Continued*)

Donkey

See also NATURE—Animals—
  Ass; Mule

Mr. Toad Set Out on a Journey.....	I	68
The Cuckoo and the Donkey........	I	122
Mary and the Christ-Child..........	I	218
The Donkey and the Lap Dog......	II	50
Illustration	II	102
The Circus Parade.................	III	46
Maggie Tulliver Goes to Live with the Gypsies	VIII	189

Dormouse

The Elf and the Dormouse........	III	39
The Butterfly's Ball..............	III	162

Elephant

Illustration	I	79
Go Ask Your Mother for Fifty Cents	I	104
Jumbo Was an Elephant...........	I	105
Old Noah	I	112
The Zoo in the Park..............	I	186
The Circus Parade.................	III	46
The Foolish, Timid, Little Hare.....	III	76
Afar in the Desert.................	VIII	36
The Circus Man...................	VIII	144
Illustration	X	235

Fox

Through the Jungle................	I	79
Illustration	I	215
Johnny and the Three Goats........	II	47
The Gingerbread Man..............	II	58
The Cock, the Mouse, and the Little Red Hen	II	192
Wee Robin's Christmas Song........	II	209
Peter Rabbit Decides to Change His Name	III	49
A Story About the Little Rabbits....	III	123
Chanticleer and Partlet.............	III	176
The Golden Bird..................	VII	134

Frog

Here We Sail So Fast and Free......	I	96
Froggie Goes a-Courting...........	I	111
Turkey in the Straw............... .	I	113
Hei, Jim Along Josey..............	I	117
Over in the Meadow...............	I	138
Illustration	I	215
Reen-Reen-Reeny-Croak-Frog	II	37
The Right Time to Laugh..........	III	81
The Battle of the Frogs and the Mice	IV	104
The Lost Spear	VI	132

Giraffe

Old Noah	I	112
Illustration	II	102

Goat

Old Mother Hubbard..............	I	38
A Goat One Day Was Feeling Fine..	I	106
Would You Like to See Goats Dance on Stilts?	I	121
Illustration	I	215
Johnny and the Three Goats........	II	47
Oeyvind and Marit	III	137
Heidi in the Alpine Pasture........	V	146
Old Pipes and the Dryad..........	VI	18
The Adventures of Alexander Selkirk	IX	41
Thor's Journey to Jotun-heim.......	IX	164

Ground Hog

See NATURE—Animals—*Woodchuck*

Hare

See also NATURE—Animals—
  Rabbit

Johnny and the Three Goats........	II	47
The Hare and the Tortoise..........	II	106
The Sheep and the Pig That Made a Home	II	145
The Foolish, Timid, Little Hare.....	III	76
The Little Girl and the Hare.......	III	111

Hedgehog

Illustration	VIII	19

Hippopotamus

Old Noah	I	112
Illustration	VIII	36

Hog

See also NATURE—Animals—*Pig*

"Bow-Wow," Says the Dog........	I	21

Horse

There Was a Horse................	I	54
Get Up, Little Horsey.............	I	65
Jingle Bells, Jingle Bells...........	I	87
Over the River and Through the Woods	I	87
I'm Captain Jinks..................	I	93
The Farmer's Boy	I	108
Mary Milks the Cow..............	I	135
Uncle Mitya's Horse...............	II	46
The Gingerbread Man..............	II	58
The Strange Adventure of Baron Münchausen	II	182
The Circus Parade.................	III	46
A Quick-Running Squash...........	III	104
Christening the Baby in Russia......	IV	63
The Cowboy's Life	IV	193
Pecos Bill, the Cowboy............	IV	195
The Story of Tom Thumb..........	V	11
The Princess on the Glass Hill......	VI	80
Illustration	VI	89
The Squire's Bride.................	VI	98
Jack the Giant-Killer...............	VI	140
The Snow-Queen	VII	48
Illustration	VII	71
The Golden Bird	VII	134
My Name Is Aram.................	VII	156
David Copperfield and Little Em'ly..	VII	182
The Magic Horse..................	VIII	92
The Ballad of East and West.......	IX	129
Joan of Arc.......................	X	98
A Story of Rustem, the Hero of Persia	X	228
Illustration	XI	7
Una and the Red Cross Knight......	XI	8
The Surprising Adventures of Don Quixote of La Mancha..........	XI	90

Jackal

Through the Jungle................	I	79
Illustration	II	104
Mowgli's Brothers	V	182

Kangaroo

Old Noah	I	112
The Zoo in the Park..............	I	186
Please Give Me a Ride on Your Back	II	154
The Right Time to Laugh..........	III	81

NATURE

ANIMALS (Continued)

Lamb
See also NATURE—Animals—Sheep

Sleep, Baby, Sleep	I	20
Mary Had a Little Lamb	I	88
The Farmer's Boy	I	108
Minnie and Mattie	I	156
Illustration	I	216
Illustration	I	217
Mary and the Christ-Child	I	218
A Song for Easter	II	80
Dame Wiggins of Lee	II	188
Charlotte's Web	V	54
David, the Shepherd Boy	VII	73

Leopard
Illustration	II	104

Lion
Illustration	I	186
Illustrations	II	102, 104
The Lion and the Mouse	II	108
The Circus Parade	III	46
The Foolish, Timid, Little Hare	III	76
Bucky, the Big, Bold Fawn	III	85
The Wizard of Oz	VI	62
David, the Shepherd Boy	VII	73
The Labors of Hercules	IX	151
The Story of the Cid	X	108

Lobster
The Mock Turtle's Song	III	170
Adventures of a Water Baby	III	211

Mole
The Right Time to Laugh	III	81
The Butterfly's Ball	III	162

Mollusk
See NATURE—Animals—Snail

Monkey
See also NATURE—Animals—
Ape; Baboon; Chimpanzee

There Was a Monkey	I	52
Pop! Goes the Weasel!	I	107
Monkeys	I	142
The Zoo in the Park	I	186
The Dancing Monkeys	II	92
Illustration	II	104
The Circus Parade	III	46
The Foolish, Timid, Little Hare	III	76
The Rarest Animal of All	IV	113

Mouse
See also NATURE—Animals—Rat

Hickory, Dickory, Dock!	I	22
I Saw a Ship a-Sailing	I	35
Birds of a Feather	I	55
The Mouse Climbed Up the Candlestick	I	77
Froggie Goes a-Courting	I	111
Conversation	I	163
Illustration	I	215
The Little Red Hen and the Grain of Wheat	II	13
Ole Shut-Eyes, the Sandman	II	26
Belling the Cat	II	35
Reen-Reen-Reeny-Croak-Frog	II	37
The City Mouse and the Country Mouse	II	84
The Lion and the Mouse	II	108
The Bee, the Mouse, and the Bum-Clock	II	155
Krazy Kat	II	172
The Cock, the Mouse, and the Little Red Hen	II	192
The Tale of Nutcracker	II	218
The Battle of the Frogs and the Mice	IV	104
The Story of Tom Thumb	V	11
The Mice	VI	131
A Tramp of the Middle West	XII	147

Mule
See also NATURE—Animals—
Ass; Donkey

I Had a Little Mule	I	106
Buffalo Bill	IX	27

Muskrat
Over in the Meadow	I	138
Peter Rabbit Decides to Change His Name	III	49

Octopus
Old Stormalong	IV	183

Opossum
The Story of Li'l Hannibal	III	116
How Brer Rabbit Met Brer Tar-Baby	IV	130

Otter
Adventures of a Water Baby	III	211

Ox
Come, Lets Go to Sant' Anita	I	70
I Should Like to Plough	I	136
The Story of Big Paul Bunyan	IV	161

Panther
Mowgli's Brothers	V	182

Pig
See also NATURE—Animals—Hog

This Little Pig Went to Market	I	19
Dickery, Dickery, Dare	I	24
As I Went to Bonner	I	29
To Market, To Market	I	33
Tom, Tom, the Piper's Son	I	34
Birds of a Feather	I	55
I Had a Little Dog	I	106
There Was an Old Pig	I	107
The Farmer's Boy	I	108
The Barnyard	I	114
Minnie and Mattie	I	156
Precocious Piggy	I	196
The Little Pig	I	198
Illustration	I	215
The Little Red Hen and the Grain of Wheat	II	13
Illustration	II	102
The Sheep and the Pig That Made a Home	II	145
The Owl and the Pussy-Cat	II	180
Charlotte's Web	V	54
Peer Gynt	IX	98

Pony
See also NATURE—Animals—
Horse

O I'm a Jolly Old Cowboy	I	100
Illustration	I	101
The Little Gray Pony	II	17
The Circus Parade	III	46
Buffalo Bill	IX	27

NATURE

ANIMALS (Continued)

Porcupine

The Little Rabbit Who Wanted
Red Wings .... II 87

Porpoise

The Mock Turtle's Song........... III 170
Adventures of a Water Baby........ III 211

Prairie Dog

Illustration .... I 181

Rabbit

See also NATURE—Animals—
Hare

Annie Goes to the Cabbage Field... I 129
Illustration .... I 215
Illustration .... I 216
A Song for Easter................. II 80
The Little Rabbit Who Wanted
Red Wings .... II 87
The Tale of Peter Rabbit.......... II 112
Peter Rabbit Decides to Change His
Name .... III 49
The Story of Li'l Hannibal......... III 116
A Story About the Little Rabbits.... III 123
The Birds' St. Valentine's Day..... III 198
How Brer Rabbit Met Brer Tar-Baby IV 130
Winnie-the-Pooh .... V 68
Hiawatha's Childhood .... V 222

Raccoon

Illustration .... I 215
The Hare and the Tortoise......... II 106
Peter Rabbit Decides to Change His
Name .... III 49

Rat

See also NATURE—Animals—
Mouse

"Bow-Wow," Says the Dog .... I 21
Birds of a Feather................. I 55
Dame Wiggins of Lee.............. II 188
How the Brazilian Beetles Got Their
Gorgeous Coats .... III 172
Cinderella .... IV 12
The Pumpkin .... IV 23
Charlotte's Web .... V 54

Reindeer

The Night Before Christmas........ II 213
Hiawatha's Childhood .... V 222
The Snow-Queen .... VII 48
Peer Gynt .... IX 98
Kalevala, Land of Heroes.......... X 151

Rhinoceros

Illustration .... II 104
Afar in the Desert................. VIII 36

Salamander

The Fairyland of Science........... VI 184

Seal

The Adventures of Alexander Selkirk IX 41

Sheep

See also NATURE—Animals—
Lamb

Baa, Baa, Black Sheep............. I 29
Little Peppino .... I 62
Over the Hill to Feed My Sheep..... I 99
The Sleepy Song.................. I 119

There Was a Little Man and His
Name Was Gice................. I 126
Thus I Guard My Mother's Lambkins I 144
Illustration .... II 101
A Bohemian Evening............... II 140
A German Evening................. II 140
The Sheep and the Pig That Made a
Home .... II 145
Dame Wiggins of Lee.............. II 188
Clouds .... III 48
Old Pipes and the Dryad........... VI 18
The Youth Who Wanted Some Fun.. VII 20

Skunk

Peter Rabbit Decides to Change His
Name .... III 49

Snail

Four-and-Twenty Tailors .... I 39
Snail, Snail .... I 132
Old Shellover .... II 185
The Butterfly's Ball.............. III 162
The Mock Turtle's Song........... III 170
The Adventures of a Water Baby.... III 211

Squirrel

The Squirrel Went Out to Cut the Hay I 60
Of All the Beasts That Roam
the Woods .... I 106
Illustration .... I 215
Whisky Frisky .... II 82
The Little Rabbit Who Wanted
Red Wings .... II 87
The Nutcracker and Sugardolly Stories IV 83
Hiawatha's Childhood .... V 222
Bucky, the Big, Bold Fawn......... III 85

Starfish

The Two Crabs .... II 33
The Adventures of a Water Baby.... III 211
David Copperfield and Little Em'ly.. VII 182

Tiger

Illustration .... I 186
Illustration .... II 104
Rama and the Tigers .... II 118
The Circus Parade................. III 46
The Foolish, Timid, Little Hare..... III 76
Mowgli's Brothers .... V 182
The Greatest Show on Earth........ VIII 154a

Toad

See also NATURE—Animals—*Frog*

The Toads in the Lake............ I 68
Mr. Toad Set Out on a Journey..... I 68
Turkey in the Straw............... I 113
Over in the Meadow.............. I 138
The Prince Who Rode Through
a Mousehole .... VII 96

Weasel

Pop! Goes the Weasel!............ I 107

Whale

Old Stormalong .... IV 183
A Whaling Adventure............. VIII 142a

Wolf

Little Peppino .... I 62
Johnny and the Three Goats........ II 47
How Brer Rabbit Met Brer Tar-Baby IV 130
Mowgli's Brothers .... V 182

Woodchuck (Ground hog)

The Little Rabbit Who Wanted
Red Wings .... II 87
The Hare and the Tortoise......... II 106

NATURE

ANIMALS (*Continued*)

Worm

Old Shellover .... II 185
The Fairyland of Science.......... VI 184

Zebra

Afar in the Desert................ VIII 36

BIRDS

Blackbird

Sing a Song of Sixpence........... I 49
There Were Two Blackbirds........ I 51
The Squirrel Went Out to Cut the Hay I 60
The Magpie's Nest .... II 42
The Birds' St. Valentine's Day....... III 198

Bluebird

Over in the Meadow.............. I 138
What Does Little Birdie Say?....... I 154
How the Finch Got Her Colors..... II 143

Bluejay

Two Birds and Their Nest......... II 45

Bulbul (Persian Songbird)

A Story of Rustem, the Hero of Persia X 228

Butcherbird

The Lost Spear .... VI 132

Buzzard

Peter Rabbit Decides to Change His
Name .... III 49

Canary

How the Finch Got Her Colors..... II 143

Cardinal

How the Finch Got Her Colors..... II 143

Chickens

Hickety, Pickety, My Black Hen..... I 24
Cock-a-Doodle-Doo! .... I 32
The Cock's on the Housetop........ I 42
Five Little Chicks .... I 64
The Roosters at the Old Crown Inn.. I 67
A Woman Had a Rooster.......... I 73
William T. Trinity................ I 98
The Farmer's Boy .... I 108
The Barnyard .... I 114
I Stand in the Pulpit and Preach.... I 117
At the Wedding of Miss Jenny Wren. I 125
There Was a Little Man and His
Name Was Gice................ I 126
Hark, Hark! Bow-wow!............ I 149
A White Hen Sitting.............. I 156
The Cock Is Crowing............. I 208
The Clucking Hen................. I 214
Illustration .... I 215
The Little Red Hen and the Grain of
Wheat .... II 13
Little Gustava .... II 30
The Rooster and the Sultan......... II 52
The Little Rooster and the Little Hen II 71
A Song for Easter................. II 80
Two Children .... II 138
The Sheep and the Pig That Made a
Home .... II 145
There Was an Old Man With a Beard II 154
The Cock, the Mouse, and the Little
Red Hen .... II 192
Chanticleer and Partlet........... III 176
The Nutcracker and Sugardolly Stories IV 83

Crane

O My Dame Had a Lame Tame
Crane .... I 95

Crow

"Bow-Wow," Says the Dog......... I 21
There Was a Crow Sat on a Stone... I 54
The Squirrel Went Out to Cut the Hay I 60
Otto Would a-Riding Go........... I 75
I Saw a Crow a-Flying Low........ I 107
At the Wedding of Miss Jenny Wren. I 125
Over in the Meadow.............. I 138
Little Gustava .... II 30
Peter Rabbit Decides to Change His
Name .... III 49

Cuckoo

"Bow-Wow," Says the Dog......... I 21
In Spring the Birds Do Sing........ I 57
Charley, Barley, Buck and Rye...... I 94
The Cuckoo and the Donkey........ I 122
How Strong, How Strong a Bridge
Have You? .... I 129
When I Was a Baby............... I 145
The Birds' St. Valentine's Day...... III 198

Dove

Little Gustava .... II 30
Noah's Ark .... II 101
Answer to a Child's Question....... II 142

Duck

"Bow-Wow," Says the Dog......... I 21
I Saw a Ship a-Sailing............. I 35
The Cock's on the Housetop........ I 42
The Farmer's Boy .... I 108
The Barnyard .... I 114
Would You Like to See Goats
Dance on Stilts?................. I 121
There Were Three Duckies......... I 127
Auntie, Where Are You Going?..... I 128
Illustration .... I 215
The Little Red Hen and the Grain of
Wheat .... II 13
Reen-Reen-Reeny-Croak-Frog ...... II 37
The Little Rabbit Who Wanted
Red Wings .... II 87
Shingebiss .... II 96
The Ugly Duckling................ II 131
Please Give Me a Ride on Your Back II 154
The Bee, the Mouse, and the Bum-
Clock .... II 155
Ducks' Ditty .... III 62
The Birds' St. Valentine's Day...... III 198
The Rarest Animal of All.......... IV 113

Eagle

Illustrations .... II 143,
　　　　　　　　　　　　　　　　　144
The Birds' St. Valentine's Day...... III 198
Snow-white and Rose-red.......... IV 34
Rhodopis and Her Gilded Sandals... VII 84
Marko, the Champion of Serbian
Liberty .... XI 29

Falcon

The Birds' St. Valentine's Day...... III 198

Finch

How the Finch Got Her Colors..... II 143

Flamingo

Illustration .... II 102
The Exile of Rama................ X 175

NATURE

BIRDS (Continued)

Goldfinch
The Goldfinch .... II 45

Goose
Goosey, Goosey, Gander .... I 22
Old Mother Goose................. I 23
Auntie, Where Are You Going?..... I 128
Illustration .... II 41
Illustration .... II 101
The Ugly Duckling................ II 131
The Sheep and the Pig That Made a
Home .... II 145
The Bee, the Mouse, and the Bum-
Clock .... II 155
A Boy in the Island of Bali........ II 176
The Turtle Who Could Not Stop
Talking .... II 178
The Birds' St. Valentine's Day...... III 198
Charlotte's Web .... V 54

Grackle
How the Finch Got Her Colors..... II 143

Grouse
Hie Away, Hie Away .... VI 70

Hawk
Wee Robin's Christmas Song .... II 209
The Birds' St. Valentine's Day...... III 198

Heron
The Honest Woodman .... III 114
Illustration .... VII 87

Lark
Answer to a Child's Question....... II 142
There Was an Old Man with a Beard II 154

Lyrebird
The Right Time to Laugh.......... III 81

Macaw
Illustration .... I 68
Illustration .... II 69

Magpie
The Magpie's Nest................. II 42

Nightingale
At the Wedding of Miss Jenny Wren. I 125

Ostrich
Afar in the Desert................. VIII 36
Illustration .... VIII 153

Owl
Old Mother Goose .... I 23
There Was an Owl................. I 50
A Song of the Railroad Men....... I 181
The Twilight .... II 41
The Magpie's Nest................. II 42
There Was an Old Man with a Beard II 154
The Owl and the Pussy-Cat........ II 180
The Owl .... III 28
The Owl's Answer to Tommy....... III 29
Hiawatha's Childhood .... V 222
A Tramp of the Middle West....... XII 147

Parrot
See also NATURE—Birds—Macaw
How the Finch Got Her Colors..... II 143
How the Brazilian Beetles Got Their
Gorgeous Coats .... III 172

Peacock
King Hilary and the Beggarman .... III 70
The Exile of Rama................ X 175

Pelican
Illustration .... II 102

Penguin
Illustration .... II 102

Raven
Noah's Ark .... II 101
Hiawatha's Fasting .... IX 89

Robin
Little Robin Redbreast............. I 23
A Story About Abe Lincoln........ V 133

Rooster
See NATURE—Birds—Chickens

Sandpiper
Adventures of a Water Baby........ III 211

Sea Gull
Illustration .... I 61
Illustration .... I 184
A Sea-Song from the Shore........ I 202
Little Gulliver .... V 103
The Sea Gull .... V 111

Sparrow
"Bow-Wow," Says the Dog......... I 21
A Little Cock Sparrow............. I 52
Little Gustava .... II 30
The Magpie's Nest................. II 42
The Tale of Peter Rabbit.......... II 112
Answer to a Child's Question....... II 142

Stork
Krazy Kat .... II 172
The Little Toy Land of the Dutch... IV 56

Sugarbird
The Lost Spear................... VI 132

Swallow
At the Wedding of Miss Jenny Wren I 125
Here We Come, We Children Come. I 204

Swan
The Ugly Duckling................ II 131
The Right Time to Laugh.......... III 81
How Jack Sought the Golden Apples V 76
The Six Swans.................... VII 126
The Trumpet of the Swan.......... IX 106
Lohengrin .... X 89

Thrush
Of Speckled Eggs the Birdie Sings... I 158
The Magpie's Nest................. II 42
Answer to a Child's Question....... II 142
Old Shellover .... II 185

Turkey
A Woman Had a Turkey.......... I 73
The Farmer's Boy .... I 108
Turkey in the Straw.............. I 113
The Ugly Duckling............... II 131
The Owl and the Pussy-Cat........ II 180
The Story of Li'l Hannibal......... III 116
The First Thanksgiving Day........ V 113

Turtledove
The Magpie's Nest................. II 42

Woodpecker
At the Wedding of Miss Jenny Wren. I 125

Wren
At the Wedding of Miss Jenny Wren. I 125
There Was an Old Man with a Beard II 154
Wee Robin's Christmas Song........ II 209

NATURE (*Continued*)

BIRD CALLS

In Spring the Birds Do Sing........	I	57
A Song of the Railroad Men.......	I	181
The Twilight	II	41
The Magpie's Nest.................	II	42
Note	III	42
Hansel and Grethel................	IV	73

BROOK

What the Children Do in Summer...	I	212
Come, Little Leaves................	II	70

CATARACT

The Cataract of Lodore............	VII	47
The Bugle Song....................	XI	7

CLOUDS

If I Could Walk...................	I	62
Pretty, See the Cloud Appear!.......	I	81
Illustration	I	194
The Bow That Bridges Heaven......	II	105
Snow	II	208
Illustration	III	11
Clouds	III	48
The Cloud	VII	95

CREEK

See NATURE—River or Creek

DESERT

Afar in the Desert................	VIII	36

FIELD AND MEADOW

Little Boy Blue...................	I	33
The Cock's on the Housetop.......	I	42
Willie Boy, Willie Boy	I	45
Little Peppino	I	62
I Took a Walk One Evening.......	I	75
Over in the Meadow..............	I	138
The Cock Is Crowing.............	I	208
Laughing Song	II	75
A Swedish Evening................	II	141

FISH

Row, Row! A-Fishing We'll Go!.....	I	61
There Was a Naughty Boy..........	I	152
Shingebiss	II	96

Eel

The Right Time to Laugh..........	III	81
The Adventures of a Water Baby....	III	211

Goldfish

Clytie	III	151

Minnow

The Little Turtle	I	162

Salmon

The Adventures of a Water Baby....	III	211

Sea Horse

A Sea-Song from the Shore........	I	202
Illustration	II	33
The Sea Shell....................	III	150
Old Stormalong	IV	183

Sunfish

The Adventures of a Water Baby....	III	211

Trout

Over in the Meadow..............	I	138
The Adventures of a Water Baby....	III	211

Whiting

The Mock Turtle's Song...........	III	170

FLOWERS

See also NATURE—Garden

Buttercup

A Milkweed and a Buttercup........	IV	118

Cactus

The Plains' Call...................	IV	211

Canterbury Bells

Dainty Little Maiden	I	155

Clover

Illustration	II	163

Cowslip

Go Out, Children..................	I	185
A Milkweed and a Buttercup	IV	118
Illustration (*Ariel's Song*)..........	VIII	35

Crocus

Crocus Flowers Bloom Like Fire....	I	205

Daffodil

Daffy-Down-Dilly	I	25
Crocus Flowers Bloom Like Fire....	I	205

Geranium

Illustration	III	128

Hollyhock

Illustration	III	128

Lavender

Lavender's Blue	I	56

Lily

Dainty Little Maiden...............	I	155
My Beloved Is Gone Down Into His Garden	II	78
Illustration (*Water Lily*)	III	211

Milkweed

A Milkweed and a Buttercup.......	IV	118

Morning Glory

Illustration	I	123

Narcissus

Crocus Flowers Bloom Like Fire....	I	205

Rose

Little Girl, Little Girl.............	I	56
Dainty Little Maiden...............	I	155
Where Are My Roses?.............	I	205
The Snow-Queen	VII	48

Silver Bells

Mary, Mary, Quite Contrary........	I	25

Sunflower

Clytie	III	151

Violet

Where Are My Roses?.............	I	205

Zinnia

Illustration	I	189

FOG

The Fog	I	184

FOREST OR JUNGLE

When Woods Awake..............	I	57
The Twilight	II	41
Rama and the Tigers	II	118
Building the Bridge..............	II	149
The Foolish, Timid, Little Hare.....	III	76
Christening the Baby in Russia......	IV	63
Hansel and Grethel................	IV	73
The Story of Big Paul Bunyan......	IV	161
Old Johnny Appleseed	IV	213
Mowgli's Brothers	V	182
Hiawatha's Childhood	V	222

	VOL.	PAGE

NATURE

FOREST OR JUNGLE (*Continued*)

A Midsummer Night's Dream....... VI 38
The Strong Boy.................... VI 71
Fairy Forests .... VI 190
The Knights of the Silver Shield..... VII 173
Exploring the Wilderness........... IX 9
The Adventures of Alexander Selkirk IX 41
Hiawatha's Fasting .... IX 89
Peer Gynt .... IX 98
As You Like It .... X 165
Una and the Red Cross Knight..... XI 8
Ye Merry Doinges of Robin Hood... XI 49
Down by the River Avon.......... XII 15

GARDEN

See also NATURE—Flowers
Mary, Mary, Quite Contrary........ I 25
Dainty Little Maiden.............. I 155
My Beloved Is Gone Down Into His
Garden .... II 78
The Tale of Peter Rabbit.......... II 112
A Child in a Mexican Garden....... IV 103
A Milkweed and a Buttercup .... IV 118

HILL

See NATURE—Mountain or Hill

INSECTS

Ant

This Little Ant Worked with Might
and Main .... I 71
The Butterfly's Ball............... III 162
The Fairyland of Science.......... VI 184

Bee

Sum-m, Sum-m, Sum-m!............ I 122
Over in the Meadow............... I 138
How Doth the Little Busy Bee...... I 143
Johnny and the Three Goats........ II 47
The Bee, the Mouse, and the Bum-
Clock .... II 155
The Song of the Bee.............. II 163
The Brook Song.................. III 161
The Butterfly's Ball............... III 162
The Nutcracker and Sugardolly Stories IV 83
The Fairyland of Science.......... VI 184

Beetle

The Bee, the Mouse, and the Bum-
Clock .... II 155
The Butterfly's Ball............... III 162
How the Brazilian Beetles Got Their
Gorgeous Coats .... III 172
The Adventures of a Water Baby.... III 211
The Fairyland of Science.......... VI 184

Butterfly

Butterflies, Butterflies .... I 81
The Butterfly's Ball............... III 162
The Lost Spear................... VI 132

Caddis fly (Caddis worm)

The Adventures of a Water Baby.... III 211
The Fairyland of Science.......... VI 184

Caterpillar

The Adventures of a Water Baby.... III 211
The Fairyland of Science.......... VI 184

Cricket

Over in the Meadow............... I 138
Come, Little Leaves.............. II 70

	VOL.	PAGE

Dragonfly

The Brook Song.................. III 161
The Butterfly's Ball............... III 162
The Adventures of a Water Baby.... III 211

Firefly

The Battle of the Firefly and the Apes III 59
Twinkling Bugs .... III 61
The Butterfly's Ball............... III 162
Hiawatha's Childhood .... V 222
The Moon-Maiden .... VI 222

Flea

The Little Turtle .... I 162
The Song of the Flea............. II 185

Fly

Baby Bye, Here's a Fly............ I 90

Grasshopper

Laughing Song .... II 75
Grasshopper Green .... II 76
An Explanation of the Grasshopper.. II 77
The Butterfly's Ball............... III 162

Hornet

The Butterfly's Ball............... III 162

Katydid

Fairy and Child.................. III 25

Ladybird

Fairy Forests .... VI 190

Locust

The Fairyland of Science.......... VI 184

Mosquito

The Little Turtle................. I 162
The Battle of the Firefly and the Apes III 59

Moth

The Butterfly's Ball .... III 162

Spider

Little Miss Muffet................ I 40
Over in the Meadow.............. I 138
Grasshopper Green .... II 76
Charlotte's Web .... V 54
The Fairyland of Science.......... VI 184
Robert Bruce, Scotland's Hero...... X 21

Wasp

The Butterfly's Ball............... III 162

JUNGLE

See NATURE—Forest or Jungle

LAKE

The Cock Is Crowing............. I 208
Shingebiss .... II 96
The Honest Woodman .... III 114
Hiawatha's Fasting .... IX 89

LIGHTNING

Thunder and Lightning........... I 195

MEADOW

See NATURE—Field and Meadow

MOON

Hey Diddle Diddle .... I 22
Boys and Girls, Come Out to Play... I 39
Note .... I 40
There Was an Old Woman Tossed
Up in a Basket.................. I 41
Sweet and Low.................. I 118
Wynken, Blynken, and Nod........ II 24

VOL. PAGE

NATURE

MOON (*Continued*)

Moon, So Round and Yellow.......	II	40
Krazy Kat	II	172
A Boy in the Island of Bali........	II	176
The Owl and the Pussy-Cat........	II	180
Old Shellover	II	185
The Owl's Answer to Tommy.......	III	29
Three Jovial Huntsmen............	III	110
The Daring Prince.................	III	127
The Pumpkin	IV	23
Tippity Witchit's Hallowe'en........	IV	145
Hiawatha's Childhood	V	222
The Moon-Maiden	VI	222
The Sky at Night.................	VII	72
The First Moon Landing..........	XII	30

MOUNTAIN OR HILL

Illustration	I	17
If I Could Walk	I	62
A Japanese Lullaby................	I	78
Illustration	I	180
Crocus Flowers Bloom Like Fire....	I	205
The Little Engine That Could......	II	200
Heidi in the Alpine Pasture........	V	146
Old Pipes and the Dryad..........	VI	18
The Man Who Loved Hai Quai.....	VI	127
The Moon-Maiden	VI	222
The Maiden, the Knight, and the Waterfall	VII	40
A Rover in the Catskills...........	XII	99
The Poet of the Sierras............	XII	143

PLAIN

See NATURE—Prairie and Plain

PLANTS

Beanstalk

Jack and the Beanstalk............	V	20

Cabbage

Annie Goes to the Cabbage Field....	I	129
The Little Girl and the Hare........	III	111

Cactus

Illustration	I	71
Illustration	I	80
Illustration	IX	39

Cattail

Illustration	I	150
Illustration	II	180
Illustration	III	62
Illustration	III	93
Illustration	III	161

Cornstalk

Pretty, See the Cloud Appear!.......	I	81

Fern

Hie Away, Hie Away (*Lady Fern*)...	VI	70

Parsley

Where Are My Roses?.............	I	205

Pumpkin

The Pumpkin	IV	23
The Acorn and the Pumpkin........	VII	132

Squash

A Quick-Running Squash...........	III	104

Strawberries

What the Children Do in Summer...	I	212
The Little Rooster and the Little Hen	II	71

VOL. PAGE

PRAIRIE AND PLAIN

A Song of the Railroad Men........	I	181
The Village of Cream Puffs.........	II	124
Buffalo Bill	IX	27
A Boy in Russia (*Steppes*)..........	XII	190

RAIN

It's Raining	I	67
The Toads in the Lake.............	I	68
This Little Ant Worked with Might and Main	I	71
Pretty, See the Cloud Appear!.......	I	81
When That I Was But a Little Tiny Boy	I	149
The Big Umbrella and the Little Rubbers	I	190
Rain	I	191
Thunder and Lightning.............	I	195
It Is God That Hath Made Us......	I	216
Noah's Ark	II	101
April	VI	96

RAINBOW

Illustration	I	61
Noah's Ark	II	101
The Bow That Bridges Heaven......	II	105
Illustration	II	144
The Labors of Hercules............	IX	151
Kalevala, Land of Heroes	X	151

REPTILES

Alligator

Aruman, a Hero of Java...........	VI	202

Crocodile

Dreamland Opens Here	I	91

Lizard

Over in the Meadow...............	I	138
The Adventures of a Water Baby....	III	211
The Lost Spear	VI	132

Serpent

The Labors of Hercules............	IX	151

Snake

A Song of the Railroad Men (*Rattlesnake*)	I	181
Pecos Bill, the Cowboy (*Rattlesnake*)	IV	195
A Midsummer Night's Dream.......	VI	38

Turtle

The Little Turtle..................	I	162
The Hare and the Tortoise..........	II	106
The Turtle Who Could Not Stop Talking	II	178
Illustration	III	114
Clytie	III	151
The Mock Turtle's Song............	III	170

RIVER OR CREEK

The Boatman He's a Lucky Man....	I	97
The Gingerbread Man	II	58
Ducks' Ditty	III	62
Where Go the Boats?.............	III	94
A Song of the Canadian Lumberjack	IV	180
How Robert Fulton Harnessed the Giant	V	48
The Strong Boy...................	VI	71
The Snow-Queen	VII	48
Recollections of The Arabian Nights.	VIII	108
Pushing Westward with Lewis and Clark	IX	25
A Chronicle of Kiev..............	IX	118

SEA

I Saw a Ship a-Sailing.............	I	35

NATURE

SEA (Contin. 1)

Bobby Shaft s Gone to Sea	I	44
Rub-a-Dub-Dub	I	48
Here We Sail So ϛ st and Free	I	96
Sweet and Low	I	118
O Sailor, Come Ashore	I	157
Of Speckled Eggs the Birdie Sings	I	158
When I Was Down Beside the Sea	I	159
My Boat	I	163
Look, See the Boat!	I	184
A Sea-Song from the Shore	I	202
The Two Crabs	II	33
The Sea Shell	III	150
Clytie	III	151
The Sea	III	155
Little Blue Apron	III	210
The Adventures of a Water Baby	III	211
Old Stormalong	IV	183
Little Gulliver	V	103
The Sea Gull	V	111
All About Columbus	V	112
Why the Sea Is Salt	V	140
The Merman	VI	182
A Tropical Morning at Sea	VI	201
White Horses	VII	144
David Copperfield and Little Em'ly	VII	182
A Song of Drake's Men	VIII	7
A Boy on the High Seas	VIII	8
Sea Fever	VIII	35
Gulliver's Travels to Lilliput	VIII	38
A Wanderer's Song	VIII	91
Mr. Hampden's Shipwreck	VIII	172
A Christmas Song at Sea	VIII	187
Solitude	IX	65
Señor Kon-Tiki	XII	30

SEASONS

Spring

In Spring the Birds Do Sing	I	57
Here We Come, We Children Come	I	204
Crocus Flowers Bloom Like Fire	I	205
It's Spring	I	208
God Hath Made Me to Laugh	I	217
Mary and the Christ-Child	I	218
Little Gustava	II	30
Behold the Fig Tree	II	78
A Song for Easter	II	80
The Song of Solomon	III	136
The Birds' St. Valentine's Day	III	198
April	VI	97
Song on May Morning	VII	171
The Stealing of Iduna	IX	172
How the Goddess of Spring Came to Scoring	IX	176

Summer

O 'Twas on a Bright Mornin' in Summer	I	59
Ice-Cold Lemonade	I	88
When I Was a Baby	I	145
Grasshopper Green	II	76
The Shaking of the Pear Tree	III	146
Old Pipes and the Dryad	VI	18
A Midsummer Night's Dream	VI	38

Autumn

Come, Little Leaves	II	70
The Kitten and Falling Leaves	III	133
The Pumpkin	IV	23

Winter

There Were Two Little Boys	I	74
Jingle Bells, Jingle Bells	I	87
It Snows and It Blows	I	87
Over the River and Through the Woods	I	87
Three Old Maids a-Skating Went	I	110
A,B,C, Kitty's in the Snow I See!	I	120
I-Yay! I-Yay! I-Yay!	I	131
Cold, Son of Wind and Snow	I	145
The Snow Man	I	192
White Fields	I	193
It Is God That Hath Made Us	I	216
Shingebiss	II	96
Jack Frost	II	186
Snow	II	208
Little Diamond and the North Wind	IV	119
Snow	VI	196
Off We'll Go	VI	196
Willows in the Snow	VI	197
Snow Blossoms	VI	197
The Snow-Queen	VII	48
The Bells	VII	71
Stopping By Woods on a Snowy Evening	VII	172
Pushing Westward with Lewis and Clark	IX	25
How Peary Reached the North Pole	IX	127

SNOW

See NATURE—Seasons—Winter

STAR

Illustration	I	39
Many, Many Stars Are in the Skies	I	86
Star Light, Star Bright	I	86
It Is God That Hath Made Us	I	216
Mary and the Christ-Child	I	218
Wynken, Blynken, and Nod	II	24
The Star	II	83
Illustration	III	127
The Sky at Night	VII	72

SUN

Clytie	III	151
The Wind and the Sun	III	196
How Yehl, the Hero, Freed the Beaming Maiden	VI	102
The Fisherman Who Caught the Sun	VI	198
A Tropical Morning at Sea	VI	201
Rhodopis and Her Gilded Sandals	VII	84
Phaeton	VII	90

THUNDER

Thunder and Lightning	I	195
How Yehl, the Hero, Freed the Beaming Maiden	VI	102
Thor's Journey to Jotun-heim	IX	164

TREES

Apple

Up in the Green Orchard	I	30
Old Johnny Appleseed	IV	213

Birch

Cold, Son of Wind and Snow	I	145
Illustration	III	93
Christening the Baby in Russia	IV	63

Cherry

Little Maid of Far Japan	III	164

Elder

The Kitten and Falling Leaves	III	133

Fig

Behold the Fig Tree	II	78
Aruman, a Hero of Java (*Waringin*)	VI	202

VOL. PAGE

NATURE
  TREES (*Continued*)
    Greenwood
      Under the Greenwood Tree......... XI 72
    Hemlock
      Bucky, the Big, Bold Fawn (Illus.).. III 85
    Linden
      The Little Rooster and the Little Hen II 71
    Mango
      How the Brazilian Beetles Got Their
        Gorgeous Coats .... III 172
    Nut
      I Had a Little Nut Tree............ I 37
    Oak
      Old Pipes and the Dryad........... VI 18
      The Acorn and the Pumpkin........ VII 132
    Palm
      The Foolish, Timid, Little Hare..... III 76
    Pear
      A Pie Sat on a Pear Tree.......... I 27
      The Shaking of the Pear Tree....... III 146
    Pine
      Illustration .... II 41
      Illustration .... II 45
      Building the Bridge............... II 149
      Christening the Baby in Russia...... IV 63
      Hiawatha's Childhood .... V 222
  VOLCANO
    The Trial by Fire................. VII 26
    The Dog of Pompeii............... VII 145
  WIND
    Blow, Wind, Blow, and Go, Mill, Go! I 31
    My Lady Wind.................... I 46
    Old Mother Wind................. I 76
    Sweet and Low................... I 118
    Cold, Son of Wind and Snow....... I 145
    My Boat .... I 163
    A Story of the Wind.............. I 200
    Who Has Seen the Wind?.......... I 201
    Come, Little Leaves............... II 70
    Awake, O North Wind............. II 79
    The Wind Bloweth Where it Listeth.. II 79
    Shingebiss .... II 96
    The Village of Cream Puffs........ II 124
    The Wind and the Sun............. III 196
    Little Diamond and the North Wind. IV 119

NEW YEAR'S DAY
  See HOLIDAYS—New Year's Day

NEW ZEALAND
  See COUNTRIES OF THE WORLD—
  New Zealand

**NOBEL PRIZE WINNERS IN
MY BOOK HOUSE**
  Björnstjerne, Björnson—*Norwegian*
    (1832-1910)
      For Literature—1903
  Buck, Pearl S.—*American*
    (1892-   )
      For Literature—1938
  Einstein, Albert—*German*
    (1879-1955)
      For Physics—1921
  Galsworthy, John—*English*
    (1867-1933)
      For Literature—1932

VOL. PAGE

  Kipling, Rudyard—*English*
    (1865-1936)
      For Literature—1907
  Roosevelt, Theodore—*American*
    (1858-1919)
      For Peace—1906
  Tagore, Rabindranath—*Bengali*
    (1861-1941)
      For Literature—1913
  Wilson, T. Woodrow—*American*
    (1856-1924)
      For Peace—1919

NORWAY
  See COUNTRIES OF THE WORLD—
  Norway

NUMBER EXPERIENCES
  See COUNTING RHYMES; *also* IN
  YOUR HANDS—Chapter X

NURSERY RHYMES
  See also IN YOUR HANDS—
  Chapters II, IV
    African .... I 146,
                        147
    American .... I 80-
                        117
    Canadian .... I 130,
                        131
    Chinese .... I 76,
                        77
    Czechoslovakian .... I 128,
                        129
    Dutch .... I 126,
                        127
    East Indian .... I 79
    English .... I 18-
                     57, 199
    Finnish .... I 144
    French .... I 124,
                        125
    German .... I 120-
                        123
    Greek .... I 205
    Hungarian .... I 136
    Irish .... I 59
    Italian .... I 62,
                        63
    Mexican .... I 70,
                        71
    Norse .... I 60,
                  61, 134, 135
    Polish .... I 72,
                        73
    Russian .... I 132,
                        133
    Scottish .... I 58
    South American................... I 68,
                        69
    Spanish .... I 64,
                        65
    Swedish .... I 74,
                        75
    Swiss .... I 66,
                        67
    Welsh .... I 58

OCCUPATIONS
  ASTRONAUT
    The First Moon Landing........... XII 30

OCCUPATIONS (*Continued*)

ATHLETE
The Loneliest Battler............... XII 79
The Man Who Made Adolf Hitler Run XII 104
The Lone Star Team of Texas....... XII 170

BAKER
Pat-a-Cake, Pat-a-Cake, Baker's Man! I 19
Blow, Wind, Blow, and Go, Mill, Go! I 31
Rub-a-Dub-Dub .... I 48
The Story of Big Paul Bunyan...... IV 161

BARBER
First Adventures .... I 160

BLACKSMITH
O Will You Shoe Our Pony, Pray?... I 66
The Little Gray Pony.............. II 17
The Blacksmith .... IV 159

BUILDER
The Sheep and the Pig That Made a
Home .... II 145
Building the Bridge............... II 149

BUTCHER
Rub-a-Dub-Dub .... I 48
I'm a Butcher.................... I 128

COBBLER
Giuseppi, the Cobbler.............. I 63
The Little Rooster and the Little Hen II 71
The Shoemaker and the Elves....... III 95

COOK
The King's Cream................. VI 209

COWBOY
O I'm a Jolly Old Cowboy......... I 100
The Cowboy's Life .... IV 193
There Goes a Scout............... IV 194
Pecos Bill, the Cowboy........... IV 195
The Rough Rider................. IX 72

DRIVER
The Big Street in the Big City
(*Bus, Taxi, Truck*) .... I 170

ELEVATOR OPERATOR
The Elevator .... I 183

FARMER
Willie Boy, Willie Boy............ I 45
My Maid Mary .... I 51
Dame Durden .... I 58
The Farmer in the Dell........... I 102
The Farmer's Boy .... I 108
Ride, Ride a Horsey............. I 116
The Boy Who Made Hay.......... I 134
I Should Like to Plough.......... I 136
When I Was a Baby.............. I 145
The Ploughman He's a Bonnie Lad.. I 153
The Little Gray Pony............. II 17
The Gingerbread Man .... II 58
Evening at the Farm............. X 79

FISHERMAN
Row, Row! A-Fishing We'll Go!..... I 61
O Well for the Fisherman's Boy..... I 154
The Fisherman Who Caught the Sun. VI 198

HOUSEWIFE
Polly, Put the Kettle On........... I 31
We've Come to See Miss Jenny Jones I 89
Knitting Still .... I 128
Thus I Guard My Mother's Lambkins I 144
Child, I Must Sweep the Hut Today.. I 147
Mix a Pancake................... I 157

LUMBERJACK
The Honest Woodman............. III 114
The Story of Big Paul Bunyan...... IV 161
A Song of the Canadian Lumberjack. IV 180

MAILMAN
Mister Postman .... I 182

MILKMAID OR MILKMAN
Little Maid, Pretty Maid.......... I 56
O 'Twas on a Bright Mornin'
in Summer .... I 59
Mary Milks the Cow.............. I 135
Where Be You Going, You Devon
Maid? .... I 152
Good Morning, Peter............. I 165
The Big Street in the Big City....... I 170
A Belgian Morning................ II 141

MILLER
Blow, Wind, Blow, and Go, Mill, Go! I 31
The Little Gray Pony.............. II 17

MINER
The Little Gray Pony.............. II 17
An American Miner's Song......... II 23
The Poet of the Sierras........... XII 143

ORGAN GRINDER
Of Speckled Eggs the Birdie Sings... I 158

PHYSICIAN
Pioneer in Surgery................ XII 154

PIPER
Old Pipes and the Dryad.......... VI 18

POLICEMAN
Policeman Joe (*Traffic*)........... I 173

RAILROAD MAN
A Song of the Railroad Men .... I 181
Casey Jones .... V 64
John Henry, the Big Steel-Drivin' Man V 139

SAILOR
Little Beppo Pippo .... I 63
Here Come Three Jolly, Jolly Sailor
Boys .... I 96
Illustration .... I 118
O Well for the Fisherman's Boy..... I 154
O Sailor, Come Ashore........... I 157
Of Speckled Eggs the Birdie Sings... I 158
My Boat .... I 163
A Sea-Song from the Shore........ I 202
Old Stormalong .... IV 183
A Boy on the High Seas.......... VIII 8
Sea Fever .... VIII 35
Gulliver's Travels to Lilliput........ VIII 38
John Paul Jones................. VIII 82
Young Midshipman David Farragut.. VIII 84

SCIENTIST
The Gentle Genius................ XII 218

SCISSORS GRINDER
Ting-a-Ling-Ling .... I 84

SHEPHERD
Little Bo-Peep .... I 32
Little Boy Blue .... I 33
Little Peppino .... I 62
Over the Hill to Feed My Sheep.... I 99
Thus I Guard My Mother's Lambkins I 144
Mary and the Christ-Child......... I 218
The Youth Who Wanted Some Fun.. VII 20

SHOEMAKER
See OCCUPATIONS—*Cobbler*

OCCUPATIONS (*Continued*)

STEAM SHOVEL OPERATOR
Biting Marion .... I 174

STOREKEEPER
The Little Gray Pony.............. II 17

SURVEYOR
George Rogers Clark and the Conquest
of the Northwest................ IX 66

TAILOR
Four-and-Twenty Tailors .... I 39
King Stephen Was a Worthy Peer... I 149
Of a Tailor and a Bear............ III 134

WEAVER
Down in a Cottage................ I 59
Frithjof, the Viking (*Ingeborg*)...... X 130
The Home-Coming of Odysseus
(*Penelope and Calypso*).......... X 217

ORGAN GRINDER
See OCCUPATIONS—Organ
Grinder

PALESTINE
See COUNTRIES OF THE WORLD—
Palestine

PANTOMIME
Krazy Kat .... II 172
Columbine and Her Playfellows of the
Italian Pantomime .... VII 119
Note .... IX 177

PARADES
Yankee Doodle .... I 101
Bang-Whang-Whang .... I 185
The Circus Parade................. III 46
Comment .... VIII 151
Comment .... VIII 169

PATRIOTIC SELECTIONS
Yankee Doodle .... I 101
George Washington and the First
American Flag .... V 116
The Fourth of July.............. V 129
Robert E. Lee .... XI 170c
Lincoln's Gettysburg Address .... XI 170d
The New Colossus.................. XI 172
The Melting Pot .... XI 173
Your America .... XI 216

PERSIA
See COUNTRIES OF THE WORLD—
Persia

PHILIPPINE ISLANDS
See COUNTRIES OF THE WORLD—
Philippine Islands

PIANO
See MUSICAL INSTRUMENTS—
Piano

PIONEER DAYS IN AMERICA
Old Johnny Appleseed.............. IV 213
The First Thanksgiving Day......... V 113
George Washington and the First
American Flag .... V 118
The Yankee Peddler................ V 130
Exploring the Wilderness............ IX 9
Pushing Westward with Lewis
and Clark .... IX 25

Buffalo Bill .... IX 27
George Rogers Clark and the Conquest
of the Northwest................. IX 66
Princess Nelly and the Seneca Chief... IX 78
Little House in the Big Woods........ IX 119

PIPER
See OCCUPATIONS—Piper

PIRATES
A Boy on the High Seas............ VIII 8
Wolfert Webber, or Golden Dreams... XI 107

PLAIN
See NATURE—Prairie and Plain

PLANTS
See NATURE—Plants

POEMS
See EXPERIENCE STORIES AND
POEMS; and FAIRY TALES AND
POEMS

POETS IN MY BOOK HOUSE
See AUTHORS, TITLES, AND LEAD-
ING CHARACTERS INDEX—Bacon;
Rosemary Benét; Stephen Vincent Benét;
Blake; Brotherton; Elizabeth Browning;
Robert Browning; Gelett Burgess; Burns;
Byron; Cammaerts; Carey; Carroll; Ca-
wein; Chamisso; Chaucer; Coleridge;
Grace Conkling; Hilda Conkling;
Cooper; Craik; De la Mare; Dickinson;
Dodge; Drake; Eaton; Emerson; Field;
Fröding; Frost, Fyleman; Galsworthy;
Greenaway; Hendry; Herford; Herrick;
Hogg; Hood; Howitt; Hughes; Keats;
Kingsley; La Fontaine; Lazarus; Lear;
Lindsay; Longfellow; Lowell; Masefield;
Miller; Milne; Milton; Moore; Morley;
Morrison; Newell; Noyes; Peabody;
Percy; Poe; Pombo; Pope; Pringle;
Rands; Richards; Riley; Rossetti; Rus-
kin; Sandburg; Schiller; Scott; Setoun;
Shakespeare; Sharpe; Shelley; Shepard;
Sill; Southey; Stephens; Stevenson;
Taylor; Teasdale; Tennyson; Thaxter;
Thayer; Tippett; Trowbridge; Under-
wood; Wadsworth; Watts; White; Whit-
man; Whittier; Wilson; Wordsworth;
Wynne

POLAND
See COUNTRIES OF THE WORLD—
Poland

POLICEMAN
See OCCUPATIONS—Policeman

PRAIRIE
See NATURE—Prairie and Plain

**PULITZER PRIZE WINNERS IN
MY BOOK HOUSE**
Benét, Stephen Vincent—*American*
(1898-1943)
For Poetry—1929
For Poetry—1944
Buck, Pearl S.—*American* (1892-   )
For Literature—1932
Frost, Robert—*American* (1874-1963)
For Poetry—1924
For Poetry—1931
For Poetry—1937
For Poetry—1943

PULITZER PRIZE WINNERS IN MY BOOK HOUSE
(Continued)

Lowell, Amy—*American* (1874-1925)
    For Poetry—1926
Richards, Laura E.—*American*
    (1850-1943)
    For Biography—1917
Sandburg, Carl—*American* (1878-1967)
    For History—1940
    For Poetry—1951
Shepard, Odell—*American* (1884-1967)
    For Biography (with Marquis
    James)—1938

**PUPPETS, MARIONETTES, AND
  SHADOW PLAYS**
See also IN YOUR HANDS—
  Chapter XXII, pages 181-183
Little Hansworst (*Dutch*) .... II 164
Comment and Note (*Javanese*) .... VI 208

RAILROAD MAN
See OCCUPATIONS—Railroad Man

RAIN
See NATURE—Rain

RAINBOW
See NATURE—Rainbow

REPETITIVE RHYMES AND STORIES
Polly, Put the Kettle On .... I 31
To Market, To Market .... I 33
Old Mother Hubbard .... I 38
Teddy Bear, Teddy Bear .... I 91
The Farmer in the Dell .... I 102
The Farmer's Boy .... I 108
Three Old Maids a-Skating Went ...... I 110
Old Noah .... I 112
The Barnyard .... I 114
There Was a Little Man and His
  Name Was Gice .... I 126
There Were Three Duckies .... I 127
Here Is the Key .... I 127
Over in the Meadow .... I 138
First Adventures .... I 160
The Three Trucks .... I 177
The Zoo in the Park .... I 186
The Orchestra .... I 187
Precocious Piggy .... I 196
The Little Pig .... I 198
Where Are My Roses? .... I 205
The Little Red Hen and the Grain of
  Wheat .... II 13
The Little Gray Pony .... II 17
The Magpie's Nest .... II 42
Johnny and the Three Goats .... II 47
The Rooster and the Sultan .... II 52
The Gingerbread Man .... II 58
The Little Rooster and the Little Hen .. II 71
Ten Little Indians .... II 94
The Sheep and the Pig That Made a
  Home .... II 145
The Bee, the Mouse, and the Bum-
  Clock .... II 155
The Cock, the Mouse, and the Little
  Red Hen .... II 192
The Little Engine That Could .... II 200
The Wee, Wee Mannie and the Big,
  Big Coo .... III 99
Three Jovial Huntsmen .... III 110
Rosy Posy .... III 128

REPTILES
See NATURE—Reptiles

RHYTHMS
See GAMES AND RHYTHMS

RIVER
See NATURE—River or Creek

ROUMANIA
See COUNTRIES OF THE WORLD—
  Roumania

RUSSIA
See COUNTRIES OF THE WORLD—
  Russia

SAILOR
See OCCUPATIONS—Sailor

ST. PATRICK'S DAY
See COUNTRIES OF THE WORLD—
  Ireland

ST. VALENTINE'S DAY
See HOLIDAYS—St. Valentine's Day

SCIENCE
The First Moon Landing .... XII 30
Pioneer in Surgery .... XII 154
The Gentle Genius .... XII 218

SCISSORS GRINDER
See OCCUPATIONS—Scissors Grinder

SCOTLAND
See COUNTRIES OF THE WORLD—
  Scotland

SEASONS
See NATURE—Seasons

SHADOW PLAYS
See IN YOUR HANDS—
  Chapter XX

SHEPHERD
See OCCUPATIONS—Shepherd

SLEIGH
See TRANSPORTATION—Sleigh

SPACE
Fiction
  The Boy Who Saved the World ..... VI 170
Non-Fiction
  The First Moon Landing .... XII 30

SPAIN
See COUNTRIES OF THE WORLD—
  Spain

SPORTS
New Heroes .... VII 144
Babe Ruth, the Home-Run King of
  Baseball .... VII 144a
Casey at the Bat .... VII 144c
Casey's Comeback .... VII 144f
The Loneliest Battler .... XII 79
The Man Who Made Adolf Hitler Run XII 104
The Lone Star Team of Texas .... XII 170

STAR
See NATURE—Star

STOREKEEPER
See OCCUPATIONS—Storekeeper

SUN
See NATURE—Sun

SURVEYOR
See OCCUPATIONS—Surveyor

SWEDEN
See COUNTRIES OF THE WORLD—
Sweden

SWITZERLAND
See COUNTRIES OF THE WORLD—
Switzerland

TAILOR
See OCCUPATIONS—Tailor

THANKSGIVING DAY
See HOLIDAYS—Thanksgiving Day

THUNDER
See NATURE—Thunder

TOY CARVER
See OCCUPATIONS—Toy Carver

TOYS
See also IN YOUR HANDS—
Chapters VII, XX
ANIMALS (Wooden)
  Little Hansworst .... II 164
BALL
  Roll It, Bowl It.................... I 130
  O Lady Mary Ann .... I 153
  Sally's Blue Ball.................. I 188
BLOCKS
  What Are You Able to Build with
    Your Blocks? .... I 164
  O I'll Build a Square with My Pretty
    Red Blocks .... I 164
BOAT
  Little Beppo Pippo (*Sailboat*)....... I 63
  My Boat .... I 163
  Paper Boats .... II 139
  Jack Frost (*Sailboat*).............. II 186
  The Brownies in the Toy Shop...... III 40
  Where Go the Boats?.............. III 94
BUCKET AND SPADE
  Illustration .... I 184
  When I Was Down Beside the Sea... I 159
CHRISTMAS TOYS
  Hark, the Christmas Bells Are Ringing I 133
  A Rhyme from Santo Domingo ..... I 224
  The Little Engine That Could....... II 200
  The Tale of Nutcracker............ II 218
  The Brownies in the Toy Shop...... III 40
DOG
  A Japanese Lullaby................ I 78
  The Sugar-Plum Tree (*Gingerbread
    dog*) .... II 223
DOLL
  A Japanese Lullaby................ I 78
  Illustration .... II 153
  Little Hansworst (*Puppets*)......... II 164
  The Brownies in the Toy Shop...... III 40
  The Doll Under the Briar Rosebush. III 204
  The Nutcracker and Sugardolly Stories IV 83
DOLL CARRIAGE
  Don't Run Away My Kitty......... I 132
DRUM
  A Japanese Lullaby................ I 78
  The Children and the Bear......... I 206
  What They Say.................... I 207
FLUTE
  A Japanese Lullaby................ I 78
GUN
  The Children and the Bear .... I 206
  The Brownies in the Toy Shop...... III 40

HOOPS
  Illustration .... I 185
  Illustration .... V 128
HORSE
  Illustration (*Hobby-horse*) .... I 19
  Ride a Cock-Horse to Banbury Cross I 28
  Smiling Girls, Rosy Boys (*Ginger-
    bread horses*) .... I 30
  Ride, Ride Away (*Hobby-horse*).... I 60
  Jokeli (*Cock-horse*) .... I 66
  O Will You Shoe Our Pony, Pray?
    (*Hobby-horse*) .... I 66
  Go to Sleepy, Little Baby........... I 90
  Hop, My Horsey, Leap and Spring
    (*Cock-horse*) .... I 123
  The Brownies in the Toy Shop
    (*Rocking-horse*) .... III 40
  A Happy Day in the City.......... III 181
JACK-IN-THE-BOX
  The Brownies in the Toy Shop...... III 40
MUSIC-BOX
  The Brownies in the Toy Shop...... III 40
NOAH'S ARK
  Little Hansworst .... II 164
PUPPETS
  See TOYS—Doll
SLIDE
  A Happy Day in the City.......... III 181
SOLDIERS
  Little Hansworst .... II 164
  The Brownies in the Toy Shop...... III 40
TEDDY BEAR
  Teddy Bear, Teddy Bear............ I 91
  O I'll Build a Square with My Pretty
    Red Blocks .... I 164
  Good Morning, Peter .... I 165
  The Teddy Bears' Picnic .... II 57
TOP
  O If My Top Would Only Spin..... I 130
  The Brownies in the Toy Shop...... III 40
TRAIN
  A Rhyme from Santo Domingo ..... I 224
TRUMPET
  What They Say.................... I 207

TRAIN
See TRANSPORTATION—Train

TRANSPORTATION
AIRPLANE
  The Airplane .... I 194
  Wilbur Wright and Orville Wright
    (*First real airplane*) .... V 66
AUTOMOBILE
  The Big Street in the Big City ...... I 170
BALLOON
  The Daring Prince................. III 127
BOATS
Ark
  Old Noah .... I 112
  Noah's Ark .... II 101
Barge
  Life in Concord .... XII 122
Canoe
  Ten Little Indians .... II 94
  A Song of the Canadian Lumberjack. IV 180
  How Yehl, the Hero, Freed the
    Beaming Maiden .... VI 102

TRANSPORTATION

BOATS (*Continued*)

The Strong Boy .... VI 71
The Fisherman Who Caught the Sun. VI 198
Illustration (*Outrigger canoe*) .... VI 201

Flatboat
The Boatman He's a Lucky Man.... I 97
A Story About Abe Lincoln........ V 133

Lifeboat
Gulliver's Travels to Lilliput........ VIII 38

Ocean Liner
Look, See the Boat!............... I 184

Paddle Wheel
How Robert Fulton Harnessed the
Giant Raft .... V 48

Raft
Señor Kon-Tiki .... XII 45

Rowboat
Row, Row! A-Fishing We'll Go!..... I 61
Illustration .... I 202
Illustration .... VII 56
The Enchanted Island (*Galley*) ..... VIII 134
Mr. Hampden's Shipwreck.......... VIII 172

Sailing Vessel
I Saw a Ship a-Sailing (*Galleon*).... I 35
Here We Sail So Fast and Free...... I 96
O Well for the Fisherman's Boy
(*Sailboat*) .... I 154
Illustration (*Clipper*) .... I 202
The Owl and the Pussy-Cat (*Sailboat*) II 180
Old Stormalong (*Clipper; Whaling
Vessel*) .... IV 183
Vladimir's Adventures in Search
of Fortune .... VII 102
A Song of Drake's Men (*Galleon*)... VIII 7
A Boy on the High Seas (*Sailboat*).. VIII 8
The Tempest .... VIII 18
Gulliver's Travels to Lilliput (*Galleon*) VIII 38
Young Midshipman David Farragut
(*Frigate*) .... VIII 84
A Wanderer's Song (*Clipper*)....... VIII 91
The Adventures of General
Tom Thumb .... VIII 155
The Adventures of Alexander Selkirk
(*Galley*) .... IX 41
How Beowulf Delivered Heorot
(*Viking*) .... X 80
Frithjof, the Viking (*Dragon ship*).. X 130
Illustration (*Galley*) .... X 207

Steamship or Steamboat
When Uncle Henry Was a Little
Tiny Boy .... I 97
A Happy Day in the City.......... III 181
The Steamboat and the Locomotive.. V 96
Mr. Hampden's Shipwreck.......... VIII 172
Illustration .... XI 172
The Melting Pot................... XI 173

BUS
The Big Street in the Big City....... I 170
Big Bus, Stop!.................... I 173
A Happy Day in the City.......... III 181

CARAVAN
The Peddler's Caravan............. IV 11
Illustration (*Gypsy caravan*) .... VII 172
Gideon, the Warrior (*Camel caravan*) IX 134

CARRIAGE
The Snow-Queen .... VII 48

CART
Come, Let's Go to Sant' Anita
(*Mexican ox cart*).............. I 70
Illustration .... I 75
Mary Milks the Cow.............. I 135
Illustration (*English ox cart*) .... II 67
A Belgian Morning (*Belgian milk
cart*) .... II 141
The Little Toy Land of the Dutch
(*Dutch dog cart*)............... IV 56
The Boy Hero of Harlem (*Dutch
dog cart*) .... IV 57
Christening the Baby in Russia...... IV 63
David Copperfield and Little Em'ly.. VII 182

CHARIOT
Joseph and His Brethren........... X 48
Cuculain, the Irish Hound.......... X 188
Illustration .... X 216
The Home-Coming of Odysseus ..... X 217

MOTORCYCLE
The Big Street in the Big City....... I 170

SLEIGH
Jingle Bells, Jingle Bells............ I 87
Over the River and Through the Woods I 87
The Snow-Queen .... VII 48
The Bells .... VII 71
Kalevala, Land of Heroes .... X 151

TAXI
The Big Street in the Big City....... I 170

TRAIN
Engine, Engine Number Nine....... I 85
Hurry Up, Engine................. I 92
When I Go a-Courting............. I 92
The Big Engine................... I 179
A Song of the Railroad Men........ I 181
The Little Engine That Could....... II 200
Pecos Bill, the Cowboy............ IV 195
Casey Jones .... V 64
The Steamboat and the Locomotive.. V 96
John Henry, the Big Steel-Drivin' Man V 139
Illustration .... VIII 168

TROLLEY CAR
A Happy Day in the City.......... III 181

TRUCK
Good Morning, Peter (*Milk truck*).. I 165
The Big Street in the Big City....... I 170
The Three Trucks .... I 177

WAGON
Illustration (*Hay wagon*) .... I 113
The Little Gray Pony.............. II 17
The Story of Big Paul Bunyan....... IV 161
Pecos Bill, the Cowboy (*Covered
wagon*) .... IV 195
Illustration (*Covered wagon*)........ V 128
Illustration (*Covered wagon*)........ V 133
The King's Cream................. VI 209
Illustration (*Gypsy wagon*)......... VIII 218
Buffalo Bill (*Covered wagon*)....... IX 27
'Way Down South in Dixie (*Farm
wagon*) .... XII 138
A Tramp of the Middle West
(*Gypsy wagon*) .... XII 147

TREES
See NATURE—Trees

TROLLEY CAR
See TRANSPORTATION—Trolley
Car

TRUCK
See TRANSPORTATION—Truck

TRUE STORIES
See also BIOGRAPHICAL SKETCHES;
and HERO AND HEROINE STO-
RIES—True
The Little Dog Waltz............... II 150
Jamie Watt and the Giant in the
Teakettle .... V 45
How Robert Fulton Harnessed the
Giant .... V 48
Wilbur Wright and Orville Wright..... V 66
The First Thanksgiving Day.......... V 113
George Washington and the First
American Flag .... V 118
A Story About Abe Lincoln .... V 133
Babe Ruth, the Home-Run King of
Baseball .... VII 144a
John Paul Jones, the First American
Naval Hero .... VIII 82
Young Midshipman David Farragut.... VIII 84
The Adventures of General Tom Thumb VIII 155
Exploring the Wilderness............ IX 9
Pushing Westward with Lewis and
Clark .... IX 25
Buffalo Bill .... IX 27
The Adventures of Alexander Selkirk.. IX 41
George Rogers Clark and the Con-
quest of the Northwest............ IX 66
Princess Nelly and the Seneca Chief... IX 78
How Peary Reached the North Pole... IX 127
Robert Bruce, Scotland's Hero........ X 21
The Children's Crusade .... X 30
Joan of Arc .... X 98
Marko, the Champion of Serbian
Liberty .... XI 29
Lincoln's Gettysburg Address......... XI 170a
Robert E. Lee, a Hero in War and in
Peace .... XI 170c

TRUMPET
See MUSICAL INSTRUMENTS—
Trumpet

UKULELE
See MUSICAL INSTRUMENTS—
Ukulele

See COUNTRIES OF THE WORLD—
United States of America

VIOLIN
See MUSICAL INSTRUMENTS—
Violin

VOLCANO
See NATURE—Volcano

WAGON
See TRANSPORTATION—Wagon

WALES
See COUNTRIES OF THE WORLD—
Wales

WASHINGTON'S BIRTHDAY
See HOLIDAYS—Washington's
Birthday

WEAVER
See OCCUPATIONS—Weaver

WESTERN HEROES
O I'm a Jolly Old Cowboy—*American
Rhyme* .... I 100
Cowboy's Life, The—*American
Cowboy Song* .... IV 193
There Goes a Scout—*Poem about
Buffalo Bill* .... IV 194
Pecos Bill, The Cowboy—*Tale of
American Cowboys* .... IV 195
Exploring the Wilderness—*Biog. Sketch
of Daniel Boone*................. IX 9
Pushing Westward with Lewis and
Clark .... IX 25
Buffalo Bill .... IX 27
George Rogers Clark and the Conquest
of the Northwest................. IX 66

WEST INDIES
See COUNTRIES OF THE WORLD—
West Indies

WIND
See NATURE—Wind

YUGOSLAVIA
See COUNTRIES OF THE WORLD—
Yugoslavia

ZOO
The Zoo in the Park................. I 186
Snowflake the Gorilla............... VI 159

Character Building Index
A Guide for Parents

This index is exclusively for the use of parents or teachers. The stories in MY BOOK HOUSE were carefully chosen for elements which would influence the formation of desirable character qualities, behavior patterns and work habits; and, graded to each stage of the child's growing needs from babyhood through adolescence. Because a young child unconsciously imitates the story characters he loves and admires, they will give him good patterns to follow and through these stories he will see the causes and effects of certain types of behavior. Under the heading, *Perseverance,* for example, are listed stories, not only of such perseverance as that of "The Little Engine That Could," but also that of Robert Bruce who learned perseverance from watching a spider try, try again.

Some of the character qualities listed are *undesirable* and the influence of the selections referred to should show the child their undesirability—subtly, without any obvious moralizing.

While there may be, at times, certain qualities a parent wishes to help a child overcome, the greatest value of our Plan lies in the *prevention* of undesirable behavior habits before they develop. During the early, impressionable years while the child is *forming* his habits and his concepts of what is good, bad, ugly, beautiful, desirable or undesirable, these stories will furnish good patterns to imitate.

All selections in this index are listed under specific headings in the progressive order of volumes. Since each child develops at his own individual rate, we cannot specify at what age a given child is ready for any one particular volume. However, for the most part we recommend for the preschool child material chiefly from the first two or three volumes. The child, himself, will indicate by his interest and attention span, when he is ready to progress to more advanced stories.

	VOL.	PAGE
ALERTNESS		
Policeman Joe	I	173
The Little Rooster and the Little Hen..	II	71
Wee Robin's Christmas Song.........	II	209
The Twelve Dancing Princesses	IV	28
The Boy Hero of Harlem............	IV	57
Jamie Watt and the Giant in the Tea-kettle	V	45
Telegraph Boy—*A Story of Andrew Carnegie*	XII	60
AMBITION		
Dick Whittington and His Cat........	V	33
The Wonderland of an Artist's Workshop	VI	164
The Circus Man—*Biog. Sketch of Phineas T Barnum*................	VIII	144
Sir Beaumains, the Kitchen Knight....	X	8
Down by the River Avon—*Biog. Sketch of William Shakespeare*......	XII	15
Señor Kon-Tiki—*A Story of Thor Heyerdahl*	XII	45
Telegraph Boy—*A Story of Andrew Carnegie*	XII	60
London Streets—*Biog. Sketch of Charles Dickens*	XII	102
Learning To Be Free—*A Story of Frederick Douglass*	XII	198
The Man Who Made Adolf Hitler Run —*Biog. Sketch of Jesse Owens*......	XII	104
Pioneer in Surgery—*Biog. Sketch of Dr. Daniel Hale Williams*.........	XII	154
ANGER		
See also SELF-CONTROL		
The Rooster and the Sultan..........	II	52
The Birds' St. Valentine's Day........	III	198
Old Pipes and the Dryad............	VI	18
Richard Feverel and the Hay-Rick.....	X	54
Frithjof, the Viking.................	X	130
APPRECIATION		
See also GRATITUDE		
The Bow That Bridges Heaven........	II	105
The Cap That Mother Made.........	III	12
Heidi in the Alpine Pasture..........	V	146
The Nuremberg Stove...............	V	162
The Wonderland of an Artist's Workshop	VI	164
ATTENTION GETTING		
Tommy Was a Silly Boy.............	I	150
The Donkey and the Lap Dog........	II	50
Yes, That's the Girl That Struts About.	III	26
BOASTFULNESS		
Tommy Was a Silly Boy.............	I	150
Belling the Cat...................	II	35
The Gingerbread Man	II	58
The City Mouse and the Country Mouse	II	84
The Dancing Monkeys..............	II	92
The Hare and the Tortoise..........	II	106
Rama and the Tigers—*A Tale of India*.	II	118
The Battle of the Firefly and the Apes.	III	59
How the Brazilian Beetles Got Their Gorgeous Coats	III	172
The Boaster	III	175
The Wind and the Sun.............	III	196
Charlotte's Web	V	54

	VOL.	PAGE
Phaeton	VII	90
The Acorn and the Pumpkin..........	VII	132
Peer Gynt	IX	98
CARELESSNESS		
Cock-a-Doodle-Doo!	I	32
Three Little Kittens.................	I	53
A-Tisket, A-Tasket	I	89
CHEERFULNESS		
See also HAPPINESS		
Billy, Billy, Come and Play..........	I	47
O I'm a Jolly Old Cowboy..........	I	100
Over in the Meadow................	I	138
Jog On, Jog On...................	I	148
O Well for the Fisherman's Boy......	I	154
Of Speckled Eggs the Birdie Sings.....	I	158
At Christmas Play and Make Good Cheer	II	217
Heap on More Wood...............	II	217
I Heard the Bells on Christmas Day...	II	217
The Story of Tom Thumb............	V	11
Winnie-the-Pooh	V	68
CHILD'S DAILY ACTIVITIES		
(Selections to encourage the formation of right habits and attitudes that will help the child in the day's routine.)		
Getting Up		
Wake Up, Jacob	I	84
Lazy Old Mary	I	98
Catherine, My Dearie..............	I	124
Dressing		
Oh, Here's a Leg for a Stocking.....	I	20
Johnny Shall Have a New Bonnet...	I	20
When Mrs. Bird Wants Mr. Bird....	I	68
Cinderella Dressed in Green........	I	83
King Dagobert	I	124
Good Morning, Peter..............	I	165
The Little Girl and the New Dress..	I	168
The Big Umbrella and the Little Rubbers	I	190
Rama and the Tigers—*A Tale of India*	II	118
Little Blue Apron	III	210
Eating		
Hickety, Pickety, My Black Hen....	I	24
Up in the Green Orchard..........	I	30
Blow, Wind, Blow, and Go, Mill, Go!	I	31
Little King Boggin.................	I	40
Little Tommy Tucker..............	I	42
Pease-Porridge Hot	I	47
Reinar Was Watching His Cows.....	I	61
I'm Going to Lady Washington's....	I	82
Get Out of the Way..............	I	93
One, Two, Three, Four.............	I	99
Open Your Beak, My Little Bird....	I	146
Mix a Pancake...................	I	157
The Friendly Cow All Red and White	I	159
Animal Crackers	I	162
Dame Wiggins of Lee.............	II	188
Drinking Milk		
The Boy Who Made Hay..........	I	134
Mary Milks the Cow	I	135
Going to Bed		
Wee Willie Winkie	I	28
Diddle, Diddle, Dumpling	I	37
Teddy Bear, Teddy Bear...........	I	91

	VOL.	PAGE
The Sleepy Song	I	119
Sleep, Sleep, My Little One!	I	146
Ole Shut-Eyes, the Sandman	II	26
A Bohemian Evening	II	140
Late	II	153
The Sugar-Plum Tree	II	223
A Trip to the Barber Shop		
First Adventures	I	160
Crossing the Street (Traffic Lights)		
The Big Street in the Big City	I	170
The Green Bus	I	173
Policeman Joe	I	173
A Trip to the City		
A Happy Day in the City	III	181

COMPLAINING
See CONTENTMENT

CONSIDERATION OF OTHERS
See also GENEROSITY; KINDNESS
The attitudes of thoughtfulness, of kindliness, of regard for others must be learned by the child as he develops if he is to find joy and satisfaction in being with other people. *Co-operation, Helpfulness,* and *Fair Play* help develop this respect for others. In a broad sense, it might be *Tolerance* or *Kindness* or *Generosity.* Consideration may be displayed outwardly in such qualities as *Courtesy* or *Hospitality.* Whatever the interpretation may be, the listings under all of these headings, as well as the stories listed below, should be helpful in developing the quality of *Consideration of Others.*

	VOL.	PAGE
Two Birds and Their Nest	II	45
How the Finch Got Her Colors	II	143
Old Johnny Appleseed	IV	213
The Red Ettin	V	90
My Name Is Aram	VII	156
Princess Nelly and the Seneca Chief	IX	78
Old Pipes and the Dryad	VI	18
Joseph and His Brethren	X	48
The Last of the Dragons	X	89

CONTENTMENT

	VOL.	PAGE
The World Is So Full	I	17
What Are You Able to Build with Your Blocks?	I	164
Laughing Song	II	75
Nurse's Song	II	152
Evening at the Farm	X	79

CO-OPERATION
See also HELPFULNESS

	VOL.	PAGE
Robin and Richard Were Two Pretty Men	I	26
My Maid Mary	I	51
The Squirrel Went Out to Cut the Hay	I	60
O I'll Build a Square with My Pretty Red Blocks	I	164
The Little Gray Pony	II	17
The Sheep and the Pig That Made a Home	II	145
Late	II	153
The Story of Li'l Hannibal	III	116
Wilbur Wright and Orville Wright	V	66
The First Moon Landing	XII	30

COURAGE
See also FEARLESSNESS

	VOL.	PAGE
The Battle of the Firefly and the Apes	III	59
Of a Tailor and a Bear	III	134
The Boy Hero of Harlem	IV	57
Jack and the Beanstalk	V	20
Little Gulliver	V	103
The Nuremberg Stove	V	162
Aruman, a Hero of Java	VI	202
Vladimir's Adventures in Search of Fortune	VII	102
The Knights of the Silver Shield	VII	173
A Boy on the High Seas—*Biog. Sketch of Joshua Barney*	VIII	8
Exploring the Wilderness—*Biog. Sketch of Daniel Boone*	IX	9
George Rogers Clark and the Conquest of the Northwest	IX	66
Princess Nelly and the Seneca Chief	IX	78
Old Yeller	IX	98
The Labors of Hercules	IX	151
Sir Beaumains, the Kitchen Knight	X	8
The Song of Roland	X	38
How Beowulf Delivered Heorot	X	80
Joan of Arc	X	98
The Story of the Cid	X	108
As You Like It	X	165
Cuculain, the Irish Hound	X	188
A Story of Rustem, the Hero of Persia	X	228
Una and the Red Cross Knight	XI	8
Marko, the Champion of Serbian Liberty	XI	29
The Tale of the Rhine-Gold	XI	73
Dante's Voyage to the Inferno, Purgatory, and Paradise	XI	156
The First Moon Landing	XII	30
Señor Kon-Tiki—*A Story of Thor Heyerdahl*	XII	45
The Loneliest Battler—*Biog. Sketch of Jackie Robinson*	XII	79
The Man Who Made Adolf Hitler Run —*Biog. Sketch of Jesse Owens*	XII	104
The Lone Star Team of Texas—*Biog. Sketch of Babe Didrikson*	XII	170
Learning To Be Free—*A Story of Frederick Douglass*	XII	198

COURTESY
See also CONSIDERATION OF OTHERS

	VOL.	PAGE
Pussy Sits Beside the Fire	I	36
Old Mother Hubbard	I	38
One Misty, Moisty Morning	I	42
Billy, Billy, Come and Play	I	47
Three Little Kittens	I	53
When I See a Lady	I	69
I Took a Walk One Evening	I	75
Quaker, Quaker, How Is Thee?	I	82
The Village of Cream Puffs	II	124
Two Children	II	138
How the Finch Got Her Colors	II	143
How the Brazilian Beetles Got Their Gorgeous Coats	III	172

COWARDICE
See also COURAGE

	VOL.	PAGE
The Battle of the Frogs and the Mice	IV	104
The Wizard of Oz	VI	62
Opportunity	X	18

	VOL.	PAGE

CRITICISM
The Two Crabs.................... II 33
The Battle of the Firefly and the Apes. III 59
How the Brazilian Beetles Got Their
   Gorgeous Coats .... III 172

CRUELTY
See also KINDNESS
The Ugly Duckling.................. II 131
The Red Ettin.................... V 90
How Yehl, the Hero, Freed the
   Beaming Maiden .... VI 102
The Legend of William Tell......... X 44

CRYING AND WHINING
The Mouse Climbed Up the
   Candlestick .... I 77
Johnny and the Three Goats......... II 47
Elsa and the Ten Elves............. IV 45
The Girl Who Used Her Wits........ IV 137

DECEIT
See also HONESTY
The Battle of the Frogs and the Mice.. IV 104
How Jack Sought the Golden Apples.. V 76
The Trial by Fire................. VII 26
Gigi and the Magic Ring............ VII 199
Una and the Red Cross Knight....... XI 8

DETERMINATION
The Little Engine That Could........ II 200
All About Columbus .... V 112
John Henry, the Big Steel-Drivin' Man. V 139
The Strong Boy..................... VI 71
A Boy on the High Seas—*Biog. Sketch
   of Joshua Barney*................. VIII 8
The Circus Man—*Biog. Sketch of
   Phineas T. Barnum*................ VIII 144
The Loneliest Battler—*Biog. Sketch of
   Jackie Robinson* .... XII 79
The Man Who Made Adolf Hitler Run
   —*Biog. Sketch of Jesse Owens*...... XII 104
Pioneer in Surgery—*Biog. Sketch of
   Dr. Daniel Hale Williams*......... XII 154
The Lone Star Team of Texas—*Biog.
   Sketch of Babe Didrikson*.......... XII 170

DISCONTENTMENT
See also CONTENTMENT
The Poor Old Lady................. II 68
The City Mouse and the Country
   Mouse .... II 84
The Little Rabbit Who Wanted Red
   Wings .... II 87
Peter Rabbit Decides to Change His
   Name .... III 49
Clytie......................... III 151
The Steamboat and the Locomotive.... V 96
The Three Wishes.................. VI 92

DISHONESTY
See also HONESTY
The Mouse Climbed Up the
   Candlestick .... I 77
Uncle Mitya's Horse................ II 46
Teeny-Tiny .... IV 143
How Jack Sought the Golden Apples.. V 76
The Trial by Fire................. VII 26
The Golden Bird.................... VII 134

My Name Is Aram.................. VII 156
Joseph and His Brethren............ X 48
Richard Feverel and the Hay-Rick .... X 54
Kalevala, Land of Heroes........... X 151

DISLOYALTY
See LOYALTY

DISOBEDIENCE
See also OBEDIENCE
Reen-Reen-Reeny-Croak-Frog .... II 37
The Gingerbread Man .... II 58
The Tale of Peter Rabbit........... II 112
King Hilary and the Beggarman....... III 70
The Nutcracker and Sugardolly Stories. IV 83
Tippity Witchit's Hallowe'en......... IV 145
The Golden Bird.................... VII 134
Maggie Tulliver Goes to Live with
   the Gypsies .... VIII 189
The Trumpet of the Swan........... IX 106
Thor's Journey to Jotun-heim......... IX 164

EGOTISM
See SELF-IMPORTANCE

ENVY
See also JEALOUSY
The Little Rabbit Who Wanted Red
   Wings .... II 87
The Three Wishes.................. VI 92
The Story of the Talking Bird........ VIII 109
The Exile of Rama.................. X 175

FAIR PLAY
The Rough Rider—*Biog. Sketch of
   Theodore Roosevelt* .... IX 72
Ye Merry Doinges of Robin Hood..... XI 49

FAITH
See also REVERENCE
The Babe Moses.................... III 156
Old Johnny Appleseed............... IV 213
David, the Shepherd Boy............. VII 73
Gideon, the Warrior................. IX 134
Joseph and His Brethren............ X 48
Joan of Arc .... X 98

FAITHFULNESS
See also LOYALTY; TRUSTWORTHINESS
Two Birds and Their Nest............ II 45
The Trial by Fire................. VII 26
East o' the Sun and West o' the Moon. VII 31
Sir Beaumains, the Kitchen Knight.... X 8
The Wanderings of Aeneas........... X 203
The Home-Coming of Odysseus....... X 217
Una and the Red Cross Knight....... XI 8
The Man Who Lived in the World of
   Dreams—*A story about Dante
   Alighieri* .... XI 152

FAULTFINDING
See CRITICISM

FEARLESSNESS
See also COURAGE
An American Miner's Song........... II 23
Shingebiss .... II 96
Snow-white and Rose-red............. IV 34
Old Johnny Appleseed............... IV 213
How Jack Sought the Golden Apples.. V 76
The Red Ettin .... V 90

	VOL.	PAGE
The Sleeping Beauty	VI	11
The Lost Spear	VI	132
Jack the Giant-Killer	VI	140
The Fisherman Who Caught the Sun	VI	198
The Trial by Fire	VII	26
David, the Shepherd Boy	VII	73
The Little-Man-As-Big-As-Your-Thumb-With-Mustaches-Seven-Miles-Long	VII	112
Buffalo Bill—*A Story of William Cody*	IX	27
The Adventures of Perseus	IX	140
The Legend of William Tell	X	44

FEARS

A child is likely to fear things he does not understand, such as darkness, rain, and wind. Such verses as "Teddy Bear" (BH: I, 91) will make a game of turning out the light, while selections such as "Thunder and Lightning" (BH: I, 195), and others listed under *Nature—Rain; Wind; Thunder,* etcetera, in the Special Subjects Index will help dispel any fears of such natural phenomena.

Fears may be caused by a feeling of insecurity. In such instances, stories under headings such as the *Protecitve Power of God or Love for Children* may give reassurance. Fears may often be *prevented* by preparing a child for a new experience before he meets it. In the *Special Subjects Index,* under *Experience Stories,* are listed such selections as "The Elevator" (BH: I, 183) which will prepare him for this somewhat terrifying experience, or "First Adventures" (BH: I, 160) which will eliminate fear of his first haircut. Selections listed under *Fearlessness* and *Courage* may also be helpful. In the stories listed below are examples of fears which prove groundless, in a different way in each instance.

The Ugly Duckling	II	131
The Mad Dog	III	63
The Foolish, Timid, Little Hare	III	76

FOOLISHNESS

Simple Simon Met a Pie-Man	I	50
Otto Would a-Riding Go	I	75
The Donkey and the Lap Dog	II	50
The Little Rabbit Who Wanted Red Wings	II	87
The Turtle Who Could Not Stop Talking	II	178
Peter Rabbit Decides to Change His Name	III	49
The Foolish, Timid, Little Hare	III	76

FORGIVENESS

See also REPENTANCE

Three Little Kittens	I	53
Cinderella	IV	12
Aruman, a Hero of Java	VI	202
My Name Is Aram	VII	156
The Tempest	VIII	18
Joseph and His Brethren	X	48
The Melting Pot	XI	173

FRIENDSHIP

See also LOYALTY

Charlotte's Web	V	54
Mr. Hampden's Shipwreck	VIII	172
The Song of Roland	X	38
The Last of the Dragons	X	89
Frithjof, the Viking	X	130

	VOL.	PAGE
Life in Concord—*Biog. Sketch of Louisa May Alcott*	XII	122
The Harvard Professor—*Biog. Sketch of Henry Wadsworth Longfellow*	XII	135

GENEROSITY

See also CONSIDERATION OF OTHERS; KINDNESS

Baa, Baa, Black Sheep	I	29
Little Girl, Little Girl	I	56
Row, Row! A-Fishing We'll Go!	I	61
There Was a Little Boy	I	77
The Little Rooster and the Little Hen	II	71
The Maiden, the Knight, and the Waterfall	VII	40

GENTLENESS

I Love Little Pussy	I	143
The Wind and the Sun	III	196
Cinderella	IV	12

GETTING ALONG WITH OTHERS

See also TOLERANCE

Many factors contribute to the development of the high art of getting along with others. *Cheerfulness* is a pleasing quality. *Generosity, Fair Play, Kindness, Tolerance, Consideration of Others,* and *Courtesy* are important elements. Selections listed under these headings should be helpful in developing these characteristics. The stories listed under *Friendship* show examples of friendship—of getting along with others. By negative example, stories listed under *Self-Importance* or *Boastfulness* may help overcome these undesirable traits which often prevent one from getting along with others.

I Took a Walk One Evening	I	75
The Village of Cream Puffs	II	124
The Sheep and the Pig That Made a Home	II	145
The Mad Dog	III	63

GRATITUDE

See also APPRECIATION

The Lion and the Mouse	II	108
The Shoemaker and the Elves	III	95
Little Gulliver	V	103
The First Thanksgiving Day	V	113
We Thank Thee	V	117
Old Pipes and the Dryad	VI	18
The Lost Spear	VI	132
The Maiden, the Knight, and the Waterfall	VII	40
Vladimir's Adventures in Search of Fortune	VII	102
Evening at the Farm	X	79
The Last of the Dragons	X	89

GREED

The Man Who Has Plenty of Good Peanuts	I	95
Reen-Reen-Reeny-Croak-Frog	II	37
The Rooster and the Sultan	II	52
The Little Rooster and the Little Hen	II	71
The Dancing Monkeys	II	92
Hansel and Grethel	IV	73
The Nutcracker and Sugardolly Stories	IV	83
Why the Sea Is Salt	V	144
The Three Wishes	VI	92
The Man Who Loved Hai Quai	VI	127

	VOL.	PAGE

The Golden Touch .... VII 210
The Tale of the Rhine-Gold.......... XI 73
Wolfert Webber, or Golden Dreams... XI 107

GRUMBLING
See CONTENTMENT

HAPPINESS
See also CHEERFULNESS
The World Is So Full................ I 17
Reinar Was Watching His Cows....... I 61
Everyone's Glad in Our City Today.... I 75
I-Yay! I-Yay! I-Yay! .... I 131
Hark, the Christmas Bells Are Ringing I 133
The Boy Who Made Hay............. I 134
What Are You Able to Build with
  Your Blocks? .... I 164
Bang-Whang-Whang .... I 185
Go Out, Children .... I 185
Park Play .... I 189
Songs of Joy from the Bible......... I 216
God Hath Made Me to Laugh........ I 217
Little Gustava .... II 30
Laughing Song .... II 75
Grasshopper Green .... II 76
Nurse's Song .... II 152
Wee Robin's Christmas Song......... II 209
A Happy Day in the City........... III 181
The Fourth of July................. V 129
Heidi in the Alpine Pasture.......... V 146

HELPFULNESS
See also CO-OPERATION
Up in the Green Orchard............ I 30
Willie Boy, Willie Boy............. I 45
Row, Row! A-Fishing We'll Go!...... I 61
Three Old Maids a-Skating Went...... I 110
Thus I Guard My Mother's Lambkins. I 144
Groceries .... I 182
The Little Rooster and the Little Hen.. II 71
The Lion and the Mouse............. II 108
Dame Wiggins of Lee............... II 188
The Owl's Answer to Tommy......... III 29
The Shoemaker and the Elves........ III 95
The Doll Under the Briar Rosebush... III 204
Snow-white and Rose-red............ IV 34
The Story of Tom Thumb........... V 11
Little Gulliver .... V 103
Joseph and His Brethren............. X 48

HONESTY
The Shoemaker and the Elves......... III 95
The Honest Woodman .... III 114
Marko, the Champion of Serbian
  Liberty .... XI 29

HOSPITALITY
Little Gustava .... II 30
David Copperfield and Little Em'ly.... VII 182
The Magic Horse .... VIII 92
Ye Merry Doinges of Robin Hood.... XI 49
Down by the River Avon—*Biog.*
  Sketch of William Shakespeare...... XII 15

HUMILITY
The Gentle Genius—*Biog. Sketch of*
  Albert Einstein .... XII 218

IMAGINATIVENESS
Daffy-Down-Dilly .... I 25
Mary, Mary, Quite Contrary......... I 25

	VOL.	PAGE

I Saw a Ship a-Sailing............... I 35
My Lady Wind .... I 46
Pretty, See the Cloud Appear!........ I 81
The Fog .... I 184
Wynken, Blynken, and Nod.......... II 24
The Twilight .... II 41
Grasshopper Green .... II 76
An Explanation of the Grasshopper ... II 77
The Star .... II 83
The Bow That Bridges Heaven....... II 105
The Village of Cream Puffs.......... II 124
Paper Boats .... II 139
Jack Frost .... II 186
Snow .... II 208
The Night Before Christmas.......... II 213
The Tale of Nutcracker.............. II 218
The Sugar-Plum Tree .... II 223
The Elf and the Dormouse........... III 39
Clouds .... III 48
Clytie .... III 151
The Knight .... IV 129
Little Diamond and the North Wind... IV 119
The Assembling of the Fays.......... VI 17
A Musical Visit to Fairyland—*A*
  story about Felix Mendelssohn...... VI 59
The Fairyland of Science—*Biog.*
  Sketch of Jean Henri Fabre........ VI 184
The Surprising Adventures of Don
  Quixote of La Mancha............. XI 90

IMPATIENCE
See also PATIENCE
The Magpie's Nest .... II 42
East o' the Sun and West o' the Moon. VII 31

INDUSTRY
This Little Ant Worked with Might
  and Main .... I 71
How Doth the Little Busy Bee........ I 143
Biting Marion .... I 174
The Little Red Hen and the Grain of
  Wheat .... II 13
The City Mouse and the Country
  Mouse .... II 84
Building the Bridge.................. II 149
The Cock, the Mouse, and the Little
  Red Hen .... II 192
The Honest Woodman............... III 114
Dick Whittington and His Cat........ V 33
Jamie Watt and the Giant in the
  Teakettle .... V 45
John Henry, the Big Steel-Drivin' Man. V 139
Miska and the Man-With-The-Iron-Head VII 11
The Circus Man—*Biog. Sketch of*
  Phineas T. Barnum............... VIII 144
Little House in the Big Woods....... IX 119
Telegraph Boy—*A Story of Andrew*
  Carnegie .... XII 60

INGRATITUDE
See also GRATITUDE
Snow-white and Rose-red............ IV 34
The Nutcracker and Sugardolly Stories. IV 83
The Man Who Loved Hai Quai....... VI 127
Pigling and Her Proud Sister......... VI 191

INITIATIVE
The Little Red Hen and the Grain of
  Wheat .... II 13
Shingebiss .... II 96

	VOL.	PAGE
The Sheep and the Pig That Made a Home	II	145
Jamie Watt and the Giant in the Teakettle	V	45
How Robert Fulton Harnessed the Giant	V	48
Exploring the Wilderness—*Biog. Sketch of Daniel Boone*	IX	9
Telegraph Boy—*A Story of Andrew Carnegie*	XII	60
Pioneer in Surgery—*Biog. Sketch of Dr. Daniel Hale Williams*	XII	154

INJUSTICE
See JUSTICE

INQUISITIVENESS

What's Your Name?	I	95
Where Be You Going, You Devon Maid?	I	152
Goldilocks and the Three Bears	III	20
The Nutcracker and Sugardolly Stories.	IV	83
East o' the Sun and West o' the Moon.	VII	31

INSECURITY
See SECURITY

INTEGRITY
See HONESTY; TRUSTWORTHINESS

INTOLERANCE
See also TOLERANCE

Joan of Arc	X	98
Learning To Be Free—*A Story of Frederick Douglas*	XII	198

INVENTIVENESS
See also RESOURCEFULNESS

Jamie Watt and the Giant in the Tea-kettle	V	45
How Robert Fulton Harnessed the Giant	V	48
Wilbur Wright and Orville Wright	V	66
Jasper the Drummin' Boy	VI	108
The King's Cream	VI	209

IRRESPONSIBILITY
See also TRUSTWORTHINESS

The Owl's Answer to Tommy	III	29
Elsa and the Ten Elves	IV	45
The Girl Who Used Her Wits	IV	137
The Youth Who Wanted Some Fun	VII	20

JEALOUSY
See also ENVY

The Donkey and the Lap Dog	II	50
The Mad Dog	III	63
The Trial by Fire	VII	26
David, the Shepherd Boy	VII	73
The Six Swans	VII	126
Maggie Tulliver Goes to Live with the Gypsies	VIII	189
Joseph and His Brethren	X	48

JUSTICE
Right-Doing Rewarded

How the Finch Got Her Colors	II	143
The Honest Woodman	III	114
How the Brazilian Beetles Got Their Gorgeous Coats	III	172
Doll i' the Grass	IV	24

	VOL.	PAGE
Snow-white and Rose-red	IV	34
How Jack Sought the Golden Apples	V	76
Old Pipes and the Dryad	VI	18
The Lost Spear	VI	132
Pigling and Her Proud Sister	VI	191
Vladimir's Adventures in Search of Fortune	VII	102
The Golden Bird	VII	134
The Knights of the Silver Shield	VII	173

Wrong-Doing Punished

King Hilary and the Beggarman	III	70
The Pert Fire Engine	IV	218
The Strong Boy	VI	71
Aruman, a Hero of Java	VI	202
Phaeton	VII	90
The Six Swans	VII	126
The Story of the Talking Bird	VIII	109
The Adventures of Perseus	IX	140
The Song of Roland	X	38
The Legend of William Tell	X	44
Ye Merry Doinges of Robin Hood	XI	49
Telegraph Boy—*A Story of Andrew Carnegie*	XII	60

KINDNESS
See also CONSIDERATION OF OTHERS; GENEROSITY

The Lion and the Mouse	II	108
Dame Wiggins of Lee	II	188
The Tale of Nutcracker	II	218
The Babe Moses	III	156
Snow-white and Rose-red	IV	34
Little Gulliver	V	103
A Story About Abe Lincoln	V	133
Old Pipes and the Dryad	VI	18
The Prince Who Rode Through a Mousehole	VII	96

Kindness to Animals

I Love Little Pussy	I	143
Little Gustava	II	30
Mrs. Tabby Gray	III	129
The Rarest Animal of All	IV	113
Heidi in the Alpine Pasture	V	146
Snowflake the Gorilla	VI	159
Jane and the Wild Chimps	XII	70

LAZINESS
See also INDUSTRY

Little Boy Blue	I	33
Lazy Old Mary	I	98
The Owl's Answer to Tommy	III	29
The Story of Li'l Hannibal	III	116
Elsa and the Ten Elves	IV	45
How Brer Rabbit Met Brer Tar-Baby	IV	130

LEADERSHIP

The Knight	IV	129
The Knights of the Silver Shield	VII	173
A Boy on the High Seas—*Biog. Sketch of Joshua Barney*	VIII	8
Young Midshipman David Farragut—*Biog. Sketch*	VIII	84
Exploring the Wilderness—*Biog. Sketch of Daniel Boone*	IX	9
Buffalo Bill—*The Story of William Cody*	IX	27
Robert Bruce, Scotland's Hero—*Biog. Sketch*	X	21
Joseph and His Brethren	X	48

	VOL.	PAGE

LEADERSHIP (*Continued*)

	VOL.	PAGE
How Beowulf Delivered Heorot.......	X	80
Joan of Arc—*Biog. Sketch*..........	X	98
The Word of Igor's Armament........	X	119
The Wanderings of Aeneas..........	X	203
Marko, the Champion of Serbian Liberty	XI	29
Ye Merry Doinges of Robin Hood....	XI	49

LOVE

Love of Country
The First Thanksgiving Day........	V	113
The Fourth of July...............	V	129
Robert Bruce, Scotland's Hero— *Biog. Sketch*	X	21
Joan of Arc—*Biog. Sketch*.........	X	98
The Melting Pot..................	XI	173
Your America	XI	216

Love for Father
Late	II	153
How Jack Sought the Golden Apples	V	76
The Legend of William Tell.......	X	44
The Exile of Rama...............	X	175
The Wanderings of Aeneas.........	X	203
The Home-Coming of Odysseus.....	X	217

Love of God
See REVERENCE

Love for Home and Family
An American Miner's Song.........	II	23
A German Evening................	II	140
Christening the Baby in Russia......	IV	63
The Story of the Talking Bird.......	VIII	109
Life in Concord—*Biog. Sketch of Louisa May Alcott*..............	XII	122

Love for Mother
Chink, Chink, Chocket.............	I	70
The Cap That Mother Made........	III	12
Old Pipes and the Dryad..........	VI	18
The Strong Boy..................	VI	71
Princess Nelly and the Seneca Chief	IX	78
The Adventures of Perseus........	IX	140
The Exile of Rama...............	X	175
Life in Concord—*Biog. Sketch of Louisa May Alcott*..............	XII	122
'Way Down South in Dixie—*Biog. Sketch of Joel Chandler Harris*....	XII	138

Love for Children
Old Mother Wind.................	I	76
Sleep, Sleep, Sleep!..............	I	80
A Roumanian Lullaby.............	I	137
When I Was a Baby...............	I	145
Sleep, Sleep, My Little One!........	I	146
Mrs. Tabby Gray.................	III	129
The Babe Moses..................	III	156
Tippity Witchit's Hallowe'en........	IV	145

Love of Nature
When I Was a Baby...............	I	145
Crocus Flowers Bloom Like Fire....	I	205
It's Spring	I	208
A Song for Easter................	II	80
Answer to a Child's Question.......	II	142
The Wonderful World.............	III	11
We Thank Thee..................	V	117
How the Goddess of Spring Came to Scoring	IX	176

Love for Sister or Brother
A Boy in the Island of Bali........	II	176

	VOL.	PAGE
Wilbur Wright and Orville Wright...	V	66
A Musical Visit to Fairyland—*A story about Felix Mendelssohn*....	VI	58
The Six Swans...................	VII	126
The Story of the Talking Bird......	VIII	109
The Exile of Rama...............	X	175

LOYALTY
See also FAITHFULNESS; TRUST-WORTHINESS
The Snow-Queen	VII	48
David, the Shepherd Boy...........	VII	73
The Dog of Pompeii...............	VII	145
Old Yeller	IX	98
The Story of the Cid.............	X	108
The Exile of Rama...............	X	175

MAKE BELIEVE
See IMAGINATIVENESS

MERCY (Compassion)

Mercy is defined as "The compassionate treatment of an offender or adversary or of the unfortunate." Examples of fine acts of mercy are shown in each of the stories listed below, and from them the child will sense the bigness of spirit, the pity and compassion that moved Pharaoh's daughter to seek mercy for the Babe Moses; the tender concern of Lincoln for the starving birds; the forgiveness and mercy shown by Joseph toward his brothers who had wronged him. For a little child, the beginnings of the capacity for mercy may be influenced by such stories as are listed under *Kindness, Forgiveness, Consideration of Others,* and *Tolerance.*

The Babe Moses..................	III	156
A Story About Abe Lincoln.........	V	133
Vladimir's Adventures in Search of Fortune	VII	102
Joseph and His Brethren...........	X	48

MINDING ONE'S OWN AFFAIRS

Goldilocks and the Three Bears.......	III	20
The Battle of the Firefly and the Apes.	III	59
The Nutcracker and Sugardolly Stories	IV	83

NEATNESS

When Mrs. Bird Wants Mr. Bird......	I	68
Engine, Engine Number Nine.........	I	85
The Little Girl and the New Dress.....	I	168
A Story About the Little Rabbits......	III	123
The Little Toy Land of the Dutch....	IV	56

OBEDIENCE

Over in the Meadow...............	I	138
What Does Little Birdie Say?.........	I	154
The Big Street in the Big City........	I	170
Policeman Joe	I	173
Biting Marion	I	174
The Little Pig	I	198
Come, Little Leaves...............	II	70
Noah's Ark	II	101
A Story About the Little Rabbits......	III	123
How Jack Sought the Golden Apples..	V	76
Sir Beaumains, the Kitchen Knight....	X	8
Joan of Arc......................	X	98

OBSERVATION

To develop in the child the habit of *Observation* is to encourage his sense of alertness to everything in the world around him. In the stories listed here, for in-

OBSERVATION (*Continued*)

stance, a child will learn how Jamie Watt's alert observation of the steam from the teakettle led to the invention of the steam engine, and how Jane Goodall learned heretofore unknown facts about the habits of wild chimpanzees. Hiawatha *observed* all the loveliness of the world of nature in which he lived. From such stories, a child may develop an alertness to all that he sees and hears, and to what is going on around him.

The remarkable accuracy of detail of the illustrations in MY BOOK HOUSE will encourage the habit of observation; in the pictures the child will find with his eyes what he hears in the story and this observation will help him become *observing* in his daily experiences.

Jamie Watt and the Giant in the Tea-
kettle .... V 45
Boots and his Brothers.............. V 157
Hiawatha's Childhood .... V 222
Jane and the Wild Chimps.......... XII 70

PATIENCE
How the Finch Got Her Colors....... II 143
Cinderella .... IV 12
The Boy Hero of Harlem............. IV 57
The Prince Who Rode Through a
Mousehole .... VII 96
Sir Beaumains, the Kitchen Knight.... X 8
Jane and the Wild Chimps.......... XII 70

PATRIOTISM
Yankee Doodle .... I 101
George Washington and the First
American Flag .... V 118
The Fourth of July................. V 129
Young Midshipman David Farragut... VIII 84
George Rogers Clark and the Conquest
of the Northwest................. IX 66
The Melting Pot.................... XI 173
Your America .... XI 216

PERSEVERANCE
The Rooster and the Sultan......... II 52
The Little Rooster and the Little Hen. II 71
Shingebiss .... II 96
The Hare and the Tortoise.......... II 106
The Little Engine That Could....... II 200
Wee Robin's Christmas Song......... II 209
Jamie Watt and the Giant in the Tea-
kettle .... V 45
How Robert Fulton Harnessed the
Giant .... V 48
Wilbur Wright and Orville Wright.... V 66
The Princess on the Glass Hill....... VI 80
Rhodopis and Her Gilded Sandals..... VII 84
The Prince Who Rode Through a
Mousehole .... VII 96
The Little-Man-As-Big-As-Your-Thumb-
With-Mustaches-Seven-Miles-Long .. VII 112
The Six Swans..................... VII 126
The Circus Man—*Biog. Sketch of
Phineas T. Barnum*............... VIII 144
The Labors of Hercules............. IX 151
Sir Beaumains, the Kitchen Knight.... X 8
Robert Bruce, Scotland's Hero....... X 21
The Home-Coming of Odysseus....... X 217

Down by the River Avon—*Biog.
Sketch of William Shakespeare*...... XII 15
Jane and the Wild Chimps.......... XII 70
The Loneliest Battler—*Biog. Sketch of
Jackie Robinson* .... XII 79
The Hoosier Poet—*Biog. Sketch of
James Whitcomb Riley*............. XII 141
The Lone Star Team of Texas—*Biog.
Sketch of Babe Didrikson*.......... XII 170
The Gentle Genius—*Biog. Sketch of
Albert Einstein* .... XII 218

PITY
See MERCY

POLITENESS
See COURTESY

PREJUDICE
See TOLERANCE

PROTECTIVE POWER OF GOD
Noah's Ark .... II 101
The Babe Moses.................... III 156
Daniel in the Lions' Den............. VI 180
David, the Shepherd Boy............ VII 73
Joseph and His Brethren............. X 48

REPENTANCE
See also FORGIVENESS
The Selfish Giant................... IV 50
The Maiden, the Knight, and the
Waterfall .... VII 40
The Adventures of Alexander Selkirk.. IX 41
Richard Feverel and the Hay-Rick..... X 54
Frithjof, the Viking................. X 130
As You Like It..................... X 165

RESOURCEFULNESS
See also INVENTIVENESS
Johnny and the Three Goats......... II 47
Shingebiss .... II 96
The Cock, the Mouse, and the Little
Red Hen .... II 192
Of a Tailor and a Bear............. III 134
The Girl Who Used Her Wits........ IV 137
The Nuremberg Stove............... V 162
Jack the Giant-Killer............... VI 140
The Little-Man-As-Big-As-Your-Thumb-
With-Mustaches-Seven-Miles-Long .. VII 112
Battle Tactics .... VII 165
A Boy on the High Seas—*Biog. Sketch
of Joshua Barney*.................. VIII 8
Young Midshipman David Farragut—
Biog. Sketch .... VIII 84
The Magic Horse................... VIII 92
Mr. Hampden's Shipwreck.......... VIII 172
Exploring the Wilderness—*Biog. Sketch
of Daniel Boone*................... IX 9
The Adventures of Alexander Selkirk.. IX 41
Robert Bruce, Scotland's Hero—
Biog. Sketch .... X 21
The Exile of Rama................. X 175
Pioneer in Surgery—*Biog. Sketch of
Dr. Daniel Hale Williams*........... XII 154

REVENGE
See FORGIVENESS

REVERENCE

See also FAITH

Songs of Joy from the Bible	I	216
Mary and the Christ-Child	I	218
The First Thanksgiving Day	V	113
We Thank Thee	V	117
The Sky at Night	VII	72

RUDENESS

See COURTESY

RUNNING AWAY

While the stories listed will show a child the undesirability of running away, because in various situations the outcome is not a happy one, the important thing to determine is the *cause* of the desire to run away. This may differ with the individual child. If, for instance, the child feels he is not loved or wanted because baby sister gets more time and attention, perhaps he would find reassurance in such selections as are listed under *Love for Home and Family, Love for Children, Love for Sister or Brother.*

There are various reasons why a child might run away, such as wanting to assert independence, over-strict discipline on the part of the parents, retaliation for punishment, friction with playmates, dislike of school, and many others. Whatever the underlying reason for a desire to run away, stories may be found in MY BOOK HOUSE which will help overcome it.

Don't Run Away My Kitty	I	132
Reen-Reen-Reeny-Croak-Frog	II	37
The Gingerbread Man	II	58
The Tale of Peter Rabbit	II	112
The Story of Li'l Hannibal	III	116
The Nutcracker and Sugardolly Stories	IV	83
Tippity Witchit's Hallowe'en	IV	145
Maggie Tulliver Goes to Live with the Gypsies	VIII	189
Life in Concord—*Biog. Sketch of Louisa May Alcott*	XII	122

SECURITY

Educators all agree that a need for a feeling of security—*emotional* security—is basic to a child's well-being. He needs security in many areas—in the knowledge that he is loved and wanted—in the feeling of "belongingness" in family or play group —in feeling that he is successful in some accomplishment. Thus, to help build his feeling of security, read the selections listed under *Protective Power of God, Forgiveness, Friendship, Self-Reliance, Contentment.* To help build his security in successful accomplishment, read the stories listed under *Leadership, Resourcefulness, Perseverance,* or stories that encourage his own special interests, talents or abilities.

Old Johnny Appleseed	IV	213

SELF-CONFIDENCE

Precocious Piggy	I	196
The Little Red Hen and the Grain of Wheat	II	13
Shingebiss	II	96
The Little Engine That Could	II	200
Jack the Giant-Killer	VI	140
A Boy on the High Seas	VIII	8

SELF-CONTROL

Boots and His Brothers	V	157
The Rough Rider—*Biog. Sketch of Theodore Roosevelt*	IX	72
Sir Beaumains, the Kitchen Knight	X	8

SELF-IMPORTANCE

See also BOASTFULNESS

The Two Crabs	II	33
Yes, That's the Girl That Struts About	III	26
Peter Rabbit Decides to Change His Name	III	49
The Mice	VI	131

SELFISHNESS

See also UNSELFISHNESS

The Man Who Has Plenty of Good Peanuts	I	95
The Little Rooster and the Little Hen	II	71
The Dog in the Manger	III	197
The Selfish Giant	IV	50
The Red Ettin	V	90
How Yehl, the Hero, Freed the Beaming Maiden	VI	102
Pigling and Her Proud Sister	VI	191
My Name Is Aram	VII	156
Peer Gynt	IX	98

SELF-RELIANCE

Precocious Piggy	I	196
The Little Red Hen and the Grain of Wheat	II	13
Shingebiss	II	96
The Little-Man-As-Big-As-Your-Thumb-With-Mustaches-Seven-Miles-Long	VII	112
Battle Tactics	VII	165
A Boy on the High Seas—*Biog. Sketch of Joshua Barney*	VIII	8
Learning To Be Free	XII	198

SENSE OF HUMOR

See SPECIAL SUBJECTS INDEX—
Humorous Rhymes and Stories

The priceless attribute of humor saves many a grim situation and manages to lighten even the heaviest burden. It cannot be taught but it can be caught, and it differs in people according to their varying sense of values. There are as many different shades and degrees and types of humor as there are humorists. Thus, in MY BOOK HOUSE the child is exposed to a wide range of humorous rhymes and stories, as well as humor in the illustrations. Child and parent can chuckle together over the humor of the nursery rhymes—in which even the combinations of sounds are often funny—and share amusement over the stubbornness of the "Big, Big Coo."

Later, as the child progresses with his reading, he will discover in the selections listed under the heading, *Humorous Rhymes and Stories* (in the SPECIAL SUBJECTS INDEX), varying kinds of humor —humor implied and humor expressed—and sometimes intermingled with pathos. So his views will broaden and he will begin to feel a tolerance for, and an understanding of, some of the foolishness and the weaknesses of human behavior. As he grows in this understanding his sense of values will be influenced by such stories as are listed under *Kindness, Consideration of Others,* etcetera. He will not, then, enjoy the type of humor that is based on the misfortunes of others, but will find humor in a wide range of situations, even when the laugh is at his own expense.

SHARING
See GENEROSITY

SHYNESS
Shyness is usually caused by a feeling of insecurity in the child, the basis of which may differ in each individual case. See the explanations and suggestions given under the heading, *Security,* for help in overcoming a tendency to shyness. The stories listed under *Getting Along with Others,* as well as the suggestions for related reading, may be helpful.

A rich background of experience from living and from reading will help the child to develop a sense of confidence and adequacy. If a child has an ample vocabulary so that he can express his thoughts easily and words are a vocal outlet for his emotions, he will be less likely to withdraw into the protective shell of shyness. The selections listed under *Repetitive Rhymes and Stories* in the SPECIAL SUBJECTS INDEX will help build a vocabulary of unusual and colorful words.

STICK-TO-ITIVENESS
See PERSEVERANCE

STINGINESS
See GENEROSITY

STUBBORNNESS
The Right Time to Laugh............ III 81
The Wee, Wee Mannie and the Big,
 Big Coo .... III 99
The Pert Fire Engine................ IV 218
Phaeton .... VII 90

TEMPER
See also ANGER
Snow-white and Rose-red............ IV 34
The Adventures of Alexander Selkirk.. IX 41

THOUGHTFULNESS
See CONSIDERATION OF OTHERS

TOLERANCE
See also GETTING ALONG WITH OTHERS
The Ballad of East and West......... IX 129
The New Colossus................... XI 172
The Melting Pot .... XI 173

TRUSTWORTHINESS
See also FAITHFULNESS; LOYALTY
Little Gulliver .... V 103
The Knights of the Silver Shield...... VII 173

TRUTHFULNESS
See HONESTY

UNDERSTANDING
See TOLERANCE

UNKINDNESS
See KINDNESS

UNSELFISHNESS
Cinderella .... IV 12
Vladimir's Adventures in Search of
 Fortune .... VII 102
The Dog of Pompeii................. VII 145
How Beowulf Delivered Heorot....... X 80
Joan of Arc—*Biog. Sketch*........... X 98
Life in Concord—*Biog. Sketch of
 Louisa May Alcott* .... XII 122

VANITY
See SELF-IMPORTANCE

WILLINGNESS
My Maid Mary .... I 51
Knitting Still .... I 128
The Little Red Hen and the Grain
 of Wheat .... II 13
The Sheep and the Pig That Made a
 Home .... II 145
Dick Whittington and His Cat........ V 33

WISDOM
Stories which show the desirability of right behavior, the undesirability of wrong behavior, the outcome, and the cause and effect of different courses of action, all build toward a sense of values that should influence wise decisions. The stories listed under *Justice* exemplify the rewards of right doing. The ability to judge soundly, and the attitudes and habits of character which direct the right course of action, add up to the meaning of *Wisdom.* It is the ultimate goal of each parent for his child, and the aim of MY BOOK HOUSE is to help him toward that goal.

Conversation .... I 163
Chanticleer and Partlet.............. III 176
The Boy Hero of Harlem............ IV 57
Hansel and Grethel................. IV 73
The Girl Who Used Her Wits........ IV 137
Charlotte's Web .... V 54
The Little-Man-As-Big-As-Your-Thumb-
 With-Mustaches-Seven-Miles-Long ... VII 112
The Enchanted Island............... VIII 134
Joseph and His Brethren............. X 48
Down by the River Avon—*Biog.
 Sketch of William Shakespeare*...... XII 15

WORK HABITS
See CHILD'S DAILY ACTIVITIES;
 CO-OPERATION; HELPFULNESS;
 INDUSTRY; PERSEVERANCE;
 SELF-RELIANCE

GUIDE TO THE PRONUNCIATION OF PROPER NAMES

THE DIACRITICAL MARKS USED ARE THE SAME AS GIVEN IN WEBSTER'S NEW INTERNATIONAL DICTIONARY

ā as in *cane*	ē as in *eve*	ō as in *old*	ū as in *cube*
ă as in *add*	ĕ as in *end*	ŏ as in *odd*	ŭ as in *up*
ä as in *arm*	ē as in *maker*	ô as in *obey*	û as in *urn*
â as in *care*	ê as in *event*	ô as in *orb*	ü as in *unite*
à as in *ask*	ī as in *ice*	ōō as in *food*	th as in *then*
â as in *chaotic*	ĭ as in *ill*	ŏŏ as in *foot*	zh = z in *azure*

Aeneas, ē nē'ás
Alighieri, ä'lē gyâ'rē
Anastasia, an as tä'shi à
Andromeda, an drom'e dä
Apollo, Phoebus, à pŏl'ō, fē'bŭs
Ariel, ā'rĭ ĕl; â'rĭ ĕl
Aristophanes, ăr ĭs tŏf'à nēz
Aruman, är ū'măn
Asbjörnsen, äs byŭrn'sĕn
Ase, ā'sà
Athenaeus, ăth'ê nē'ŭs
Augean, â'jē an
Avon, ā'vŏn; ăv'ŏn
Bach, bäk
Bali, bä'lē
Basel, bä'zĕl
Baudricourt, bō'drē kòòr
Bazzini, bät sē'nê
Beatrice, bē'a trĭs
Beaumains, bō màn'
Bechuan, bĕch'ŏŏ än
Beethoven, bā'tō vĕn
Benét, bĕ nā'
Beowulf, bā'ō wŏŏlf
Berlioz, bĕr lē ôs'
Björnson, Björnstjerne, byŭrn'sŭn, byŭrn shĕr'nĕ
Boggin, bŏg'ĭn
Bois de Boulogne, bwä dē bŏŏ lôn'y
Boito, bô'ê tō
Bontemps, bôn ton'
Brahms, brämz
Bysshe, bĭsh
Cammaerts, Émile, kä'märts, â mēl'
Campania, käm pän'yä

Cawein, kā wīn'
Cervantes, sĕr văn'tēz (Eng.); thĕr vän'tās (Sp.)
Chamisso, shà mĭs'sō
Champs Elysées, shän zâ'lē zā'
Chanson de Geste, shän sôn' dē zhĕst'
Chanson de Roland, shän sôn' dē rō län'
Charlemagne, shär'lĕ mān
Chaucer, chô'sĕr
Chopin, shô'păn'
Cid, Campeador, sĭd (Eng.) thĕth (Sp.) käm pä ä thōr'
Cinque Ports, sĭngk pōrts
Circe, sûr'sē
Clymene, klĭm'ê nē
Clytie, klĭ'tē
Columbine, kol'um bĭn
Compiègné, kŏn pyĕn'y
Croesus, krē'sŭs
Cuculain, kŏŏ kōō'lĭn
Czechoslovakia, chĕk ō slō vä'kĭ à
Dagobert, dä'gō bĕrt (Eng.); dä'gô-bâr' (Fr.)
Dasent, dā'sĕnt
Dauphin, dô'fĭn
Da Vinci, dä vēn'che
David, Félicien, dà vēd'
Debeauve, dē bō vā'
Debussy, dē bü sē'
Dido, dē'dō
Don Quixote, dŏn kê hō'tä (Sp.)
Donuil Dhu, dŏn'ĭl dŏŏ'
Dovre, dŏv'rē
Dracul, drä'kŏŏl

Dvořák, dvôr'zhäk
Eloi, ā'lwä
Fabre, Jean Henri, fä'br', zhän än'rē
Firdusi, fĕr dŏŏ'sē
Fra Angelico, frä än jĕl'ê kō
Francesca da Rimini, frän ches'kä dä rē'mē nē
Frithjof, frĭth'yōf
Fröding, Gustaf, frû'dĭng, gūs täf'
Galapagos, gä lä'pä gôs
Gauguin, gô găn'
Giovanni, jō vän'nê
Giuseppi, gīz'ep pĭ
Gluck, von, glŏŏk', fŏn
Gounod, gōō'nō
Grethel, grā'tĕl
Guillaume, gē'yôm'
Händel, hĕn'dĕl
Harlequin, här'lē kwĭn
Haydn, hī'd'n
Heine, Heinrich, hī'nĕ, hīn rĭk
Hilary, hĭl'a rĭ
Hine Moa, hē'nāy mō'à
Hjalmar, yĕl'mär
Hjuki, yū'kē
Hopi, hō'pê
I Pagliacci, ē pä lyä'chê
Iduna, ē dŏŏ'nà
Il Trovatore, ĕl tro'vä tō'râ
Iroquois, ir ō kwoi'
Jeanne d'Arc, zhän' dàrk'
Jokeli, yŏ'kĕ lĭ
Jotun-heim, yŏ'tŏŏn häm
Juan Fernandez, jŏŏ'ăn fĕr năn dĕz (Eng.); hwän fĕr nän' däth (Sp.)

Kalevala, *kä lä vä'lä*
Kiev, *kē'yĕf*
L'Allegro, *lä lā'grō*
La Fontaine, Jean de, *lä fôn tĕn, zhän dĕ*
Le Coq d' Or, *lĕ kôk'dôr'*
Le Fevre, Felicite, *lĕ fĕv'r, fä lĕ sĕ tä'*
Leontes, *lĕ on'tēz*
Leprechaun, *lĕp'rē kôn'*
Liszt, *lĭst*
Longchamps, *lôn shän'*
Maoris, *mä'ô rĭz*
Massenet, *mä's'nĕ'*
Mazurka, *mȧ zûr'kȧ*
Meleager, *mĕl'ĕ ā'jēr*
Meštrović, *mĕsh'trō vich*
Michelangelo, *mī'kĕl ăn'jĕ lō*
Mignon, *mē'nyôn'*
Miller, Joaquin, *wȧ kēn'*
Milne, *mĭln*
Mjolner, *myôl'nēr*
Münchausen, *mŭn chô' zĕn* (Eng.); *müngk'hou'zĕn* (Ger.)
Nigel, *nī'jĕl*
Nobel, *nō'bĕl*
Noyes, *noiz*
Odense, *ō'thĕn sȧ*
Odysseus, *ō dis'ūs*
Odyssey, *ŏd'ĭ sĭ*

Omphale, *ŏm'fä lē*
Ouida, *wē'dȧ*
Penelope, *pē nĕl'ō pē*
Peppino, *pāy pē͞e'nō*
Perrault, *pĕ rō'*
Perseus, *pêr'sūs*
Phaeton, *fā'ĕ t'n*
Pharaoh, *fâ'rō; fā rō*
Pierrot, *pē'ēr ō; pyĕ rō'*
Pogany, *pō'gä nĭ*
Polonaise, *pō lō nāz'*
Pueblo, *pwĕb'lō*
Pulitzer, *pū'lĭt sėr*
Rajah, *rä'jȧ*
Ramayana, *rä mä'yȧ nȧ*
Ramée, De la, *rȧ mä, dĕ lä*
Reinar, *rāy ē när'*
Restrepo, Don Antonio José, *rĕs trȧ pō, dŏn ȧn tō'nĭ ō hō sāy'*
Rheims, *rēmz* (Eng.); *răns* (Fr.)
Rhodopis, *rō dō'pĭs*
Rossetti, *rō sĕt'ĕ*
Rouen, *rwän*
Rustem, *rös tem'*
Ruy Diaz, *rwē dē'äth*
Saint-Saëns, *săn-säns'*
Sancho Panza, *săng'kō pȧn'zȧ* (Eng.); *sän'chō pän'thä* (Sp.)

Shah Nameh, *shäh nä'mė*
Shingebiss, *shĭn'ge bĭs*
Sibelius, *sē bā'lĕ us*
Solveig, *sŏl'vāg*
Stuyvesant, *stī'vĕ sȧnt*
Tagore, Rabindranath, *tȧ gôr', rȧ bĭn'drȧ näth*
Tchaikovsky, *chī kôf' skĕ*
Theognis, *thĕ ŏg'nĭs*
Thomas, Ambrose, *tō'mä'*
Thoreau, *thō'rō*
Titania, *tĭ tā'nĭ ȧ*
Tolstoy, *tŏl stoi'*
Tutaneikai, *tōō'tȧ nā kāy*
Tyrol, *tĭr'ŏl*
Vachel, *vä'chĕl*
Valkyrs, *văl kĭrz*
Vancouleur, *văn kōō'lēr*
Vladimir, *vlăd'ĭ mĭr*
Von Chamisso, *fŏn shä'mĭ sō*
Wagner, *väg'nēr*
Wainamoinen, *wäinamöinen*
Warwickshire, *wŏr'ĭk shēr*
Worcester, *wŏ͞os'tēr*
Ximena, *hē mān'nä*
Yvetot, *ēv tō'*
Zuñi, *zōō'nyĕ*